# the losers:

# ante

# THE LOSERS
## ante up

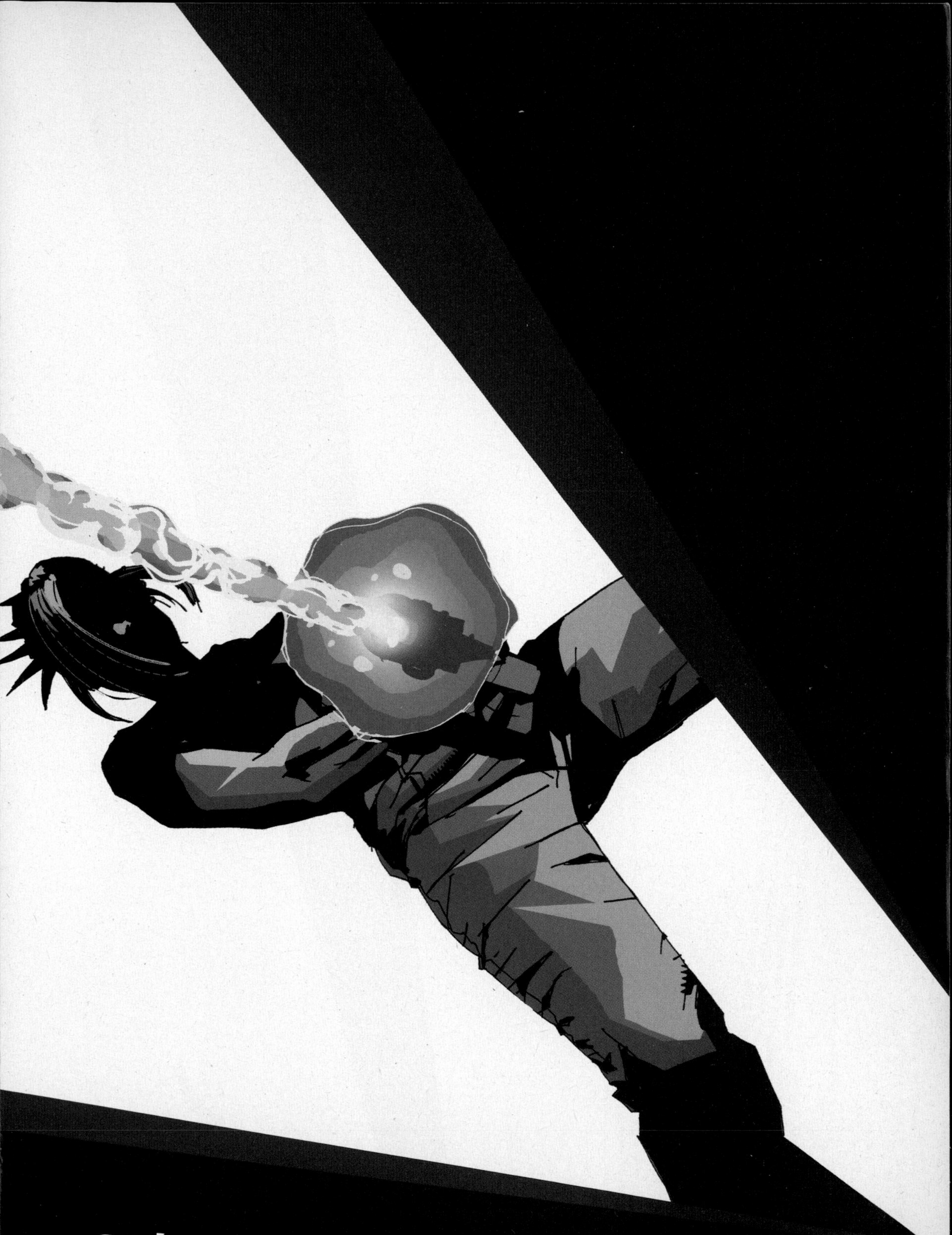

**andy diggle** WRITER **jock** ARTIST & ORIGINAL SERIES COVERS

**lee loughridge** COLORIST **clem robins** LETTERER

KAREN BERGER, VP-Executive Editor    WILL DENNIS, Editor-original series    ZACHARY RAU • PORNSAK PICHETSHOTE, Assistant Editors-original series    SCOTT NYBAKKEN, Editor-collected edition    ROBBIN BROSTERMAN, Senior Art Director
PAUL LEVITZ, President & Publisher    GEORG BREWER, VP-Design & Retail Product Development    RICHARD BRUNING, Senior VP-Creative Director    PATRICK CALDON, Senior VP-Finance & Operations    CHRIS CARAMALIS, VP-Finance
TERRI CUNNINGHAM, VP-Managing Editor    DAN DIDIO, VP-Editorial    ALISON GILL, VP-Manufacturing    LILLIAN LASERSON, Senior VP & General Counsel    JIM LEE, Editorial Director-WildStorm    DAVID McKILLIPS, VP-Advertising & Custom Publishing
JOHN NEE, VP-Business Development    GREGORY NOVECK, Senior VP-Creative Affairs    CHERYL RUBIN, VP-Brand Management    BOB WAYNE, VP-Sales & Marketing

**THE LOSERS: ANTE UP**    Published by DC Comics. Cover and compilation copyright © 2004 DC Comics. All Rights Reserved.    Originally published in single magazine form as THE LOSERS 1-6. Copyright © 2003, 2004 DC Comics.
All Rights Reserved. All characters, their distinctive likenesses and related elements featured in this publication are trademarks of DC Comics. The stories, characters and incidents featured in this publication are entirely fic-
tional. DC Comics does not read or accept unsolicited submissions of ideas, stories or artwork.  DC Comics, 1700 Broadway, New York, NY 10019  A Warner Bros. Entertainment Company  Printed in Canada. First Printing.
ISBN: 1-4012-0198-9
Cover illustration by **Jock.**
Publication design by **John J. Hill.**

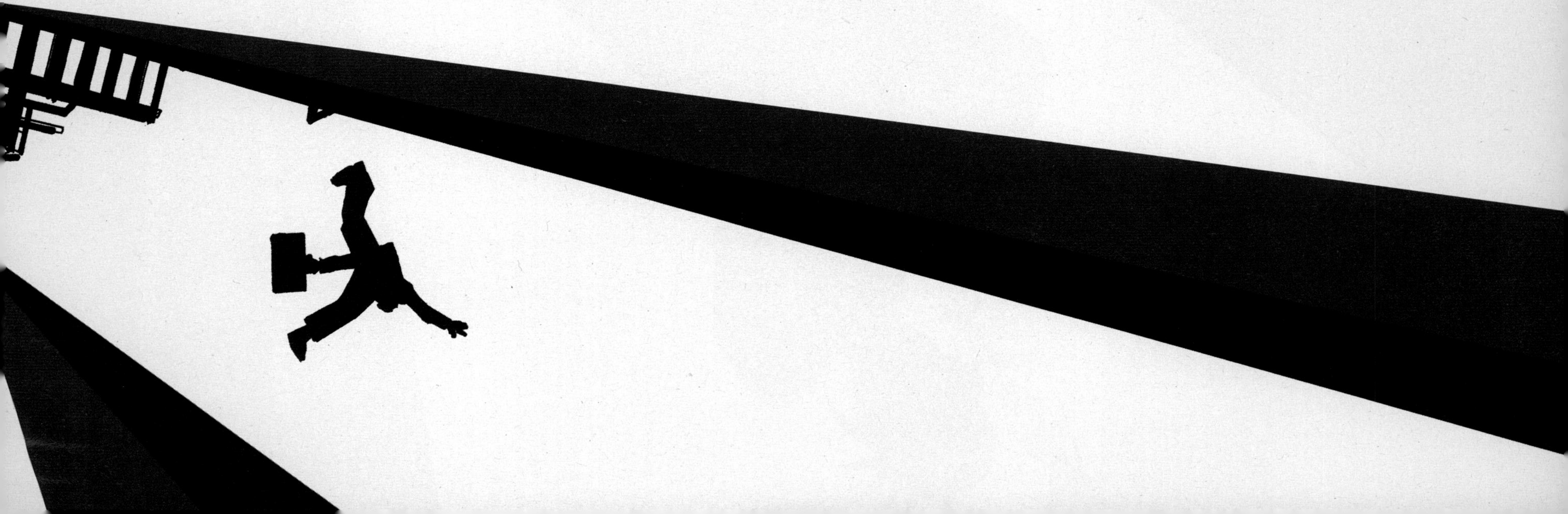

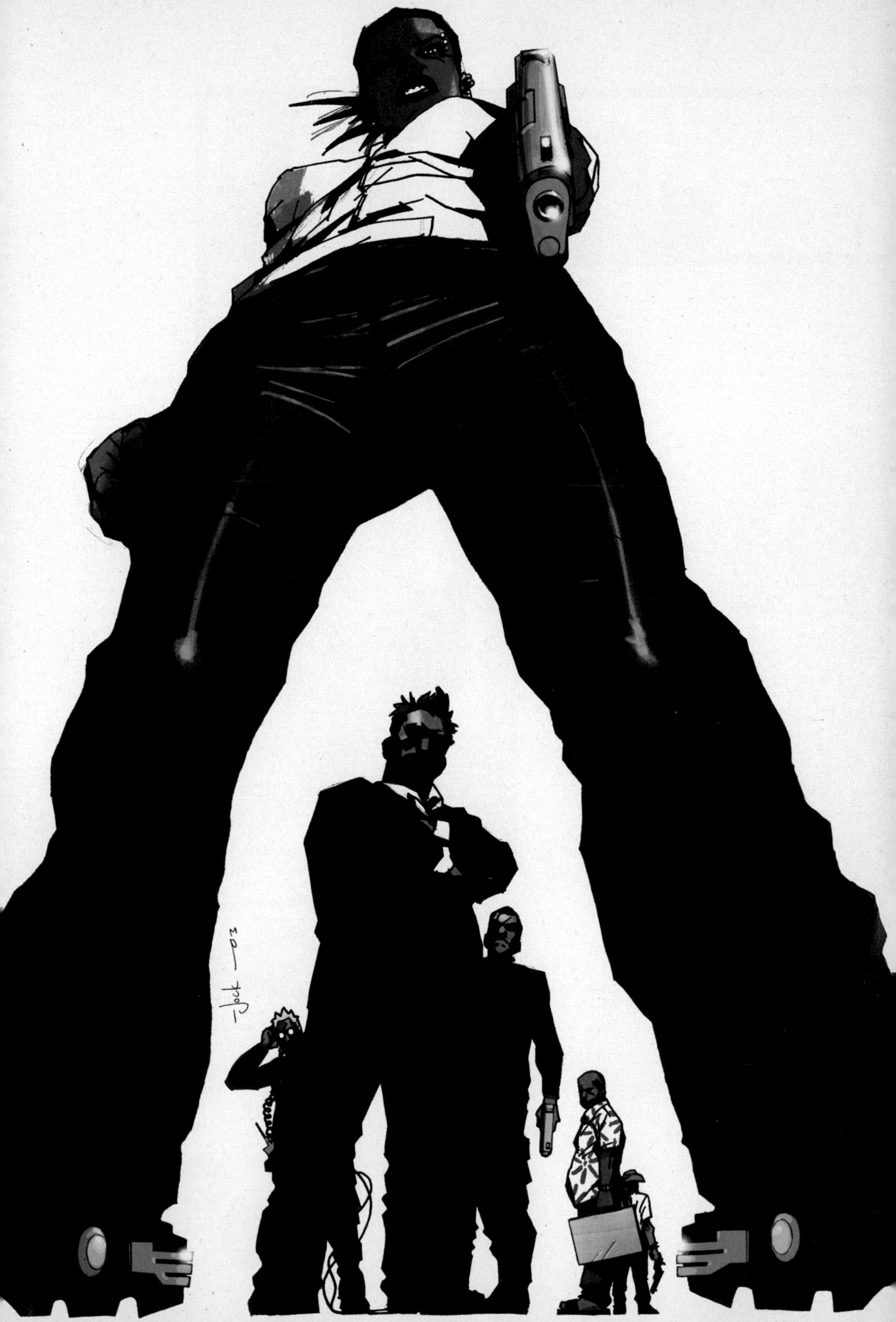

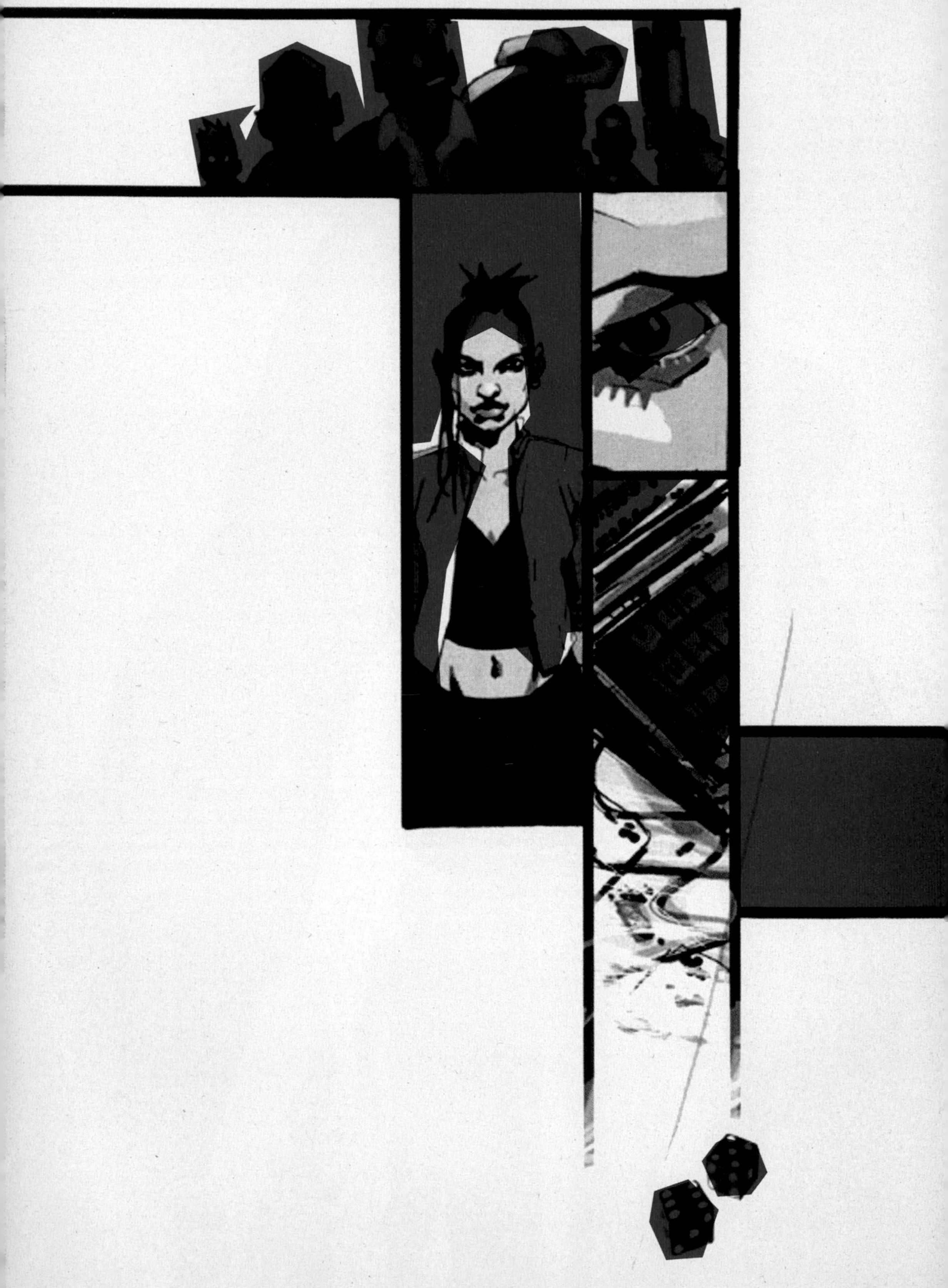

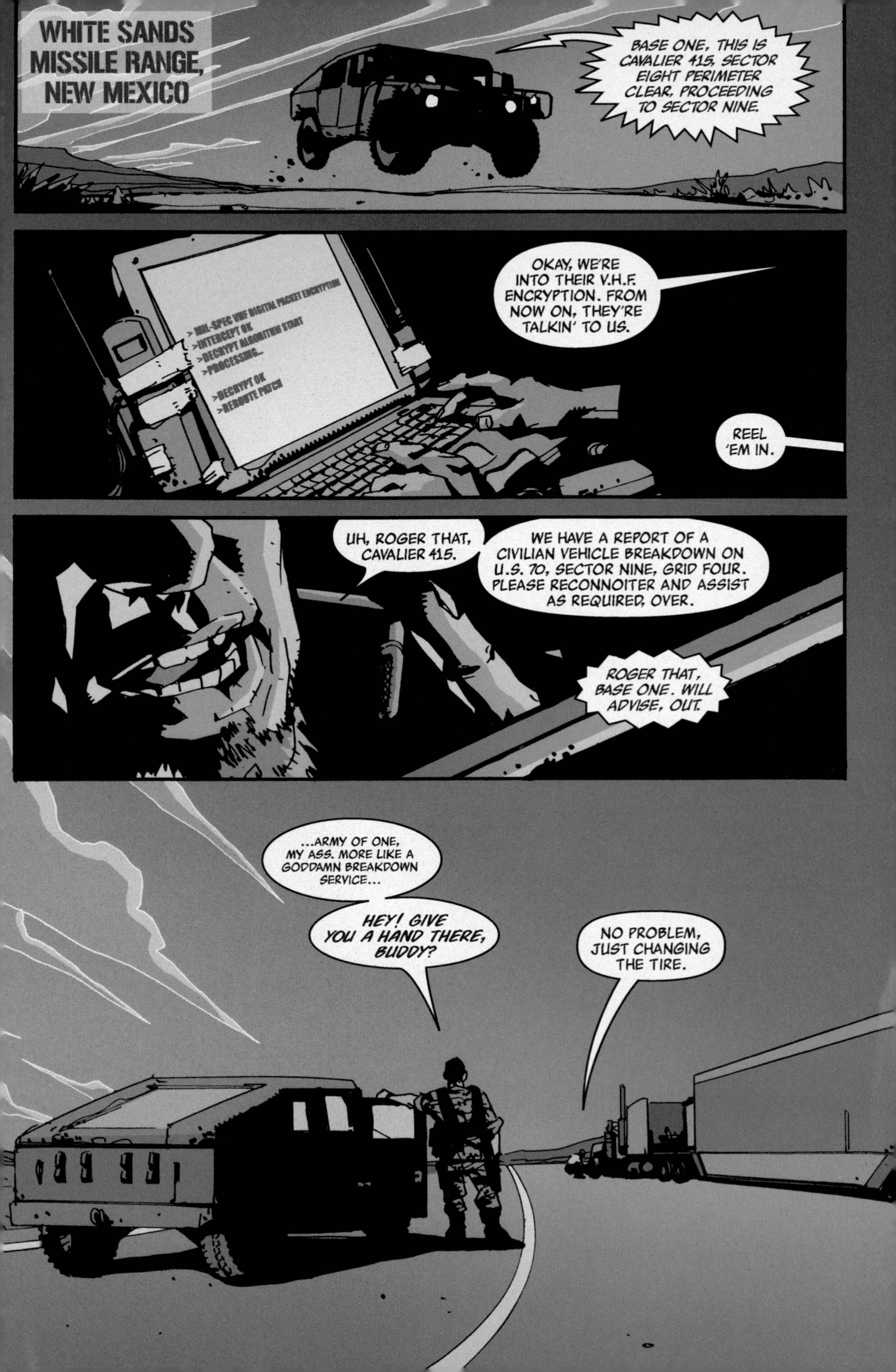
WHITE SANDS MISSILE RANGE, NEW MEXICO
BASE ONE, THIS IS CAVALIER 415, SECTOR EIGHT PERIMETER CLEAR, PROCEEDING TO SECTOR NINE.
>MIL-SPEC VHF DIGITAL PACKET ENCRYPTION
>INTERCEPT OK
>DECRYPT ALGORITHM START
>PROCESSING...
>DECRYPT OK
>REROUTE PATCH
OKAY, WE'RE INTO THEIR V.H.F. ENCRYPTION. FROM NOW ON, THEY'RE TALKIN' TO US.
REEL 'EM IN.
UH, ROGER THAT, CAVALIER 415.
WE HAVE A REPORT OF A CIVILIAN VEHICLE BREAKDOWN ON U.S. 70, SECTOR NINE, GRID FOUR. PLEASE RECONNOITER AND ASSIST AS REQUIRED, OVER.
ROGER THAT, BASE ONE. WILL ADVISE, OUT.
...ARMY OF ONE, MY ASS. MORE LIKE A GODDAMN BREAKDOWN SERVICE...
HEY! GIVE YOU A HAND THERE, BUDDY?
NO PROBLEM, JUST CHANGING THE TIRE.

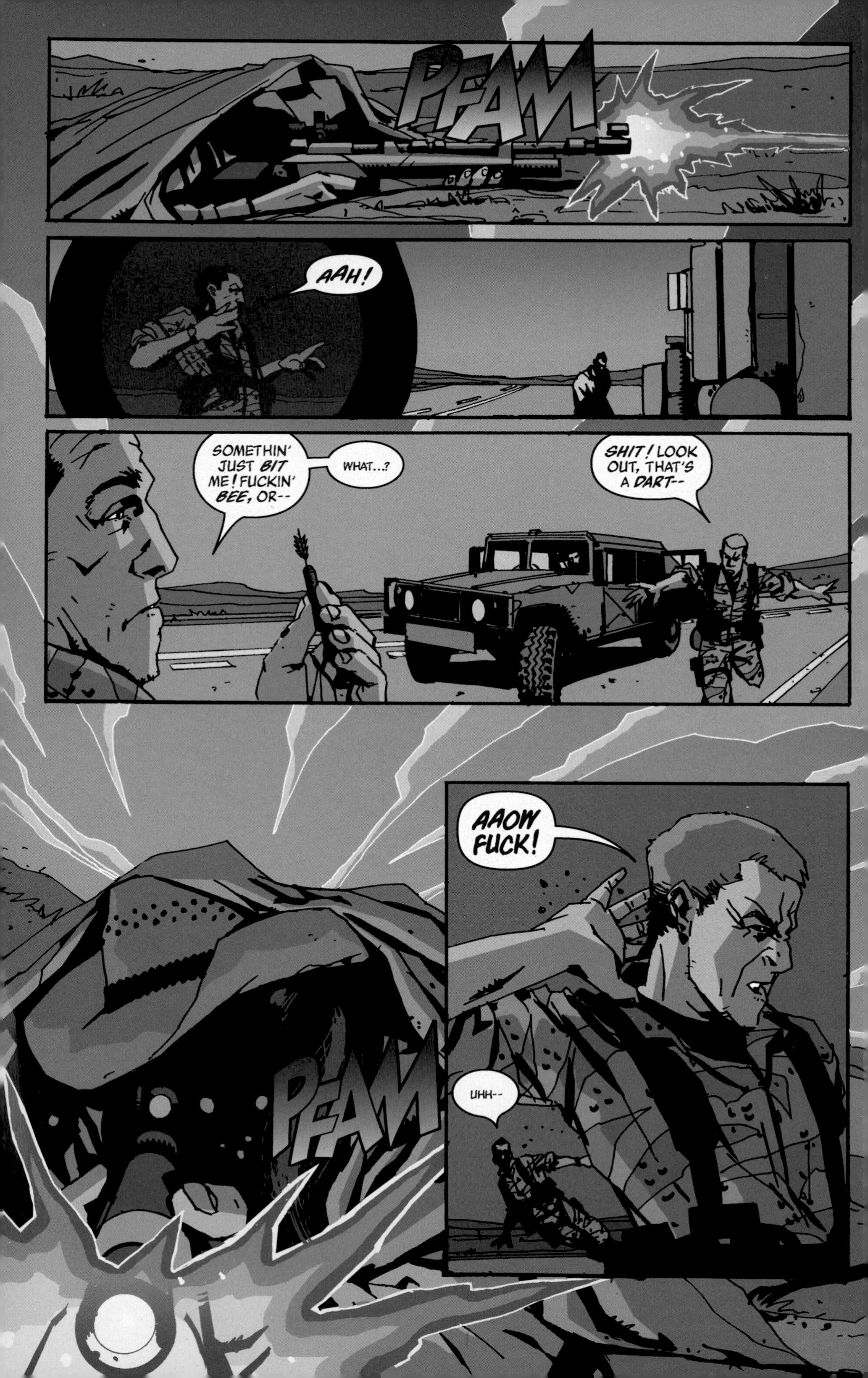
PFAM
AAH!
SOMETHIN' JUST BIT ME! FUCKIN' BEE, OR--
WHAT...?
SHIT! LOOK OUT, THAT'S A DART--
AAOW FUCK!
PFAM
UHH--

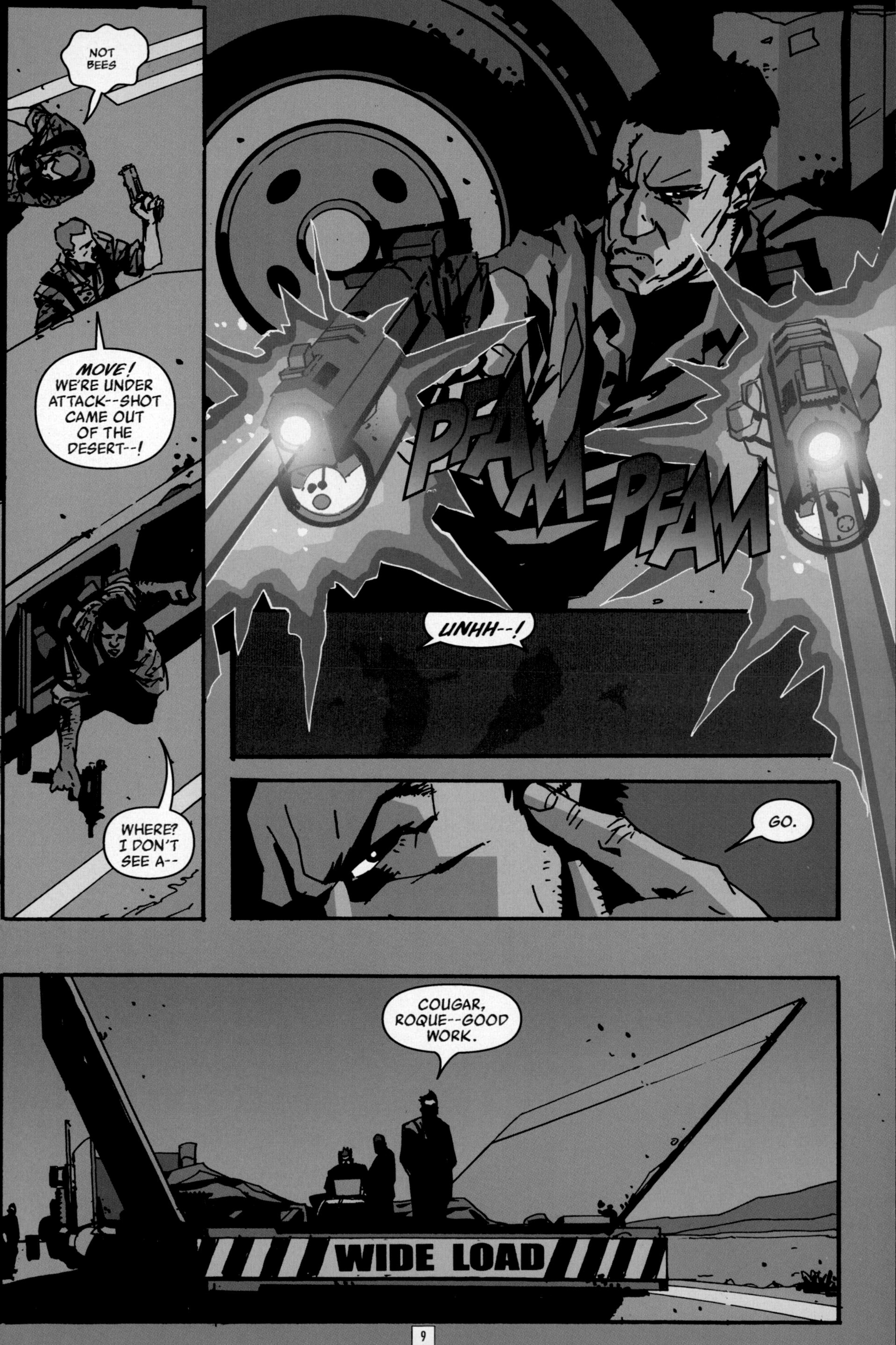
NOT BEES
MOVE! WE'RE UNDER ATTACK--SHOT CAME OUT OF THE DESERT--!
WHERE? I DON'T SEE A--
PFAM PFAM PFAM
UNHH--!
GO.
COUGAR, ROQUE--GOOD WORK.
WIDE LOAD

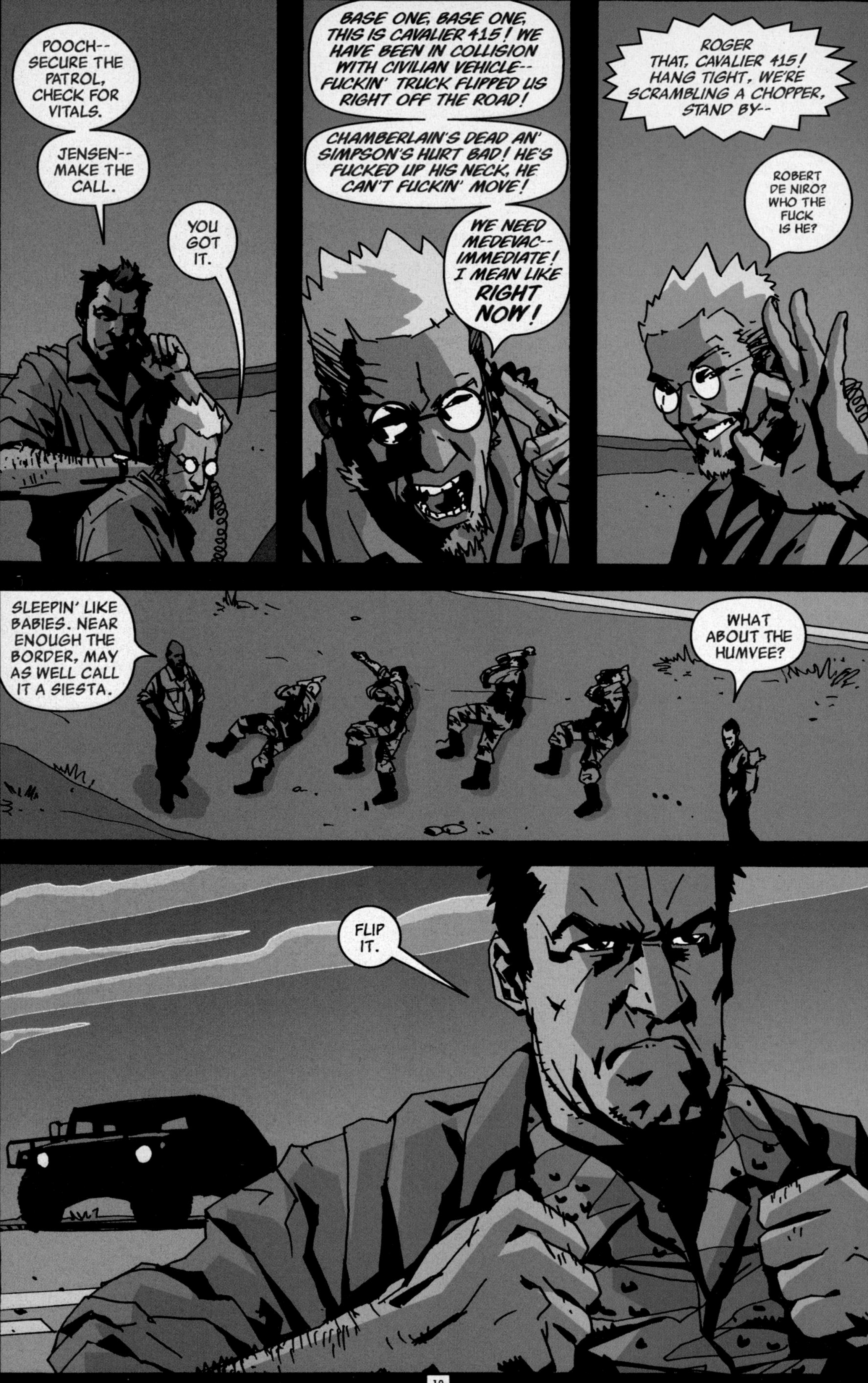
POOCH-- SECURE THE PATROL, CHECK FOR VITALS.
JENSEN-- MAKE THE CALL.
YOU GOT IT.
BASE ONE, BASE ONE, THIS IS CAVALIER 415! WE HAVE BEEN IN COLLISION WITH CIVILIAN VEHICLE-- FUCKIN' TRUCK FLIPPED US RIGHT OFF THE ROAD!
CHAMBERLAIN'S DEAD AN' SIMPSON'S HURT BAD! HE'S FUCKED UP HIS NECK, HE CAN'T FUCKIN' MOVE!
WE NEED MEDEVAC-- IMMEDIATE! I MEAN LIKE RIGHT NOW!
ROGER THAT, CAVALIER 415! HANG TIGHT, WE'RE SCRAMBLING A CHOPPER, STAND BY--
ROBERT DE NIRO? WHO THE FUCK IS HE?
SLEEPIN' LIKE BABIES. NEAR ENOUGH THE BORDER, MAY AS WELL CALL IT A SIESTA.
WHAT ABOUT THE HUMVEE?
FLIP IT.

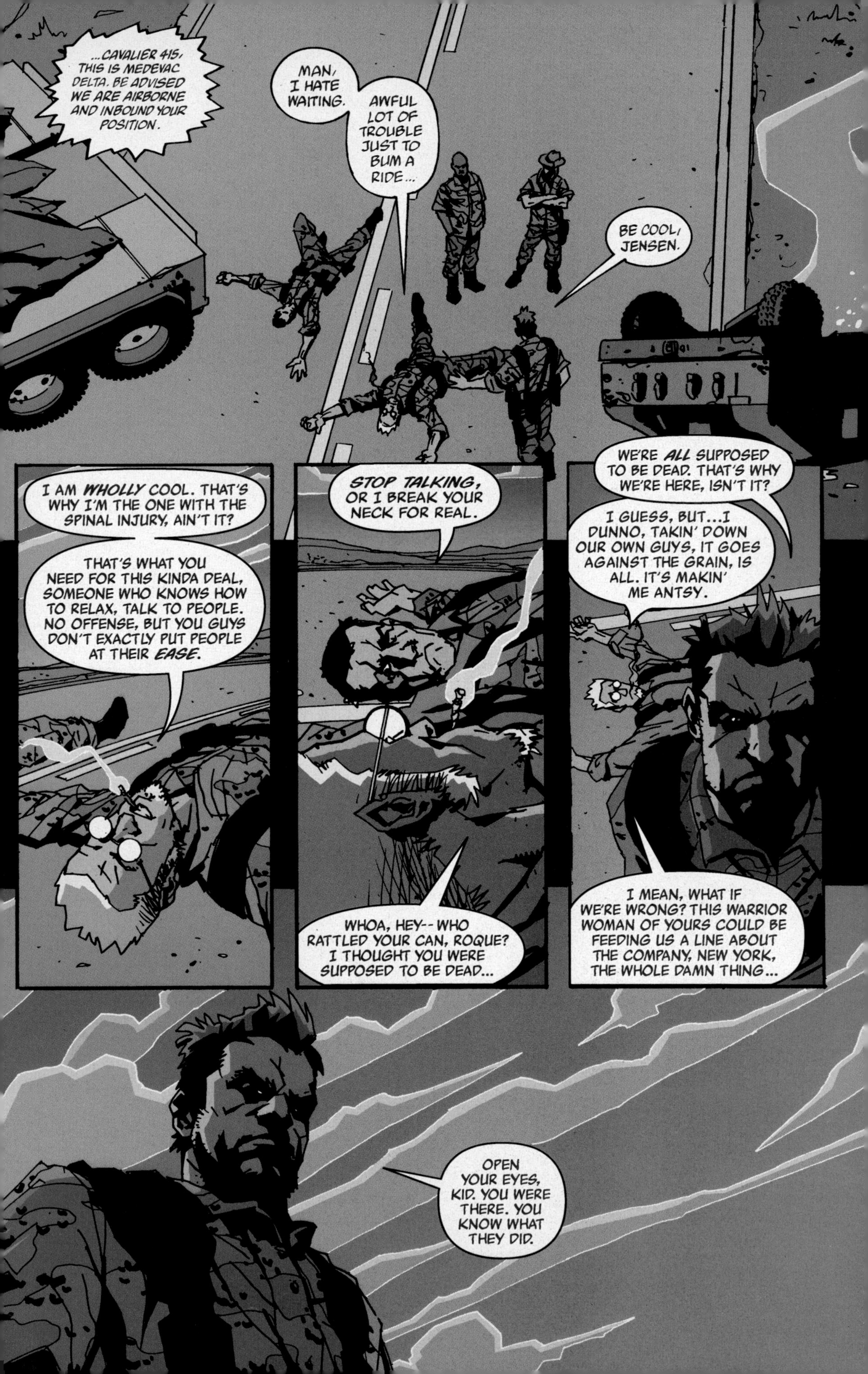
...CAVALIER 415, THIS IS MEDEVAC DELTA. BE ADVISED WE ARE AIRBORNE AND INBOUND YOUR POSITION.
MAN, I HATE WAITING.
AWFUL LOT OF TROUBLE JUST TO BUM A RIDE...
BE COOL, JENSEN.
I AM WHOLLY COOL. THAT'S WHY I'M THE ONE WITH THE SPINAL INJURY, AIN'T IT?
THAT'S WHAT YOU NEED FOR THIS KINDA DEAL, SOMEONE WHO KNOWS HOW TO RELAX, TALK TO PEOPLE. NO OFFENSE, BUT YOU GUYS DON'T EXACTLY PUT PEOPLE AT THEIR EASE.
STOP TALKING, OR I BREAK YOUR NECK FOR REAL.
WHOA, HEY-- WHO RATTLED YOUR CAN, ROQUE? I THOUGHT YOU WERE SUPPOSED TO BE DEAD...
WE'RE ALL SUPPOSED TO BE DEAD. THAT'S WHY WE'RE HERE, ISN'T IT?
I GUESS, BUT...I DUNNO, TAKIN' DOWN OUR OWN GUYS, IT GOES AGAINST THE GRAIN, IS ALL. IT'S MAKIN' ME ANTSY.
I MEAN, WHAT IF WE'RE WRONG? THIS WARRIOR WOMAN OF YOURS COULD BE FEEDING US A LINE ABOUT THE COMPANY, NEW YORK, THE WHOLE DAMN THING...
OPEN YOUR EYES, KID. YOU WERE THERE. YOU KNOW WHAT THEY DID.

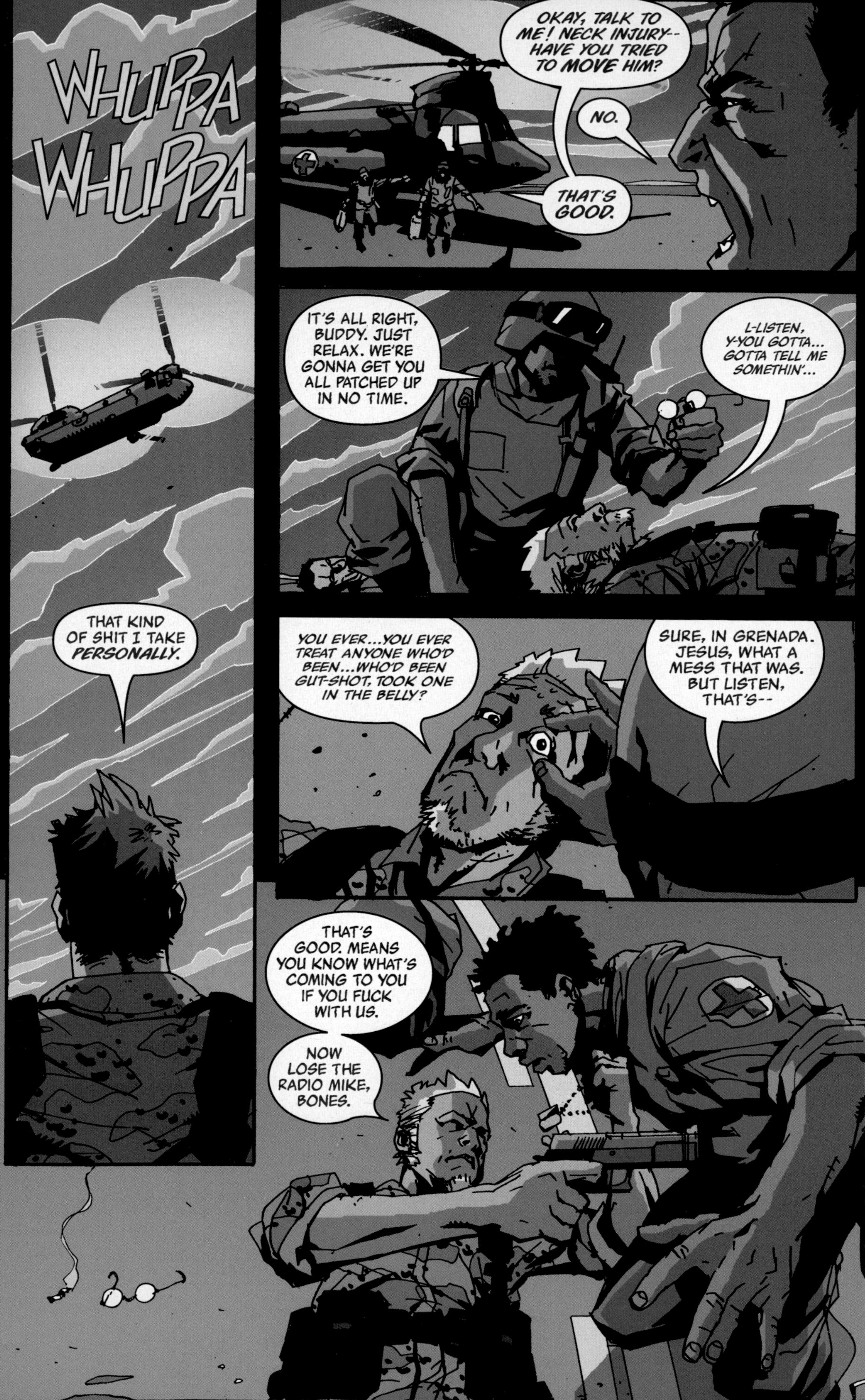

WHUPPA WHUPPA
OKAY, TALK TO ME! NECK INJURY-- HAVE YOU TRIED TO MOVE HIM?
NO.
THAT'S GOOD.
IT'S ALL RIGHT, BUDDY. JUST RELAX. WE'RE GONNA GET YOU ALL PATCHED UP IN NO TIME.
L-LISTEN, Y-YOU GOTTA... GOTTA TELL ME SOMETHIN'...
THAT KIND OF SHIT I TAKE PERSONALLY.
YOU EVER...YOU EVER TREAT ANYONE WHO'D BEEN...WHO'D BEEN GUT-SHOT, TOOK ONE IN THE BELLY?
SURE, IN GRENADA. JESUS, WHAT A MESS THAT WAS. BUT LISTEN, THAT'S--
THAT'S GOOD. MEANS YOU KNOW WHAT'S COMING TO YOU IF YOU FUCK WITH US.
NOW LOSE THE RADIO MIKE, BONES.

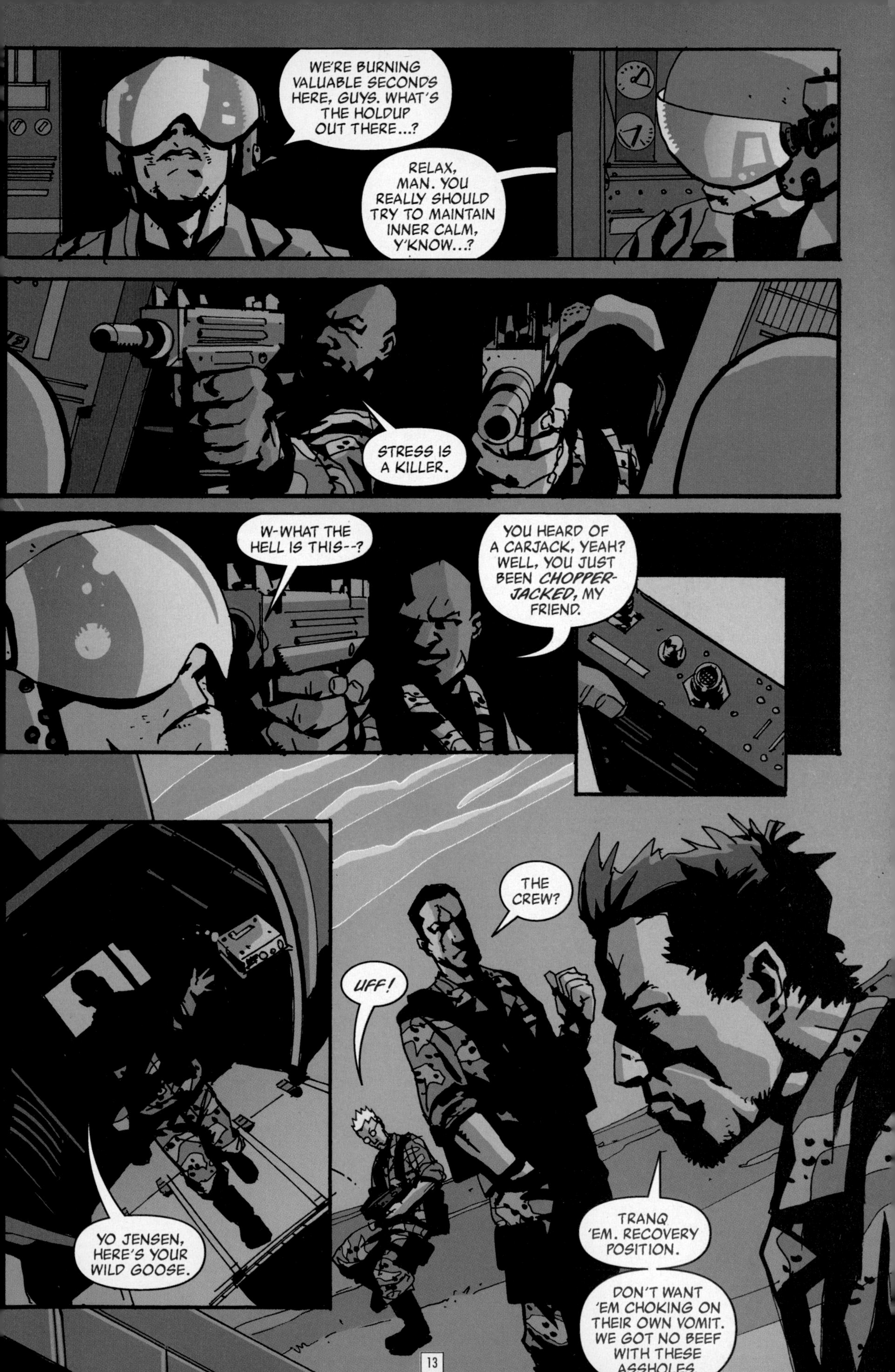
WE'RE BURNING VALUABLE SECONDS HERE, GUYS. WHAT'S THE HOLDUP OUT THERE...?
RELAX, MAN. YOU REALLY SHOULD TRY TO MAINTAIN INNER CALM, Y'KNOW...?
STRESS IS A KILLER.
W-WHAT THE HELL IS THIS--?
YOU HEARD OF A CARJACK, YEAH? WELL, YOU JUST BEEN *CHOPPER-JACKED*, MY FRIEND.
THE CREW?
*UFF!*
YO JENSEN, HERE'S YOUR WILD GOOSE.
TRANQ 'EM. RECOVERY POSITION.
DON'T WANT 'EM CHOKING ON THEIR OWN VOMIT. WE GOT NO BEEF WITH THESE ASSHOLES.

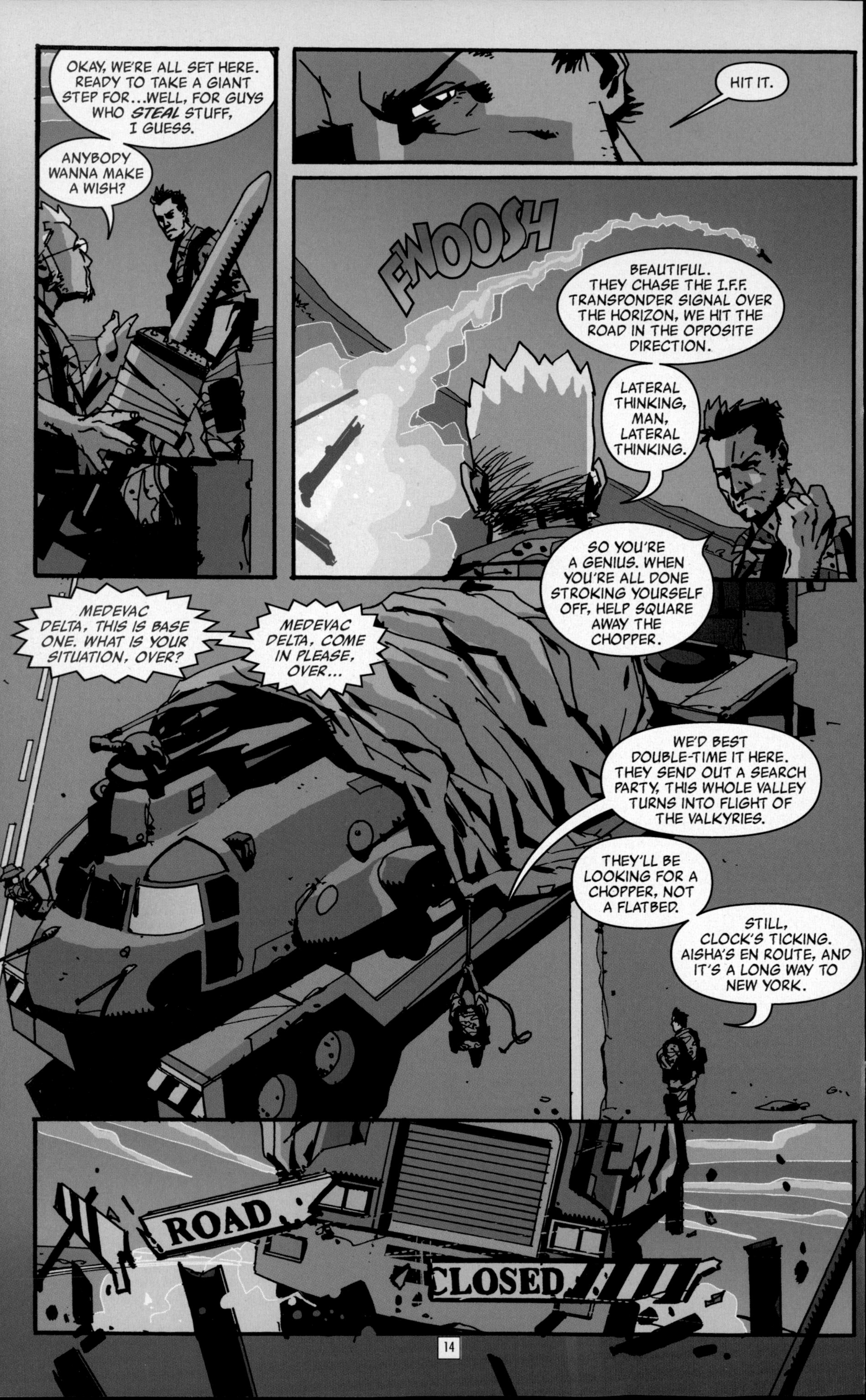
OKAY, WE'RE ALL SET HERE. READY TO TAKE A GIANT STEP FOR...WELL, FOR GUYS WHO STEAL STUFF, I GUESS.
ANYBODY WANNA MAKE A WISH?
HIT IT.
FWOOSH
BEAUTIFUL. THEY CHASE THE I.F.F. TRANSPONDER SIGNAL OVER THE HORIZON, WE HIT THE ROAD IN THE OPPOSITE DIRECTION.
LATERAL THINKING, MAN, LATERAL THINKING.
SO YOU'RE A GENIUS. WHEN YOU'RE ALL DONE STROKING YOURSELF OFF, HELP SQUARE AWAY THE CHOPPER.
MEDEVAC DELTA, THIS IS BASE ONE. WHAT IS YOUR SITUATION, OVER?
MEDEVAC DELTA, COME IN PLEASE, OVER...
WE'D BEST DOUBLE-TIME IT HERE. THEY SEND OUT A SEARCH PARTY, THIS WHOLE VALLEY TURNS INTO FLIGHT OF THE VALKYRIES.
THEY'LL BE LOOKING FOR A CHOPPER, NOT A FLATBED.
STILL, CLOCK'S TICKING. AISHA'S EN ROUTE, AND IT'S A LONG WAY TO NEW YORK.
ROAD
CLOSED

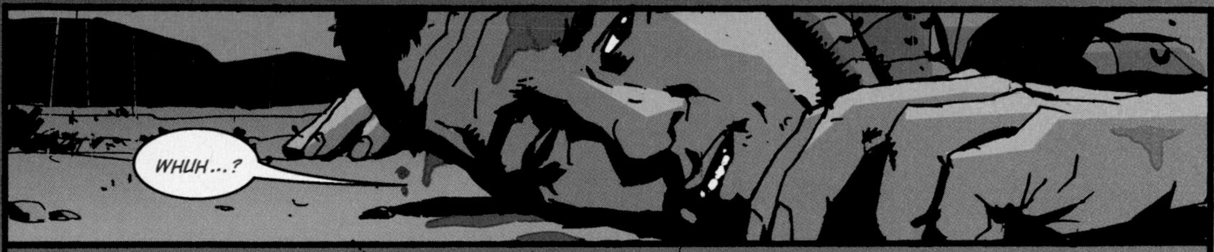
WHUH...?

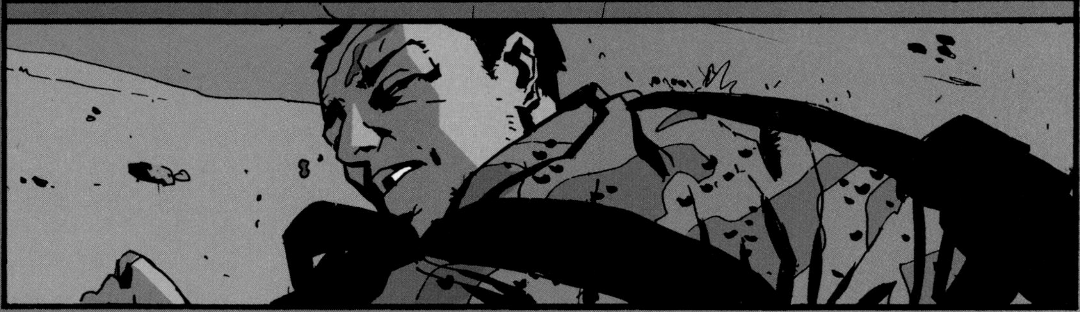

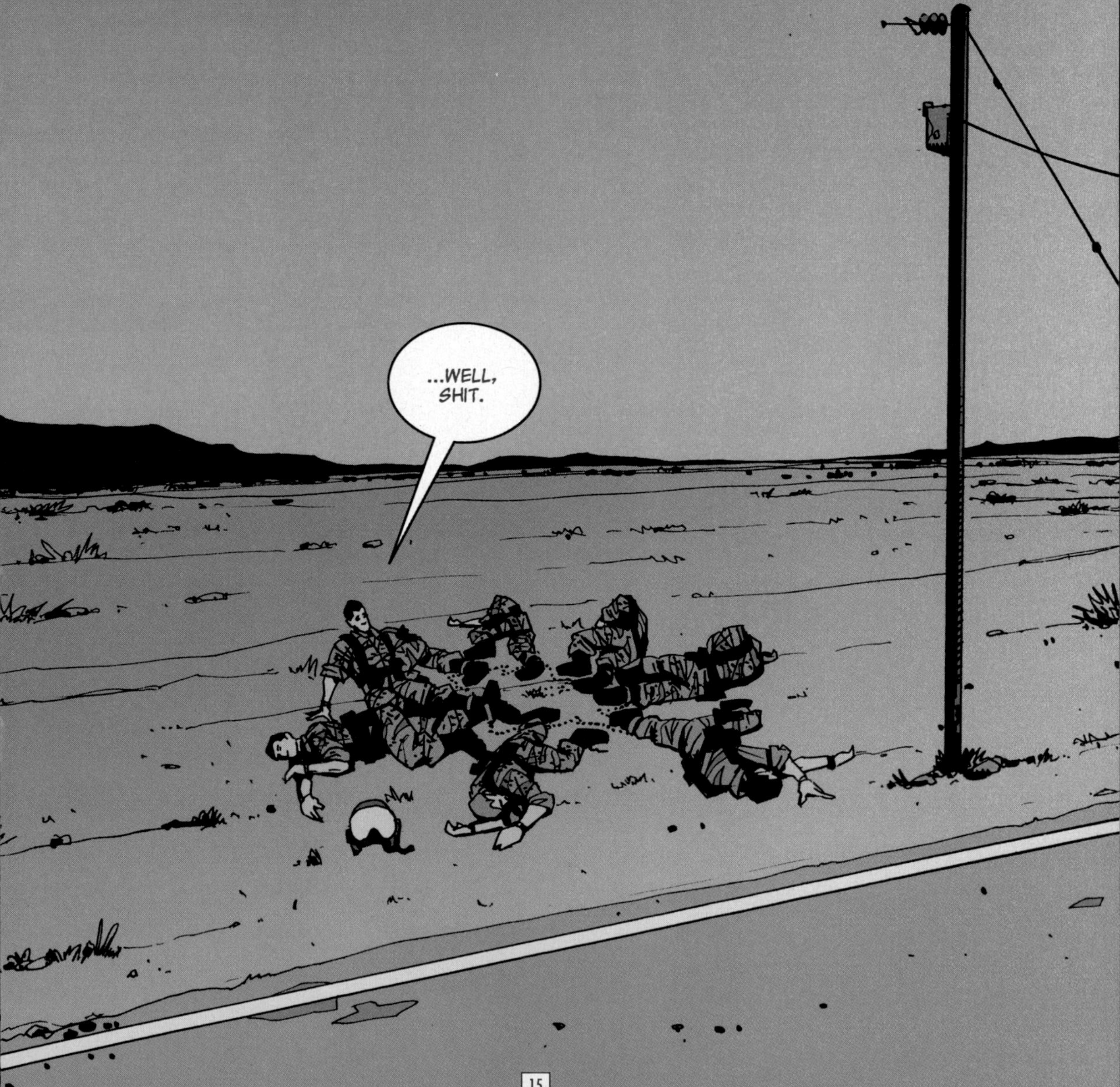
...WELL, SHIT.

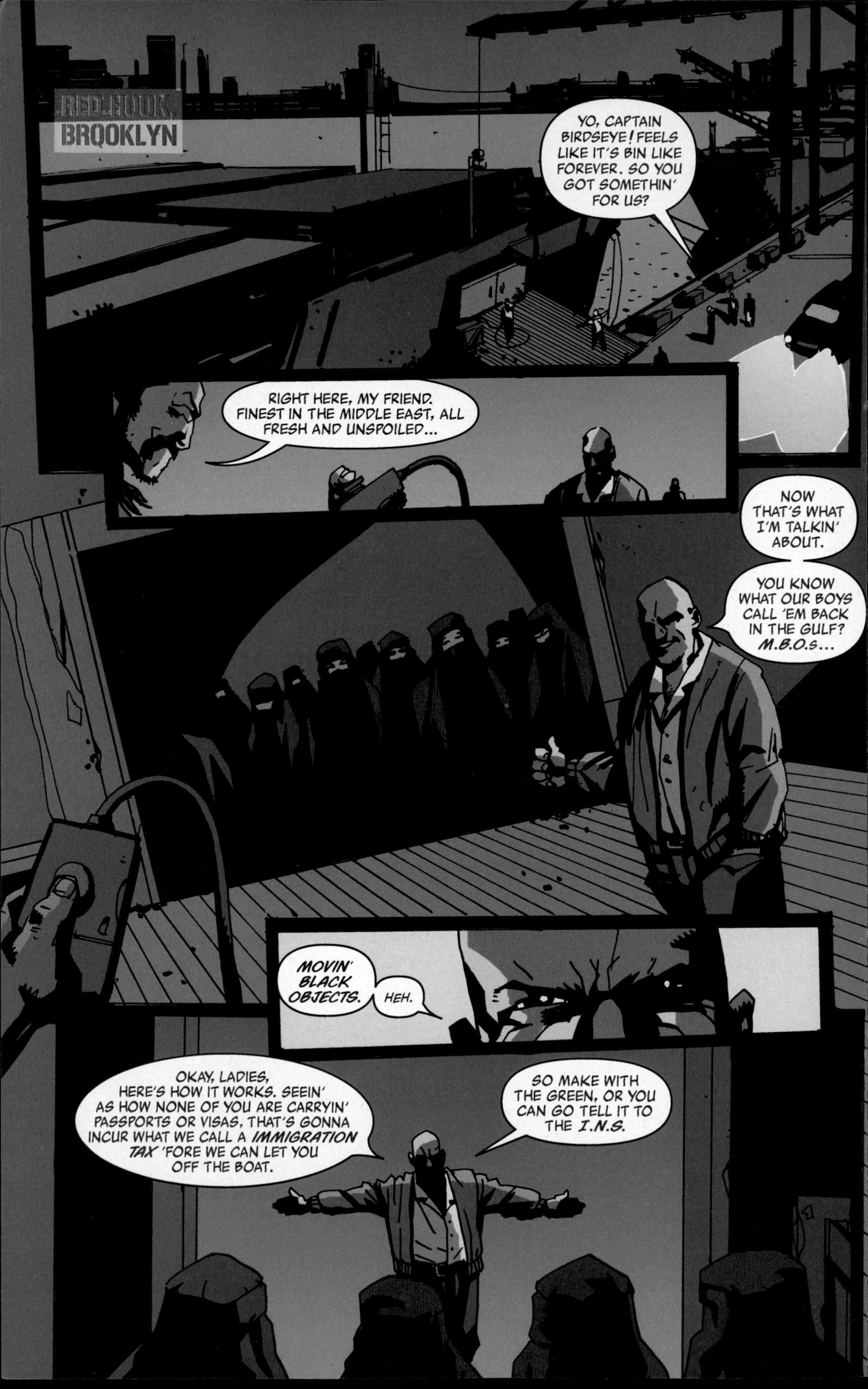
RED HOOK, BROOKLYN
YO, CAPTAIN BIRDSEYE! FEELS LIKE IT'S BIN LIKE FOREVER. SO YOU GOT SOMETHIN' FOR US?
RIGHT HERE, MY FRIEND. FINEST IN THE MIDDLE EAST, ALL FRESH AND UNSPOILED...
NOW THAT'S WHAT I'M TALKIN' ABOUT.
YOU KNOW WHAT OUR BOYS CALL 'EM BACK IN THE GULF? M.B.O.s...
MOVIN' BLACK OBJECTS.
HEH.
OKAY, LADIES, HERE'S HOW IT WORKS. SEEIN' AS HOW NONE OF YOU ARE CARRYIN' PASSPORTS OR VISAS, THAT'S GONNA INCUR WHAT WE CALL A IMMIGRATION TAX 'FORE WE CAN LET YOU OFF THE BOAT.
SO MAKE WITH THE GREEN, OR YOU CAN GO TELL IT TO THE I.N.S.

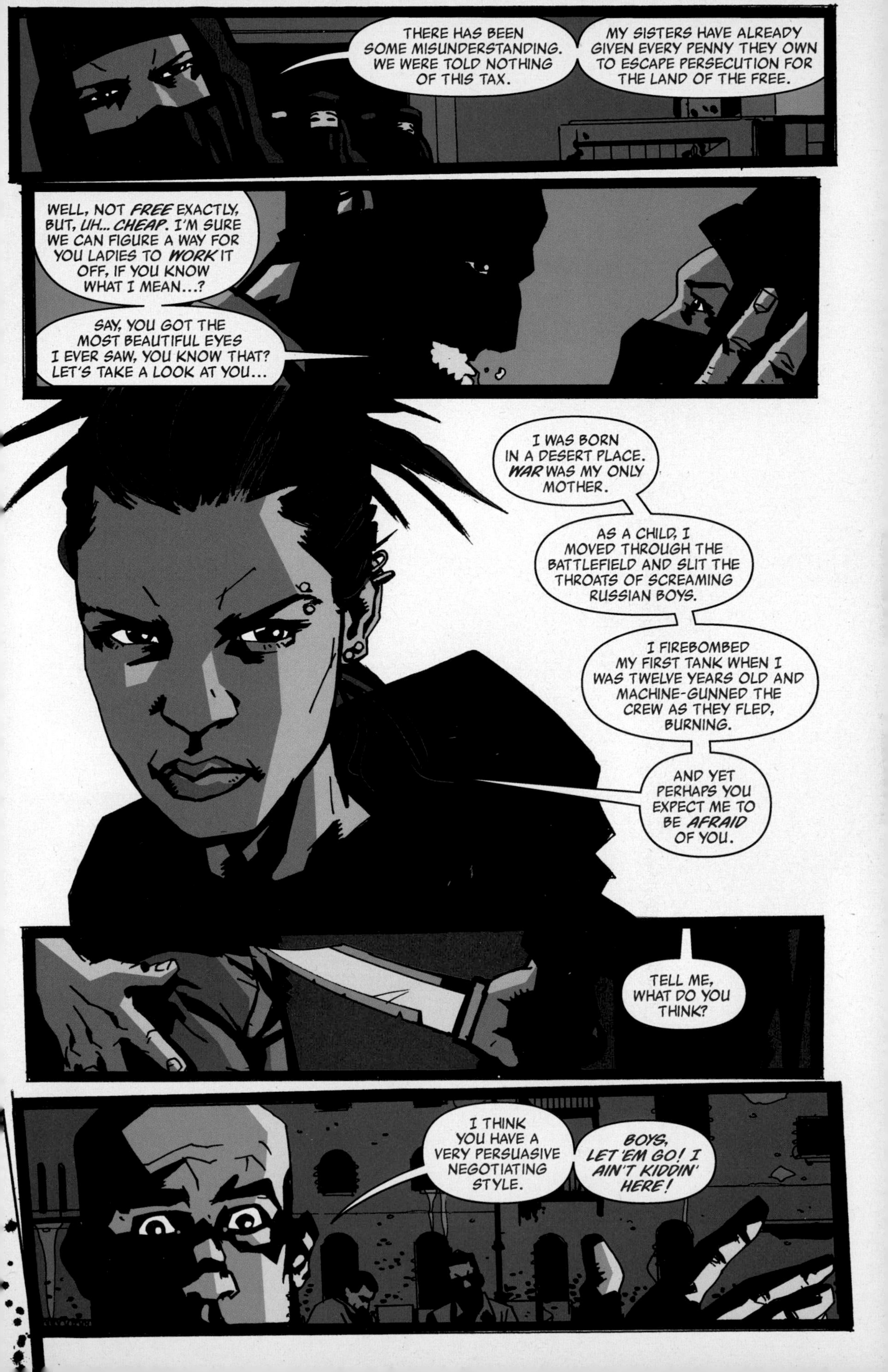
THERE HAS BEEN SOME MISUNDERSTANDING. WE WERE TOLD NOTHING OF THIS TAX.
MY SISTERS HAVE ALREADY GIVEN EVERY PENNY THEY OWN TO ESCAPE PERSECUTION FOR THE LAND OF THE FREE.
WELL, NOT FREE EXACTLY, BUT, UH... CHEAP. I'M SURE WE CAN FIGURE A WAY FOR YOU LADIES TO WORK IT OFF, IF YOU KNOW WHAT I MEAN...?
SAY, YOU GOT THE MOST BEAUTIFUL EYES I EVER SAW, YOU KNOW THAT? LET'S TAKE A LOOK AT YOU...
I WAS BORN IN A DESERT PLACE. WAR WAS MY ONLY MOTHER.
AS A CHILD, I MOVED THROUGH THE BATTLEFIELD AND SLIT THE THROATS OF SCREAMING RUSSIAN BOYS.
I FIREBOMBED MY FIRST TANK WHEN I WAS TWELVE YEARS OLD AND MACHINE-GUNNED THE CREW AS THEY FLED, BURNING.
AND YET PERHAPS YOU EXPECT ME TO BE AFRAID OF YOU.
TELL ME, WHAT DO YOU THINK?
I THINK YOU HAVE A VERY PERSUASIVE NEGOTIATING STYLE.
BOYS, LET 'EM GO! I AIN'T KIDDIN' HERE!

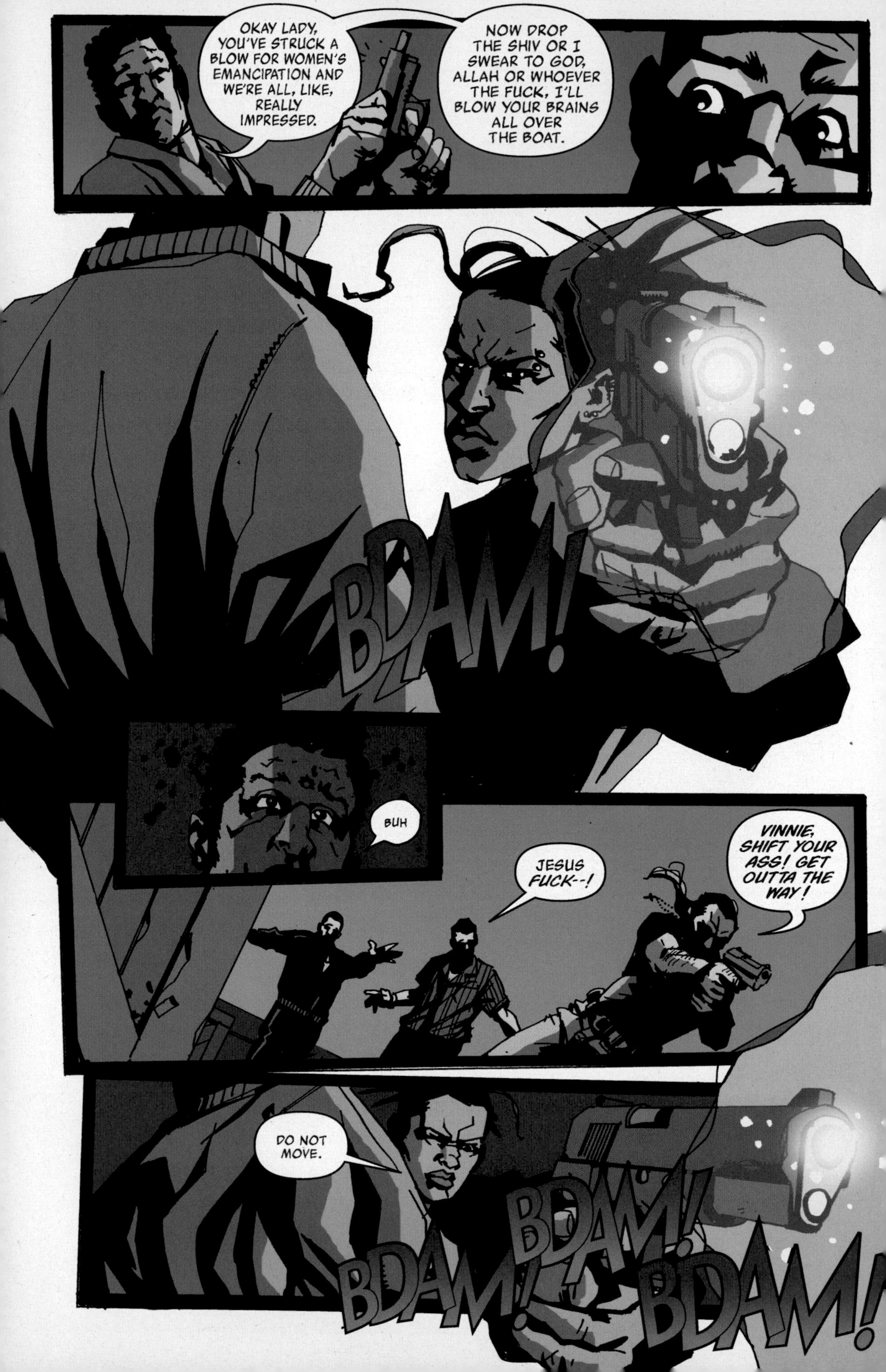
OKAY LADY, YOU'VE STRUCK A BLOW FOR WOMEN'S EMANCIPATION AND WE'RE ALL, LIKE, REALLY IMPRESSED.
NOW DROP THE SHIV OR I SWEAR TO GOD, ALLAH OR WHOEVER THE FUCK, I'LL BLOW YOUR BRAINS ALL OVER THE BOAT.
BDAM!
BUH
JESUS FUCK--!
VINNIE, SHIFT YOUR ASS! GET OUTTA THE WAY!
DO NOT MOVE.
BDAM!
BDAM!
BDAM!

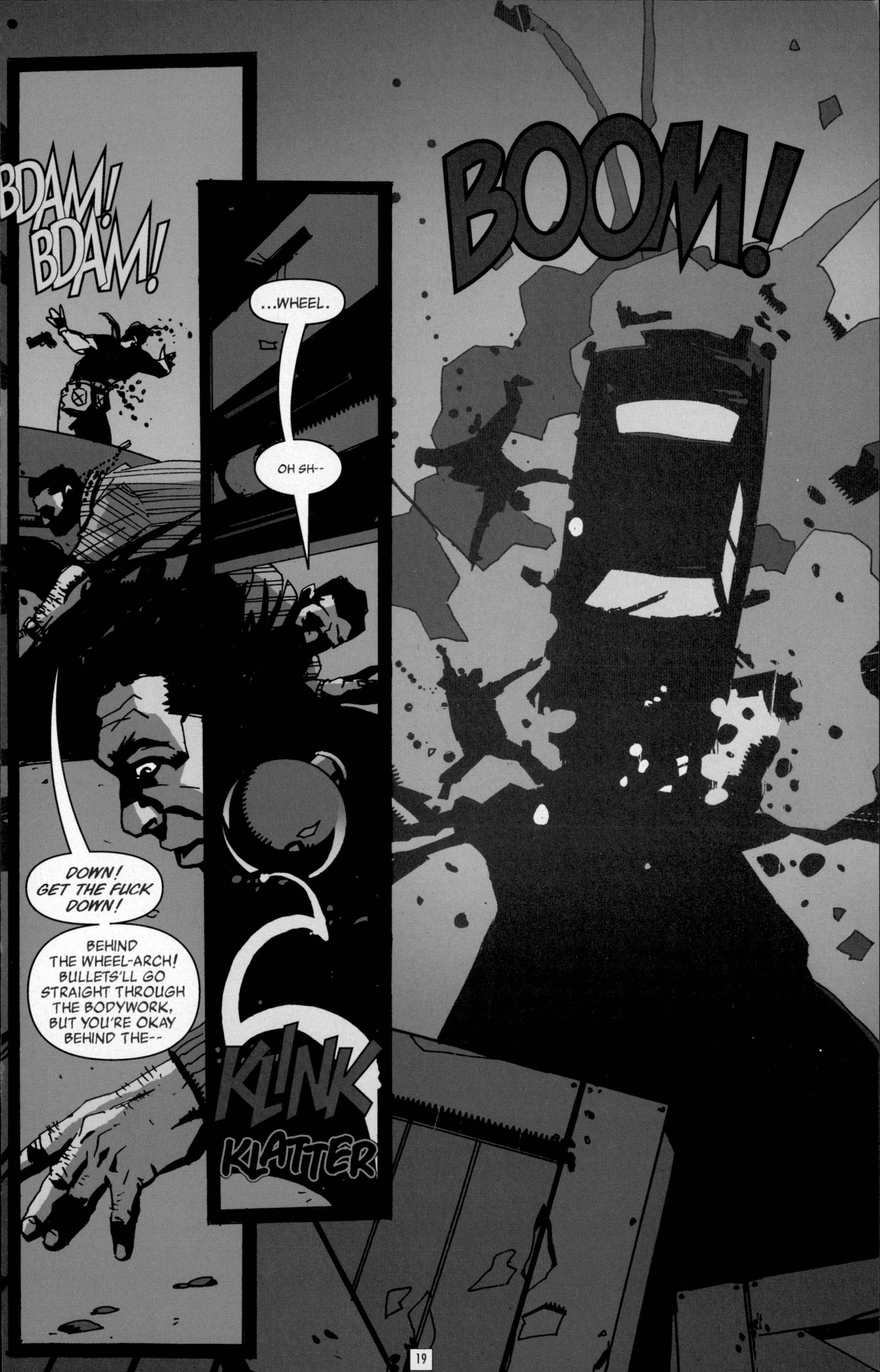
BDAM! BDAM!
...WHEEL.
OH SH--
BOOM!
DOWN! GET THE FUCK DOWN!
BEHIND THE WHEEL-ARCH! BULLETS'LL GO STRAIGHT THROUGH THE BODYWORK, BUT YOU'RE OKAY BEHIND THE--
KLINK
KLATTER

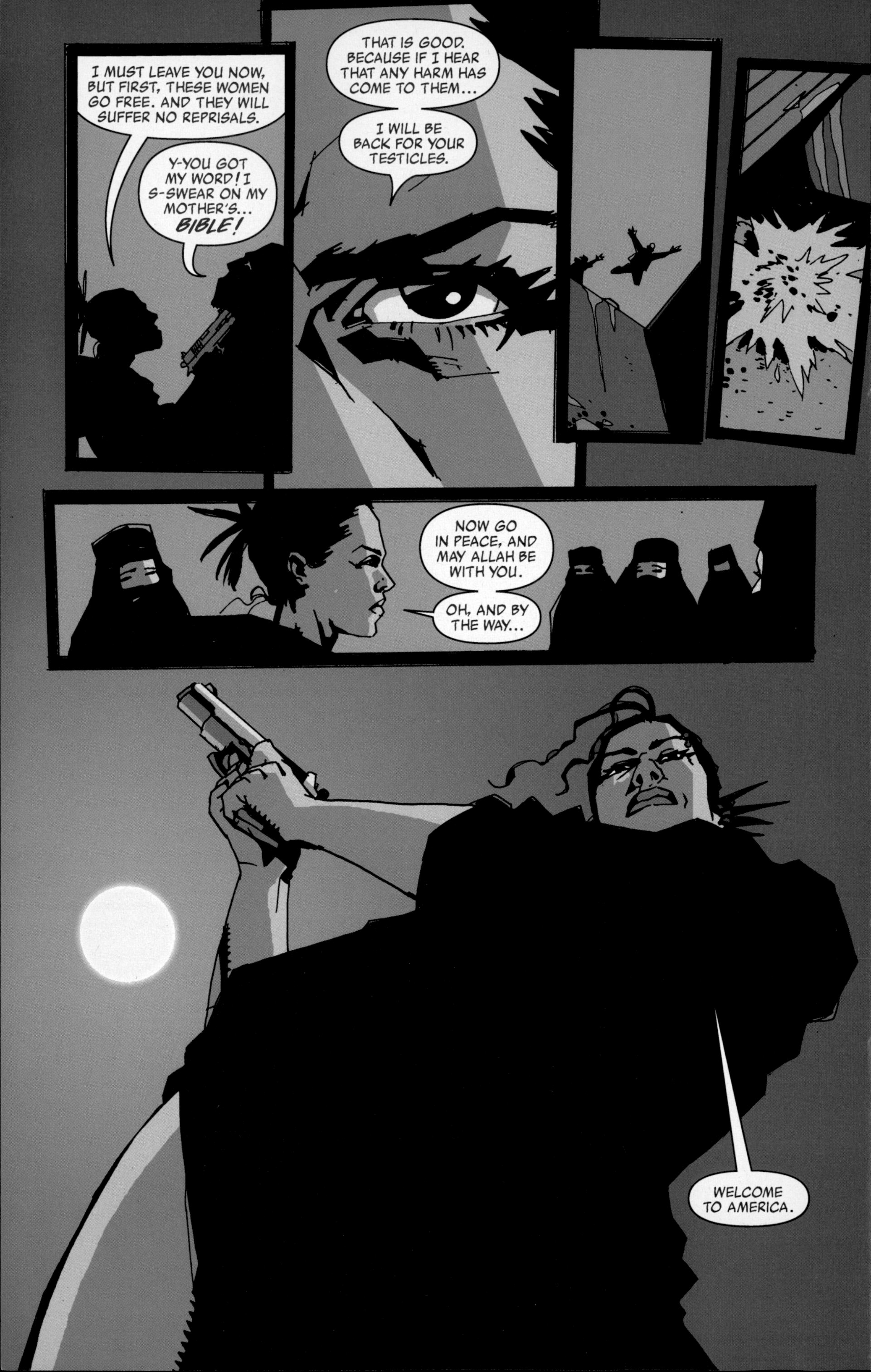
I MUST LEAVE YOU NOW, BUT FIRST, THESE WOMEN GO FREE. AND THEY WILL SUFFER NO REPRISALS.
Y-YOU GOT MY WORD! I S-SWEAR ON MY MOTHER'S... BIBLE!
THAT IS GOOD. BECAUSE IF I HEAR THAT ANY HARM HAS COME TO THEM...
I WILL BE BACK FOR YOUR TESTICLES.
NOW GO IN PEACE, AND MAY ALLAH BE WITH YOU.
OH, AND BY THE WAY...
WELCOME TO AMERICA.

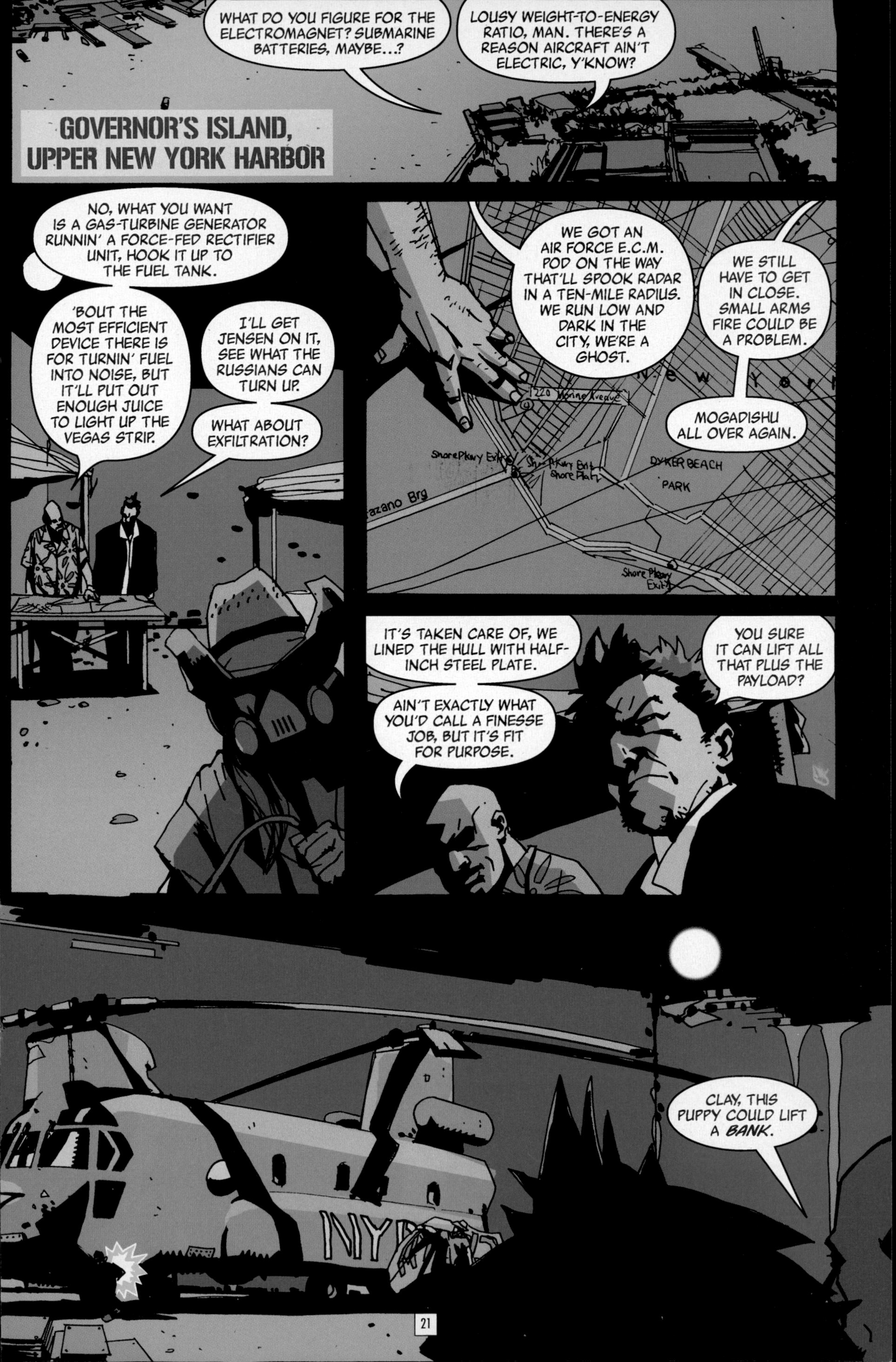
WHAT DO YOU FIGURE FOR THE ELECTROMAGNET? SUBMARINE BATTERIES, MAYBE...?
LOUSY WEIGHT-TO-ENERGY RATIO, MAN. THERE'S A REASON AIRCRAFT AIN'T ELECTRIC, Y'KNOW?
GOVERNOR'S ISLAND, UPPER NEW YORK HARBOR
NO, WHAT YOU WANT IS A GAS-TURBINE GENERATOR RUNNIN' A FORCE-FED RECTIFIER UNIT, HOOK IT UP TO THE FUEL TANK.
'BOUT THE MOST EFFICIENT DEVICE THERE IS FOR TURNIN' FUEL INTO NOISE, BUT IT'LL PUT OUT ENOUGH JUICE TO LIGHT UP THE VEGAS STRIP.
I'LL GET JENSEN ON IT, SEE WHAT THE RUSSIANS CAN TURN UP.
WHAT ABOUT EXFILTRATION?
WE GOT AN AIR FORCE E.C.M. POD ON THE WAY THAT'LL SPOOK RADAR IN A TEN-MILE RADIUS. WE RUN LOW AND DARK IN THE CITY, WE'RE A GHOST.
WE STILL HAVE TO GET IN CLOSE. SMALL ARMS FIRE COULD BE A PROBLEM.
MOGADISHU ALL OVER AGAIN.
DYKER BEACH PARK
IT'S TAKEN CARE OF, WE LINED THE HULL WITH HALF-INCH STEEL PLATE.
AIN'T EXACTLY WHAT YOU'D CALL A FINESSE JOB, BUT IT'S FIT FOR PURPOSE.
YOU SURE IT CAN LIFT ALL THAT PLUS THE PAYLOAD?
CLAY, THIS PUPPY COULD LIFT A *BANK*.

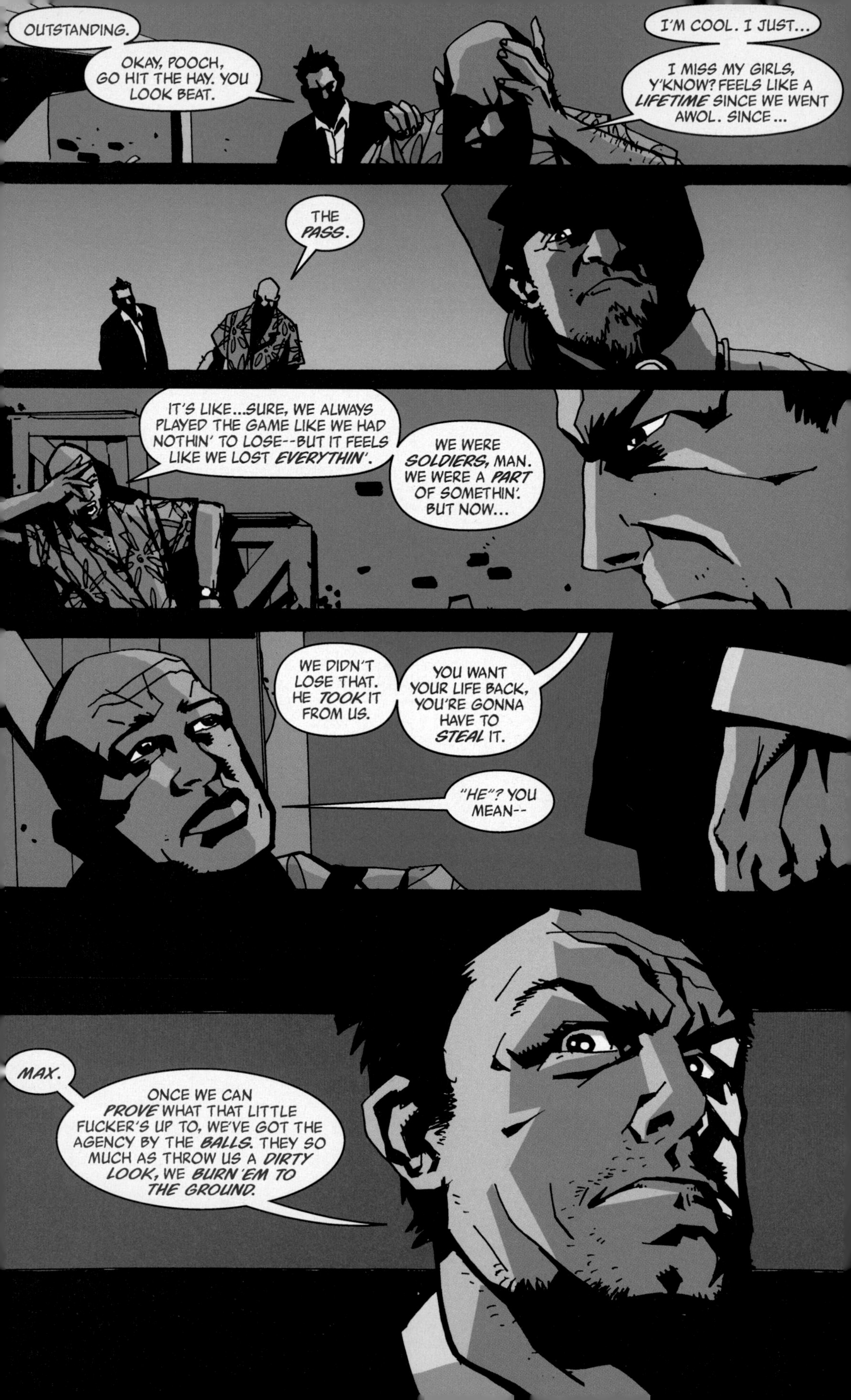
OUTSTANDING.
OKAY, POOCH, GO HIT THE HAY. YOU LOOK BEAT.
I'M COOL. I JUST...
I MISS MY GIRLS, Y'KNOW? FEELS LIKE A LIFETIME SINCE WE WENT AWOL. SINCE...
THE PASS.
IT'S LIKE...SURE, WE ALWAYS PLAYED THE GAME LIKE WE HAD NOTHIN' TO LOSE--BUT IT FEELS LIKE WE LOST EVERYTHIN'.
WE WERE SOLDIERS, MAN. WE WERE A PART OF SOMETHIN'. BUT NOW...
WE DIDN'T LOSE THAT. HE TOOK IT FROM US.
YOU WANT YOUR LIFE BACK, YOU'RE GONNA HAVE TO STEAL IT.
"HE"? YOU MEAN--
MAX.
ONCE WE CAN PROVE WHAT THAT LITTLE FUCKER'S UP TO, WE'VE GOT THE AGENCY BY THE BALLS. THEY SO MUCH AS THROW US A DIRTY LOOK, WE BURN 'EM TO THE GROUND.

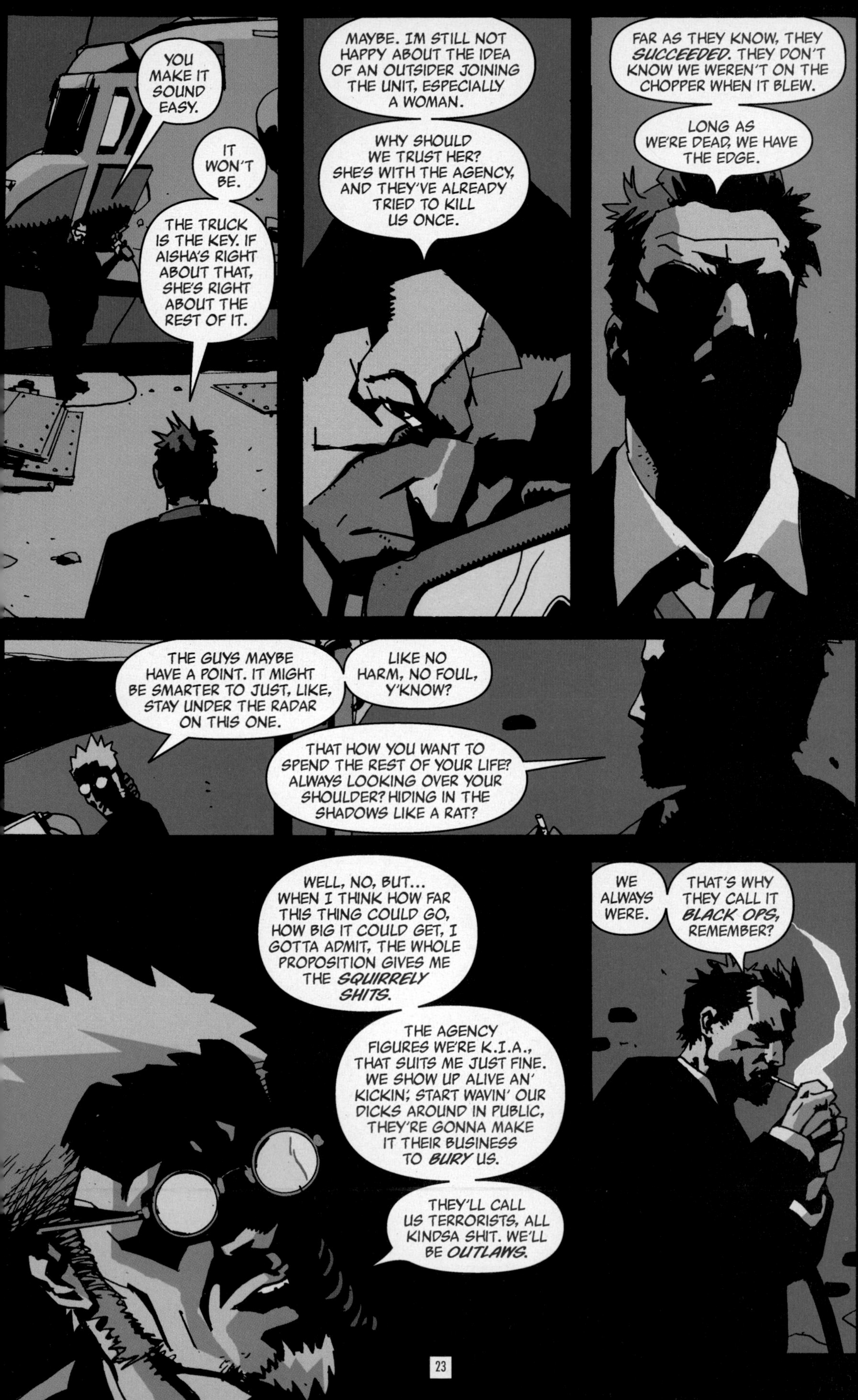
YOU MAKE IT SOUND EASY.
IT WON'T BE.
THE TRUCK IS THE KEY. IF AISHA'S RIGHT ABOUT THAT, SHE'S RIGHT ABOUT THE REST OF IT.
MAYBE. I'M STILL NOT HAPPY ABOUT THE IDEA OF AN OUTSIDER JOINING THE UNIT, ESPECIALLY A WOMAN.
WHY SHOULD WE TRUST HER? SHE'S WITH THE AGENCY, AND THEY'VE ALREADY TRIED TO KILL US ONCE.
FAR AS THEY KNOW, THEY SUCCEEDED. THEY DON'T KNOW WE WEREN'T ON THE CHOPPER WHEN IT BLEW.
LONG AS WE'RE DEAD, WE HAVE THE EDGE.
THE GUYS MAYBE HAVE A POINT. IT MIGHT BE SMARTER TO JUST, LIKE, STAY UNDER THE RADAR ON THIS ONE.
LIKE NO HARM, NO FOUL, Y'KNOW?
THAT HOW YOU WANT TO SPEND THE REST OF YOUR LIFE? ALWAYS LOOKING OVER YOUR SHOULDER? HIDING IN THE SHADOWS LIKE A RAT?
WELL, NO, BUT... WHEN I THINK HOW FAR THIS THING COULD GO, HOW BIG IT COULD GET, I GOTTA ADMIT, THE WHOLE PROPOSITION GIVES ME THE SQUIRRELY SHITS.
THE AGENCY FIGURES WE'RE K.I.A., THAT SUITS ME JUST FINE. WE SHOW UP ALIVE AN' KICKIN', START WAVIN' OUR DICKS AROUND IN PUBLIC, THEY'RE GONNA MAKE IT THEIR BUSINESS TO BURY US.
THEY'LL CALL US TERRORISTS, ALL KINDSA SHIT. WE'LL BE OUTLAWS.
WE ALWAYS WERE.
THAT'S WHY THEY CALL IT BLACK OPS, REMEMBER?

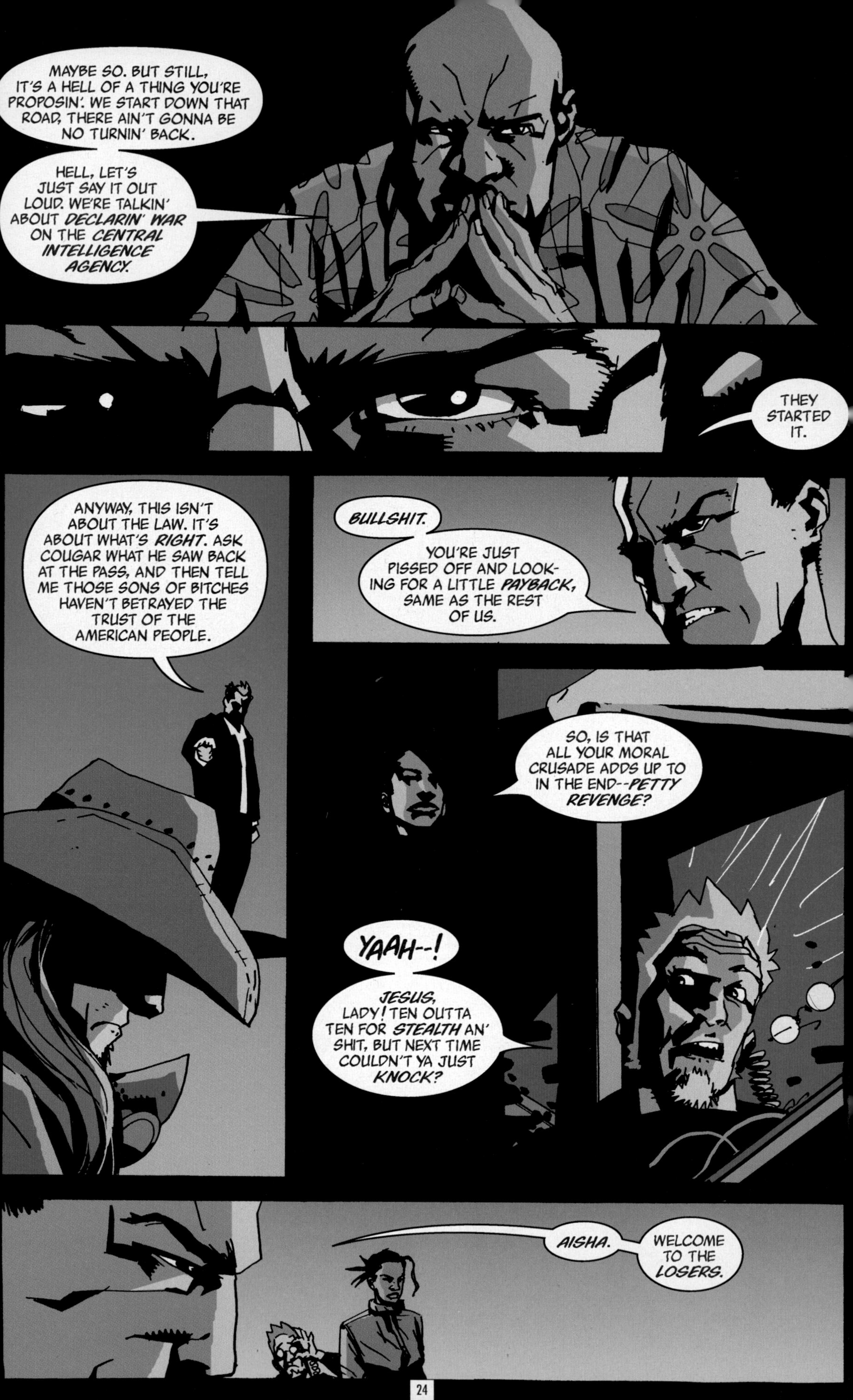
MAYBE SO. BUT STILL, IT'S A HELL OF A THING YOU'RE PROPOSIN'. WE START DOWN THAT ROAD, THERE AIN'T GONNA BE NO TURNIN' BACK.
HELL, LET'S JUST SAY IT OUT LOUD. WE'RE TALKIN' ABOUT *DECLARIN' WAR* ON THE *CENTRAL INTELLIGENCE AGENCY.*
THEY STARTED IT.
ANYWAY, THIS ISN'T ABOUT THE LAW. IT'S ABOUT WHAT'S *RIGHT*. ASK COUGAR WHAT HE SAW BACK AT THE PASS, AND THEN TELL ME THOSE SONS OF BITCHES HAVEN'T BETRAYED THE TRUST OF THE AMERICAN PEOPLE.
*BULLSHIT.*
YOU'RE JUST PISSED OFF AND LOOKING FOR A LITTLE *PAYBACK*, SAME AS THE REST OF US.
SO, IS THAT ALL YOUR MORAL CRUSADE ADDS UP TO IN THE END--*PETTY REVENGE?*
YAAH--!
*JESUS,* LADY! TEN OUTTA TEN FOR *STEALTH* AN' SHIT, BUT NEXT TIME COULDN'T YA JUST *KNOCK?*
*AISHA.*
WELCOME TO THE *LOSERS.*

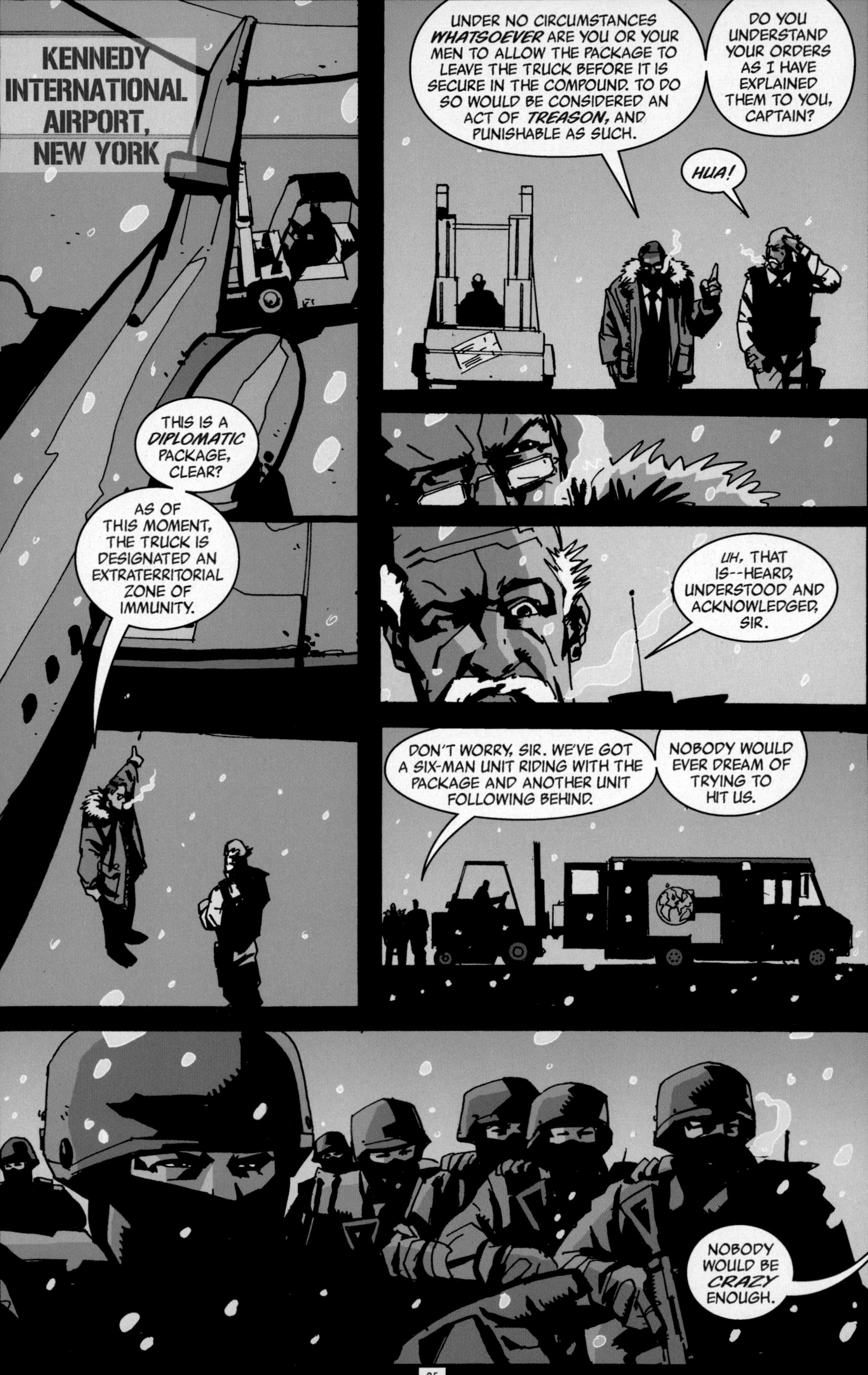
KENNEDY INTERNATIONAL AIRPORT, NEW YORK
UNDER NO CIRCUMSTANCES WHATSOEVER ARE YOU OR YOUR MEN TO ALLOW THE PACKAGE TO LEAVE THE TRUCK BEFORE IT IS SECURE IN THE COMPOUND. TO DO SO WOULD BE CONSIDERED AN ACT OF TREASON, AND PUNISHABLE AS SUCH.
DO YOU UNDERSTAND YOUR ORDERS AS I HAVE EXPLAINED THEM TO YOU, CAPTAIN?
HUA!
THIS IS A DIPLOMATIC PACKAGE, CLEAR?
AS OF THIS MOMENT, THE TRUCK IS DESIGNATED AN EXTRATERRITORIAL ZONE OF IMMUNITY.
UH, THAT IS--HEARD, UNDERSTOOD AND ACKNOWLEDGED, SIR.
DON'T WORRY, SIR. WE'VE GOT A SIX-MAN UNIT RIDING WITH THE PACKAGE AND ANOTHER UNIT FOLLOWING BEHIND.
NOBODY WOULD EVER DREAM OF TRYING TO HIT US.
NOBODY WOULD BE CRAZY ENOUGH.

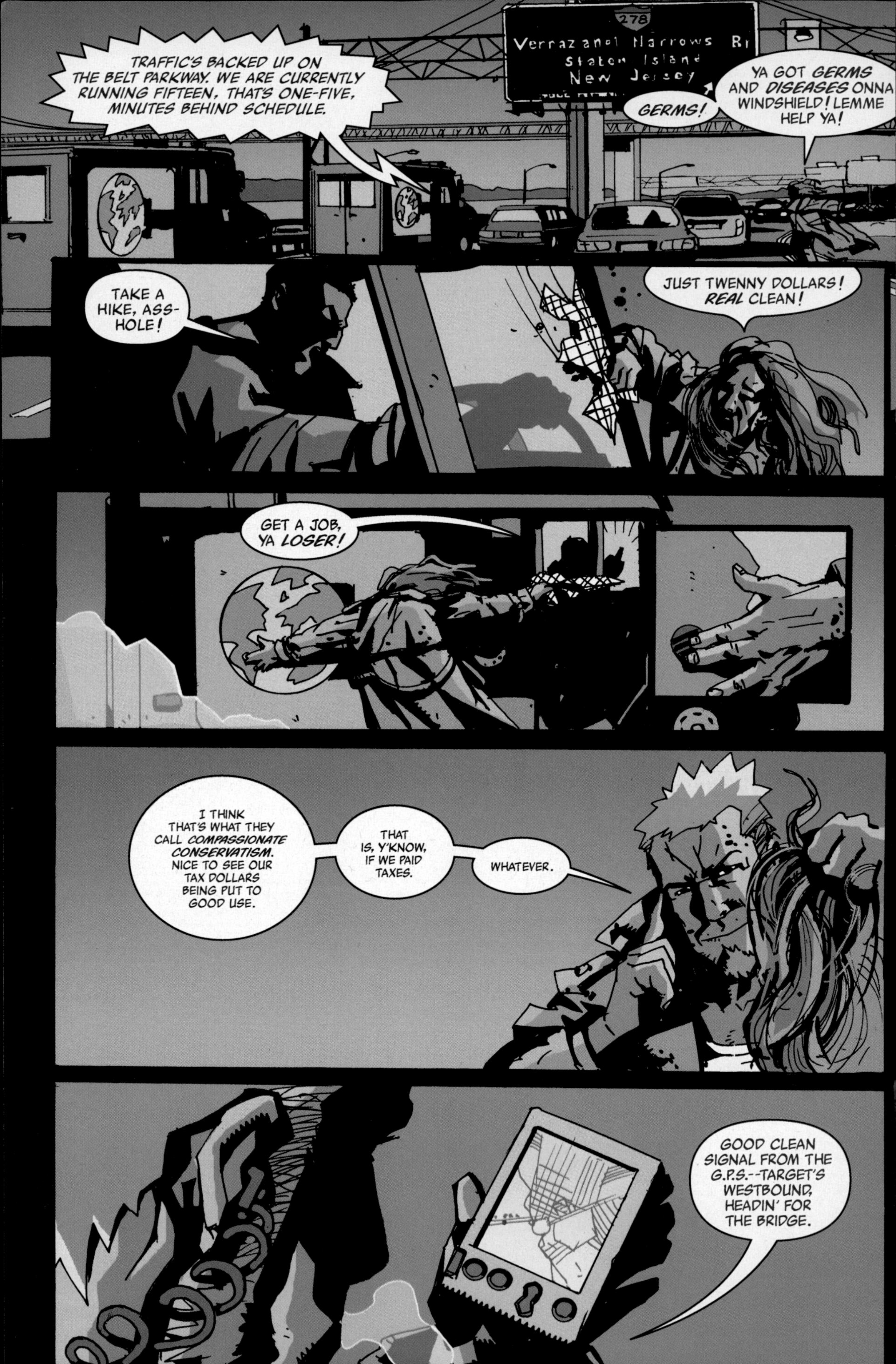
TRAFFIC'S BACKED UP ON THE BELT PARKWAY. WE ARE CURRENTLY RUNNING FIFTEEN. THAT'S ONE-FIVE, MINUTES BEHIND SCHEDULE.
278
Verrazano Narrows Br
Staten Island
New Jersey
GERMS!
YA GOT GERMS AND DISEASES ONNA WINDSHIELD! LEMME HELP YA!
TAKE A HIKE, ASS-HOLE!
JUST TWENNY DOLLARS! REAL CLEAN!
GET A JOB, YA LOSER!
I THINK THAT'S WHAT THEY CALL COMPASSIONATE CONSERVATISM. NICE TO SEE OUR TAX DOLLARS BEING PUT TO GOOD USE.
THAT IS, Y'KNOW, IF WE PAID TAXES.
WHATEVER.
GOOD CLEAN SIGNAL FROM THE G.P.S.--TARGET'S WESTBOUND, HEADIN' FOR THE BRIDGE.

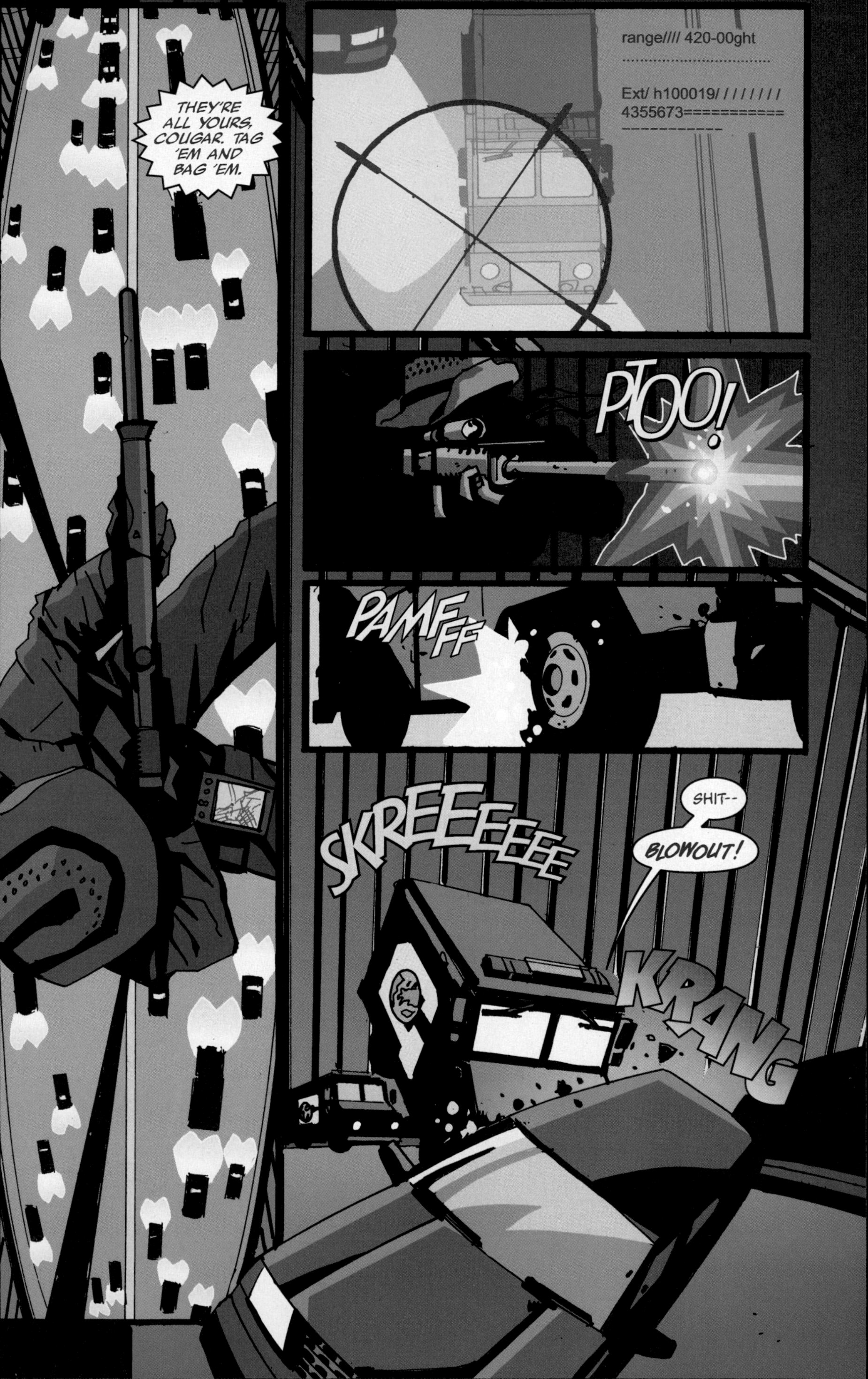
THEY'RE ALL YOURS, COUGAR. TAG 'EM AND BAG 'EM.
range//// 420-00ght
Ext/ h100019/ / / / / / / /
4355673===========
PTOO!
PAMFFF
SKREEEEEEEE
SHIT--
BLOWOUT!
KRANG

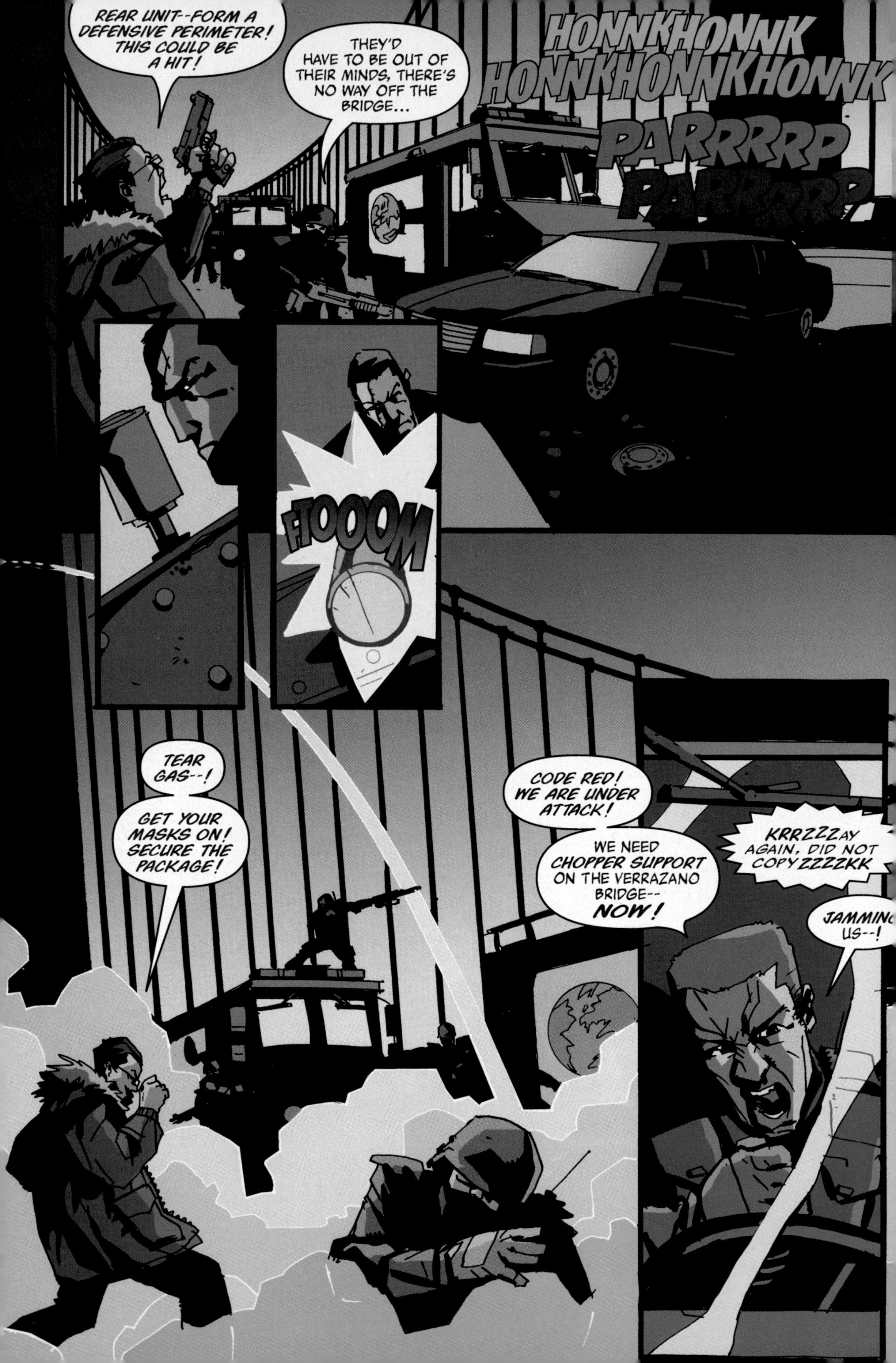
REAR UNIT--FORM A DEFENSIVE PERIMETER! THIS COULD BE A HIT!
THEY'D HAVE TO BE OUT OF THEIR MINDS, THERE'S NO WAY OFF THE BRIDGE...
HONNKHONNK
HONNKHONNKHONNK
PARRRRP
PARRRRP
FTOOOM
TEAR GAS--!
GET YOUR MASKS ON! SECURE THE PACKAGE!
CODE RED! WE ARE UNDER ATTACK!
WE NEED CHOPPER SUPPORT ON THE VERRAZANO BRIDGE-- NOW!
KRRZZZay AGAIN, DID NOT COPYZZZZKK
JAMMING US--!

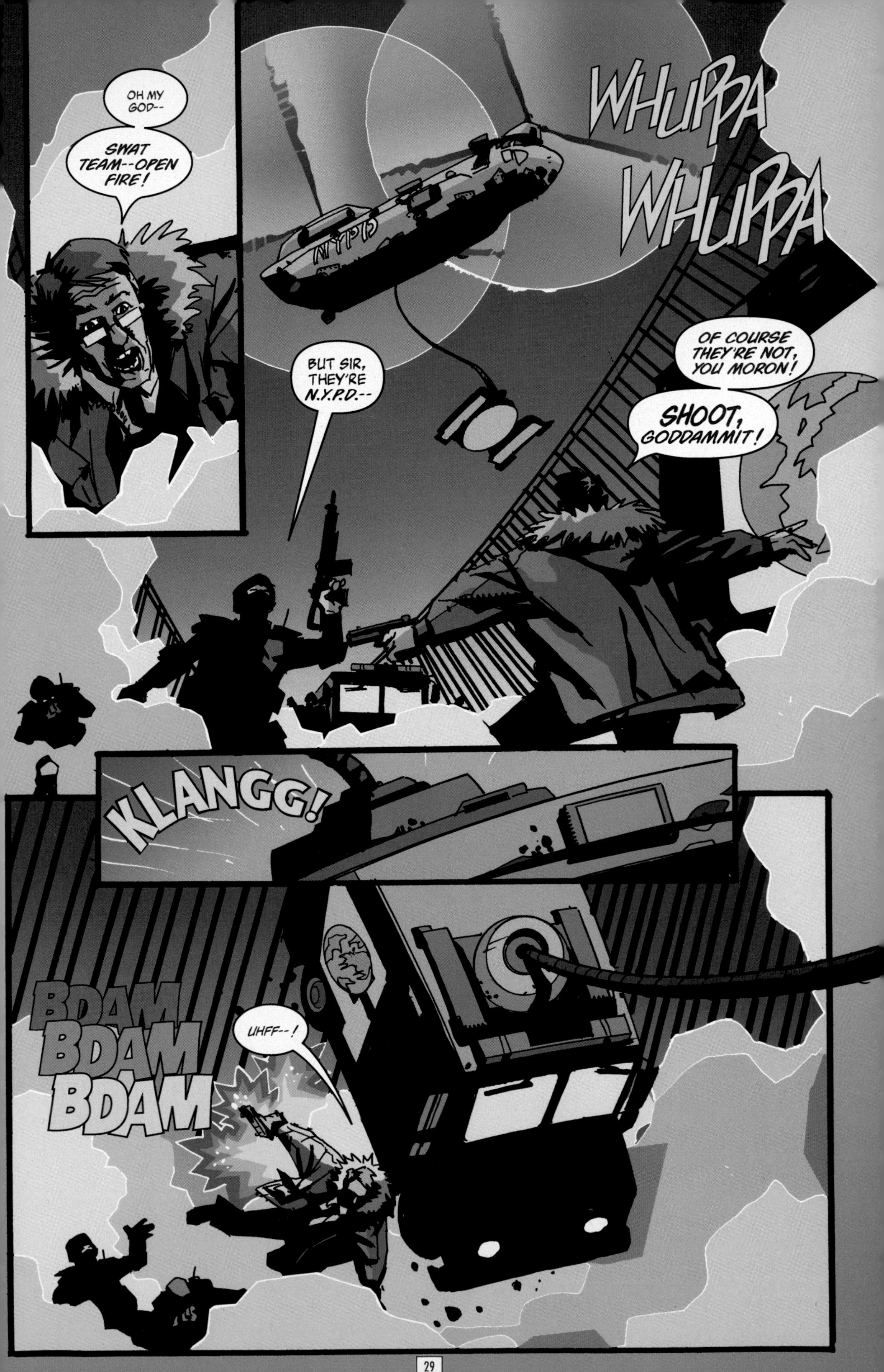
OH MY GOD--
SWAT TEAM--OPEN FIRE!
WHUPPA
WHUPPA
BUT SIR, THEY'RE N.Y.P.D.--
OF COURSE THEY'RE NOT, YOU MORON!
SHOOT, GODDAMMIT!
KLANGG!
BDAM
BDAM
BDAM
UHFF--!

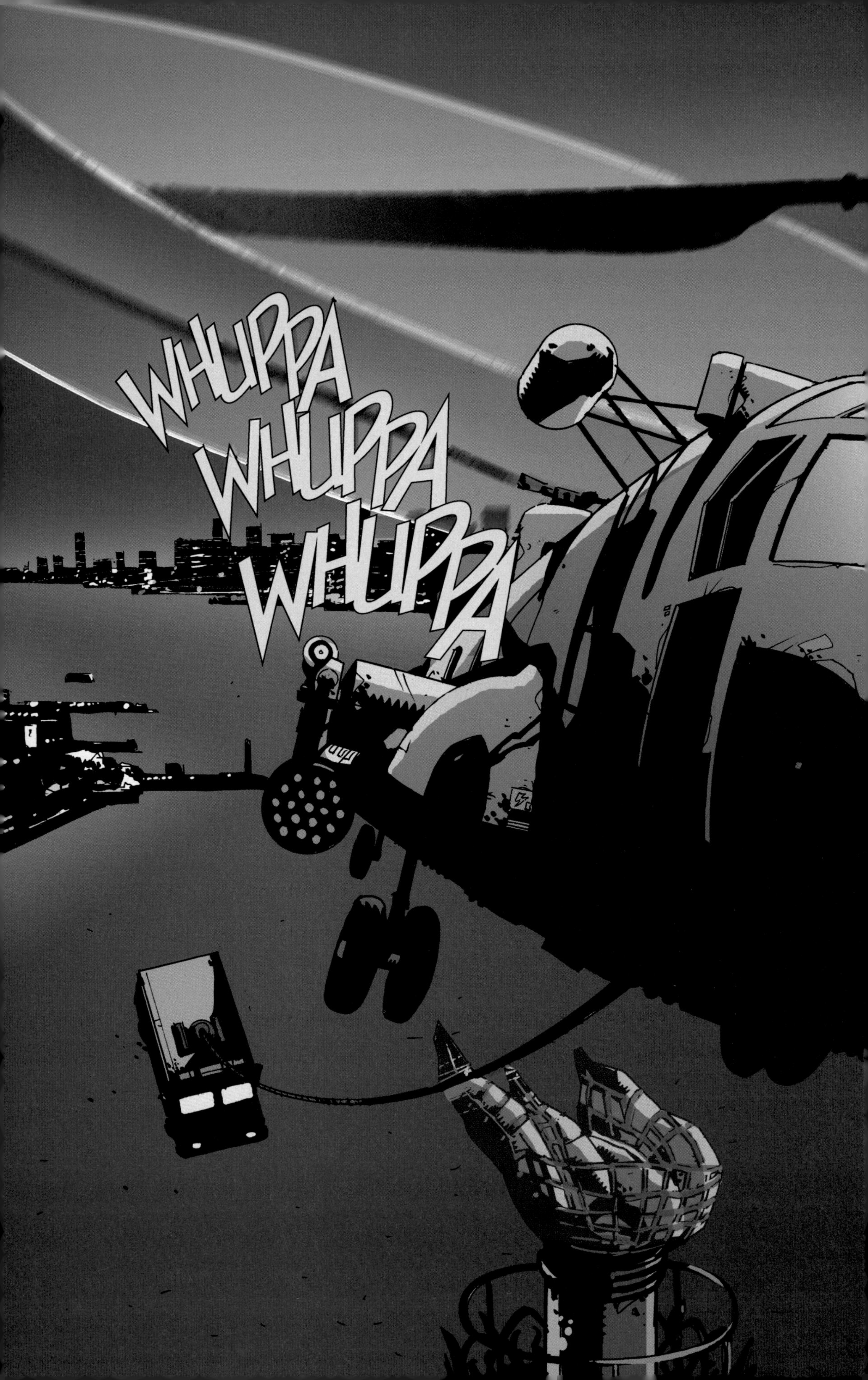
WHUPPA
WHUPPA
WHUPPA

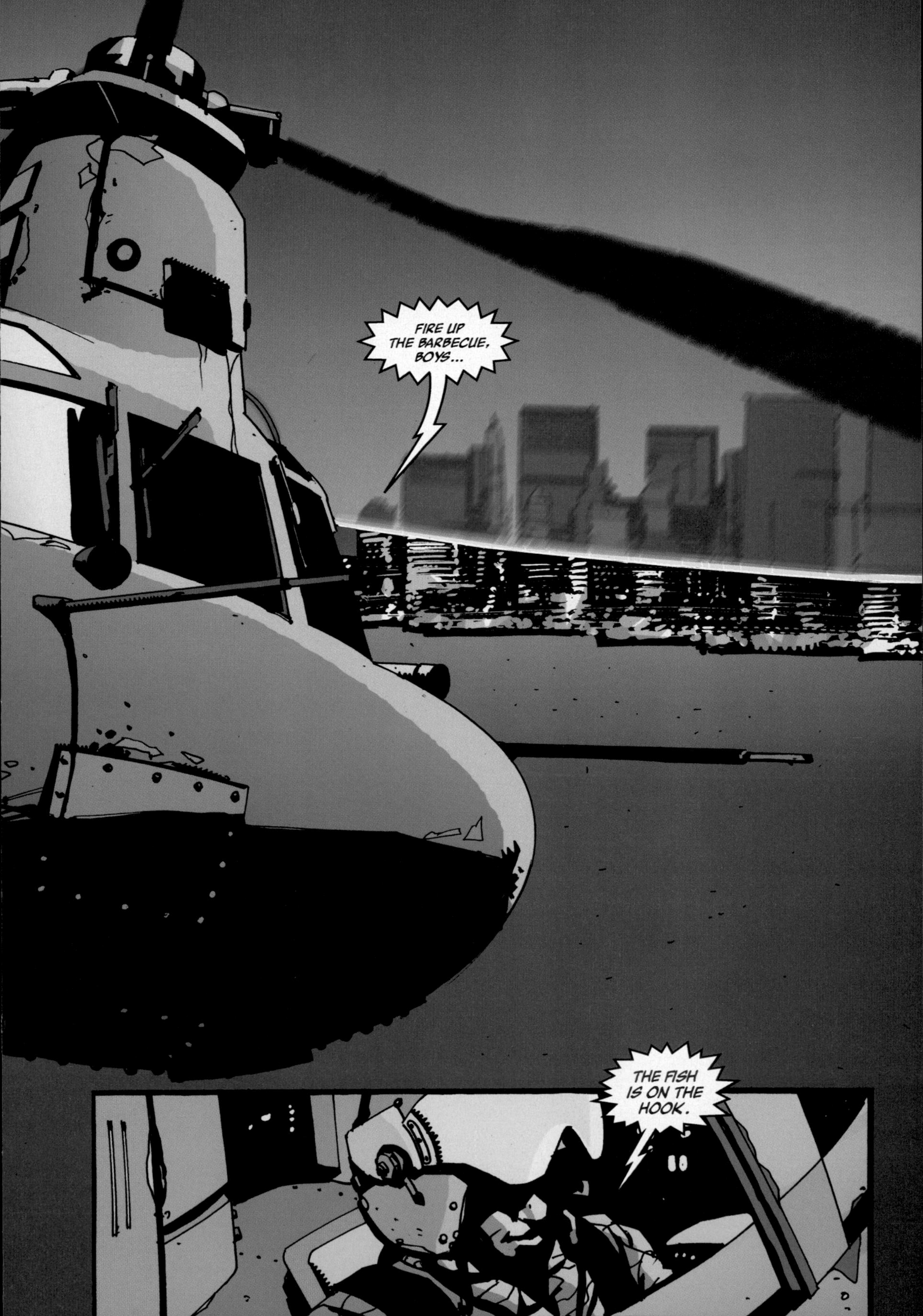
FIRE UP THE BARBECUE, BOYS...
THE FISH IS ON THE HOOK.

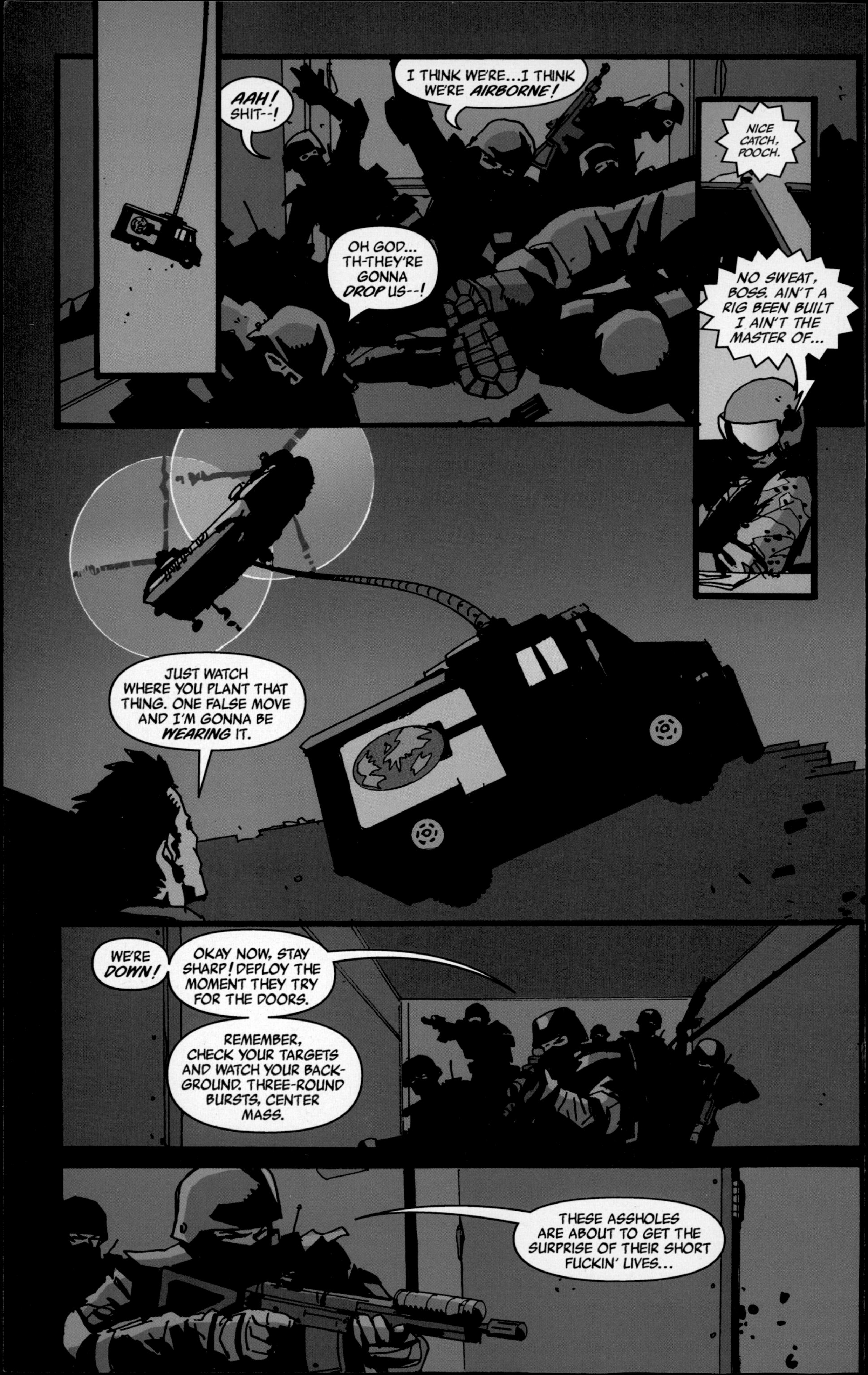
AAH! SHIT--!
I THINK WE'RE...I THINK WE'RE AIRBORNE!
OH GOD... TH-THEY'RE GONNA DROP US--!
NICE CATCH, POOCH.
NO SWEAT, BOSS. AIN'T A RIG BEEN BUILT I AIN'T THE MASTER OF...
JUST WATCH WHERE YOU PLANT THAT THING. ONE FALSE MOVE AND I'M GONNA BE WEARING IT.
WE'RE DOWN!
OKAY NOW, STAY SHARP! DEPLOY THE MOMENT THEY TRY FOR THE DOORS.
REMEMBER, CHECK YOUR TARGETS AND WATCH YOUR BACKGROUND. THREE-ROUND BURSTS, CENTER MASS.
THESE ASSHOLES ARE ABOUT TO GET THE SURPRISE OF THEIR SHORT FUCKIN' LIVES...

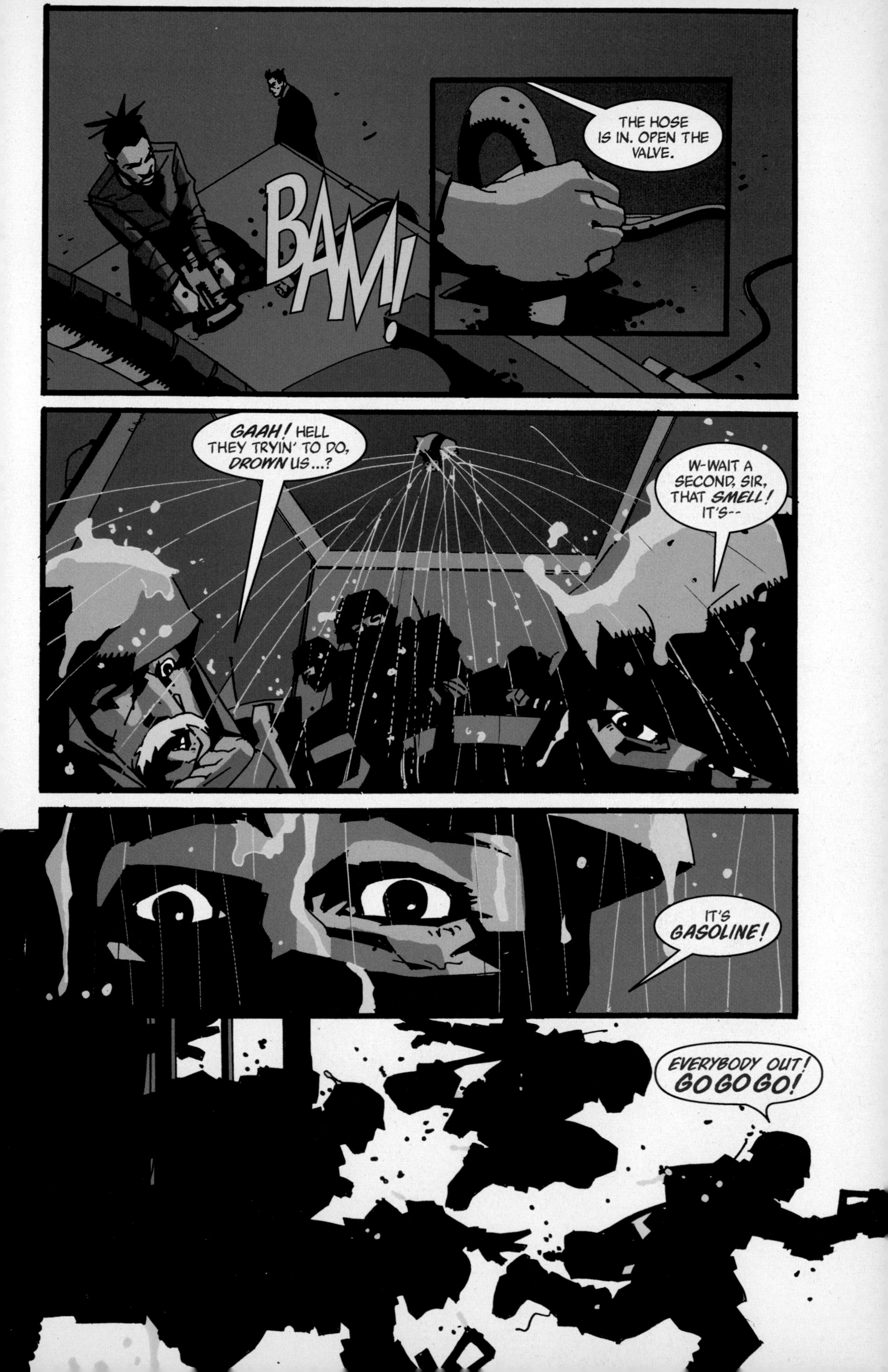
BAM!
THE HOSE IS IN. OPEN THE VALVE.
GAAH! HELL THEY TRYIN' TO DO, DROWN US...?
W-WAIT A SECOND, SIR, THAT SMELL! IT'S--
IT'S GASOLINE!
EVERYBODY OUT! GO GO GO!

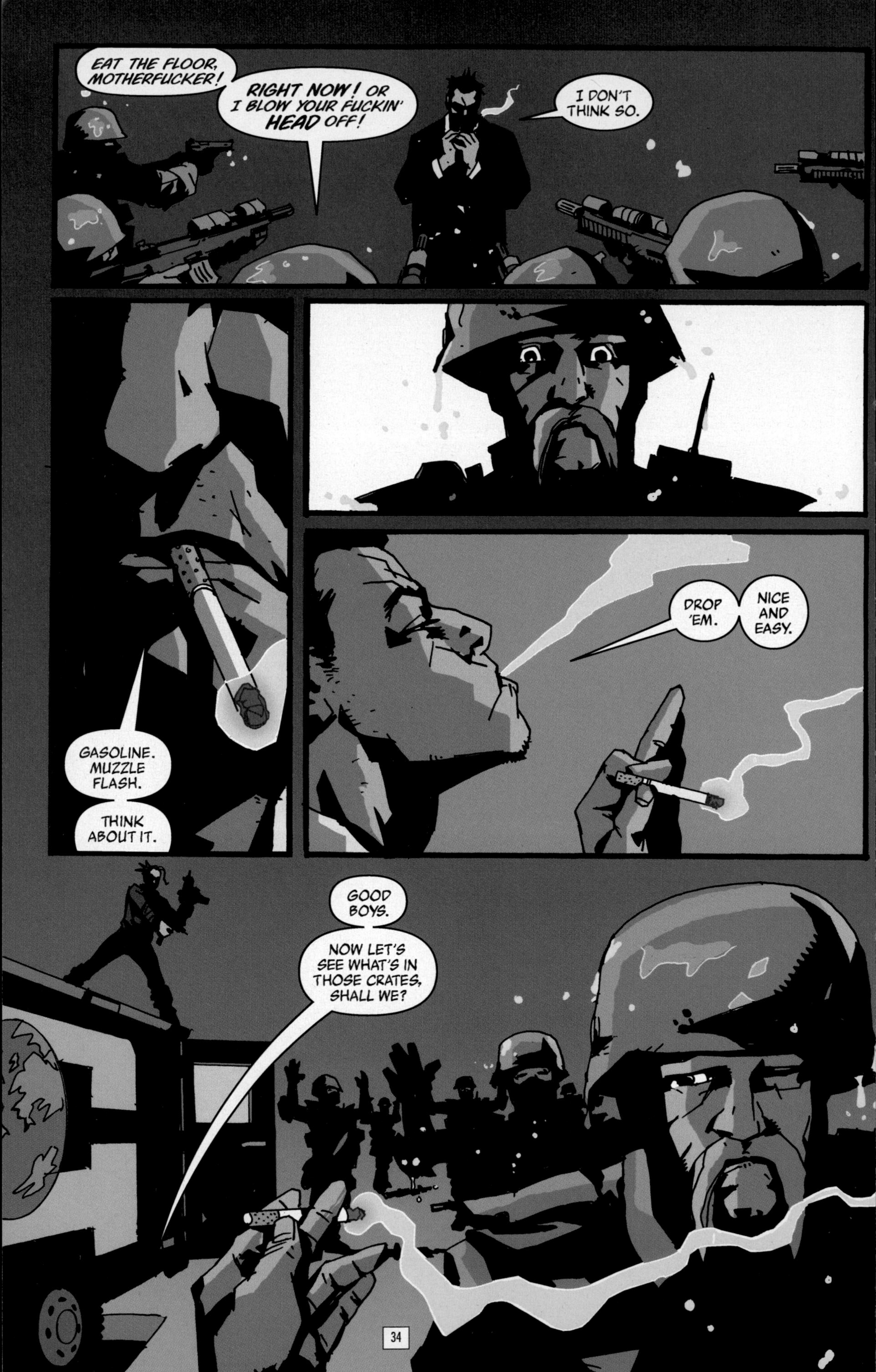
EAT THE FLOOR, MOTHERFUCKER!
RIGHT NOW! OR I BLOW YOUR FUCKIN' HEAD OFF!
I DON'T THINK SO.
GASOLINE. MUZZLE FLASH.
THINK ABOUT IT.
DROP 'EM.
NICE AND EASY.
GOOD BOYS.
NOW LET'S SEE WHAT'S IN THOSE CRATES, SHALL WE?

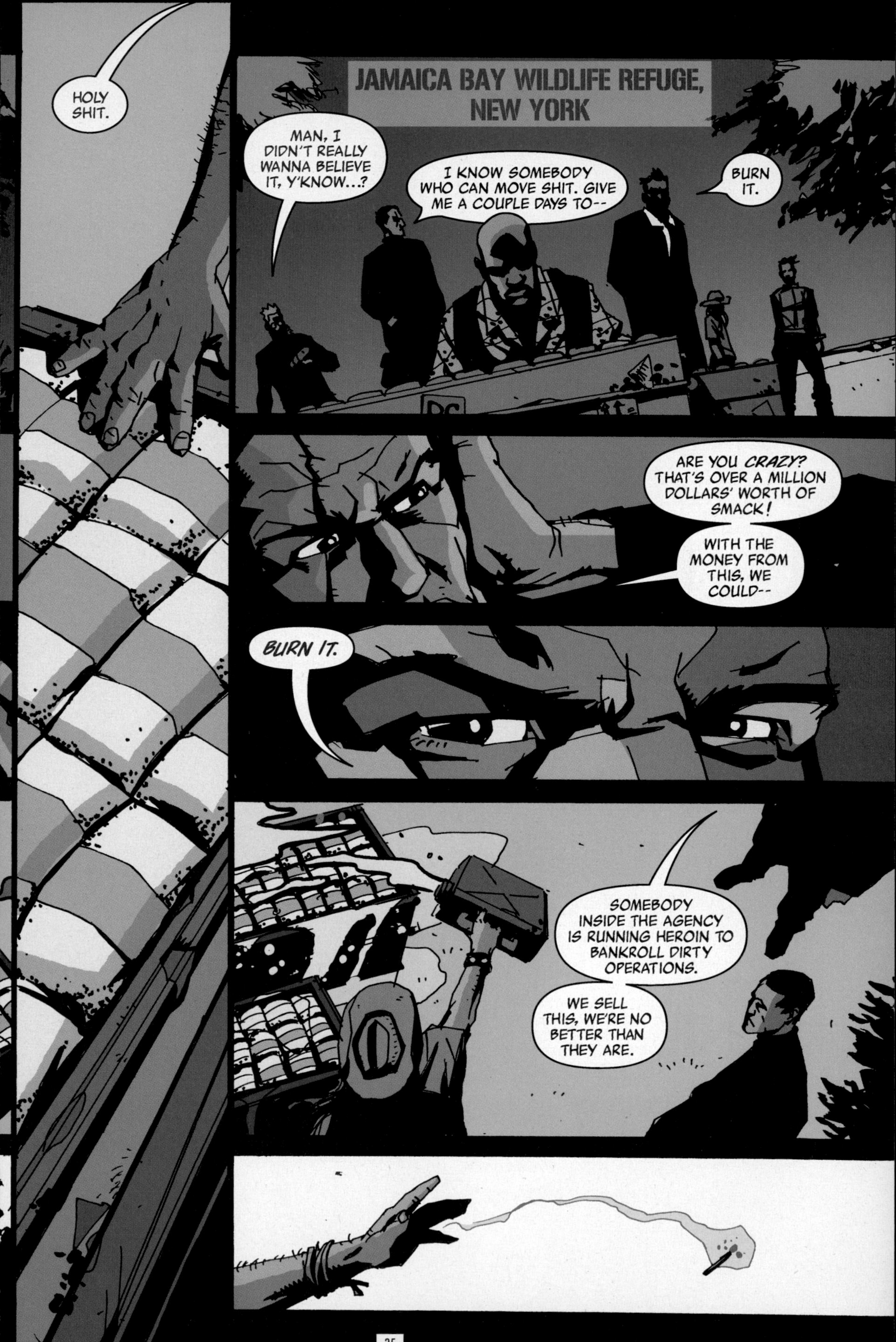
HOLY SHIT.
JAMAICA BAY WILDLIFE REFUGE, NEW YORK
MAN, I DIDN'T REALLY WANNA BELIEVE IT, Y'KNOW...?
I KNOW SOMEBODY WHO CAN MOVE SHIT. GIVE ME A COUPLE DAYS TO--
BURN IT.
ARE YOU *CRAZY*? THAT'S OVER A MILLION DOLLARS' WORTH OF SMACK!
WITH THE MONEY FROM THIS, WE COULD--
*BURN IT.*
SOMEBODY INSIDE THE AGENCY IS RUNNING HEROIN TO BANKROLL DIRTY OPERATIONS.
WE SELL THIS, WE'RE NO BETTER THAN THEY ARE.

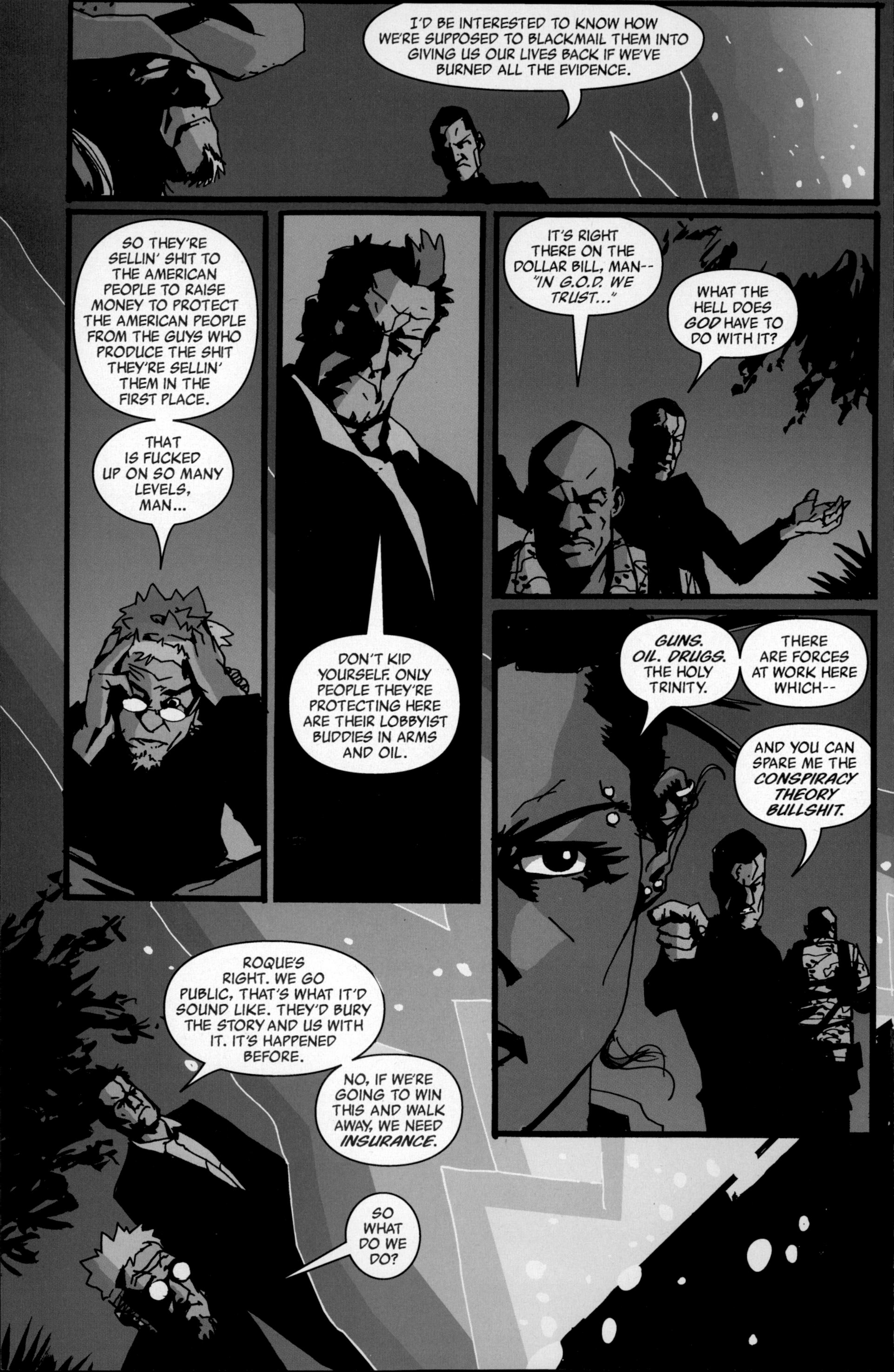
I'D BE INTERESTED TO KNOW HOW WE'RE SUPPOSED TO BLACKMAIL THEM INTO GIVING US OUR LIVES BACK IF WE'VE BURNED ALL THE EVIDENCE.
SO THEY'RE SELLIN' SHIT TO THE AMERICAN PEOPLE TO RAISE MONEY TO PROTECT THE AMERICAN PEOPLE FROM THE GUYS WHO PRODUCE THE SHIT THEY'RE SELLIN' THEM IN THE FIRST PLACE.
THAT IS FUCKED UP ON SO MANY LEVELS, MAN...
DON'T KID YOURSELF. ONLY PEOPLE THEY'RE PROTECTING HERE ARE THEIR LOBBYIST BUDDIES IN ARMS AND OIL.
IT'S RIGHT THERE ON THE DOLLAR BILL, MAN-- "IN G.O.D. WE TRUST..."
WHAT THE HELL DOES GOD HAVE TO DO WITH IT?
GUNS. OIL. DRUGS. THE HOLY TRINITY.
THERE ARE FORCES AT WORK HERE WHICH--
AND YOU CAN SPARE ME THE CONSPIRACY THEORY BULLSHIT.
ROQUE'S RIGHT. WE GO PUBLIC, THAT'S WHAT IT'D SOUND LIKE. THEY'D BURY THE STORY AND US WITH IT. IT'S HAPPENED BEFORE.
NO, IF WE'RE GOING TO WIN THIS AND WALK AWAY, WE NEED INSURANCE.
SO WHAT DO WE DO?

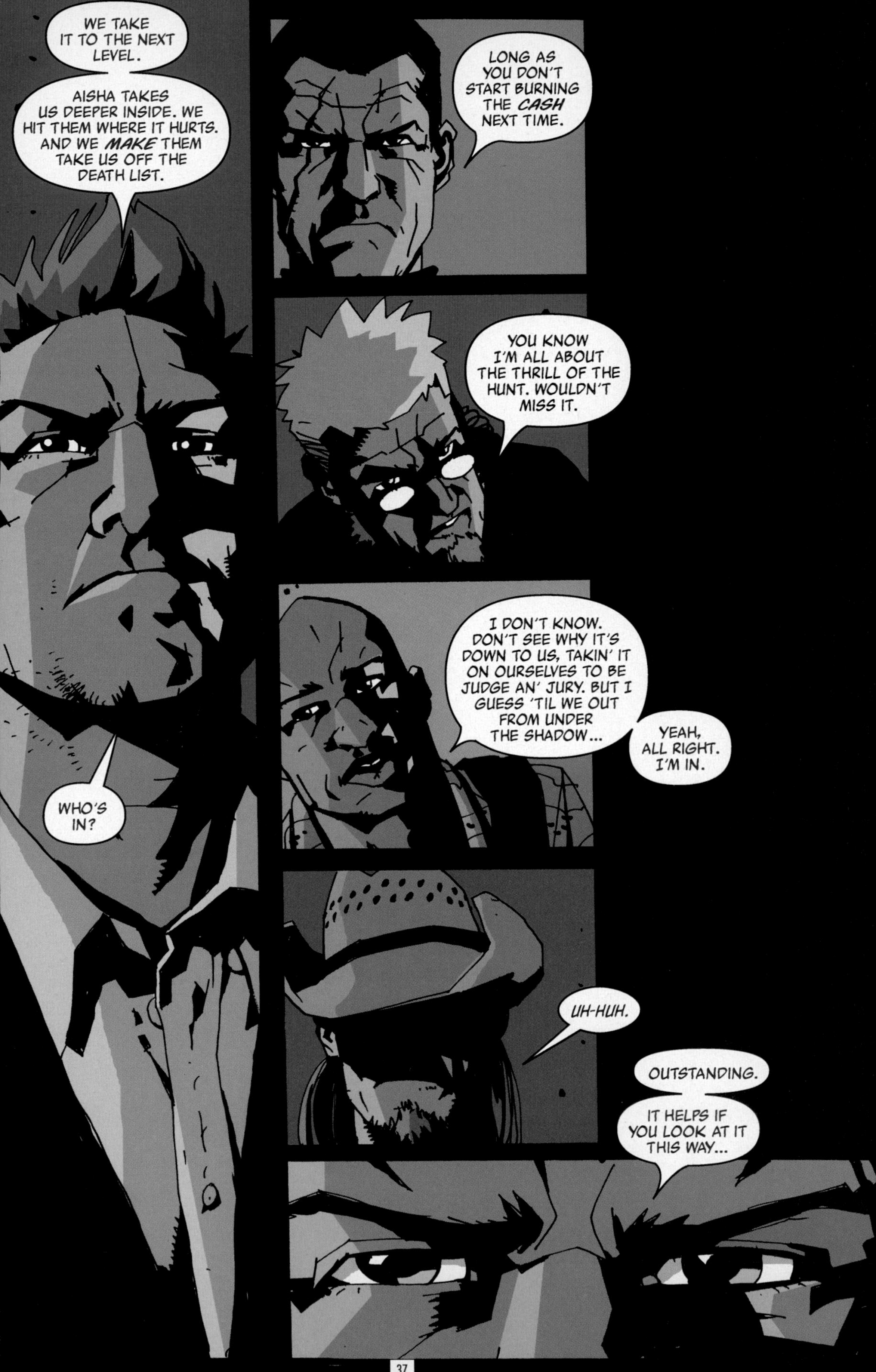
WE TAKE IT TO THE NEXT LEVEL.
AISHA TAKES US DEEPER INSIDE. WE HIT THEM WHERE IT HURTS. AND WE MAKE THEM TAKE US OFF THE DEATH LIST.
LONG AS YOU DON'T START BURNING THE CASH NEXT TIME.
YOU KNOW I'M ALL ABOUT THE THRILL OF THE HUNT. WOULDN'T MISS IT.
WHO'S IN?
I DON'T KNOW. DON'T SEE WHY IT'S DOWN TO US, TAKIN' IT ON OURSELVES TO BE JUDGE AN' JURY. BUT I GUESS 'TIL WE OUT FROM UNDER THE SHADOW...
YEAH, ALL RIGHT. I'M IN.
UH-HUH.
OUTSTANDING.
IT HELPS IF YOU LOOK AT IT THIS WAY...

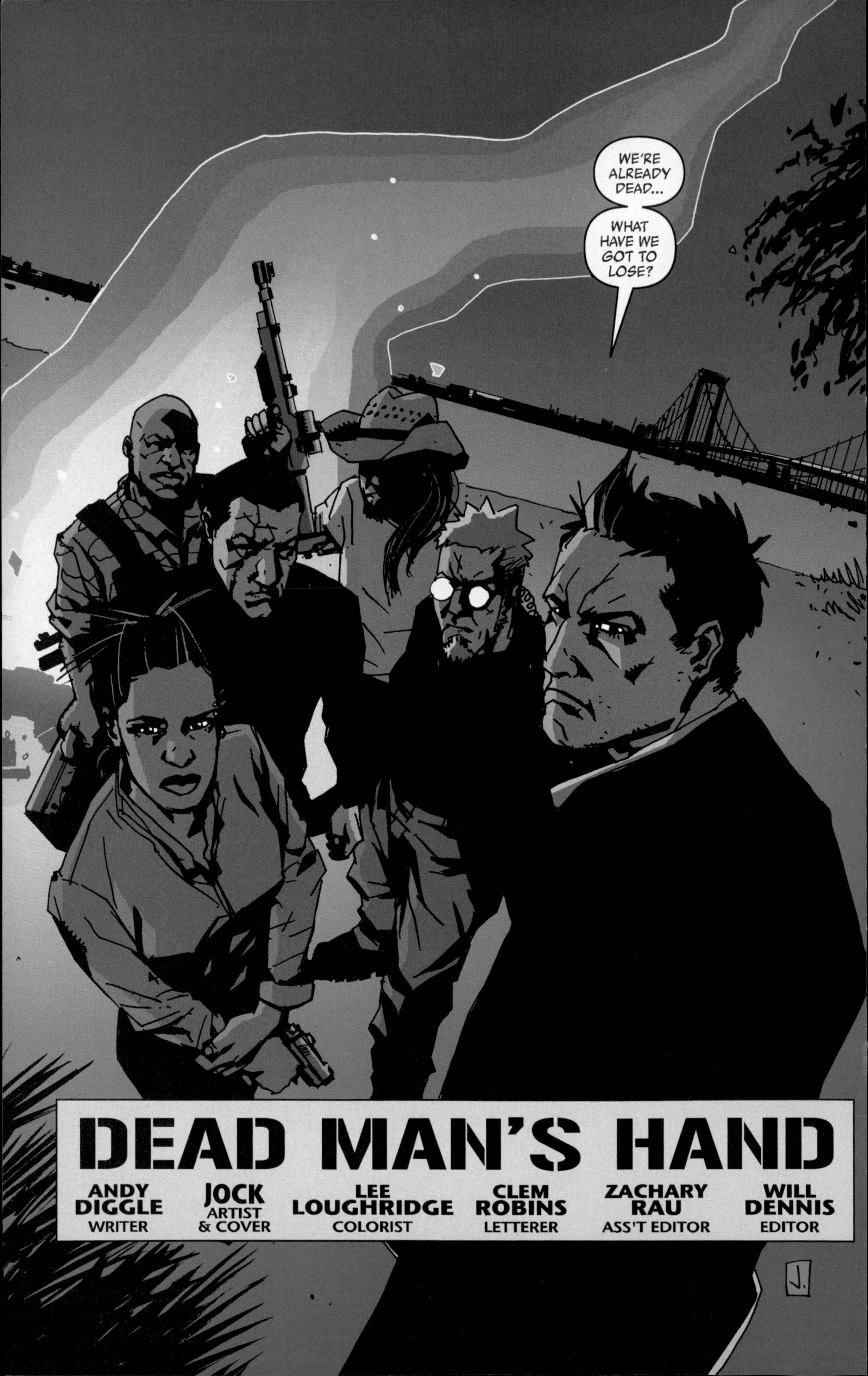
WE'RE ALREADY DEAD...
WHAT HAVE WE GOT TO LOSE?
DEAD MAN'S HAND
ANDY DIGGLE WRITER
JOCK ARTIST & COVER
LEE LOUGHRIDGE COLORIST
CLEM ROBINS LETTERER
ZACHARY RAU ASS'T EDITOR
WILL DENNIS EDITOR
J.

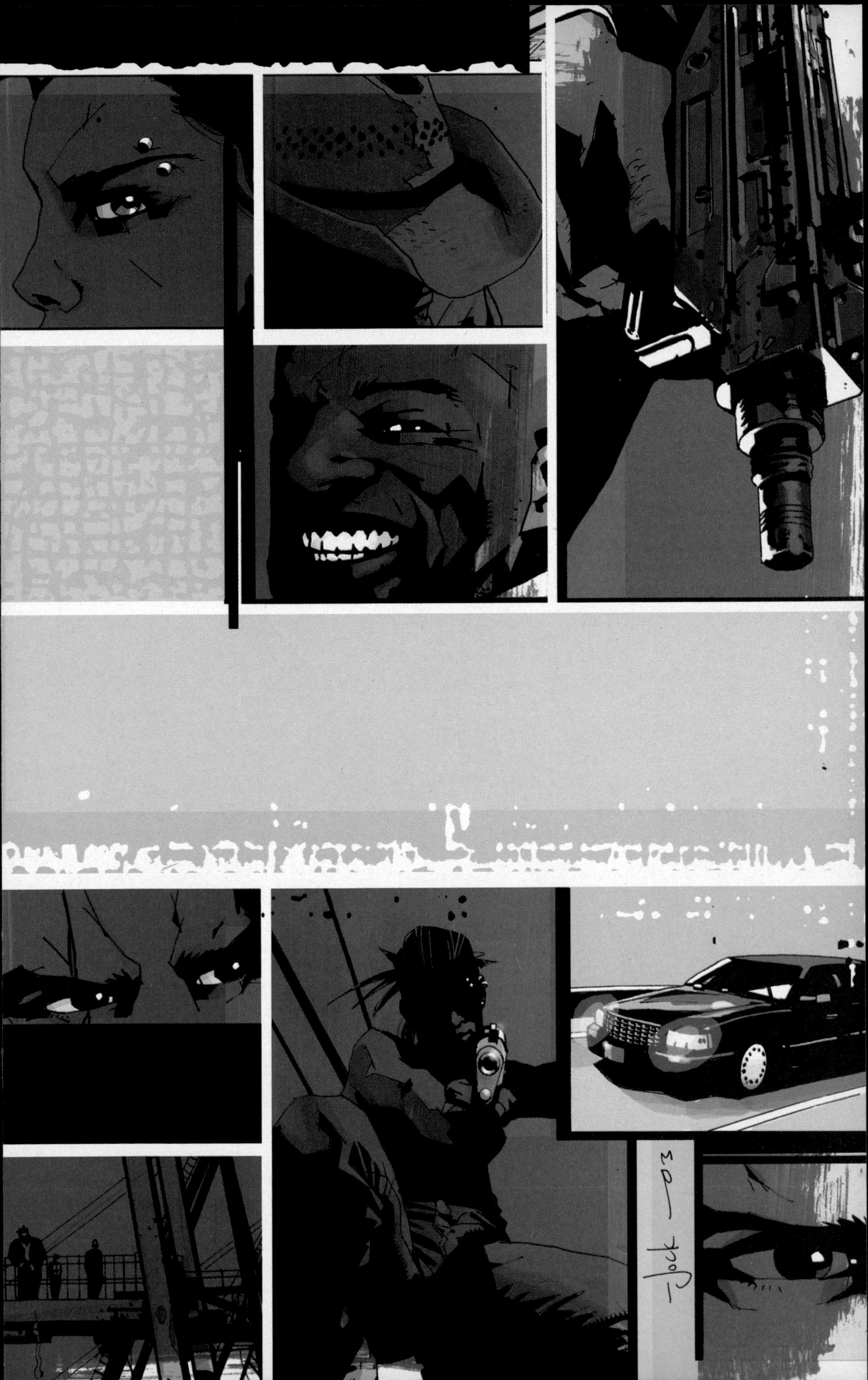
Jock

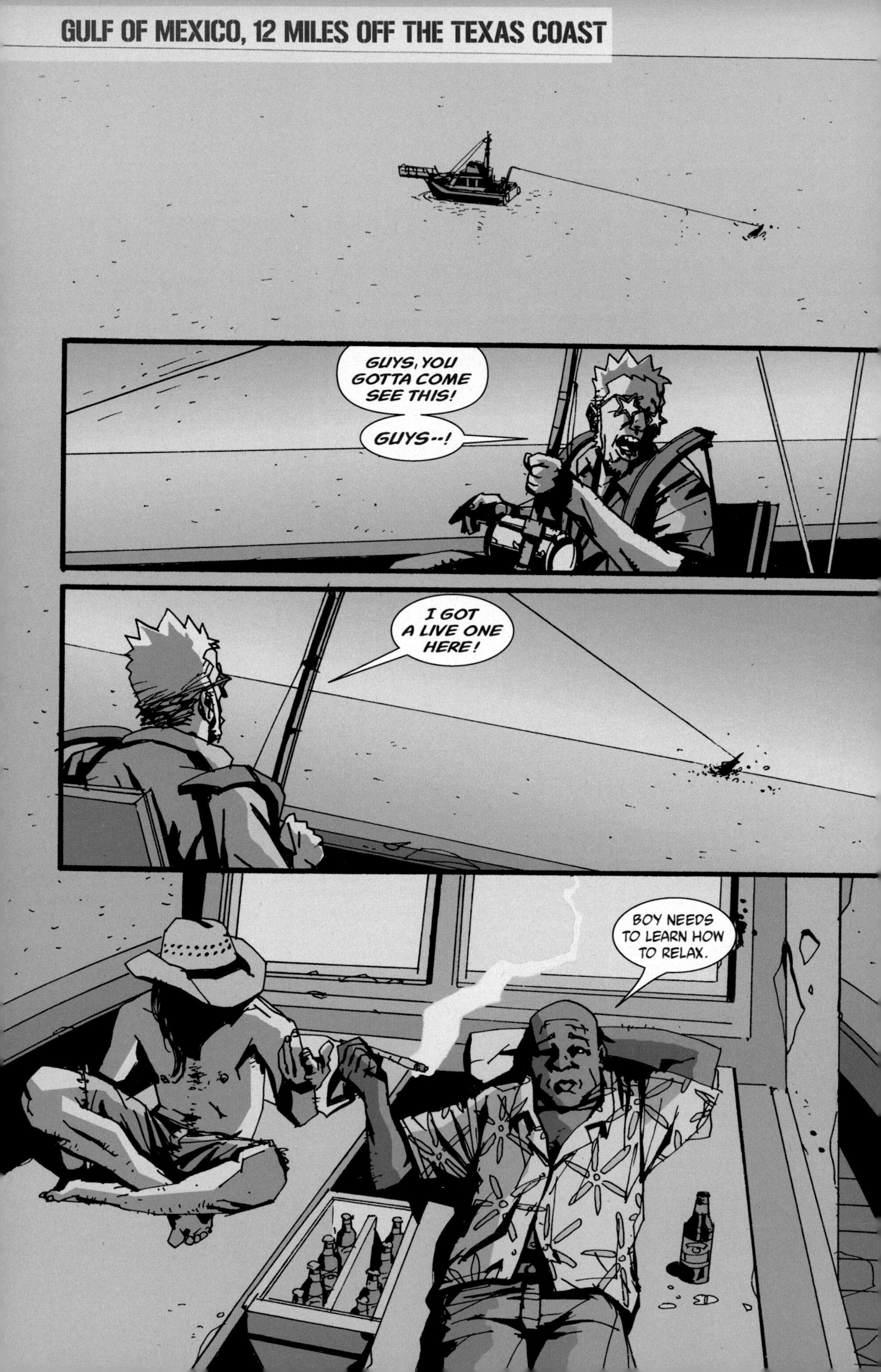
GULF OF MEXICO, 12 MILES OFF THE TEXAS COAST
GUYS, YOU GOTTA COME SEE THIS!
GUYS--!
I GOT A LIVE ONE HERE!
BOY NEEDS TO LEARN HOW TO RELAX.

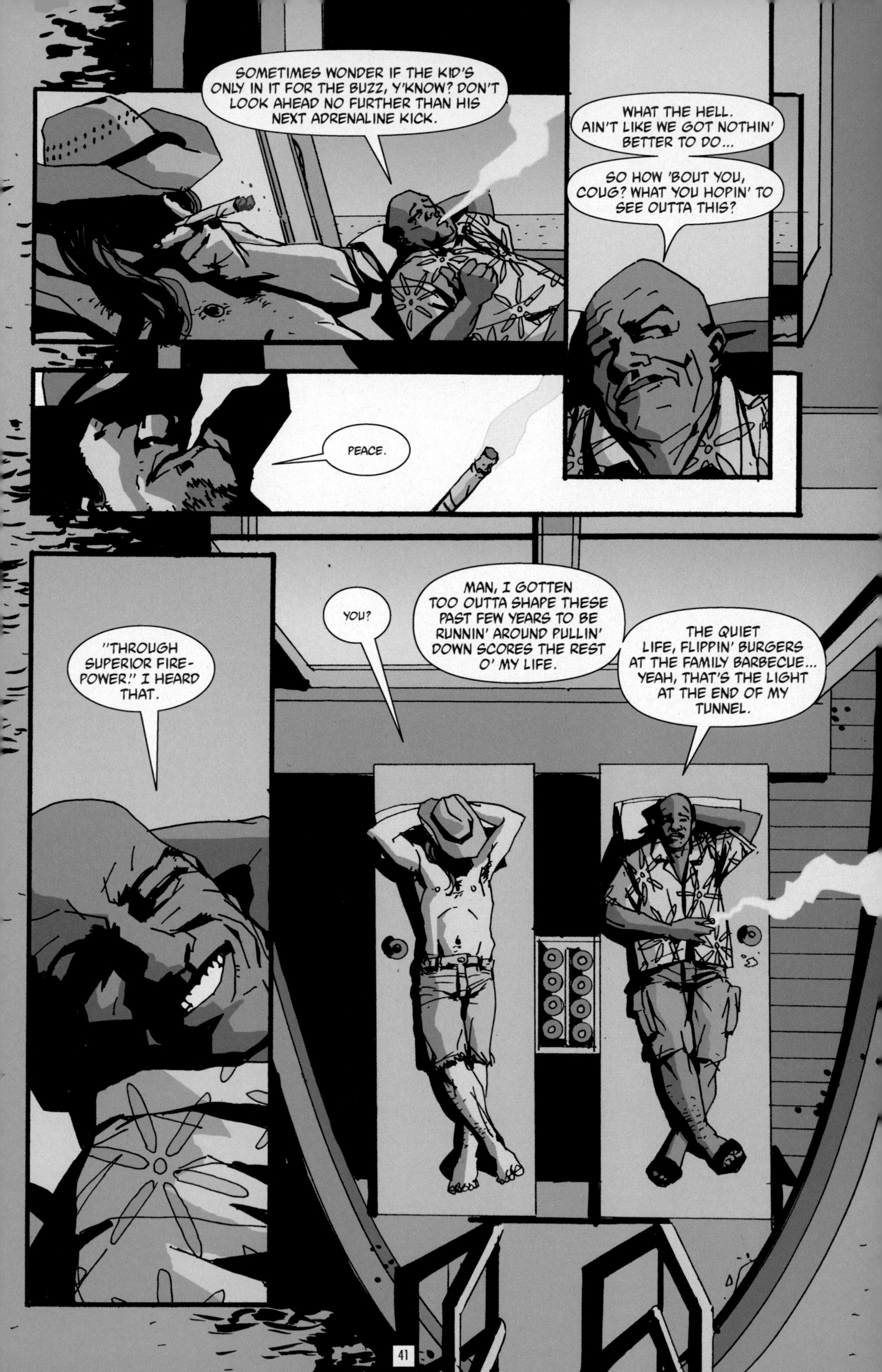
SOMETIMES WONDER IF THE KID'S ONLY IN IT FOR THE BUZZ, Y'KNOW? DON'T LOOK AHEAD NO FURTHER THAN HIS NEXT ADRENALINE KICK.
WHAT THE HELL. AIN'T LIKE WE GOT NOTHIN' BETTER TO DO...
SO HOW 'BOUT YOU, COUG? WHAT YOU HOPIN' TO SEE OUTTA THIS?
PEACE.
"THROUGH SUPERIOR FIRE-POWER." I HEARD THAT.
YOU?
MAN, I GOTTEN TOO OUTTA SHAPE THESE PAST FEW YEARS TO BE RUNNIN' AROUND PULLIN' DOWN SCORES THE REST O' MY LIFE.
THE QUIET LIFE, FLIPPIN' BURGERS AT THE FAMILY BARBECUE... YEAH, THAT'S THE LIGHT AT THE END OF MY TUNNEL.

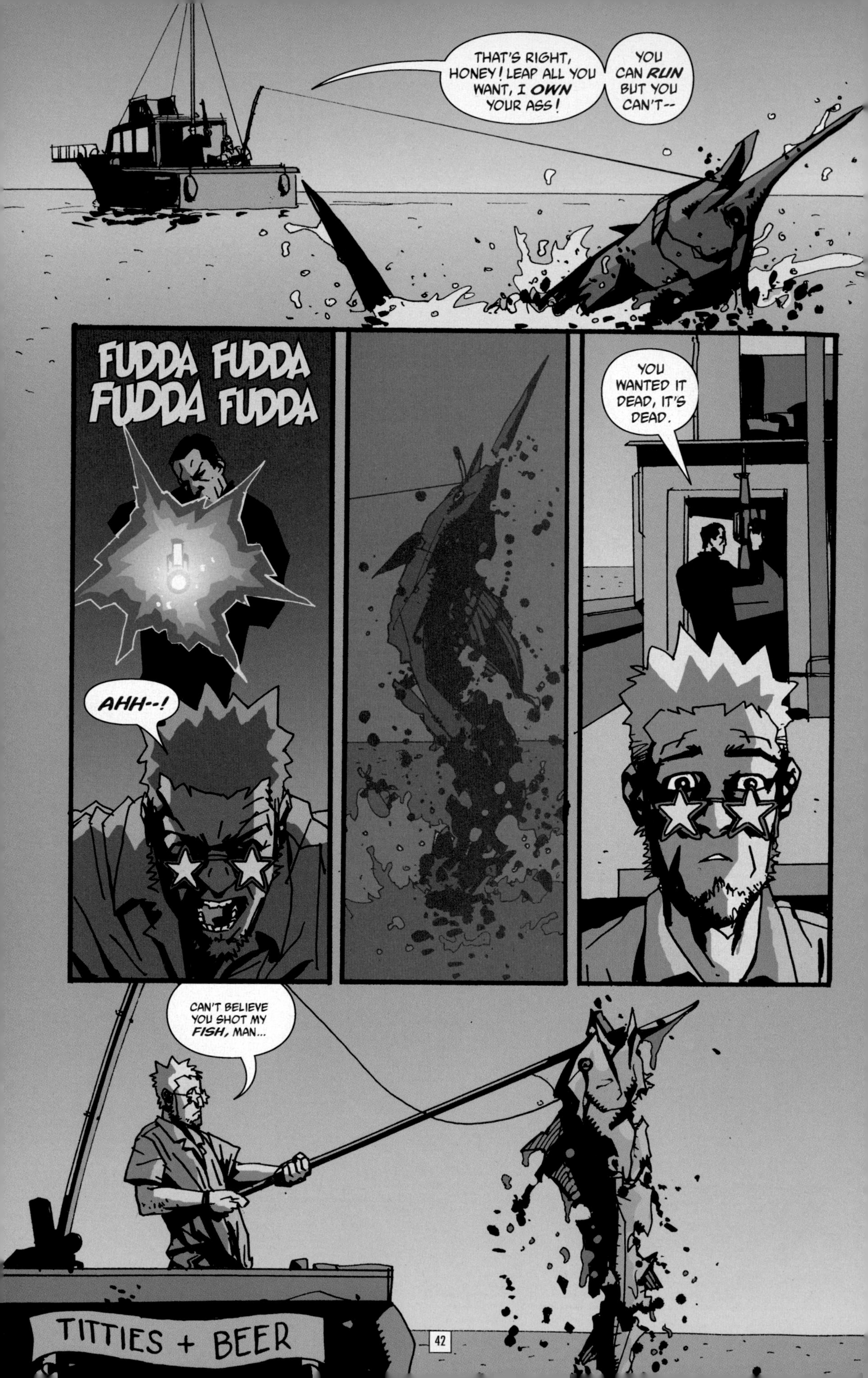
THAT'S RIGHT, HONEY! LEAP ALL YOU WANT, I OWN YOUR ASS!
YOU CAN RUN BUT YOU CAN'T--
FUDDA FUDDA FUDDA FUDDA
AHH--!
YOU WANTED IT DEAD, IT'S DEAD.
CAN'T BELIEVE YOU SHOT MY FISH, MAN...
TITTIES + BEER

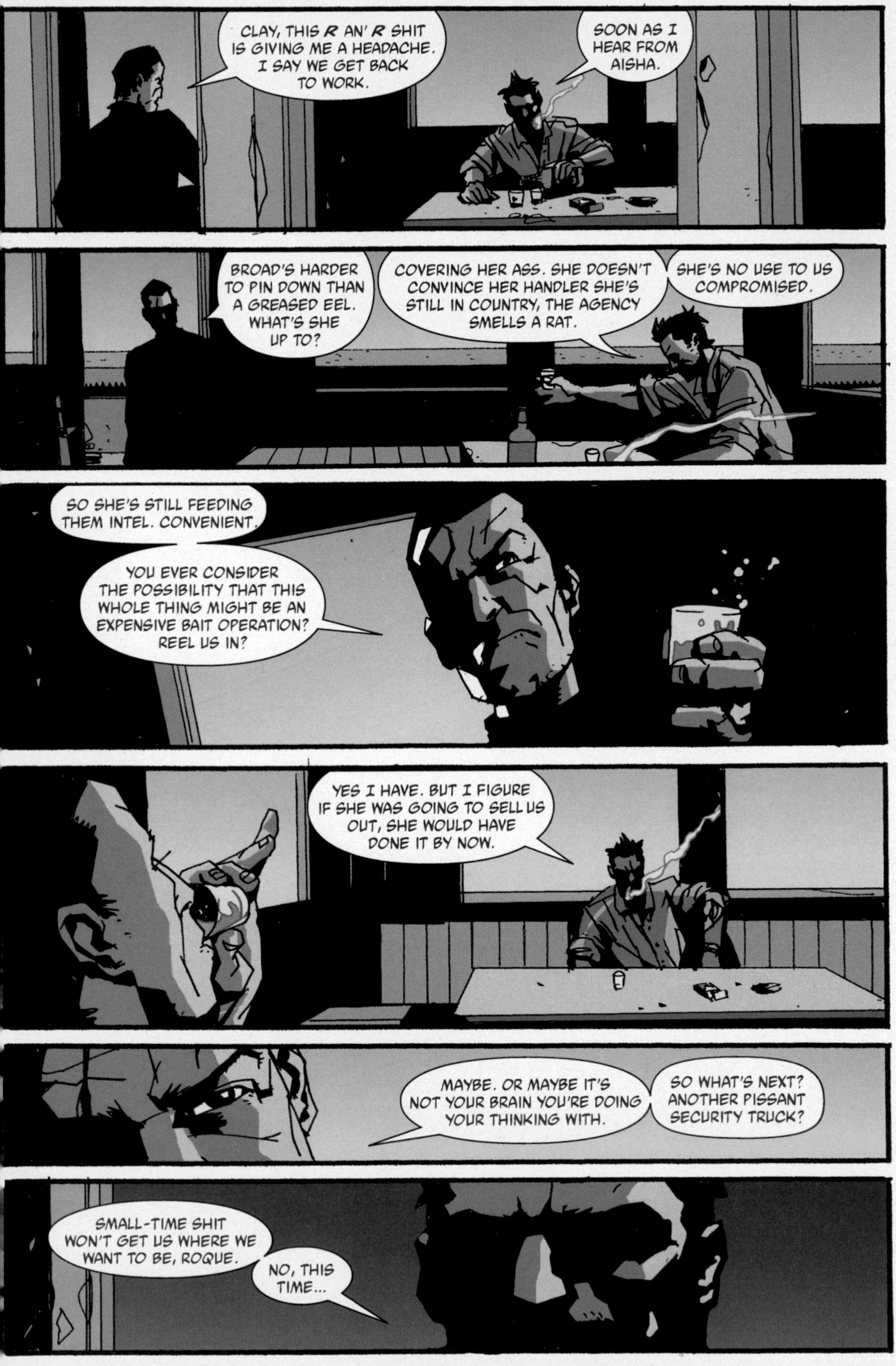
CLAY, THIS R AN' R SHIT IS GIVING ME A HEADACHE. I SAY WE GET BACK TO WORK.
SOON AS I HEAR FROM AISHA.
BROAD'S HARDER TO PIN DOWN THAN A GREASED EEL. WHAT'S SHE UP TO?
COVERING HER ASS. SHE DOESN'T CONVINCE HER HANDLER SHE'S STILL IN COUNTRY, THE AGENCY SMELLS A RAT.
SHE'S NO USE TO US COMPROMISED.
SO SHE'S STILL FEEDING THEM INTEL. CONVENIENT.
YOU EVER CONSIDER THE POSSIBILITY THAT THIS WHOLE THING MIGHT BE AN EXPENSIVE BAIT OPERATION? REEL US IN?
YES I HAVE. BUT I FIGURE IF SHE WAS GOING TO SELL US OUT, SHE WOULD HAVE DONE IT BY NOW.
MAYBE. OR MAYBE IT'S NOT YOUR BRAIN YOU'RE DOING YOUR THINKING WITH.
SO WHAT'S NEXT? ANOTHER PISSANT SECURITY TRUCK?
SMALL-TIME SHIT WON'T GET US WHERE WE WANT TO BE, ROQUE.
NO, THIS TIME...

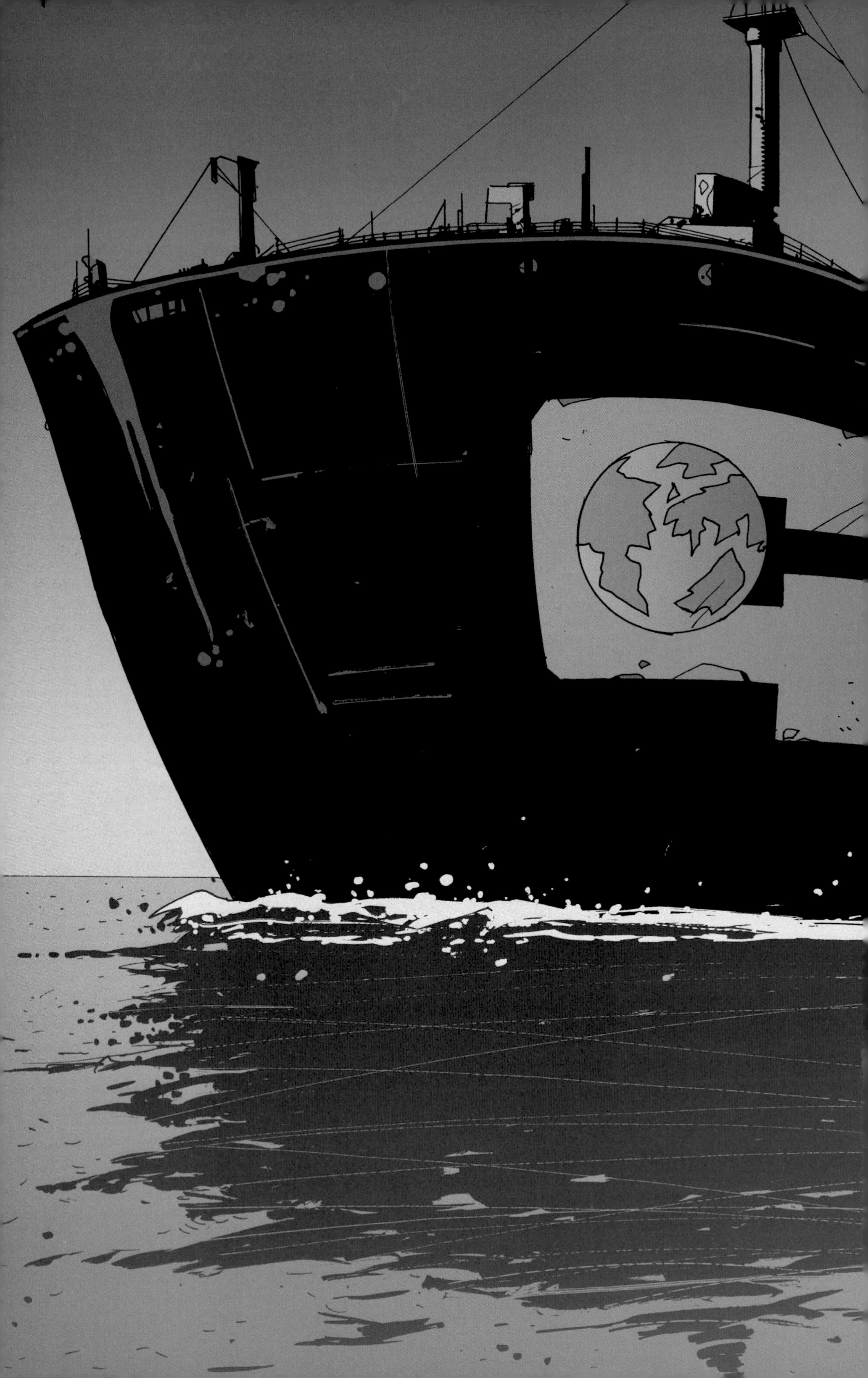

# GOLIATH
## PART ONE

**ANDY DIGGLE**, WRITER
**JOCK**, ARTIST & COVER
**LEE LOUGHRIDGE**, COLORIST
**CLEM ROBINS**, LETTERER
**ZACHARY RAU**, ASS'T EDITOR
**WILL DENNIS**, EDITOR

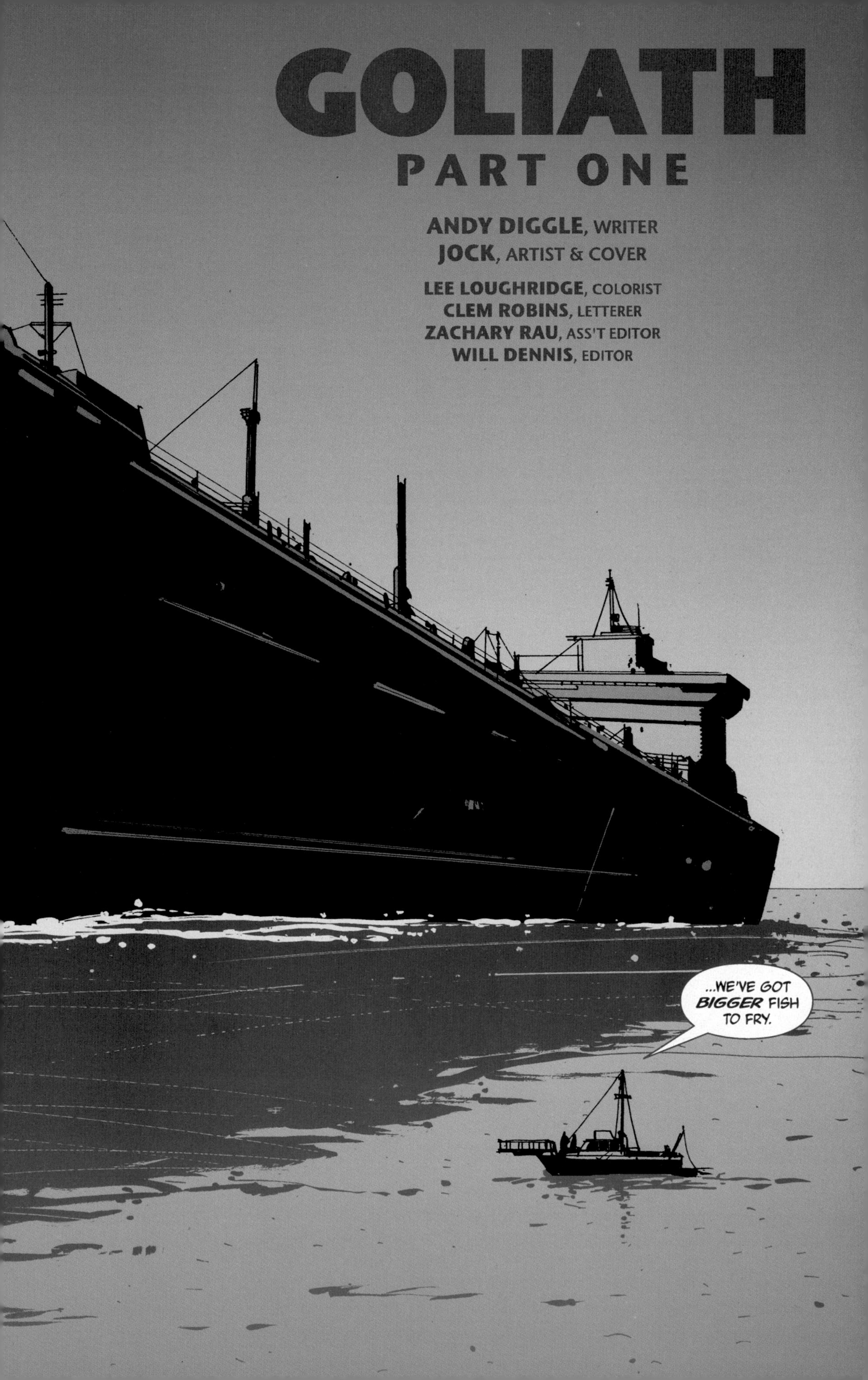
...WE'VE GOT BIGGER FISH TO FRY.

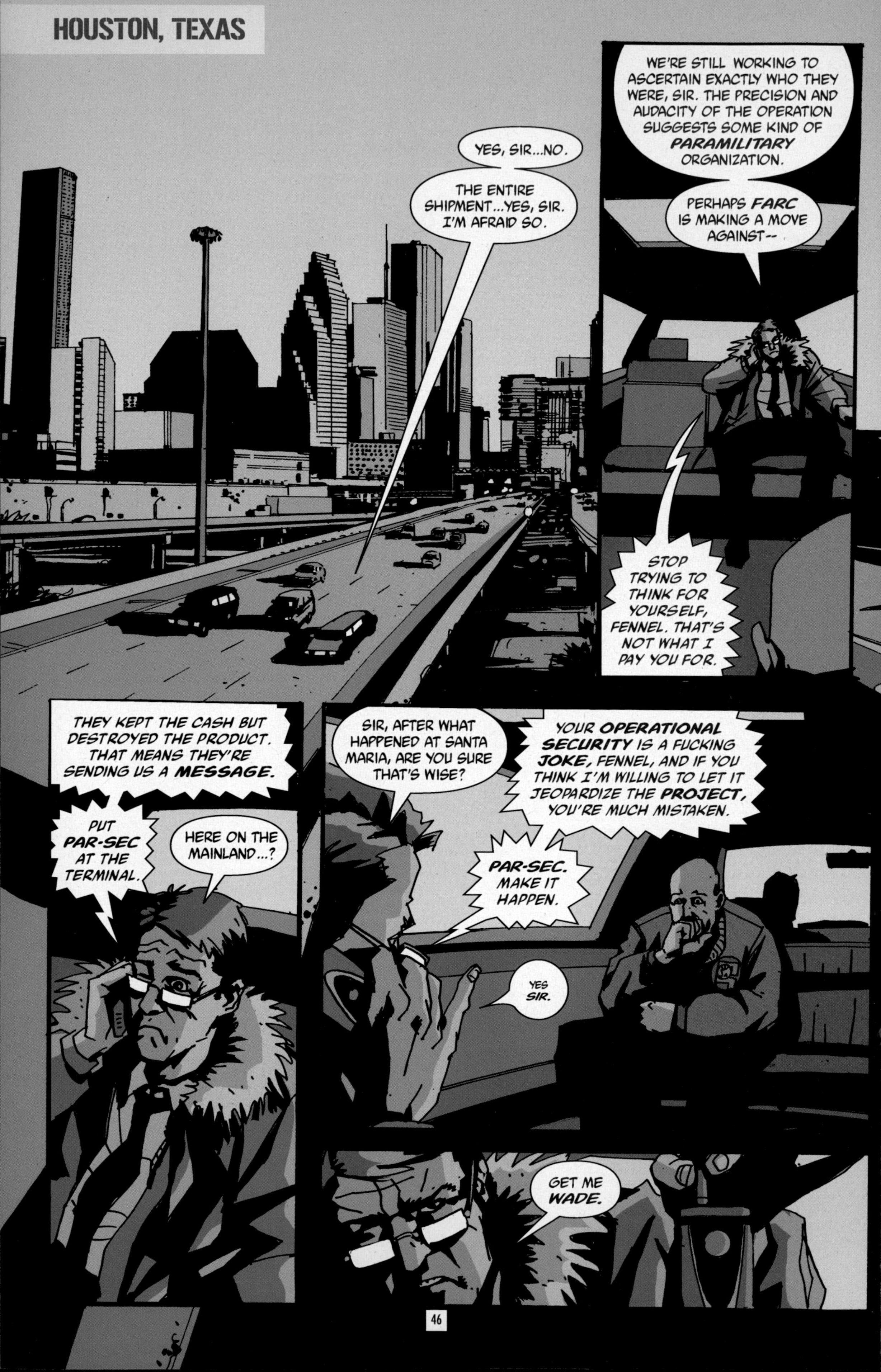
HOUSTON, TEXAS
YES, SIR...NO.
THE ENTIRE SHIPMENT...YES, SIR. I'M AFRAID SO.
WE'RE STILL WORKING TO ASCERTAIN EXACTLY WHO THEY WERE, SIR. THE PRECISION AND AUDACITY OF THE OPERATION SUGGESTS SOME KIND OF **PARAMILITARY** ORGANIZATION.
PERHAPS **FARC** IS MAKING A MOVE AGAINST--
STOP TRYING TO THINK FOR YOURSELF, FENNEL. THAT'S NOT WHAT I PAY YOU FOR.
THEY KEPT THE CASH BUT DESTROYED THE PRODUCT. THAT MEANS THEY'RE SENDING US A **MESSAGE.**
PUT **PAR-SEC** AT THE TERMINAL.
HERE ON THE MAINLAND...?
SIR, AFTER WHAT HAPPENED AT SANTA MARIA, ARE YOU SURE THAT'S WISE?
YOUR **OPERATIONAL SECURITY** IS A FUCKING **JOKE,** FENNEL, AND IF YOU THINK I'M WILLING TO LET IT JEOPARDIZE THE **PROJECT,** YOU'RE MUCH MISTAKEN.
**PAR-SEC.** MAKE IT HAPPEN.
YES SIR.
GET ME **WADE.**

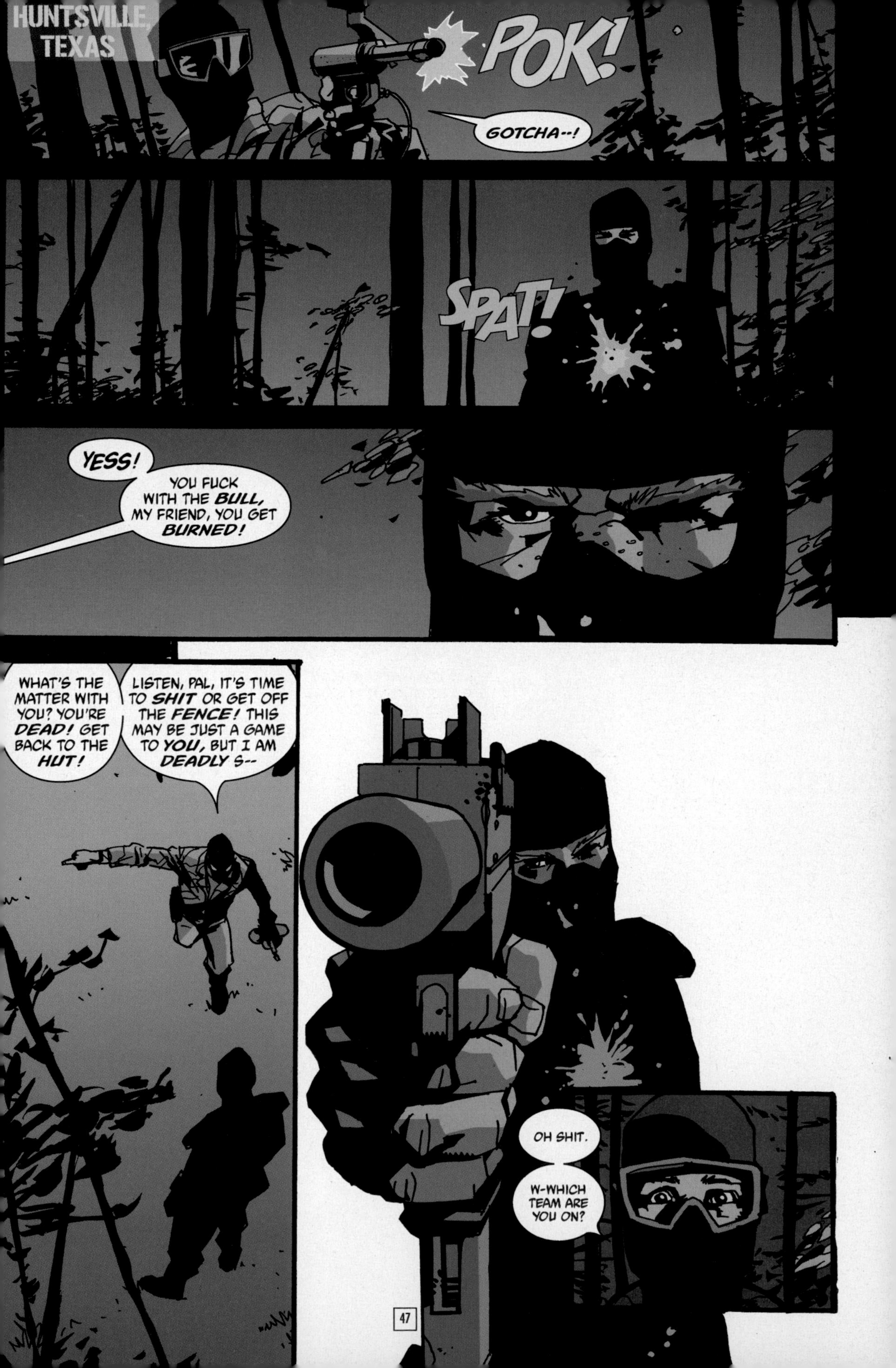

HUNTSVILLE, TEXAS
POK!
GOTCHA--!
SPAT!
YESS!
YOU FUCK WITH THE BULL, MY FRIEND, YOU GET BURNED!
WHAT'S THE MATTER WITH YOU? YOU'RE DEAD! GET BACK TO THE HUT!
LISTEN, PAL, IT'S TIME TO SHIT OR GET OFF THE FENCE! THIS MAY BE JUST A GAME TO YOU, BUT I AM DEADLY S--
OH SHIT.
W-WHICH TEAM ARE YOU ON?

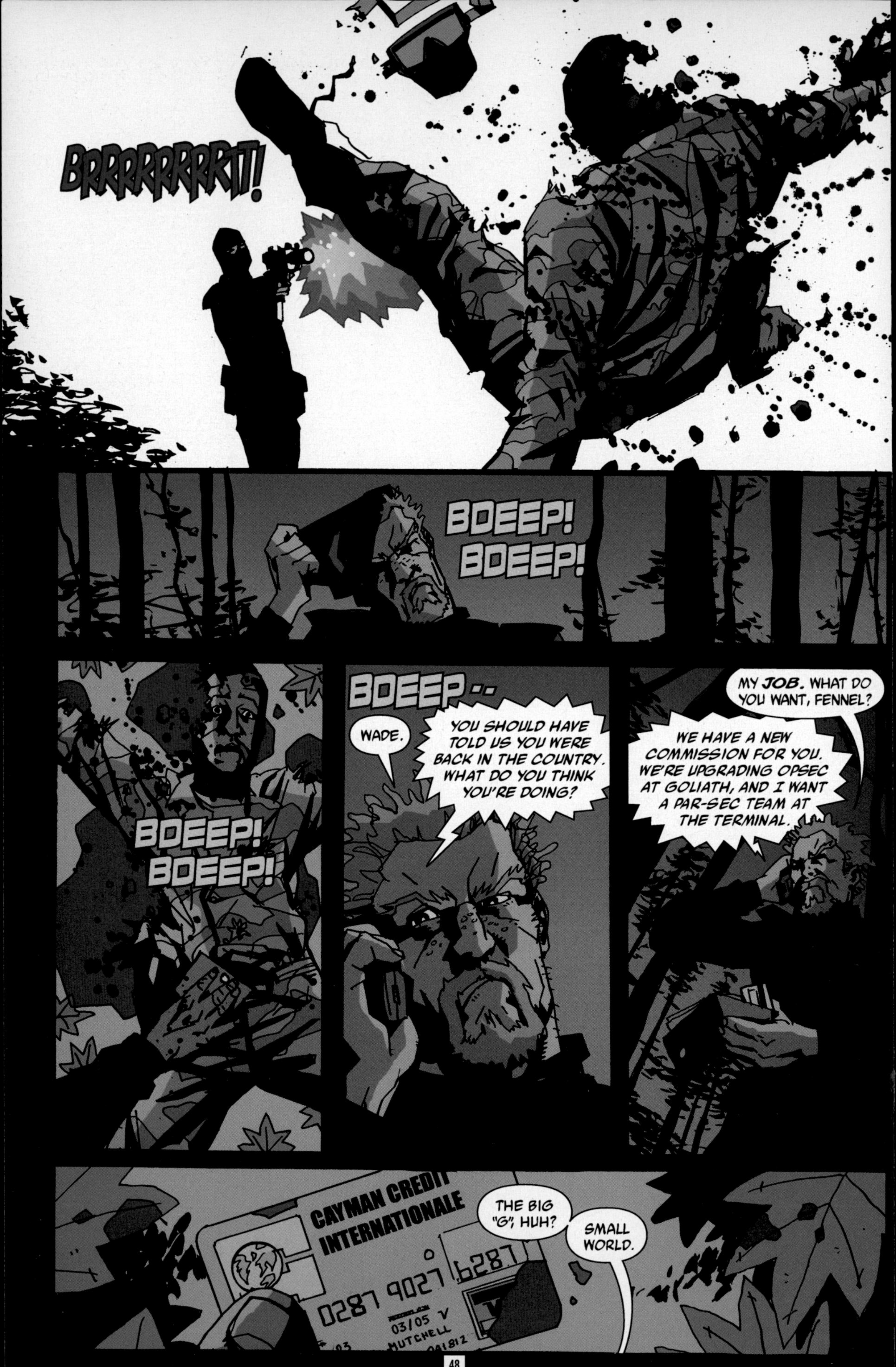
BRRRRRRRRTT!
BDEEP! BDEEP!
BDEEP! BDEEP!
BDEEP..
WADE.
YOU SHOULD HAVE TOLD US YOU WERE BACK IN THE COUNTRY. WHAT DO YOU THINK YOU'RE DOING?
MY JOB. WHAT DO YOU WANT, FENNEL?
WE HAVE A NEW COMMISSION FOR YOU. WE'RE UPGRADING OPSEC AT GOLIATH, AND I WANT A PAR-SEC TEAM AT THE TERMINAL.
CAYMAN CREDIT INTERNATIONALE
0287 9027 6287
03/05 V
MUTCHELL
THE BIG "G", HUH?
SMALL WORLD.

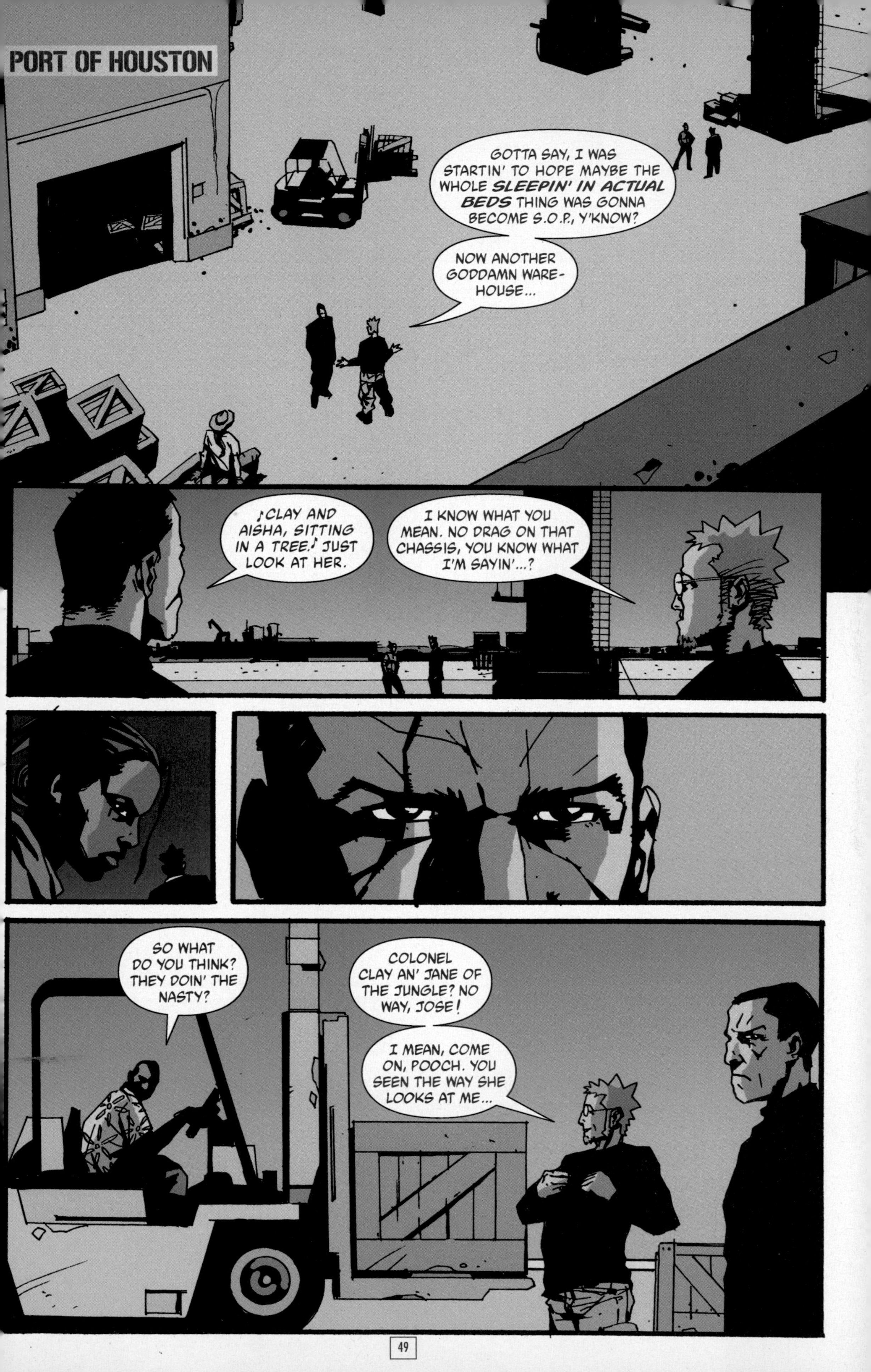
PORT OF HOUSTON
GOTTA SAY, I WAS STARTIN' TO HOPE MAYBE THE WHOLE SLEEPIN' IN ACTUAL BEDS THING WAS GONNA BECOME S.O.P., Y'KNOW?
NOW ANOTHER GODDAMN WARE-HOUSE...
♪CLAY AND AISHA, SITTING IN A TREE.♪ JUST LOOK AT HER.
I KNOW WHAT YOU MEAN. NO DRAG ON THAT CHASSIS, YOU KNOW WHAT I'M SAYIN'...?
SO WHAT DO YOU THINK? THEY DOIN' THE NASTY?
COLONEL CLAY AN' JANE OF THE JUNGLE? NO WAY, JOSE!
I MEAN, COME ON, POOCH. YOU SEEN THE WAY SHE LOOKS AT ME...

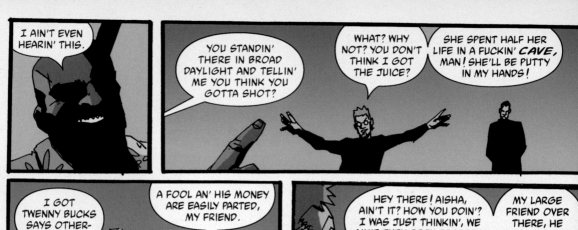

I AIN'T EVEN HEARIN' THIS.

YOU STANDIN' THERE IN BROAD DAYLIGHT AND TELLIN' ME YOU THINK YOU GOTTA SHOT?

WHAT? WHY NOT? YOU DON'T THINK I GOT THE JUICE?

SHE SPENT HALF HER LIFE IN A FUCKIN' *CAVE*, MAN! SHE'LL BE PUTTY IN MY HANDS!

I GOT TWENNY BUCKS SAYS OTHER- WISE.

A FOOL AN' HIS MONEY ARE EASILY PARTED, MY FRIEND.

HOW THEY EVER GOT TOGETHER IN THE FIRST PLACE, NOW THAT'S THE REAL QUESTION.

HEY THERE! AISHA, AIN'T IT? HOW YOU DOIN'? I WAS JUST THINKIN', WE AIN'T EVEN BEEN PROPERLY INTRODUCED YET.

MY LARGE FRIEND OVER THERE, HE CALLS HIMSELF POOCH, AND I'M--

WHAT DO YOU WANT?

WANT? ME? NOTHIN'! I JUST FIGURED, WE'RE GONNA BE WORKIN' REAL CLOSE, IT'D BE GOOD TO GET TO KNOW EACH OTHER FIRST...

SO, UH, TELL ME A LITTLE ABOUT YOURSELF. I HEARD YOU GREW UP IN THE HINDU KUSH, YEAH? THAT MUSTA BEEN ROUGH...

YES.

SO, UH...

YOU GOT ANY HOBBIES?

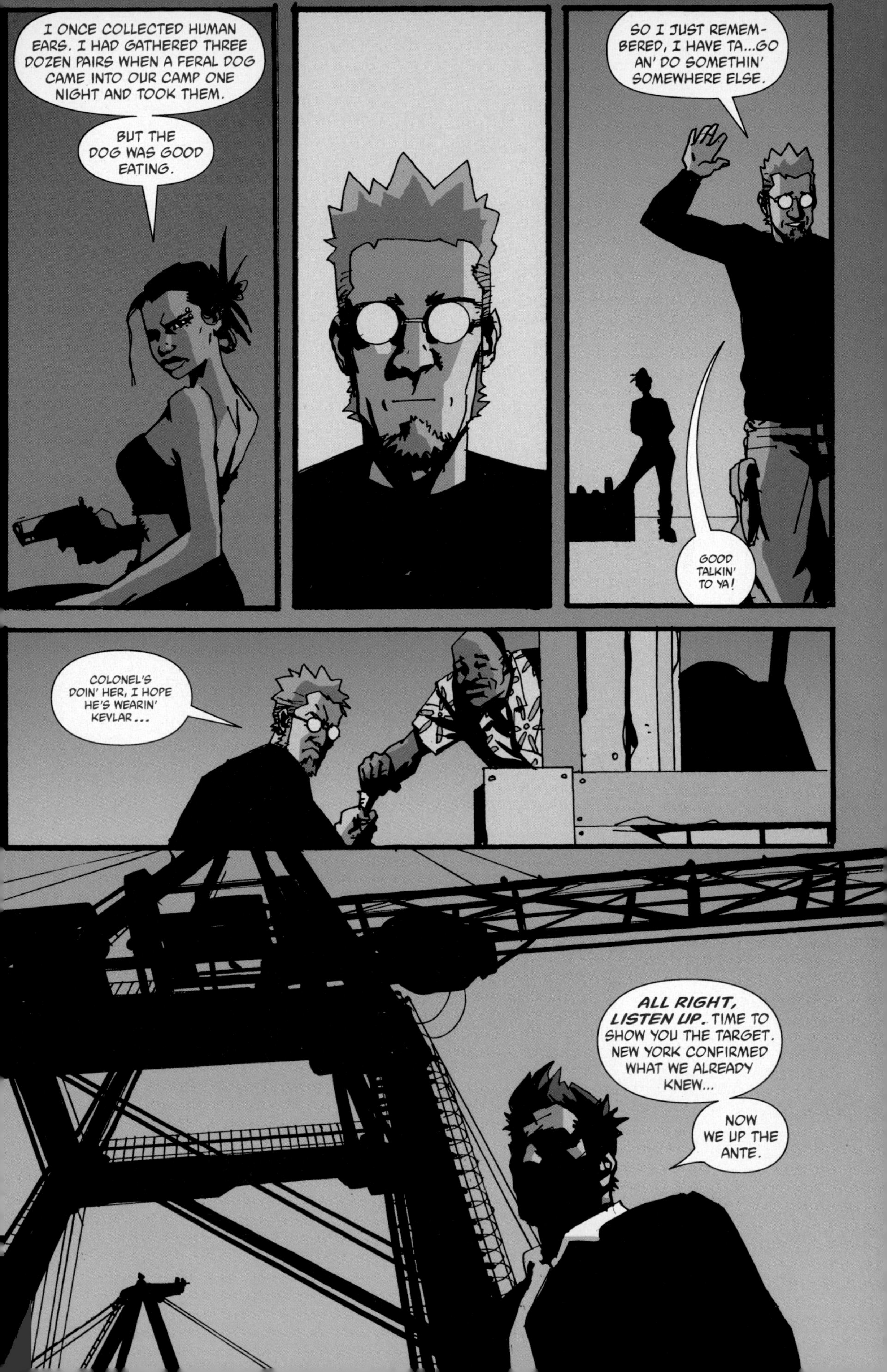
I ONCE COLLECTED HUMAN EARS. I HAD GATHERED THREE DOZEN PAIRS WHEN A FERAL DOG CAME INTO OUR CAMP ONE NIGHT AND TOOK THEM.
BUT THE DOG WAS GOOD EATING.
SO I JUST REMEMBERED, I HAVE TA...GO AN' DO SOMETHIN' SOMEWHERE ELSE.
GOOD TALKIN' TO YA!
COLONEL'S DOIN' HER, I HOPE HE'S WEARIN' KEVLAR...
ALL RIGHT, LISTEN UP.. TIME TO SHOW YOU THE TARGET. NEW YORK CONFIRMED WHAT WE ALREADY KNEW...
NOW WE UP THE ANTE.

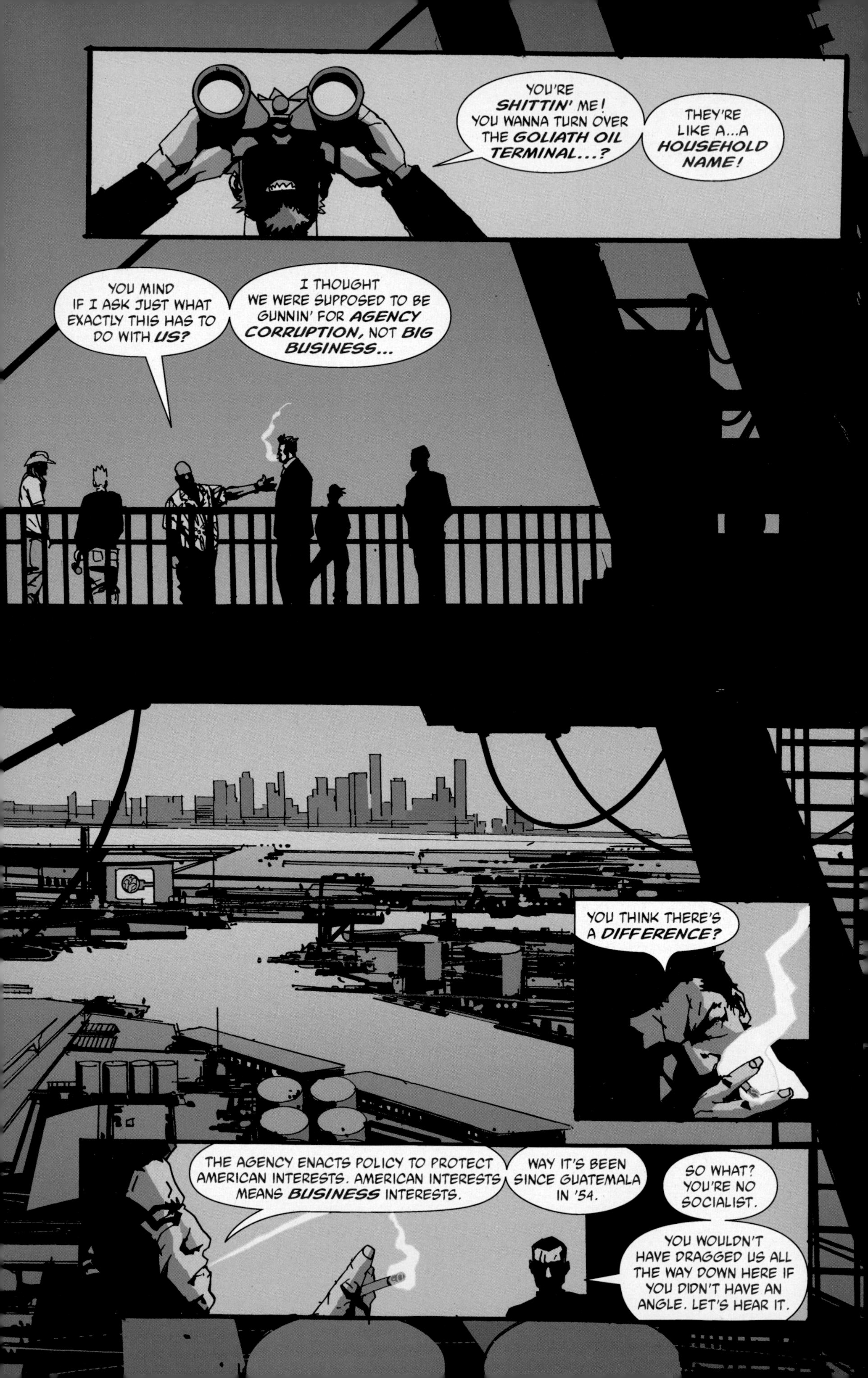
YOU'RE SHITTIN' ME! YOU WANNA TURN OVER THE GOLIATH OIL TERMINAL...?
THEY'RE LIKE A...A HOUSEHOLD NAME!
YOU MIND IF I ASK JUST WHAT EXACTLY THIS HAS TO DO WITH US?
I THOUGHT WE WERE SUPPOSED TO BE GUNNIN' FOR AGENCY CORRUPTION, NOT BIG BUSINESS...
YOU THINK THERE'S A DIFFERENCE?
THE AGENCY ENACTS POLICY TO PROTECT AMERICAN INTERESTS. AMERICAN INTERESTS MEANS BUSINESS INTERESTS.
WAY IT'S BEEN SINCE GUATEMALA IN '54.
SO WHAT? YOU'RE NO SOCIALIST.
YOU WOULDN'T HAVE DRAGGED US ALL THE WAY DOWN HERE IF YOU DIDN'T HAVE AN ANGLE. LET'S HEAR IT.

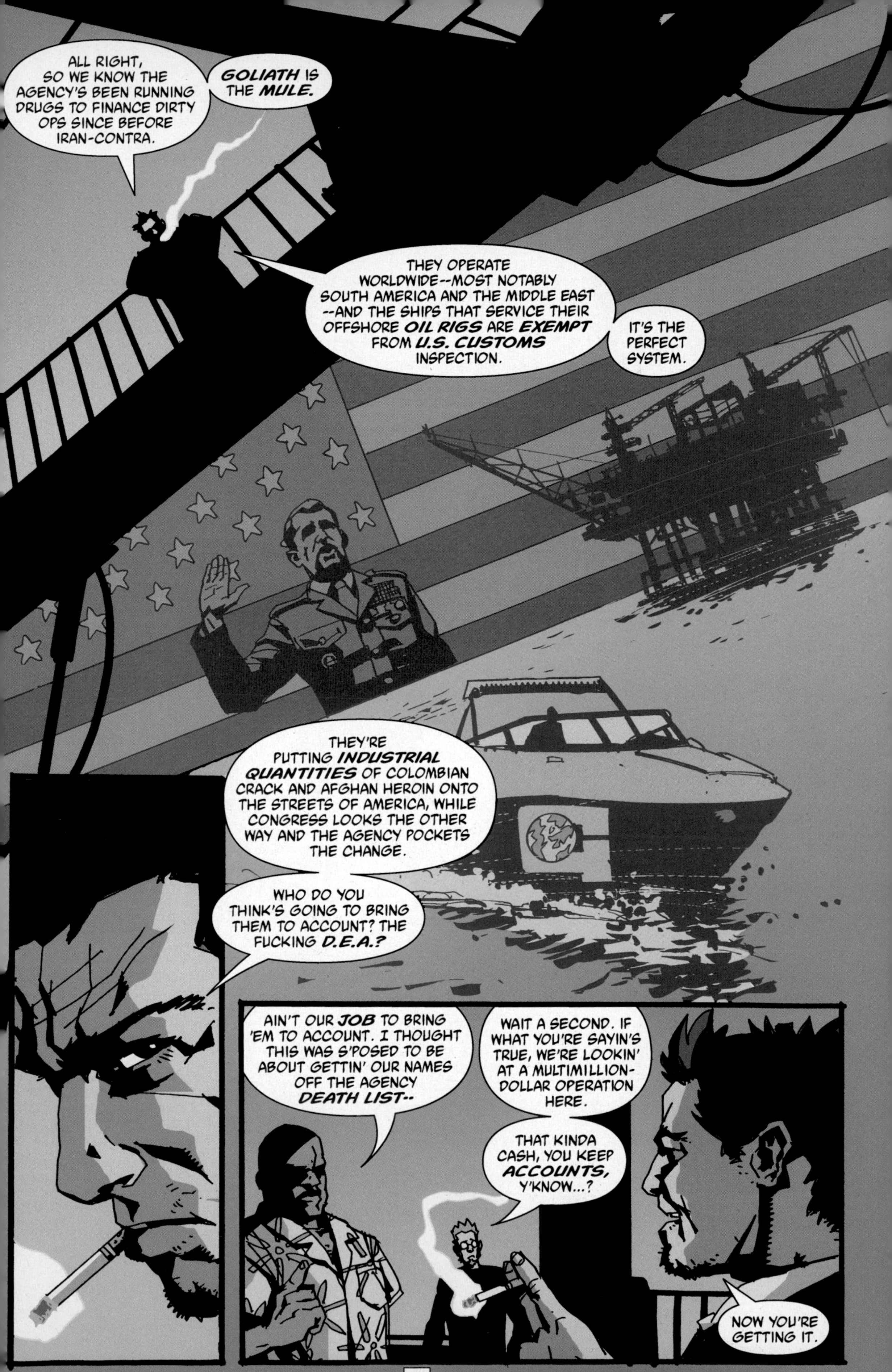
ALL RIGHT, SO WE KNOW THE AGENCY'S BEEN RUNNING DRUGS TO FINANCE DIRTY OPS SINCE BEFORE IRAN-CONTRA.
GOLIATH IS THE MULE.
THEY OPERATE WORLDWIDE--MOST NOTABLY SOUTH AMERICA AND THE MIDDLE EAST --AND THE SHIPS THAT SERVICE THEIR OFFSHORE OIL RIGS ARE EXEMPT FROM U.S. CUSTOMS INSPECTION.
IT'S THE PERFECT SYSTEM.
THEY'RE PUTTING INDUSTRIAL QUANTITIES OF COLOMBIAN CRACK AND AFGHAN HEROIN ONTO THE STREETS OF AMERICA, WHILE CONGRESS LOOKS THE OTHER WAY AND THE AGENCY POCKETS THE CHANGE.
WHO DO YOU THINK'S GOING TO BRING THEM TO ACCOUNT? THE FUCKING D.E.A.?
AIN'T OUR JOB TO BRING 'EM TO ACCOUNT. I THOUGHT THIS WAS S'POSED TO BE ABOUT GETTIN' OUR NAMES OFF THE AGENCY DEATH LIST--
WAIT A SECOND. IF WHAT YOU'RE SAYIN'S TRUE, WE'RE LOOKIN' AT A MULTIMILLION-DOLLAR OPERATION HERE.
THAT KINDA CASH, YOU KEEP ACCOUNTS, Y'KNOW...?
NOW YOU'RE GETTING IT.

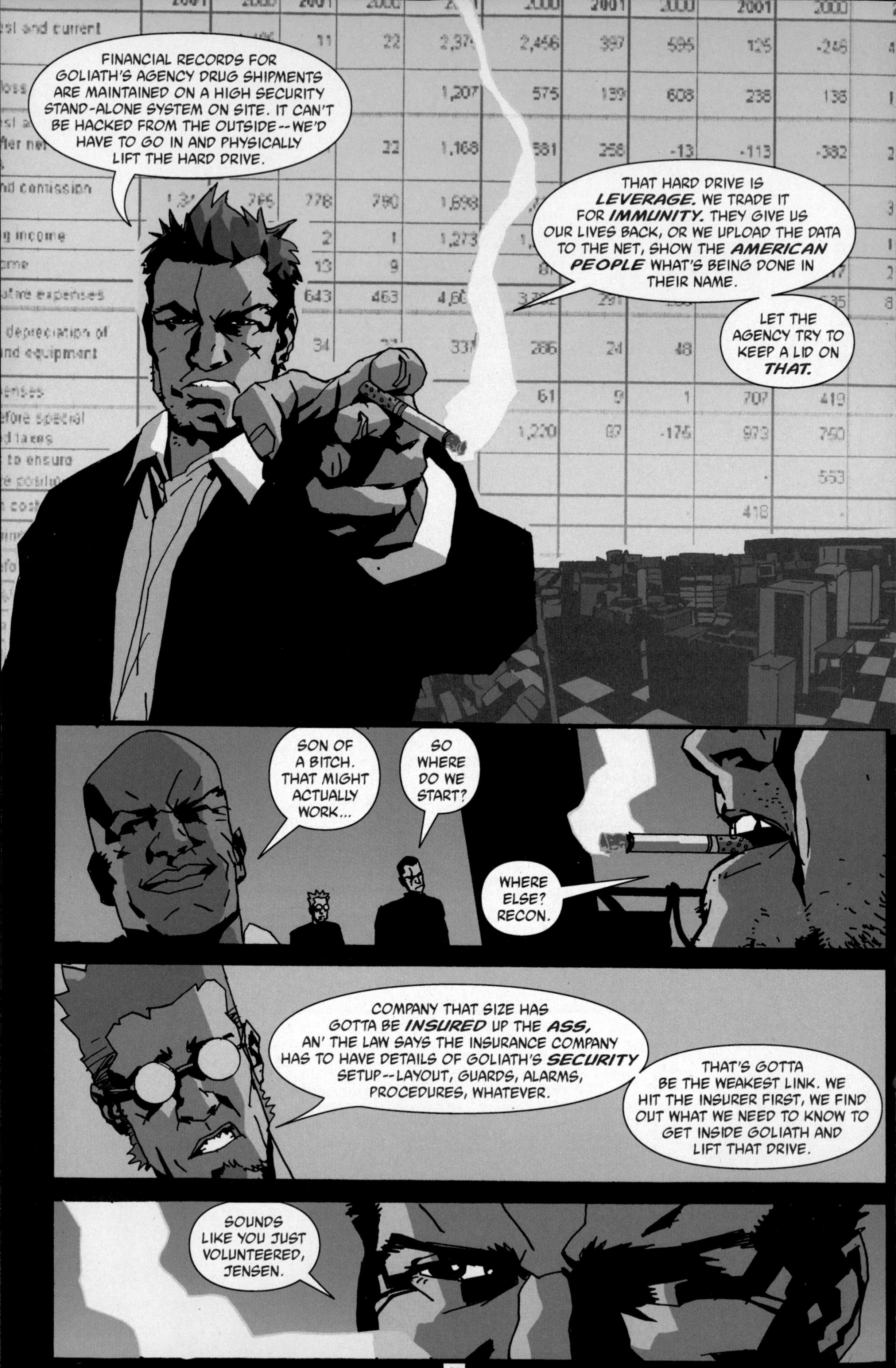
FINANCIAL RECORDS FOR GOLIATH'S AGENCY DRUG SHIPMENTS ARE MAINTAINED ON A HIGH SECURITY STAND-ALONE SYSTEM ON SITE. IT CAN'T BE HACKED FROM THE OUTSIDE--WE'D HAVE TO GO IN AND PHYSICALLY LIFT THE HARD DRIVE.
THAT HARD DRIVE IS *LEVERAGE.* WE TRADE IT FOR *IMMUNITY.* THEY GIVE US OUR LIVES BACK, OR WE UPLOAD THE DATA TO THE NET, SHOW THE *AMERICAN PEOPLE* WHAT'S BEING DONE IN THEIR NAME.
LET THE AGENCY TRY TO KEEP A LID ON *THAT.*
SON OF A BITCH. THAT MIGHT ACTUALLY WORK...
SO WHERE DO WE START?
WHERE ELSE? RECON.
COMPANY THAT SIZE HAS GOTTA BE *INSURED* UP THE *ASS,* AN' THE LAW SAYS THE INSURANCE COMPANY HAS TO HAVE DETAILS OF GOLIATH'S *SECURITY* SETUP--LAYOUT, GUARDS, ALARMS, PROCEDURES, WHATEVER.
THAT'S GOTTA BE THE WEAKEST LINK. WE HIT THE INSURER FIRST, WE FIND OUT WHAT WE NEED TO KNOW TO GET INSIDE GOLIATH AND LIFT THAT DRIVE.
SOUNDS LIKE YOU JUST VOLUNTEERED, JENSEN.

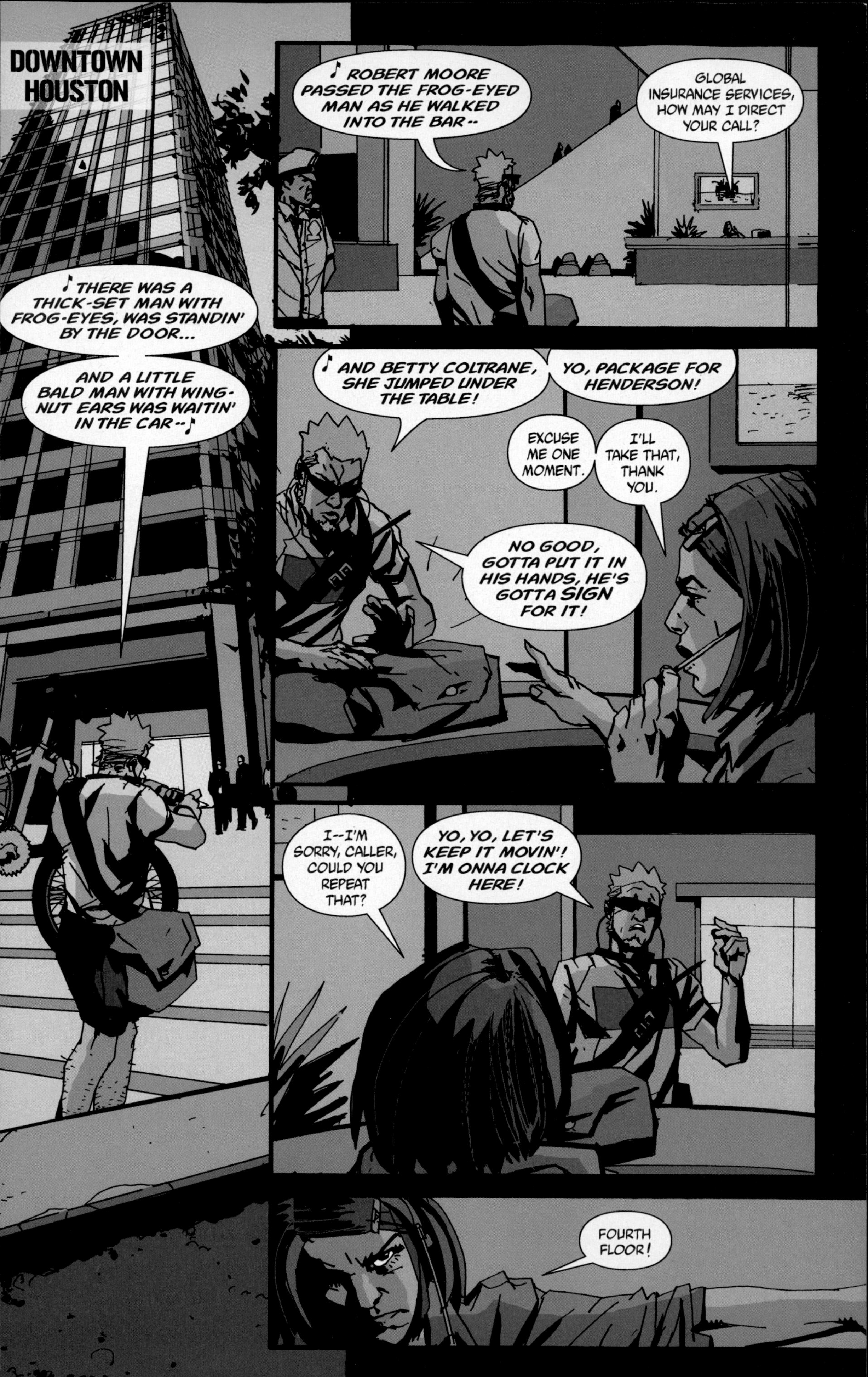
DOWNTOWN HOUSTON
♪ THERE WAS A THICK-SET MAN WITH FROG-EYES, WAS STANDIN' BY THE DOOR...
AND A LITTLE BALD MAN WITH WING-NUT EARS WAS WAITIN' IN THE CAR--♪
♪ ROBERT MOORE PASSED THE FROG-EYED MAN AS HE WALKED INTO THE BAR--
GLOBAL INSURANCE SERVICES, HOW MAY I DIRECT YOUR CALL?
♪ AND BETTY COLTRANE, SHE JUMPED UNDER THE TABLE!
YO, PACKAGE FOR HENDERSON!
EXCUSE ME ONE MOMENT.
I'LL TAKE THAT, THANK YOU.
NO GOOD, GOTTA PUT IT IN HIS HANDS, HE'S GOTTA SIGN FOR IT!
I--I'M SORRY, CALLER, COULD YOU REPEAT THAT?
YO, YO, LET'S KEEP IT MOVIN'! I'M ONNA CLOCK HERE!
FOURTH FLOOR!

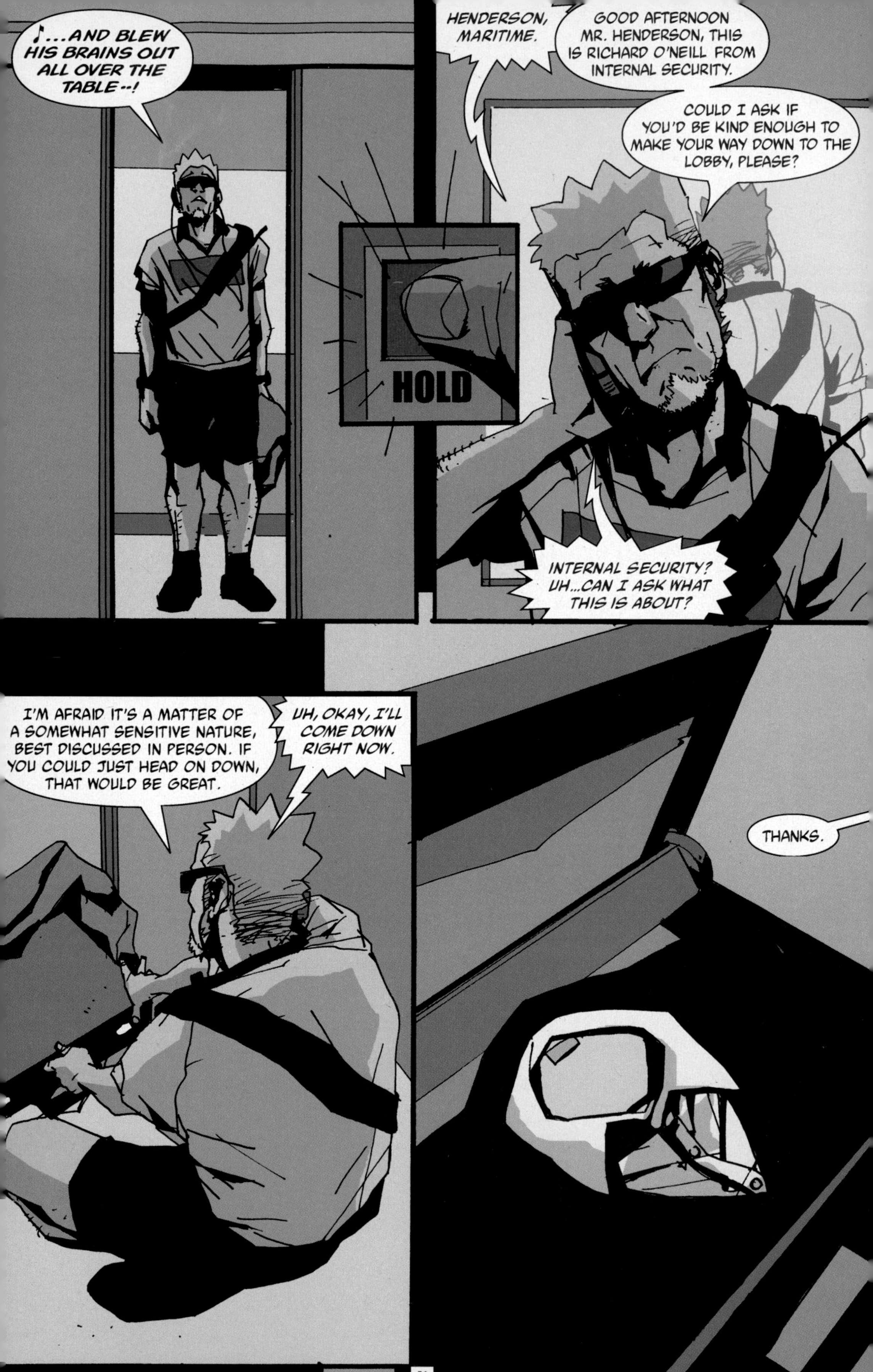
♪...AND BLEW HIS BRAINS OUT ALL OVER THE TABLE--!
HOLD
HENDERSON, MARITIME.
GOOD AFTERNOON MR. HENDERSON, THIS IS RICHARD O'NEILL FROM INTERNAL SECURITY.
COULD I ASK IF YOU'D BE KIND ENOUGH TO MAKE YOUR WAY DOWN TO THE LOBBY, PLEASE?
INTERNAL SECURITY? UH...CAN I ASK WHAT THIS IS ABOUT?
I'M AFRAID IT'S A MATTER OF A SOMEWHAT SENSITIVE NATURE, BEST DISCUSSED IN PERSON. IF YOU COULD JUST HEAD ON DOWN, THAT WOULD BE GREAT.
UH, OKAY, I'LL COME DOWN RIGHT NOW.
THANKS.

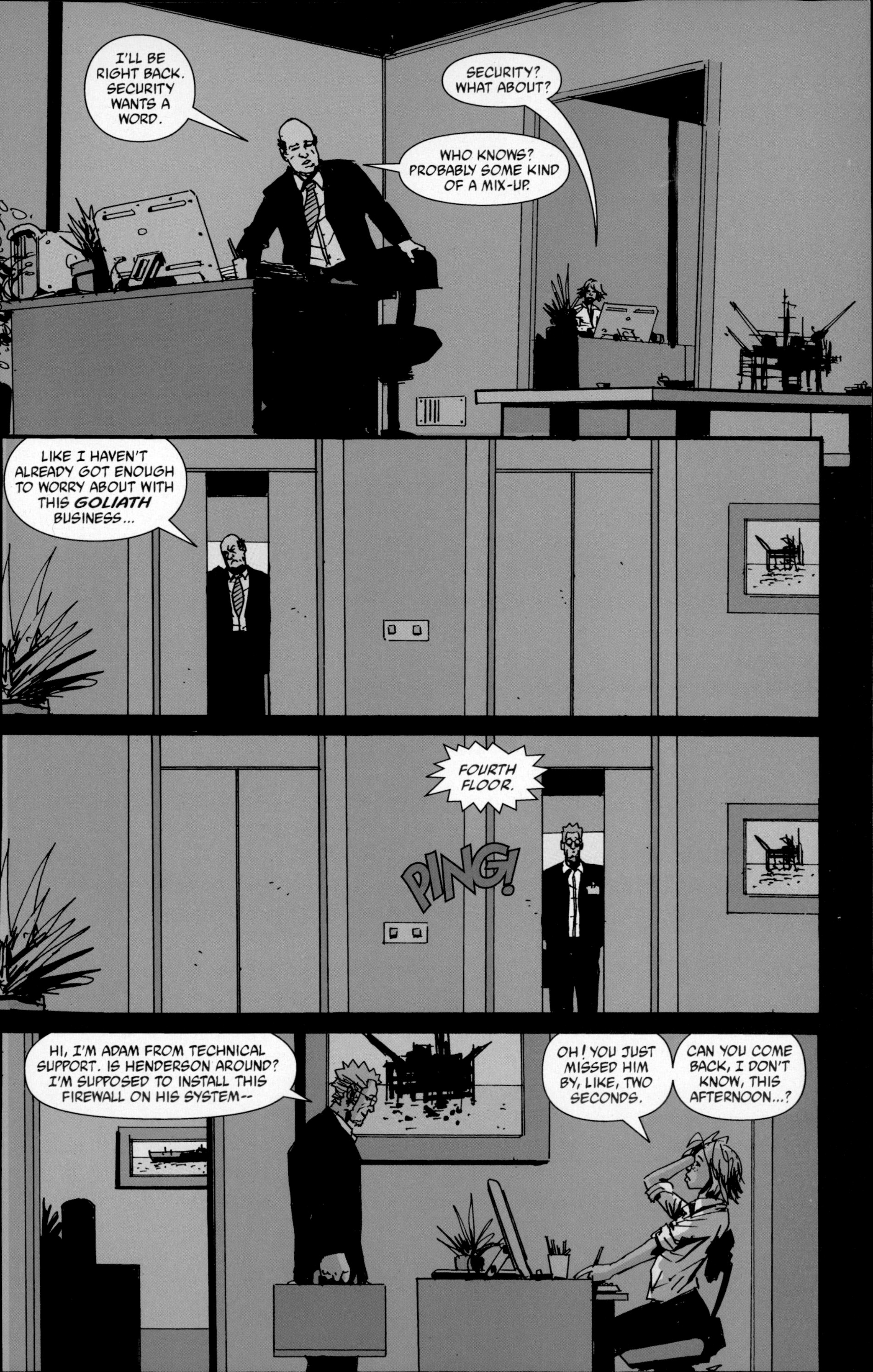
I'LL BE RIGHT BACK. SECURITY WANTS A WORD.
SECURITY? WHAT ABOUT?
WHO KNOWS? PROBABLY SOME KIND OF A MIX-UP.
LIKE I HAVEN'T ALREADY GOT ENOUGH TO WORRY ABOUT WITH THIS GOLIATH BUSINESS...
FOURTH FLOOR.
PING!
HI, I'M ADAM FROM TECHNICAL SUPPORT. IS HENDERSON AROUND? I'M SUPPOSED TO INSTALL THIS FIREWALL ON HIS SYSTEM--
OH! YOU JUST MISSED HIM BY, LIKE, TWO SECONDS.
CAN YOU COME BACK, I DON'T KNOW, THIS AFTERNOON...?

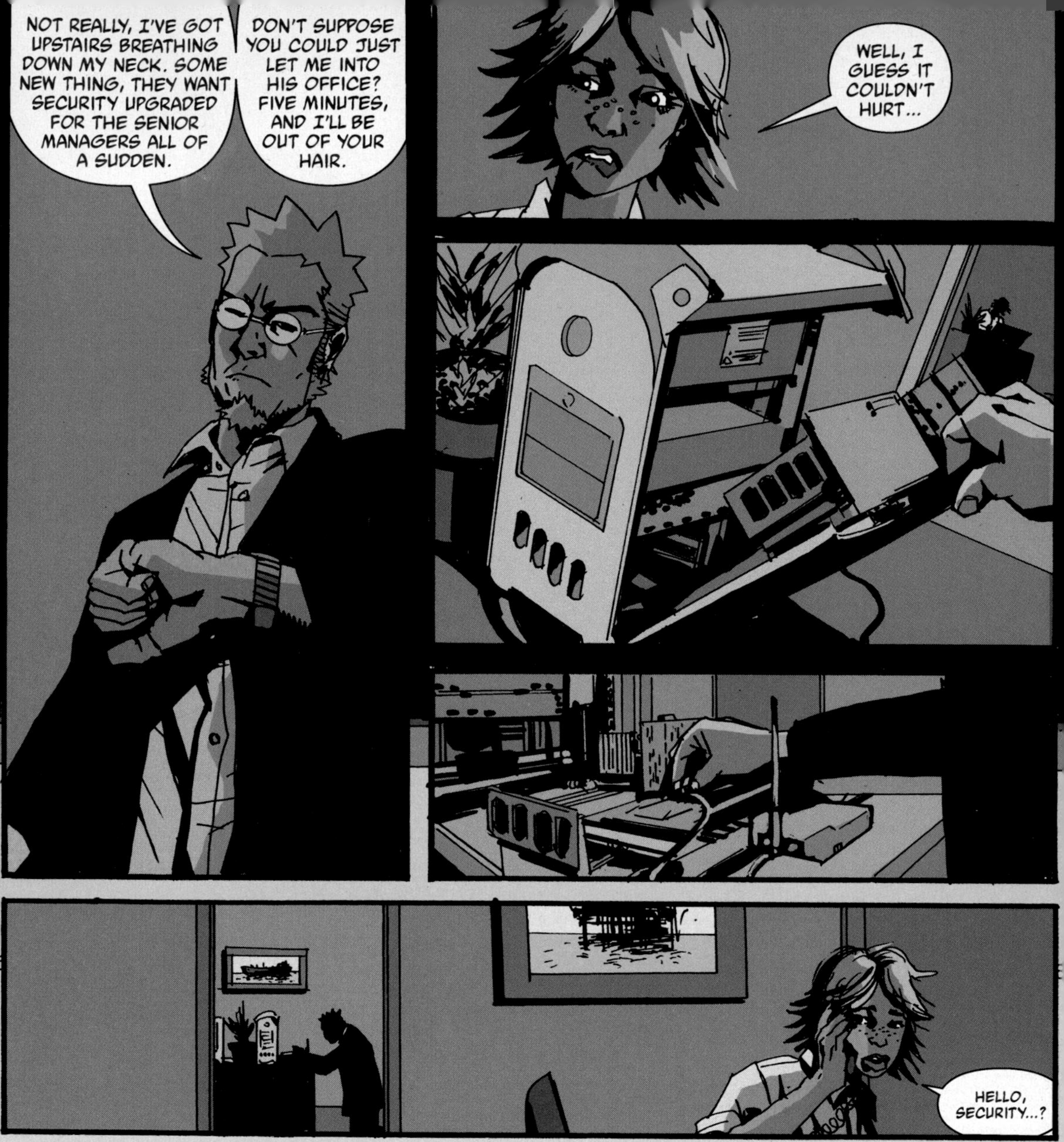
NOT REALLY, I'VE GOT UPSTAIRS BREATHING DOWN MY NECK. SOME NEW THING, THEY WANT SECURITY UPGRADED FOR THE SENIOR MANAGERS ALL OF A SUDDEN.
DON'T SUPPOSE YOU COULD JUST LET ME INTO HIS OFFICE? FIVE MINUTES, AND I'LL BE OUT OF YOUR HAIR.
WELL, I GUESS IT COULDN'T HURT...
HELLO, SECURITY...?

# GOLIATH AMALGAMATED INDUSTRIES INCORPORATE

## Port Of Houston Terminal Security Operat
## Annual Report

## Global Insurance Services
## 2003

**luction**

report has been produced for the purpose of providing a detailed a
tial aspects of port security and identifies many of the unique cha
th Port Of Houston terminal.

lso intended to provide the designated insurer Global Insurance S
non basis upon which to enforce port security standards and the o
ng those standards.

e of Contents

**time Security**

Broadband Wireless Modem Transmitting...

```
[localhost:~] chris% more /etc/daily
#!/bin/sh -
#
#       @(#)daily       8.2 (Berkeley) 1/25/94
#
PATH=/bin:/usr/bin:/sbin:/usr/sbin:/usr/local/bin
host=`hostname`
echo "Subject: $host daily run output"
bak=/var/backups

echo ""
echo "R  nv                    nk    les:"

if [ -d /var/rwho ] ; then
    cd /var/rwho && {
    find . ! -name . -mtime +7 -exec rm -f -- {} \; ; }
fi

#
#find / \( ! -fstype local -o -fstype rdonly \) -a -prune -o \
#       \( -name '[#,]*' -o -name '.#*' -o -name a.out -o -name '*.core' \
#          -o -name '*.CKP' -o -name '.emacs_[8-9]*' \) \
#               -a -atime +3 -exec rm -f -- {} \;
```

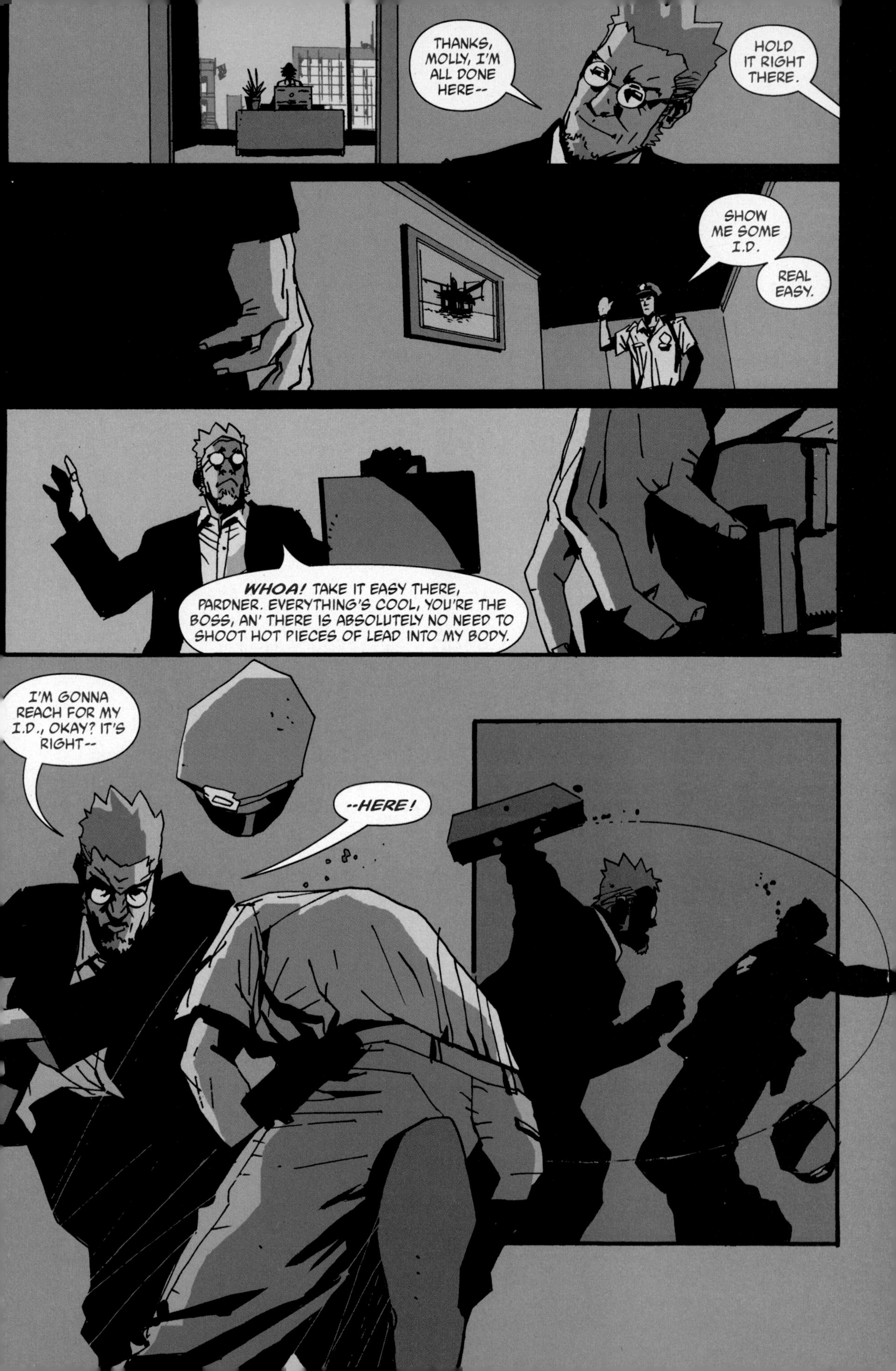
THANKS, MOLLY, I'M ALL DONE HERE--
HOLD IT RIGHT THERE.
SHOW ME SOME I.D.
REAL EASY.
WHOA! TAKE IT EASY THERE, PARDNER. EVERYTHING'S COOL, YOU'RE THE BOSS, AN' THERE IS ABSOLUTELY NO NEED TO SHOOT HOT PIECES OF LEAD INTO MY BODY.
I'M GONNA REACH FOR MY I.D., OKAY? IT'S RIGHT--
--HERE!

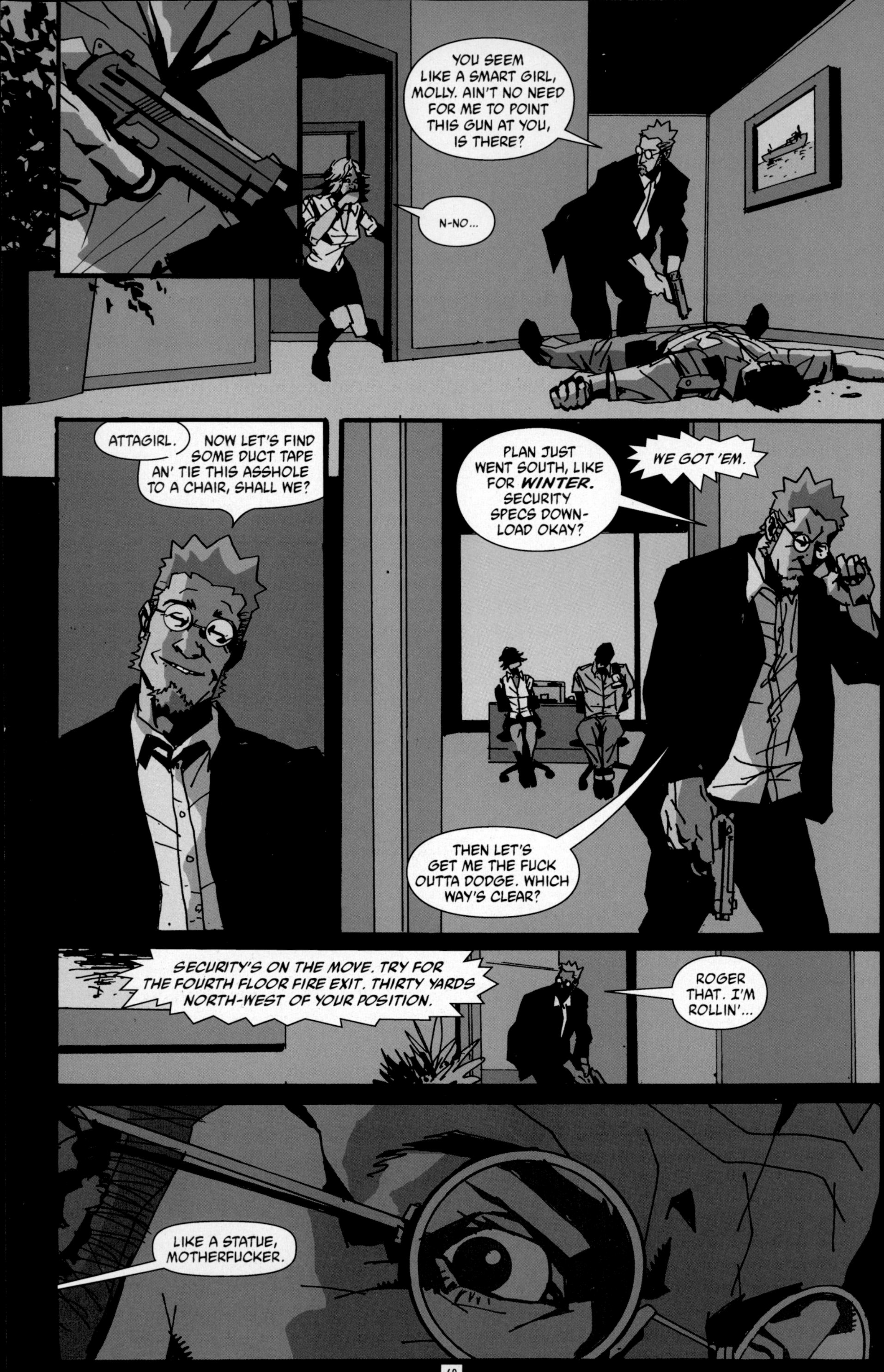
YOU SEEM LIKE A SMART GIRL, MOLLY. AIN'T NO NEED FOR ME TO POINT THIS GUN AT YOU, IS THERE?
N-NO...
ATTAGIRL.
NOW LET'S FIND SOME DUCT TAPE AN' TIE THIS ASSHOLE TO A CHAIR, SHALL WE?
PLAN JUST WENT SOUTH, LIKE FOR WINTER. SECURITY SPECS DOWN-LOAD OKAY?
WE GOT 'EM.
THEN LET'S GET ME THE FUCK OUTTA DODGE. WHICH WAY'S CLEAR?
SECURITY'S ON THE MOVE. TRY FOR THE FOURTH FLOOR FIRE EXIT. THIRTY YARDS NORTH-WEST OF YOUR POSITION.
ROGER THAT. I'M ROLLIN'...
LIKE A STATUE, MOTHERFUCKER.

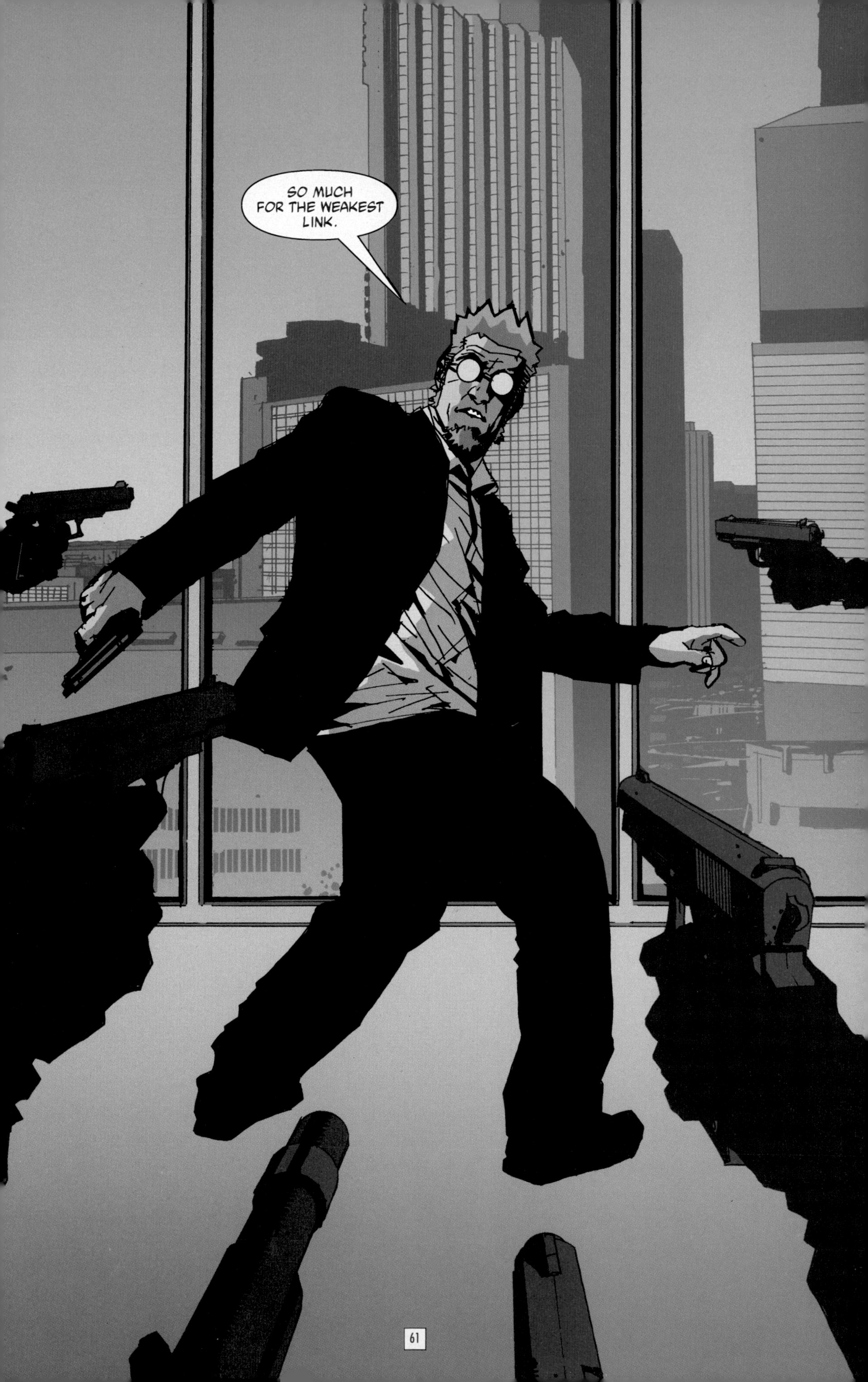
SO MUCH FOR THE WEAKEST LINK.

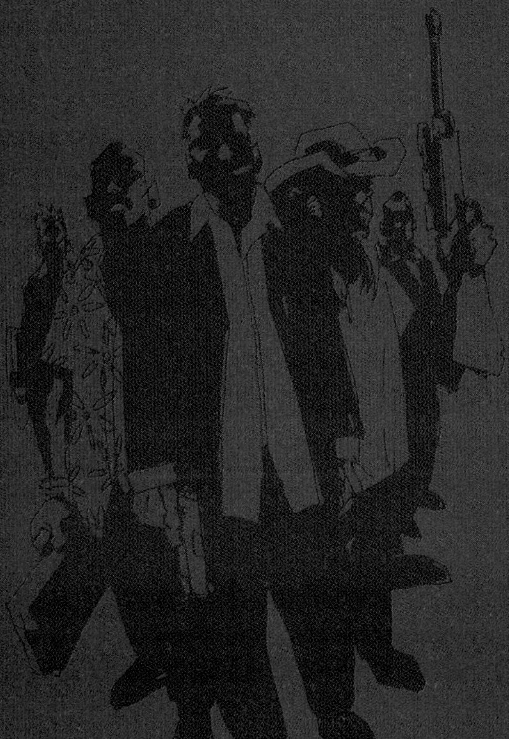

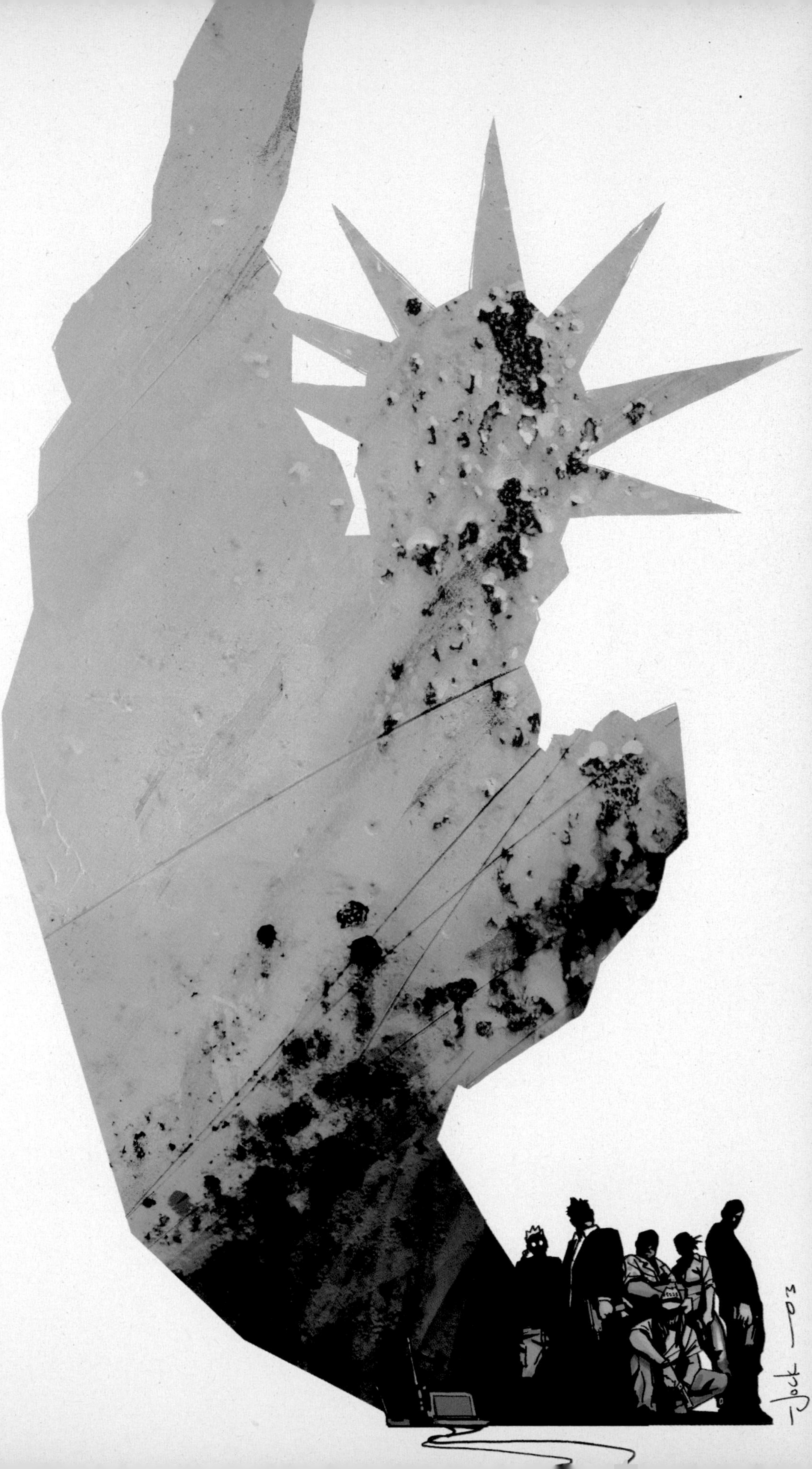

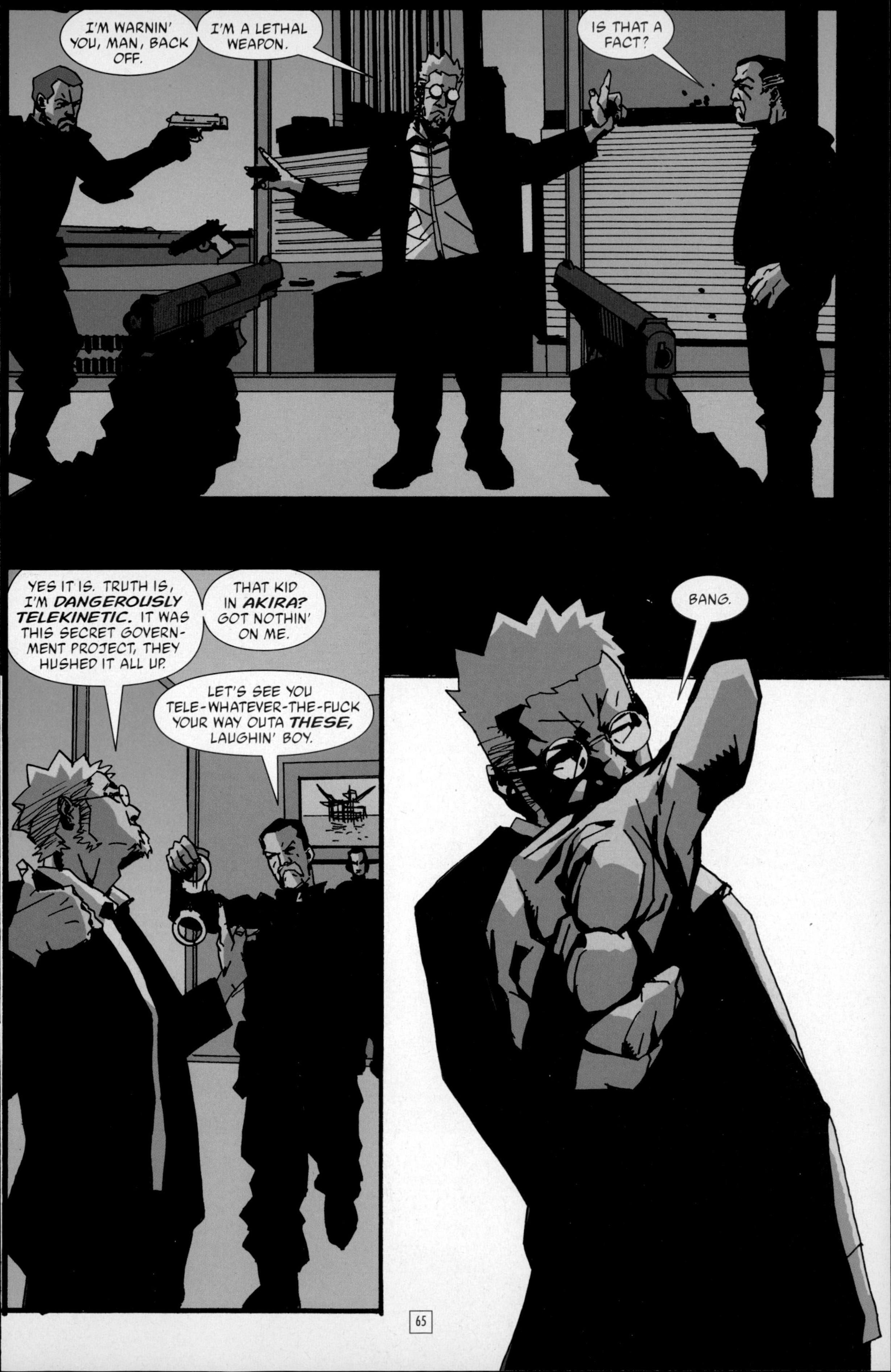
I'M WARNIN' YOU, MAN, BACK OFF.
I'M A LETHAL WEAPON.
IS THAT A FACT?
YES IT IS. TRUTH IS, I'M DANGEROUSLY TELEKINETIC. IT WAS THIS SECRET GOVERNMENT PROJECT, THEY HUSHED IT ALL UP.
THAT KID IN AKIRA? GOT NOTHIN' ON ME.
LET'S SEE YOU TELE-WHATEVER-THE-FUCK YOUR WAY OUTA THESE, LAUGHIN' BOY.
BANG.

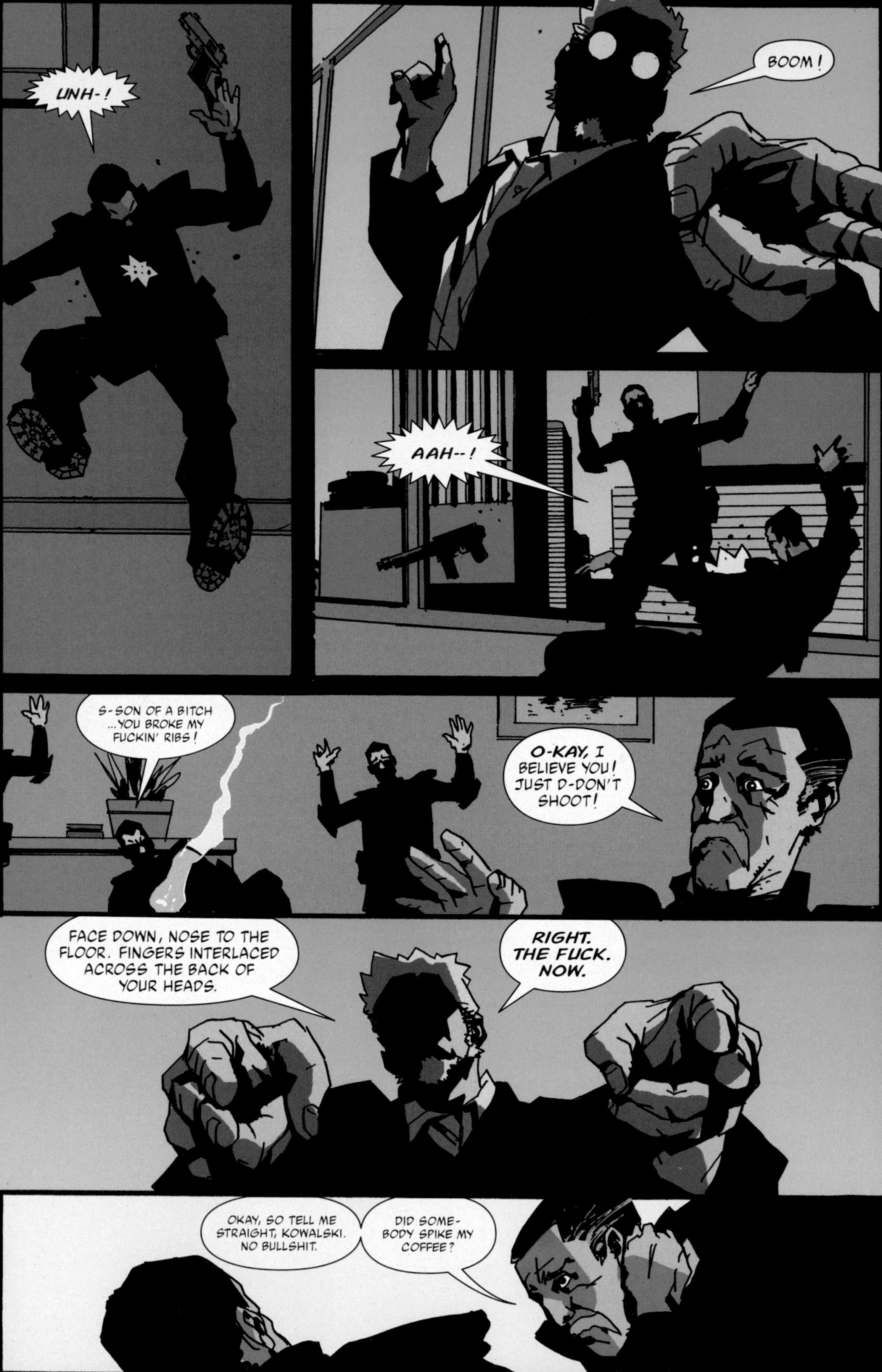
UNH-!
BOOM!
AAH--!
S-SON OF A BITCH ...YOU BROKE MY FUCKIN' RIBS!
O-KAY, I BELIEVE YOU! JUST D-DON'T SHOOT!
FACE DOWN, NOSE TO THE FLOOR. FINGERS INTERLACED ACROSS THE BACK OF YOUR HEADS.
RIGHT. THE FUCK. NOW.
OKAY, SO TELL ME STRAIGHT, KOWALSKI. NO BULLSHIT.
DID SOMEBODY SPIKE MY COFFEE?

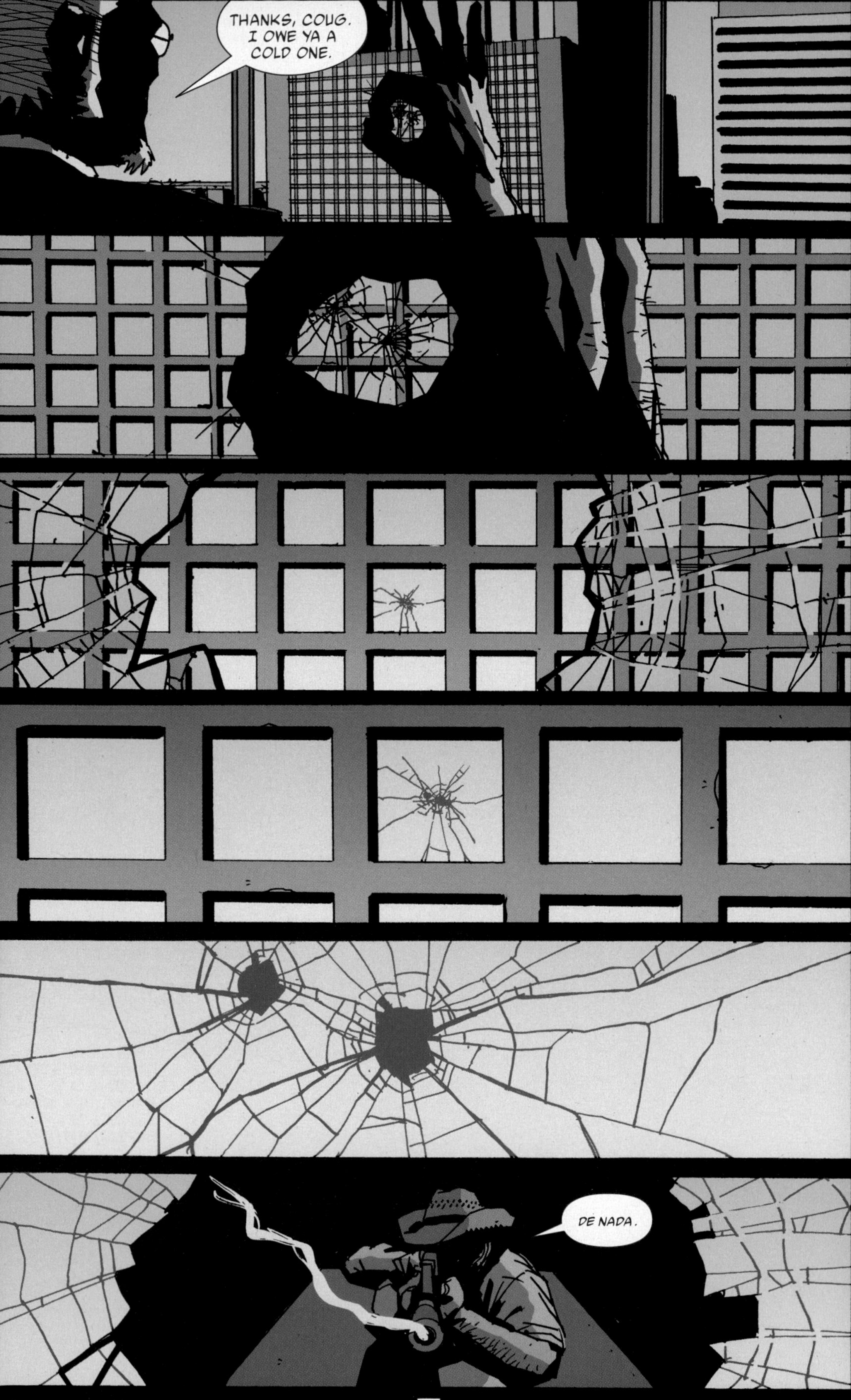
THANKS, COUG. I OWE YA A COLD ONE.
DE NADA.

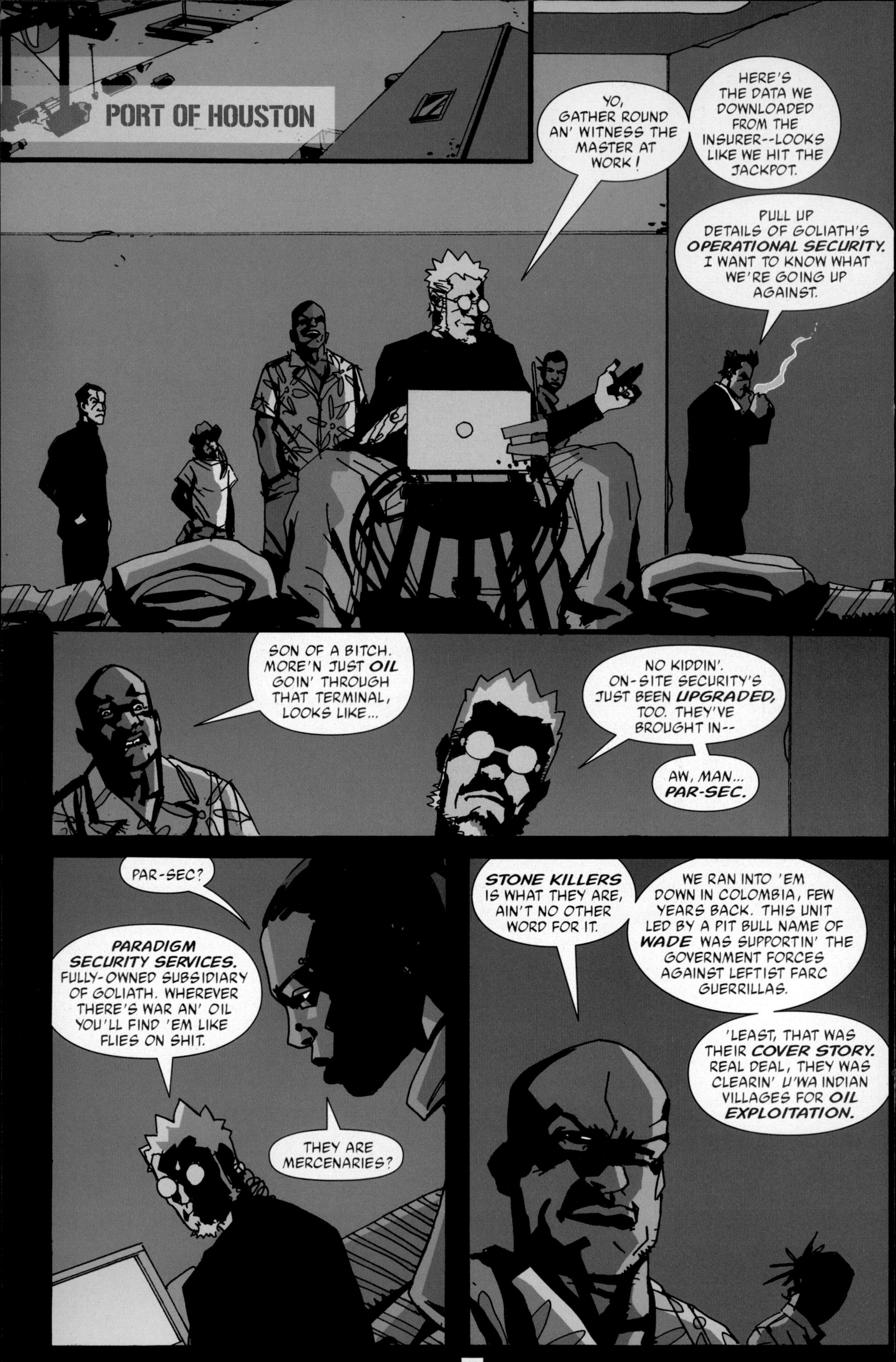

PORT OF HOUSTON
YO, GATHER ROUND AN' WITNESS THE MASTER AT WORK!
HERE'S THE DATA WE DOWNLOADED FROM THE INSURER--LOOKS LIKE WE HIT THE JACKPOT.
PULL UP DETAILS OF GOLIATH'S OPERATIONAL SECURITY. I WANT TO KNOW WHAT WE'RE GOING UP AGAINST.
SON OF A BITCH. MORE'N JUST OIL GOIN' THROUGH THAT TERMINAL, LOOKS LIKE...
NO KIDDIN'. ON-SITE SECURITY'S JUST BEEN UPGRADED, TOO. THEY'VE BROUGHT IN--
AW, MAN... PAR-SEC.
PAR-SEC?
PARADIGM SECURITY SERVICES. FULLY-OWNED SUBSIDIARY OF GOLIATH. WHEREVER THERE'S WAR AN' OIL YOU'LL FIND 'EM LIKE FLIES ON SHIT.
THEY ARE MERCENARIES?
STONE KILLERS IS WHAT THEY ARE, AIN'T NO OTHER WORD FOR IT.
WE RAN INTO 'EM DOWN IN COLOMBIA, FEW YEARS BACK. THIS UNIT LED BY A PIT BULL NAME OF WADE WAS SUPPORTIN' THE GOVERNMENT FORCES AGAINST LEFTIST FARC GUERRILLAS.
'LEAST, THAT WAS THEIR COVER STORY. REAL DEAL, THEY WAS CLEARIN' U'WA INDIAN VILLAGES FOR OIL EXPLOITATION.

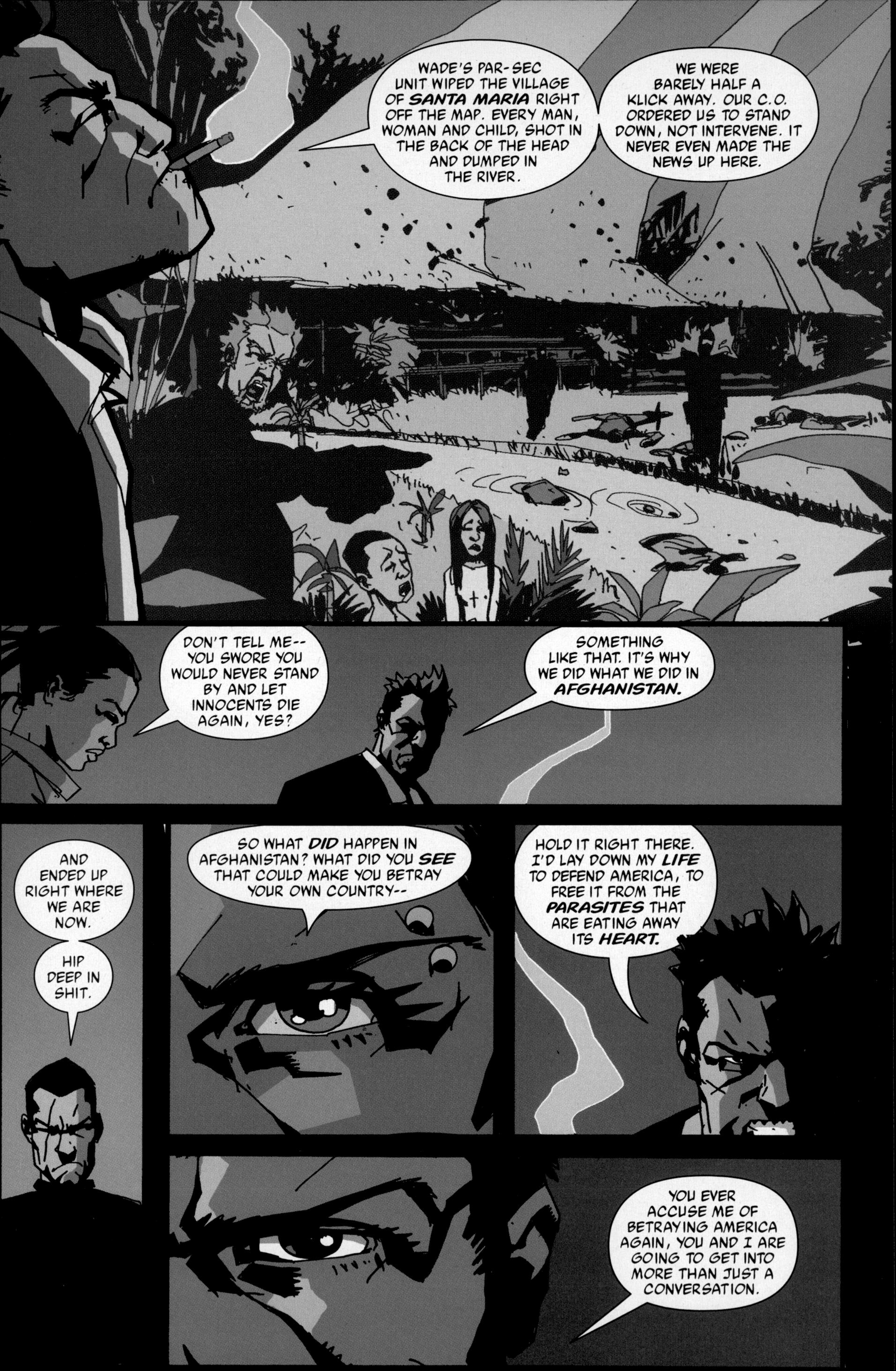
WADE'S PAR-SEC UNIT WIPED THE VILLAGE OF SANTA MARIA RIGHT OFF THE MAP. EVERY MAN, WOMAN AND CHILD, SHOT IN THE BACK OF THE HEAD AND DUMPED IN THE RIVER.
WE WERE BARELY HALF A KLICK AWAY. OUR C.O. ORDERED US TO STAND DOWN, NOT INTERVENE. IT NEVER EVEN MADE THE NEWS UP HERE.
DON'T TELL ME-- YOU SWORE YOU WOULD NEVER STAND BY AND LET INNOCENTS DIE AGAIN, YES?
SOMETHING LIKE THAT. IT'S WHY WE DID WHAT WE DID IN AFGHANISTAN.
AND ENDED UP RIGHT WHERE WE ARE NOW.
HIP DEEP IN SHIT.
SO WHAT DID HAPPEN IN AFGHANISTAN? WHAT DID YOU SEE THAT COULD MAKE YOU BETRAY YOUR OWN COUNTRY--
HOLD IT RIGHT THERE. I'D LAY DOWN MY LIFE TO DEFEND AMERICA, TO FREE IT FROM THE PARASITES THAT ARE EATING AWAY ITS HEART.
YOU EVER ACCUSE ME OF BETRAYING AMERICA AGAIN, YOU AND I ARE GOING TO GET INTO MORE THAN JUST A CONVERSATION.

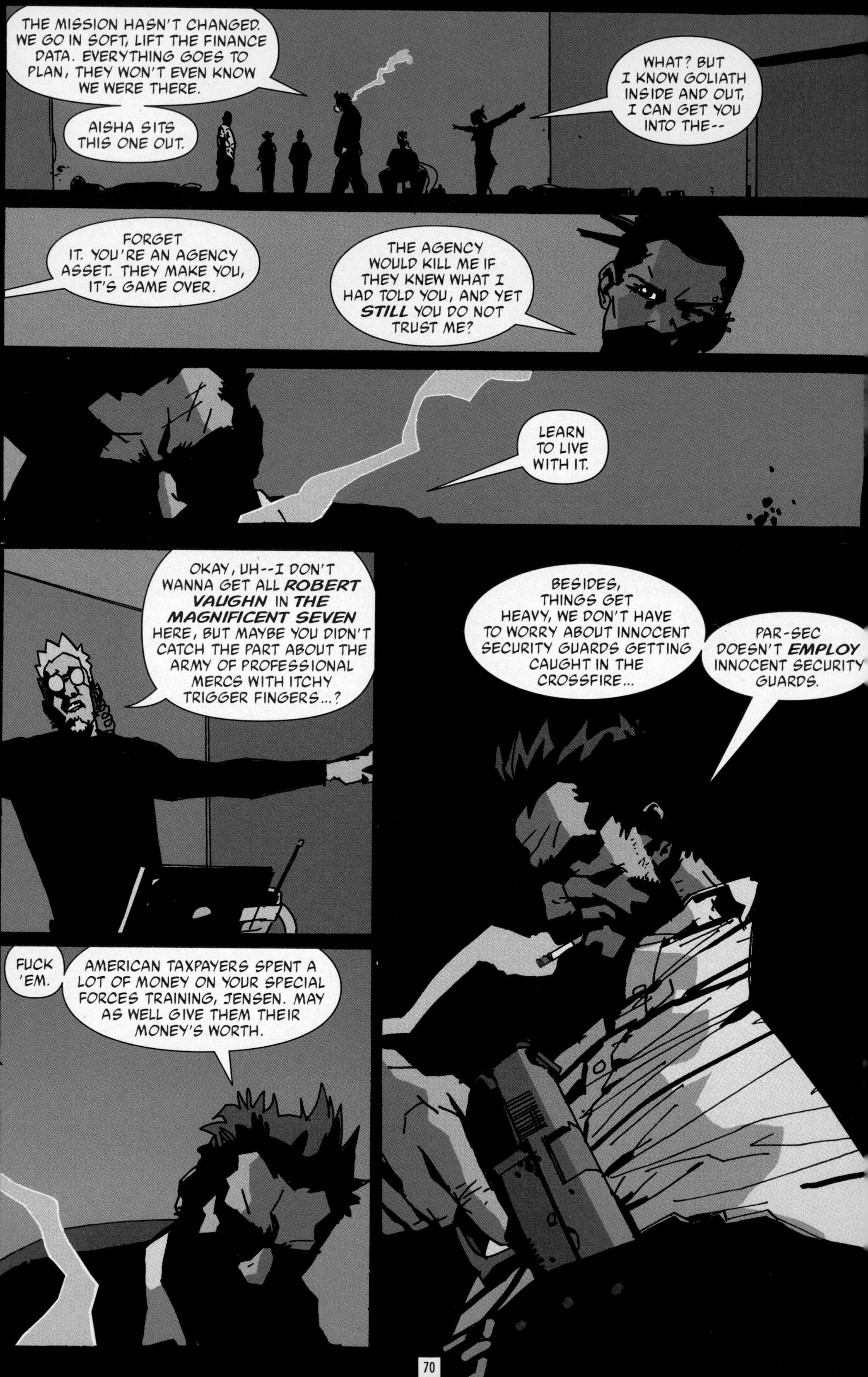
THE MISSION HASN'T CHANGED. WE GO IN SOFT, LIFT THE FINANCE DATA. EVERYTHING GOES TO PLAN, THEY WON'T EVEN KNOW WE WERE THERE.
AISHA SITS THIS ONE OUT.
WHAT? BUT I KNOW GOLIATH INSIDE AND OUT, I CAN GET YOU INTO THE--
FORGET IT. YOU'RE AN AGENCY ASSET. THEY MAKE YOU, IT'S GAME OVER.
THE AGENCY WOULD KILL ME IF THEY KNEW WHAT I HAD TOLD YOU, AND YET STILL YOU DO NOT TRUST ME?
LEARN TO LIVE WITH IT.
OKAY, UH--I DON'T WANNA GET ALL ROBERT VAUGHN IN THE MAGNIFICENT SEVEN HERE, BUT MAYBE YOU DIDN'T CATCH THE PART ABOUT THE ARMY OF PROFESSIONAL MERCS WITH ITCHY TRIGGER FINGERS...?
BESIDES, THINGS GET HEAVY, WE DON'T HAVE TO WORRY ABOUT INNOCENT SECURITY GUARDS GETTING CAUGHT IN THE CROSSFIRE...
PAR-SEC DOESN'T EMPLOY INNOCENT SECURITY GUARDS.
FUCK 'EM.
AMERICAN TAXPAYERS SPENT A LOT OF MONEY ON YOUR SPECIAL FORCES TRAINING, JENSEN. MAY AS WELL GIVE THEM THEIR MONEY'S WORTH.

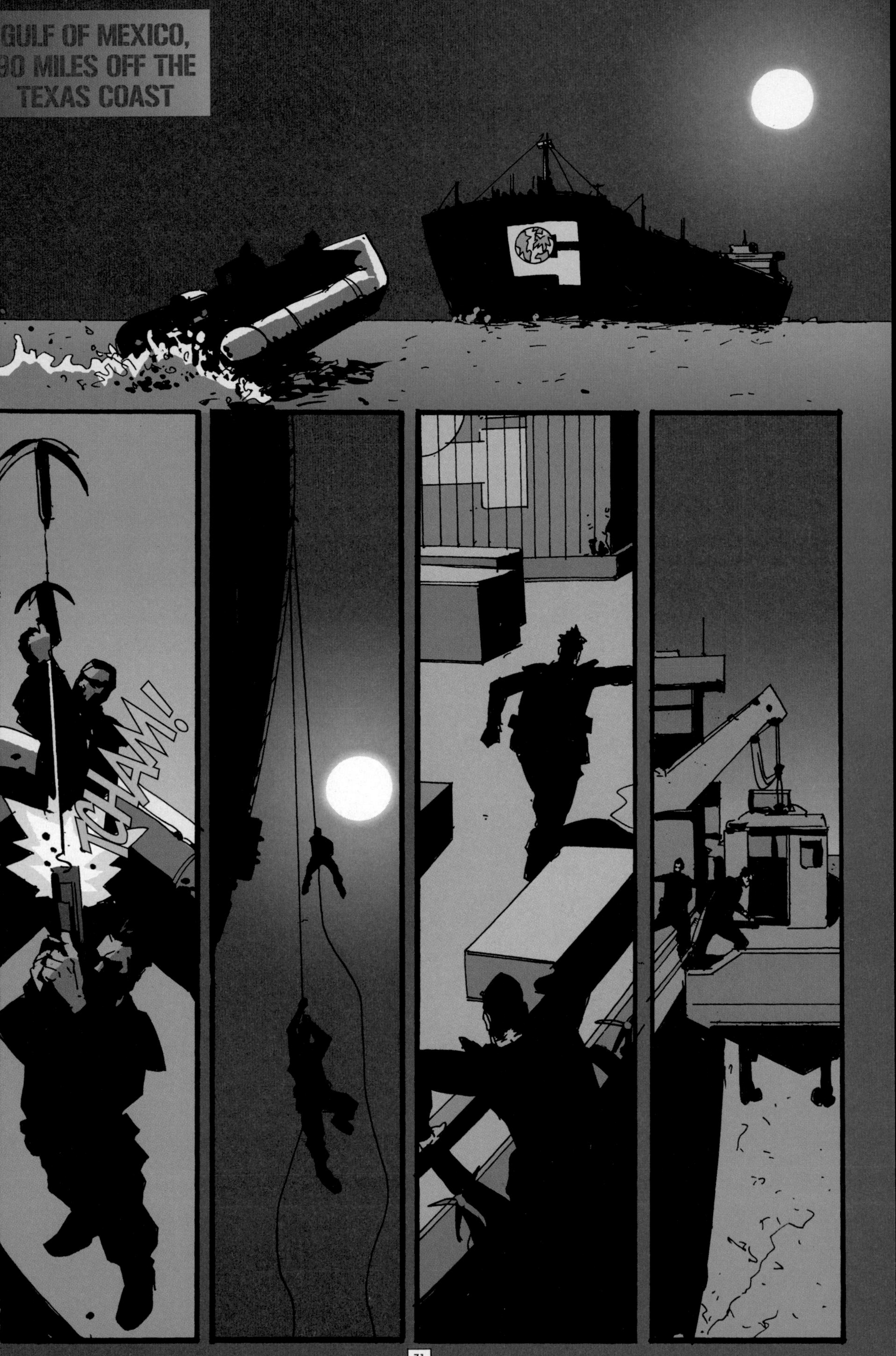
GULF OF MEXICO, 90 MILES OFF THE TEXAS COAST
TCHAM!

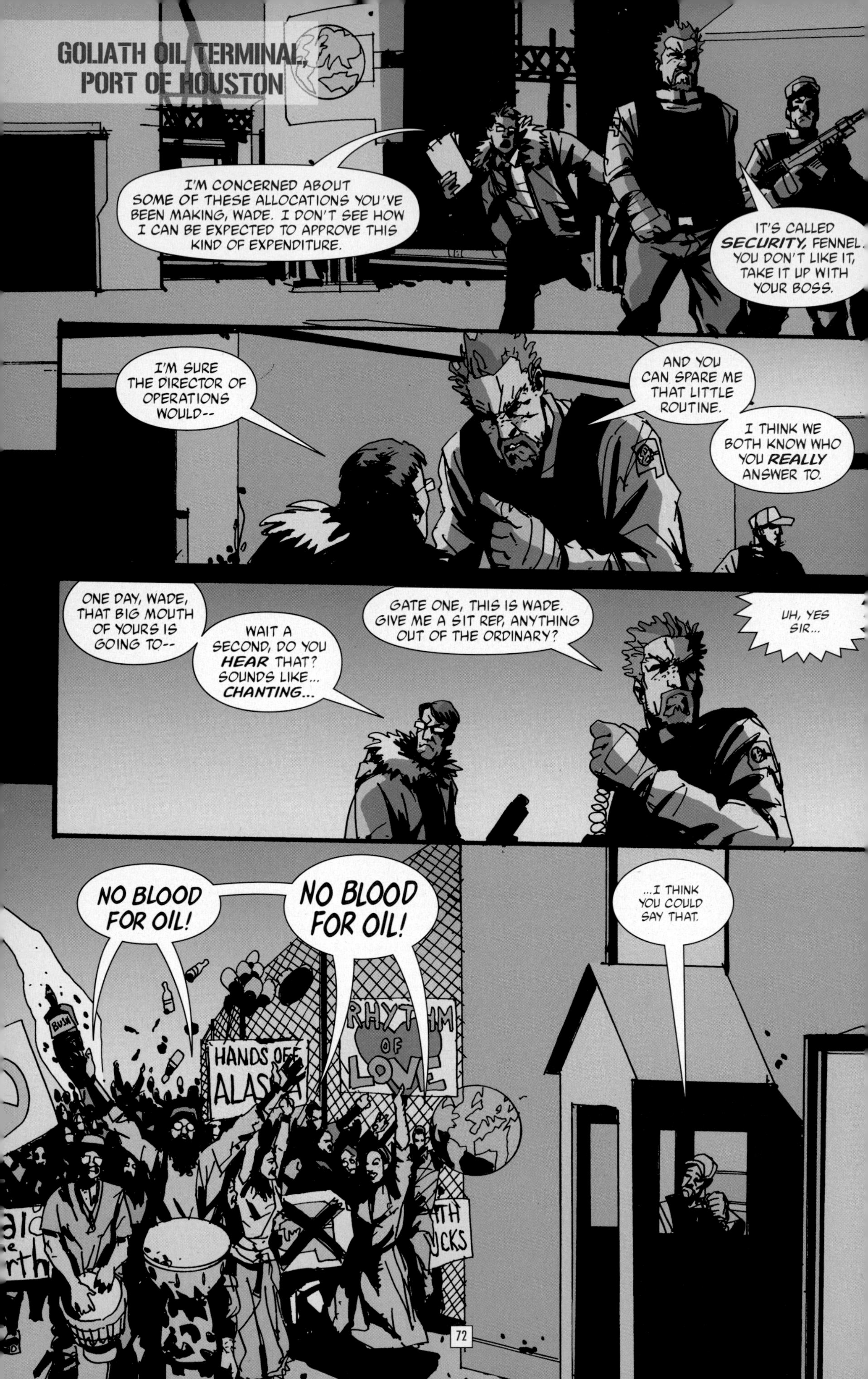
GOLIATH OIL TERMINAL, PORT OF HOUSTON
I'M CONCERNED ABOUT SOME OF THESE ALLOCATIONS YOU'VE BEEN MAKING, WADE. I DON'T SEE HOW I CAN BE EXPECTED TO APPROVE THIS KIND OF EXPENDITURE.
IT'S CALLED SECURITY, FENNEL. YOU DON'T LIKE IT, TAKE IT UP WITH YOUR BOSS.
I'M SURE THE DIRECTOR OF OPERATIONS WOULD--
AND YOU CAN SPARE ME THAT LITTLE ROUTINE.
I THINK WE BOTH KNOW WHO YOU REALLY ANSWER TO.
ONE DAY, WADE, THAT BIG MOUTH OF YOURS IS GOING TO--
WAIT A SECOND, DO YOU HEAR THAT? SOUNDS LIKE... CHANTING...
GATE ONE, THIS IS WADE. GIVE ME A SIT REP, ANYTHING OUT OF THE ORDINARY?
UH, YES SIR...
NO BLOOD FOR OIL!
NO BLOOD FOR OIL!
...I THINK YOU COULD SAY THAT.
HANDS OFF ALAS
RHYTHM OF LOVE
BUSH

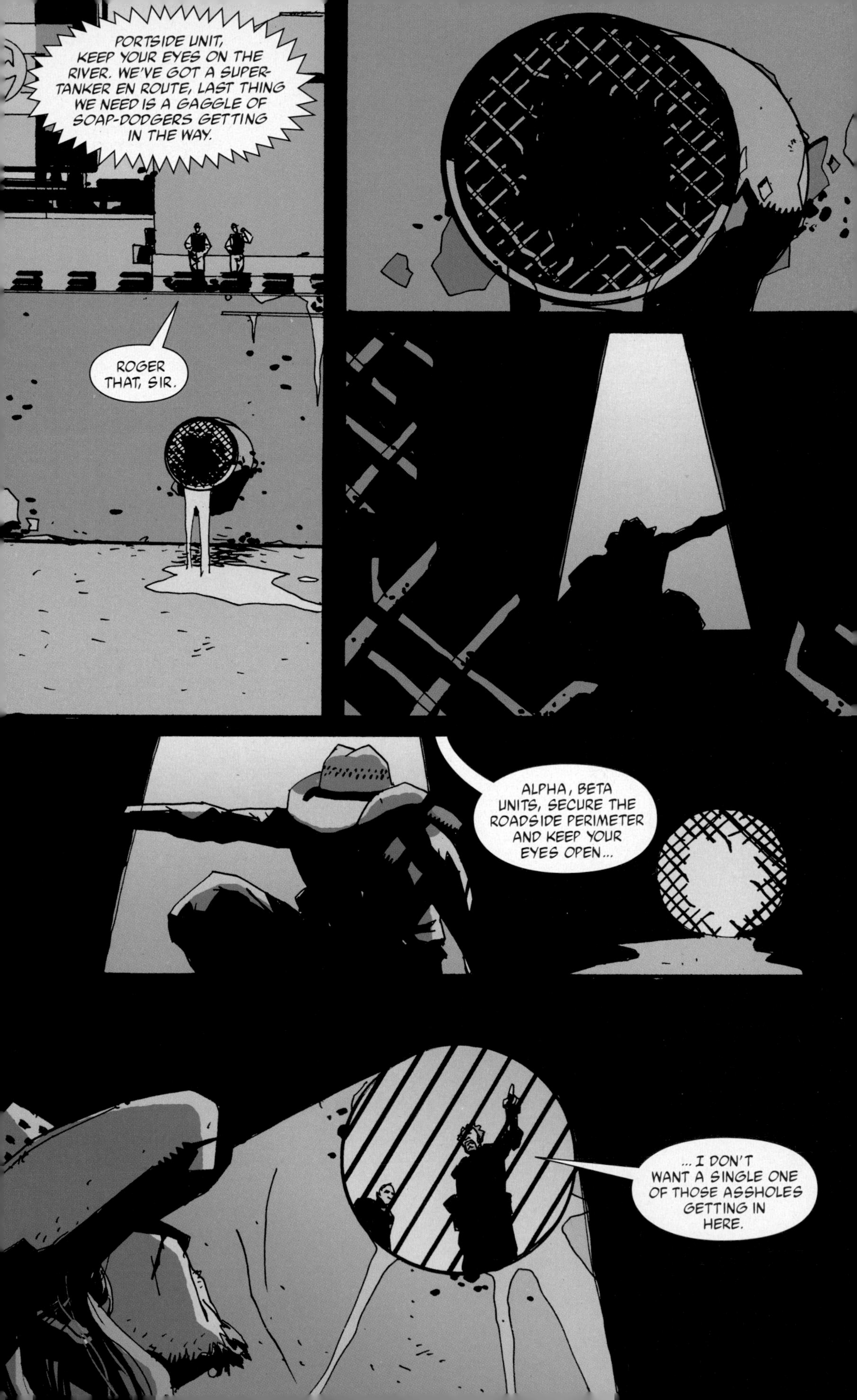
PORTSIDE UNIT, KEEP YOUR EYES ON THE RIVER. WE'VE GOT A SUPER-TANKER EN ROUTE, LAST THING WE NEED IS A GAGGLE OF SOAP-DODGERS GETTING IN THE WAY.
ROGER THAT, SIR.
ALPHA, BETA UNITS, SECURE THE ROADSIDE PERIMETER AND KEEP YOUR EYES OPEN...
...I DON'T WANT A SINGLE ONE OF THOSE ASSHOLES GETTING IN HERE.

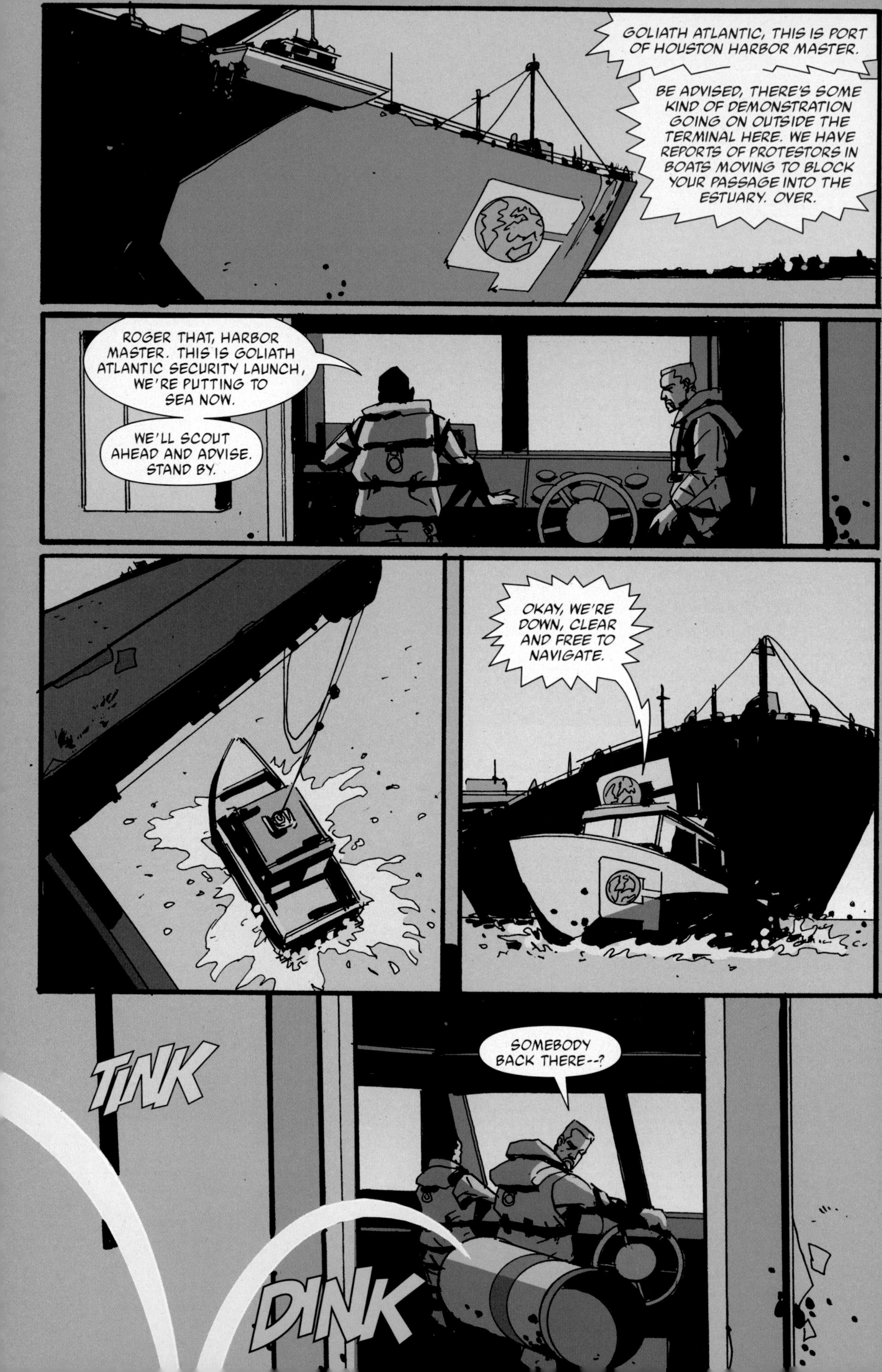
GOLIATH ATLANTIC, THIS IS PORT OF HOUSTON HARBOR MASTER.
BE ADVISED, THERE'S SOME KIND OF DEMONSTRATION GOING ON OUTSIDE THE TERMINAL HERE. WE HAVE REPORTS OF PROTESTORS IN BOATS MOVING TO BLOCK YOUR PASSAGE INTO THE ESTUARY. OVER.
ROGER THAT, HARBOR MASTER. THIS IS GOLIATH ATLANTIC SECURITY LAUNCH, WE'RE PUTTING TO SEA NOW.
WE'LL SCOUT AHEAD AND ADVISE. STAND BY.
OKAY, WE'RE DOWN, CLEAR AND FREE TO NAVIGATE.
TINK
SOMEBODY BACK THERE--?
DINK

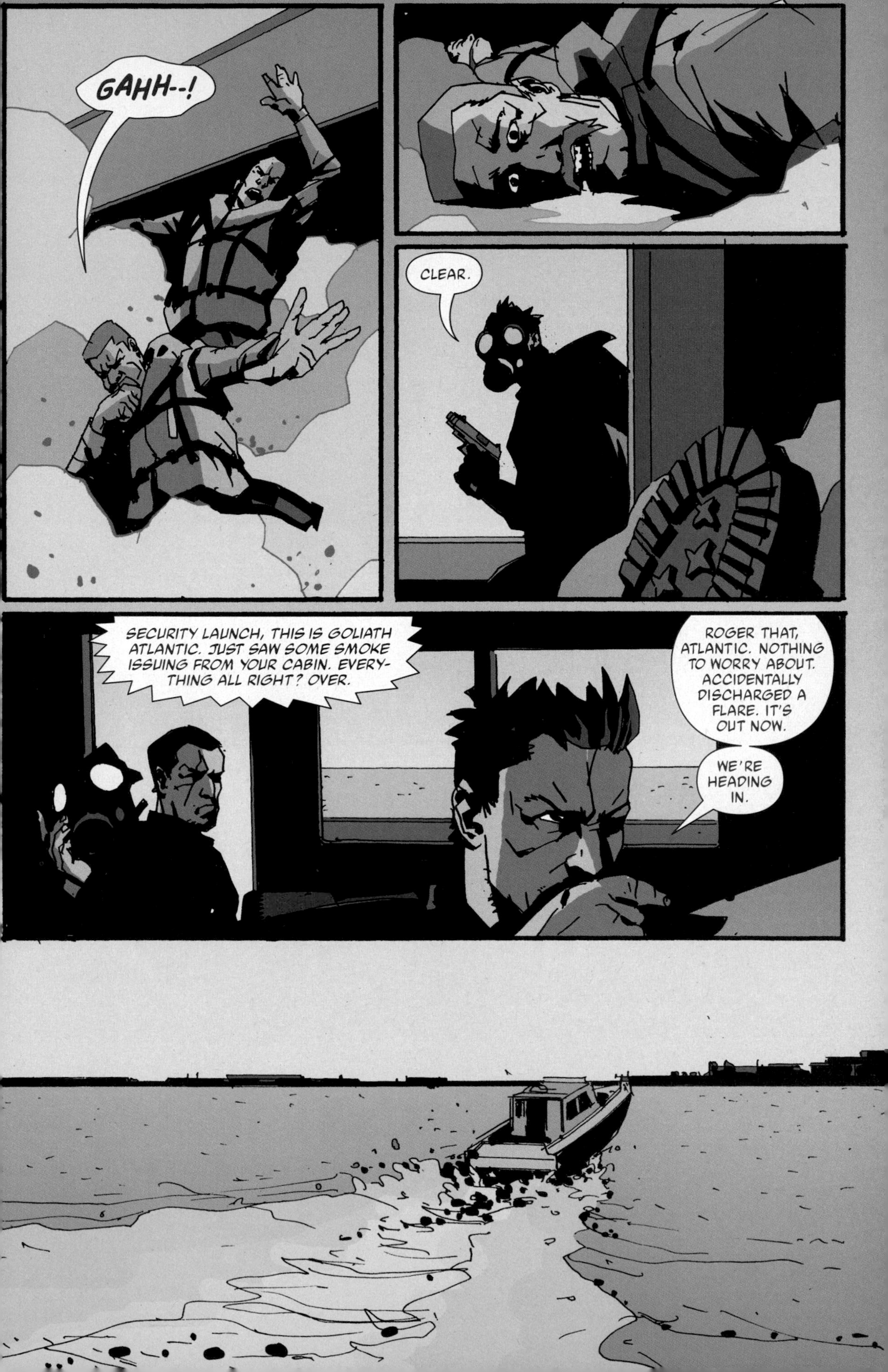
GAHH--!
CLEAR.
SECURITY LAUNCH, THIS IS GOLIATH ATLANTIC. JUST SAW SOME SMOKE ISSUING FROM YOUR CABIN. EVERYTHING ALL RIGHT? OVER.
ROGER THAT, ATLANTIC. NOTHING TO WORRY ABOUT. ACCIDENTALLY DISCHARGED A FLARE. IT'S OUT NOW.
WE'RE HEADING IN.

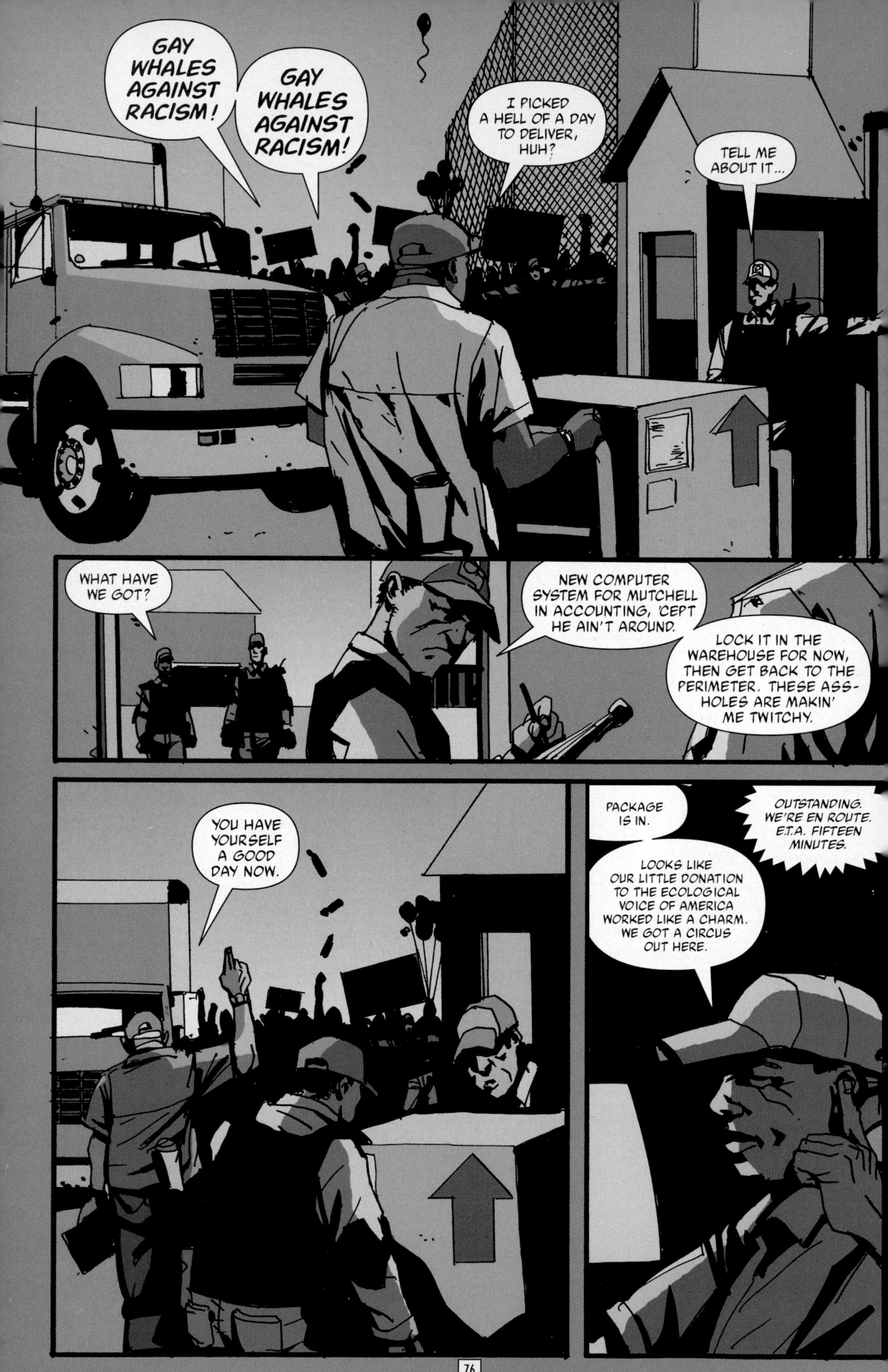
GAY WHALES AGAINST RACISM!
GAY WHALES AGAINST RACISM!
I PICKED A HELL OF A DAY TO DELIVER, HUH?
TELL ME ABOUT IT...
WHAT HAVE WE GOT?
NEW COMPUTER SYSTEM FOR MUTCHELL IN ACCOUNTING, 'CEPT HE AIN'T AROUND.
LOCK IT IN THE WAREHOUSE FOR NOW, THEN GET BACK TO THE PERIMETER. THESE ASS-HOLES ARE MAKIN' ME TWITCHY.
YOU HAVE YOURSELF A GOOD DAY NOW.
PACKAGE IS IN.
OUTSTANDING. WE'RE EN ROUTE. E.T.A. FIFTEEN MINUTES.
LOOKS LIKE OUR LITTLE DONATION TO THE ECOLOGICAL VOICE OF AMERICA WORKED LIKE A CHARM. WE GOT A CIRCUS OUT HERE.

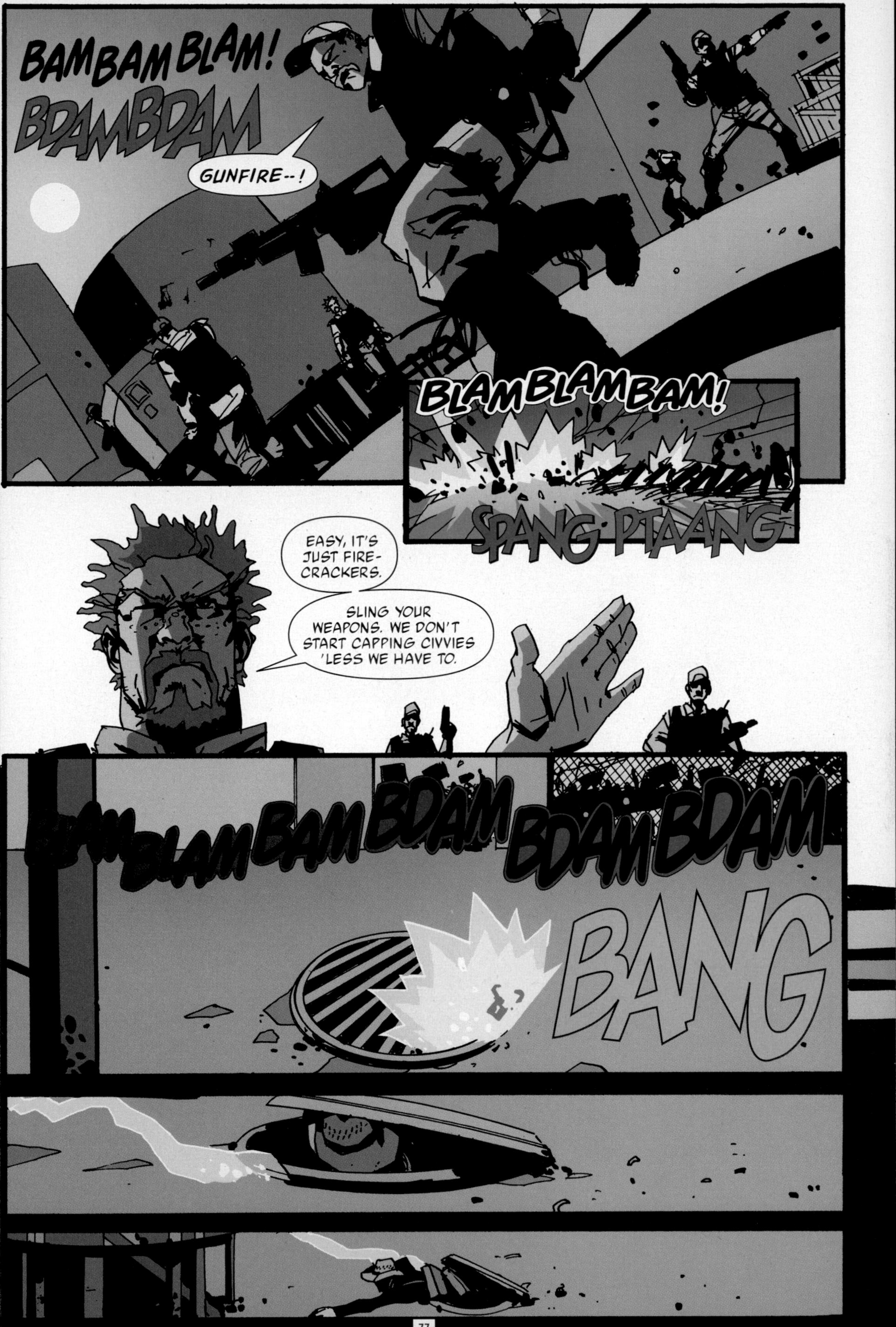
BAMBAMBLAM!
BDAMBDAM
GUNFIRE--!
BLAMBLAMBAM!
SPANG PTAANG
EASY, IT'S JUST FIRE-CRACKERS.
SLING YOUR WEAPONS. WE DON'T START CAPPING CIVVIES 'LESS WE HAVE TO.
BLAM BAM BDAM BDAM BDAM
BANG

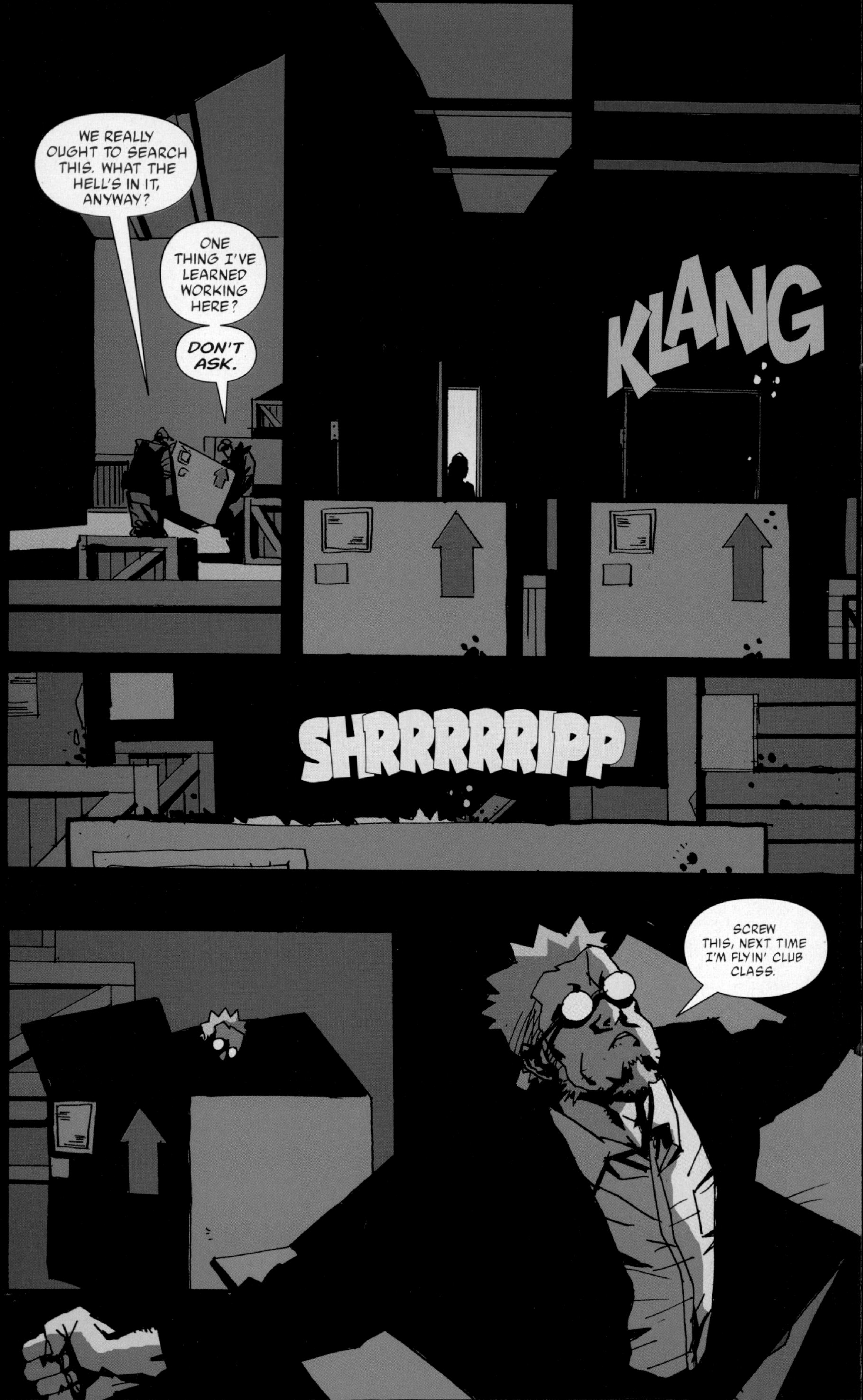

WE REALLY OUGHT TO SEARCH THIS. WHAT THE HELL'S IN IT, ANYWAY?
ONE THING I'VE LEARNED WORKING HERE?
DON'T ASK.
KLANG
SHRRRRRIPP
SCREW THIS, NEXT TIME I'M FLYIN' CLUB CLASS.

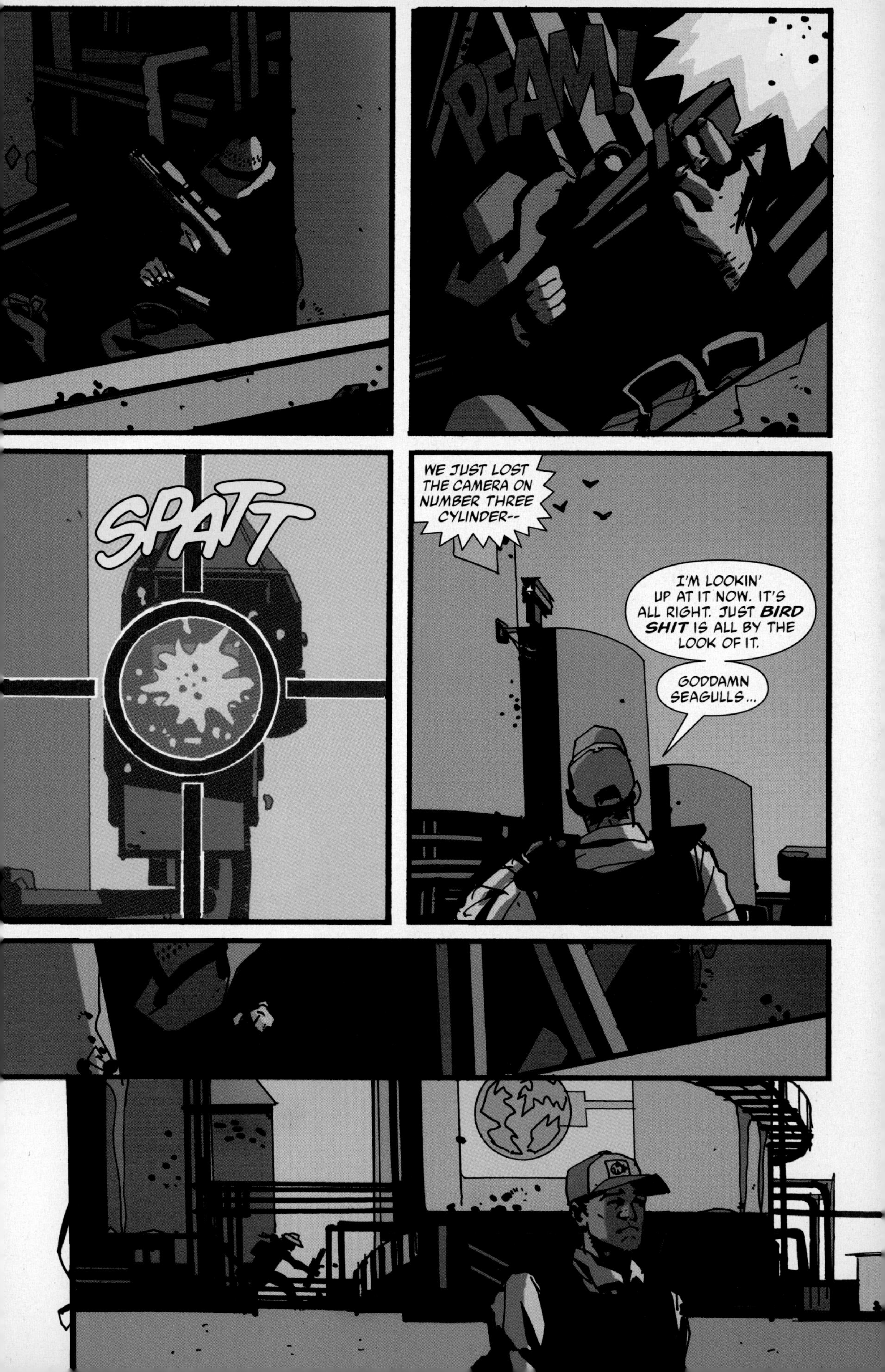
PFAM!
SPATT
WE JUST LOST THE CAMERA ON NUMBER THREE CYLINDER--
I'M LOOKIN' UP AT IT NOW. IT'S ALL RIGHT. JUST BIRD SHIT IS ALL BY THE LOOK OF IT.
GODDAMN SEAGULLS...

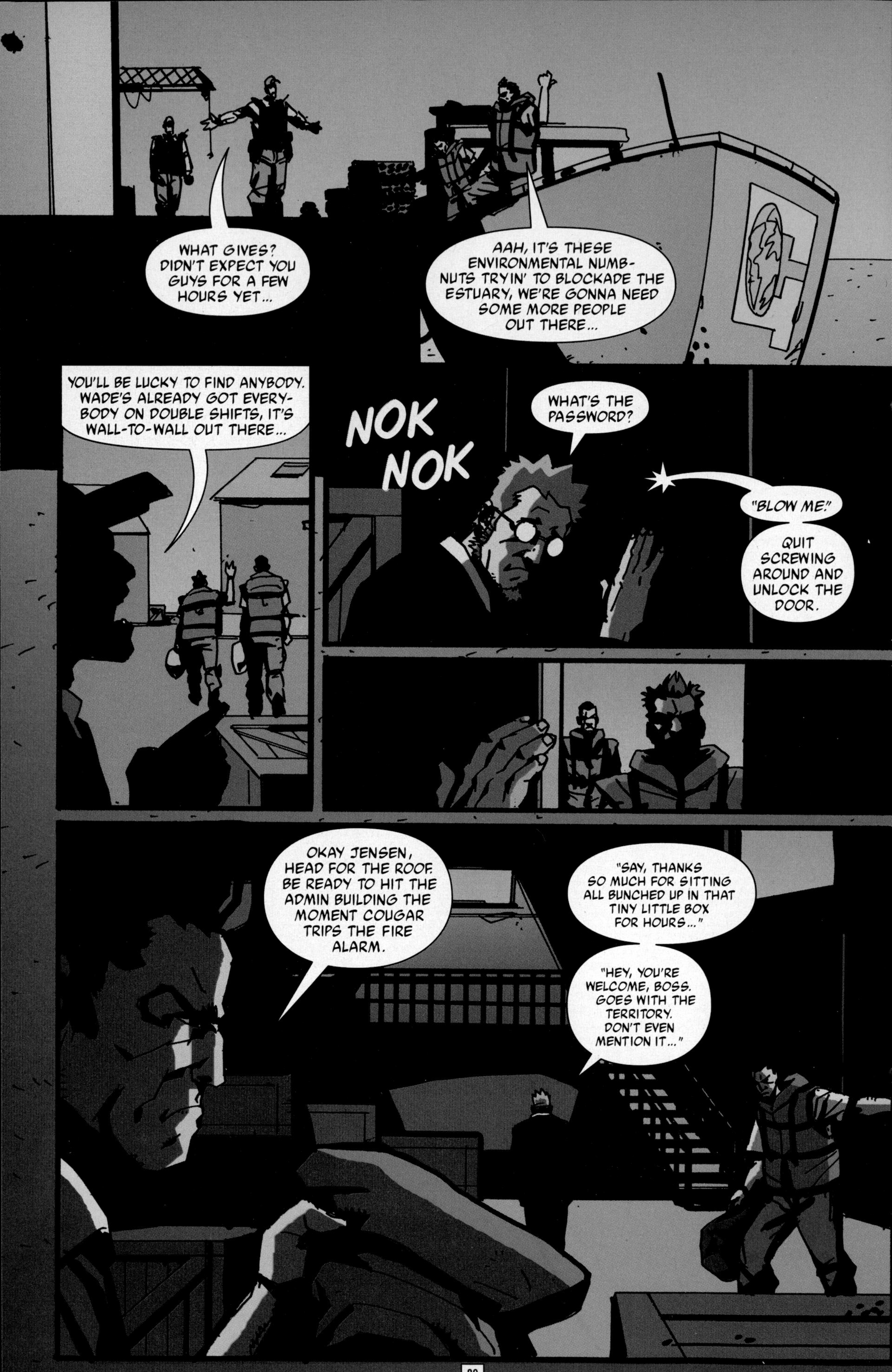
WHAT GIVES? DIDN'T EXPECT YOU GUYS FOR A FEW HOURS YET...
AAH, IT'S THESE ENVIRONMENTAL NUMB-NUTS TRYIN' TO BLOCKADE THE ESTUARY, WE'RE GONNA NEED SOME MORE PEOPLE OUT THERE...
YOU'LL BE LUCKY TO FIND ANYBODY. WADE'S ALREADY GOT EVERY-BODY ON DOUBLE SHIFTS, IT'S WALL-TO-WALL OUT THERE...
NOK NOK
WHAT'S THE PASSWORD?
"BLOW ME."
QUIT SCREWING AROUND AND UNLOCK THE DOOR.
OKAY JENSEN, HEAD FOR THE ROOF. BE READY TO HIT THE ADMIN BUILDING THE MOMENT COUGAR TRIPS THE FIRE ALARM.
"SAY, THANKS SO MUCH FOR SITTING ALL BUNCHED UP IN THAT TINY LITTLE BOX FOR HOURS..."
"HEY, YOU'RE WELCOME, BOSS. GOES WITH THE TERRITORY. DON'T EVEN MENTION IT..."

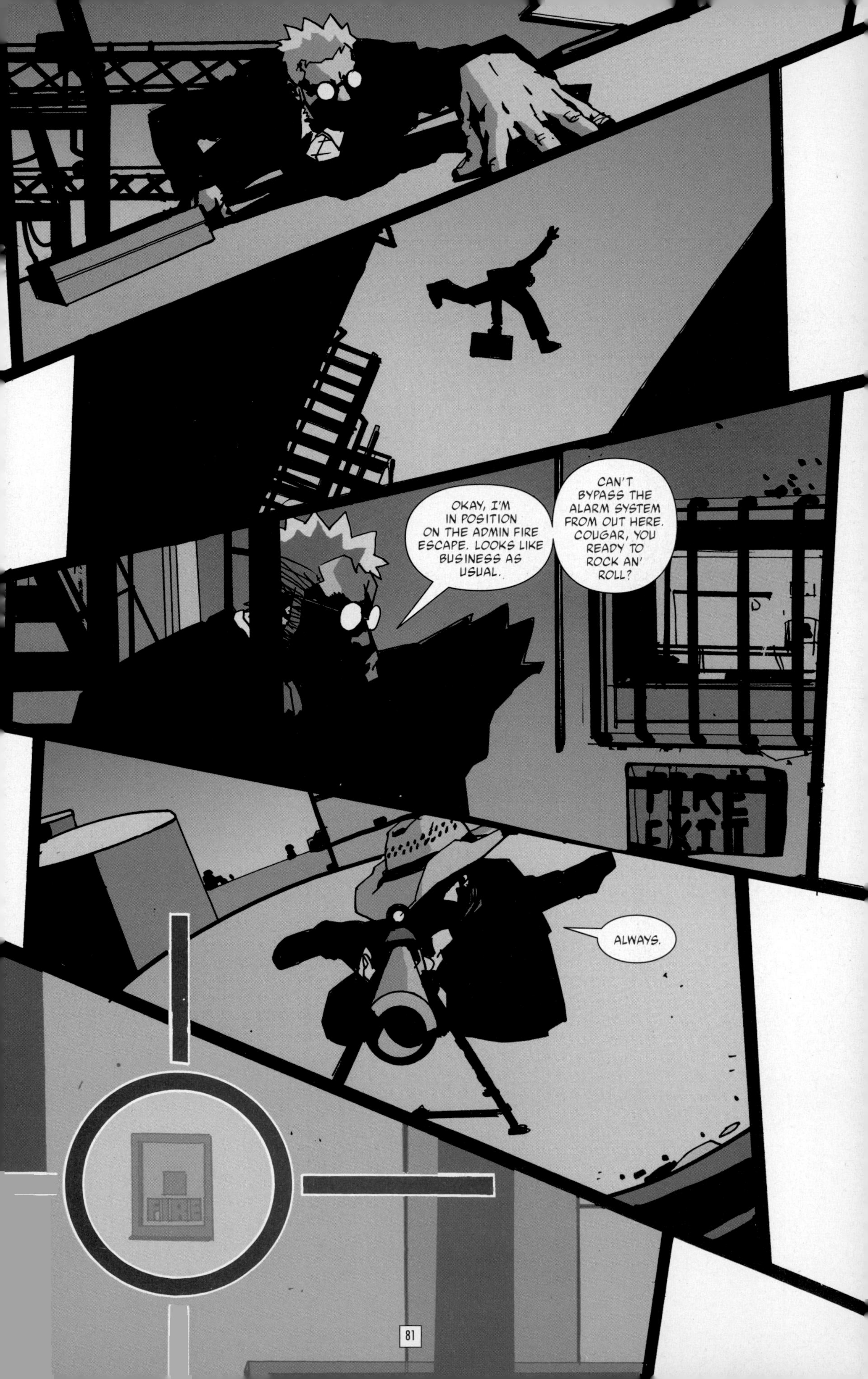
OKAY, I'M IN POSITION ON THE ADMIN FIRE ESCAPE. LOOKS LIKE BUSINESS AS USUAL.
CAN'T BYPASS THE ALARM SYSTEM FROM OUT HERE. COUGAR, YOU READY TO ROCK AN' ROLL?
ALWAYS.

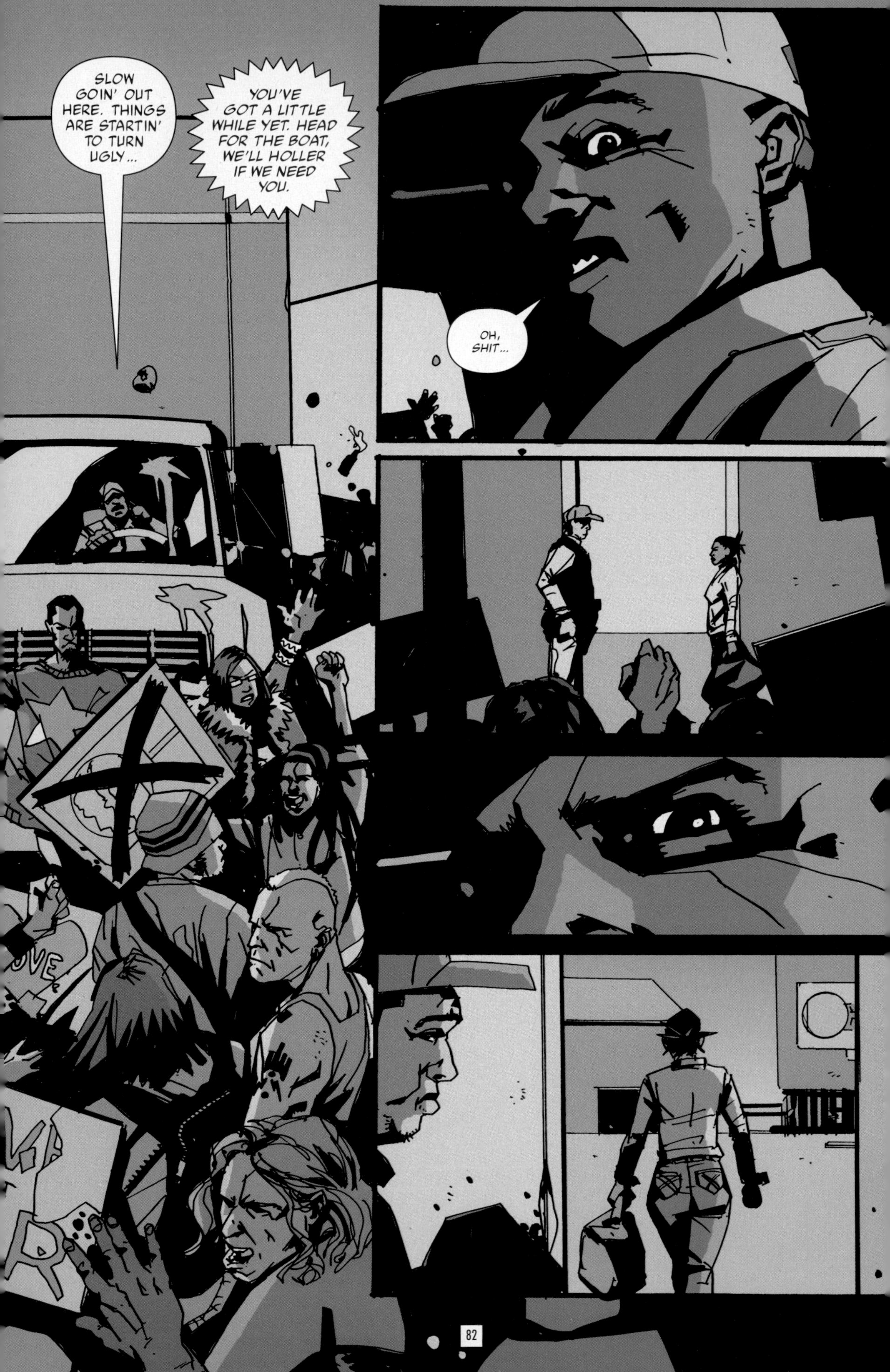
SLOW GOIN' OUT HERE. THINGS ARE STARTIN' TO TURN UGLY...
YOU'VE GOT A LITTLE WHILE YET. HEAD FOR THE BOAT, WE'LL HOLLER IF WE NEED YOU.
OH, SHIT...

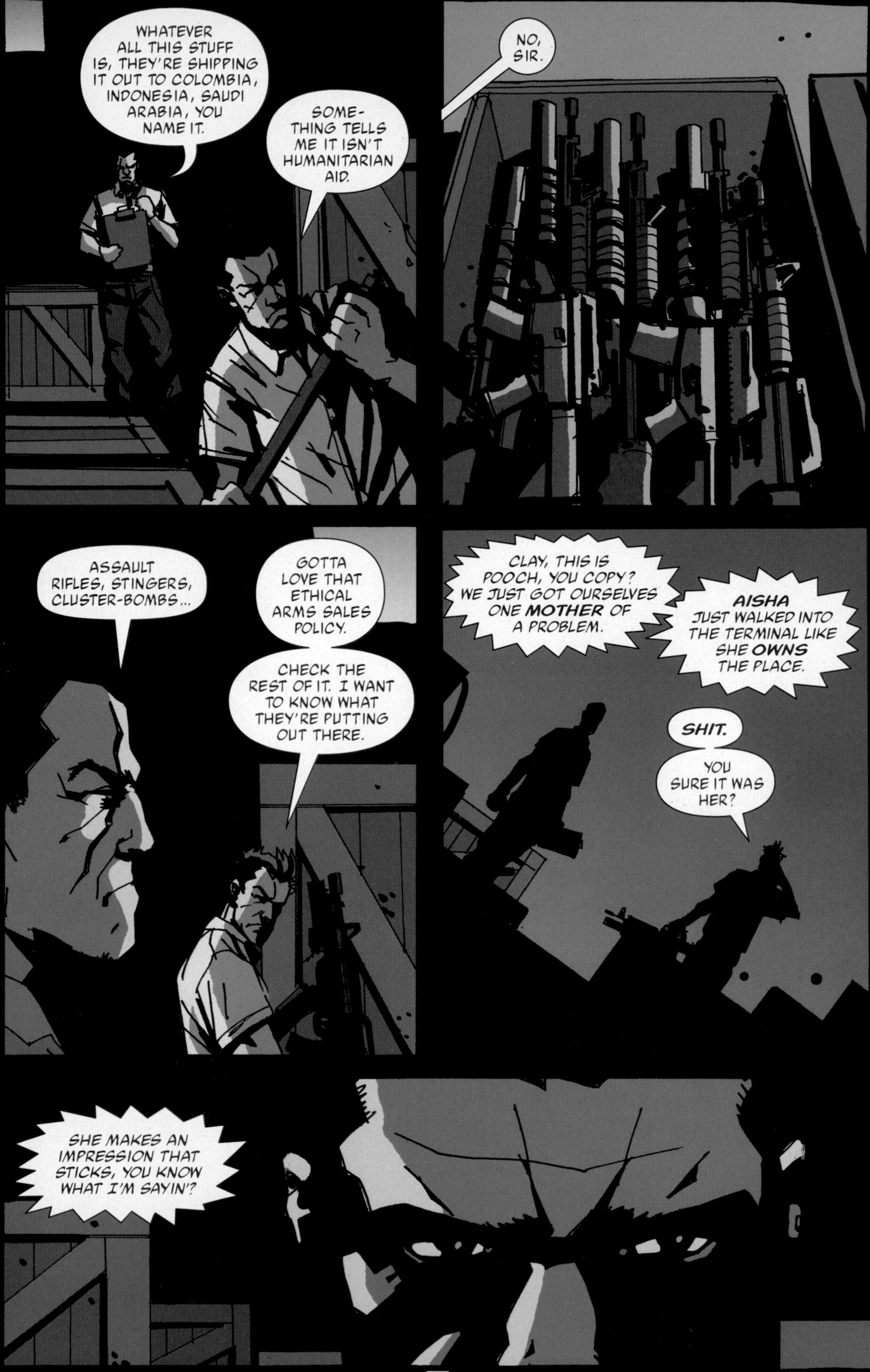

WHATEVER ALL THIS STUFF IS, THEY'RE SHIPPING IT OUT TO COLOMBIA, INDONESIA, SAUDI ARABIA, YOU NAME IT.
SOME-THING TELLS ME IT ISN'T HUMANITARIAN AID.
NO, SIR.
ASSAULT RIFLES, STINGERS, CLUSTER-BOMBS...
GOTTA LOVE THAT ETHICAL ARMS SALES POLICY.
CHECK THE REST OF IT. I WANT TO KNOW WHAT THEY'RE PUTTING OUT THERE.
CLAY, THIS IS POOCH, YOU COPY? WE JUST GOT OURSELVES ONE **MOTHER** OF A PROBLEM.
**AISHA** JUST WALKED INTO THE TERMINAL LIKE SHE **OWNS** THE PLACE.
**SHIT.**
YOU SURE IT WAS HER?
SHE MAKES AN IMPRESSION THAT STICKS, YOU KNOW WHAT I'M SAYIN'?

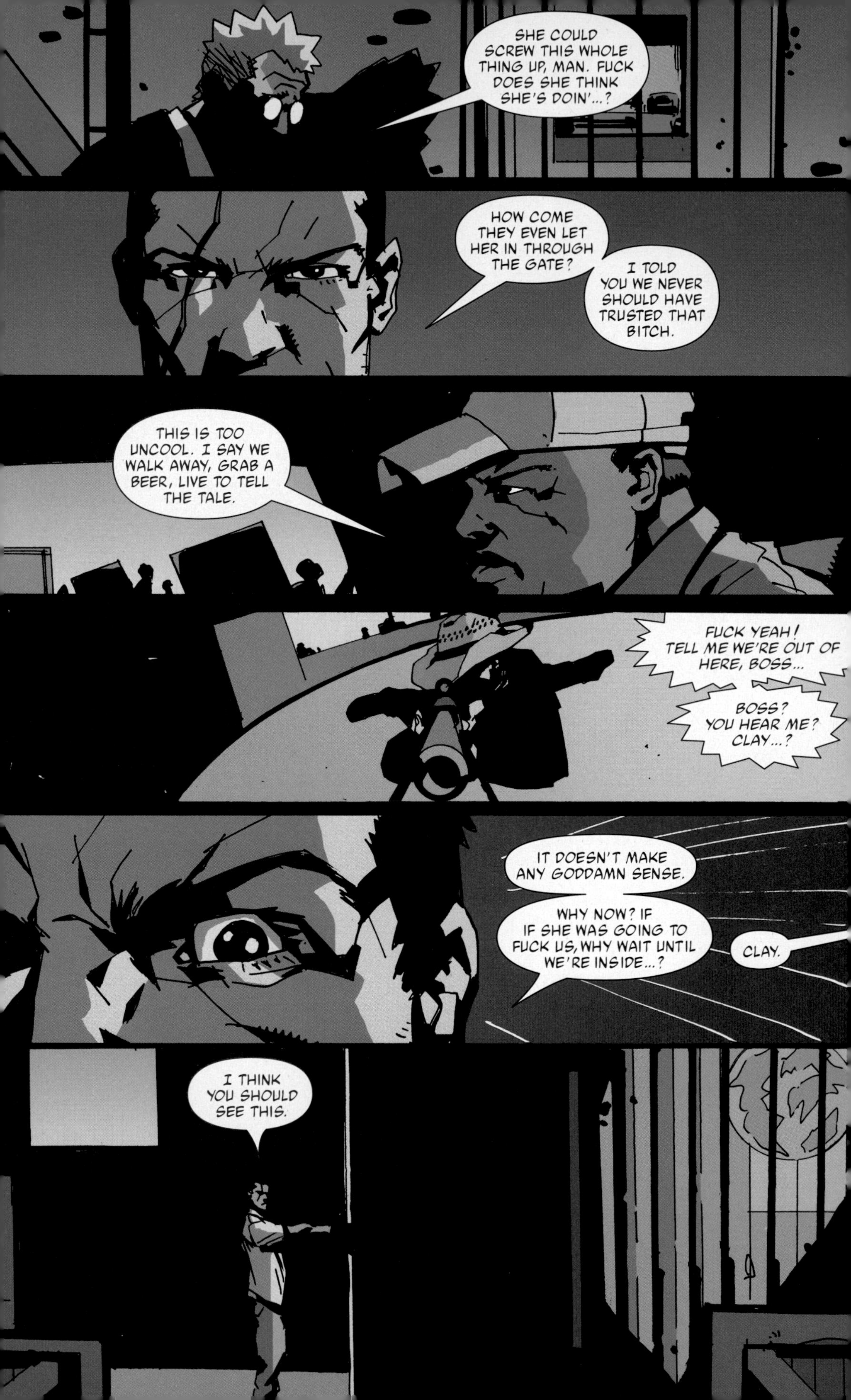
SHE COULD SCREW THIS WHOLE THING UP, MAN. FUCK DOES SHE THINK SHE'S DOIN'...?
HOW COME THEY EVEN LET HER IN THROUGH THE GATE?
I TOLD YOU WE NEVER SHOULD HAVE TRUSTED THAT BITCH.
THIS IS TOO UNCOOL. I SAY WE WALK AWAY, GRAB A BEER, LIVE TO TELL THE TALE.
FUCK YEAH! TELL ME WE'RE OUT OF HERE, BOSS...
BOSS? YOU HEAR ME? CLAY...?
IT DOESN'T MAKE ANY GODDAMN SENSE.
WHY NOW? IF IF SHE WAS GOING TO FUCK US, WHY WAIT UNTIL WE'RE INSIDE...?
CLAY.
I THINK YOU SHOULD SEE THIS.

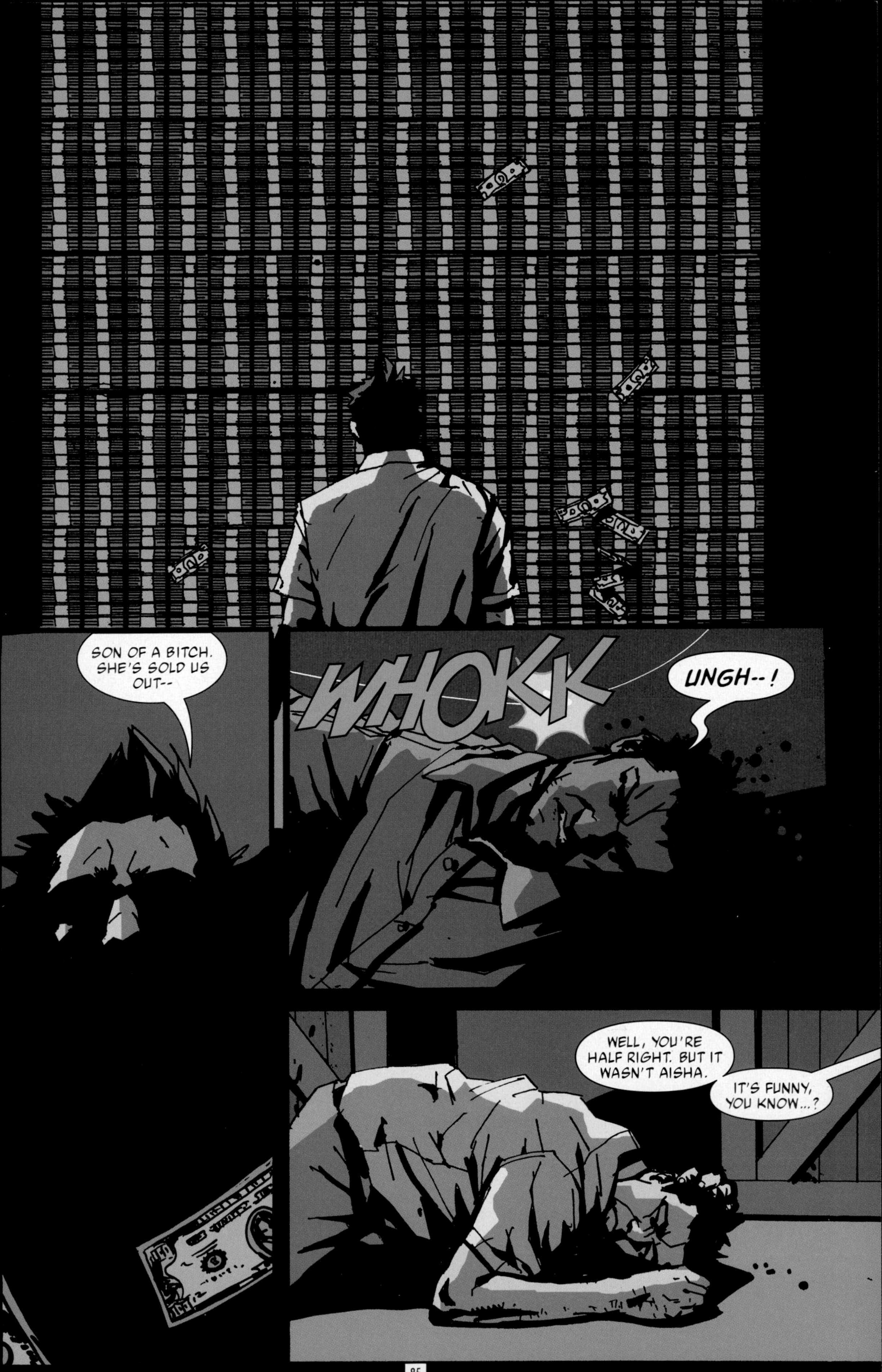
SON OF A BITCH. SHE'S SOLD US OUT--
WHOKK
UNGH--!
WELL, YOU'RE HALF RIGHT. BUT IT WASN'T AISHA.
IT'S FUNNY, YOU KNOW...?

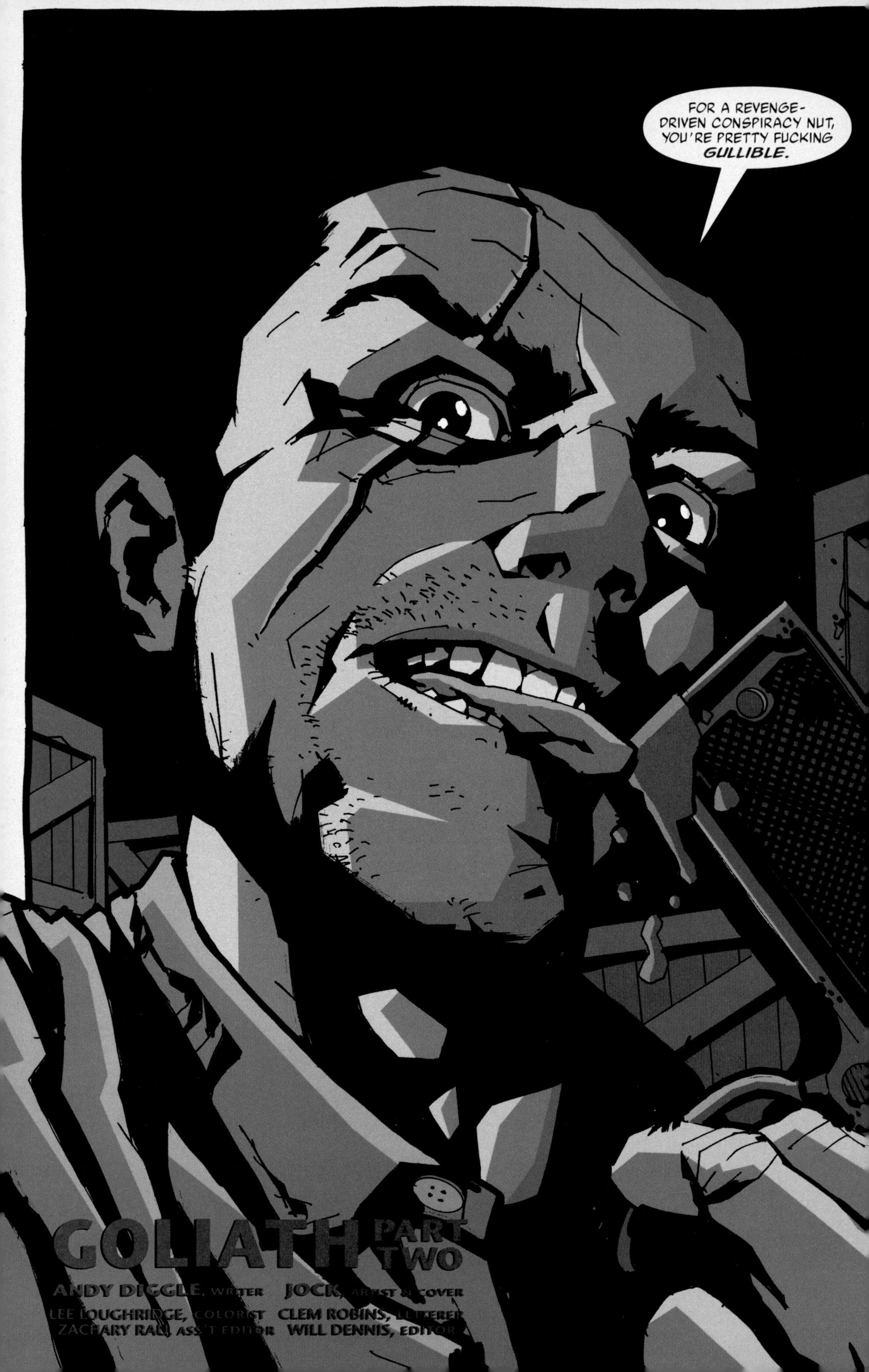
FOR A REVENGE-DRIVEN CONSPIRACY NUT, YOU'RE PRETTY FUCKING *GULLIBLE.*
GOLIATH PART TWO
ANDY DIGGLE, WRITER JOCK, ARTIST & COVER
LEE LOUGHRIDGE, COLORIST CLEM ROBINS, LETTERER
ZACHARY RAU, ASS'T EDITOR WILL DENNIS, EDITOR

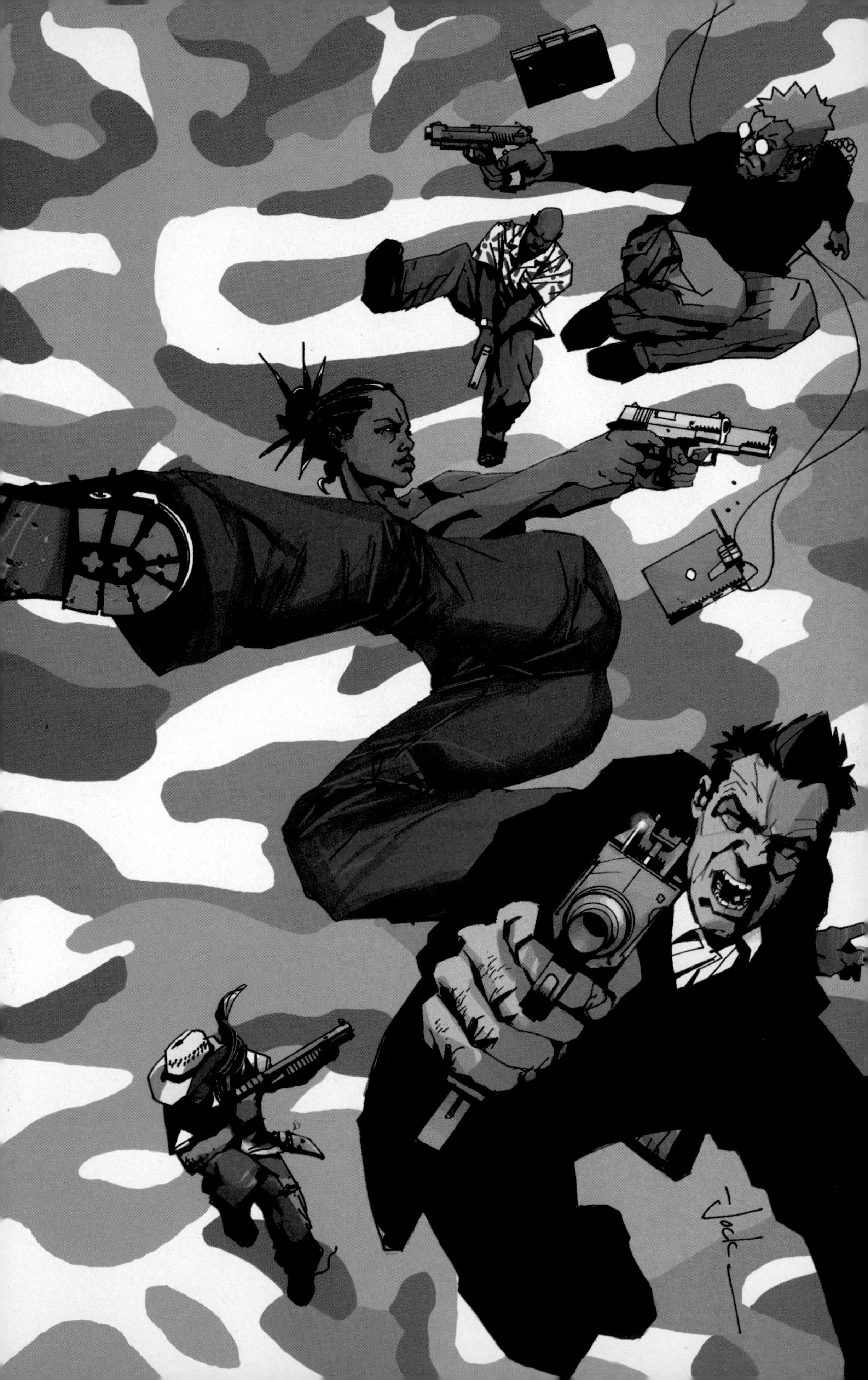
Jock

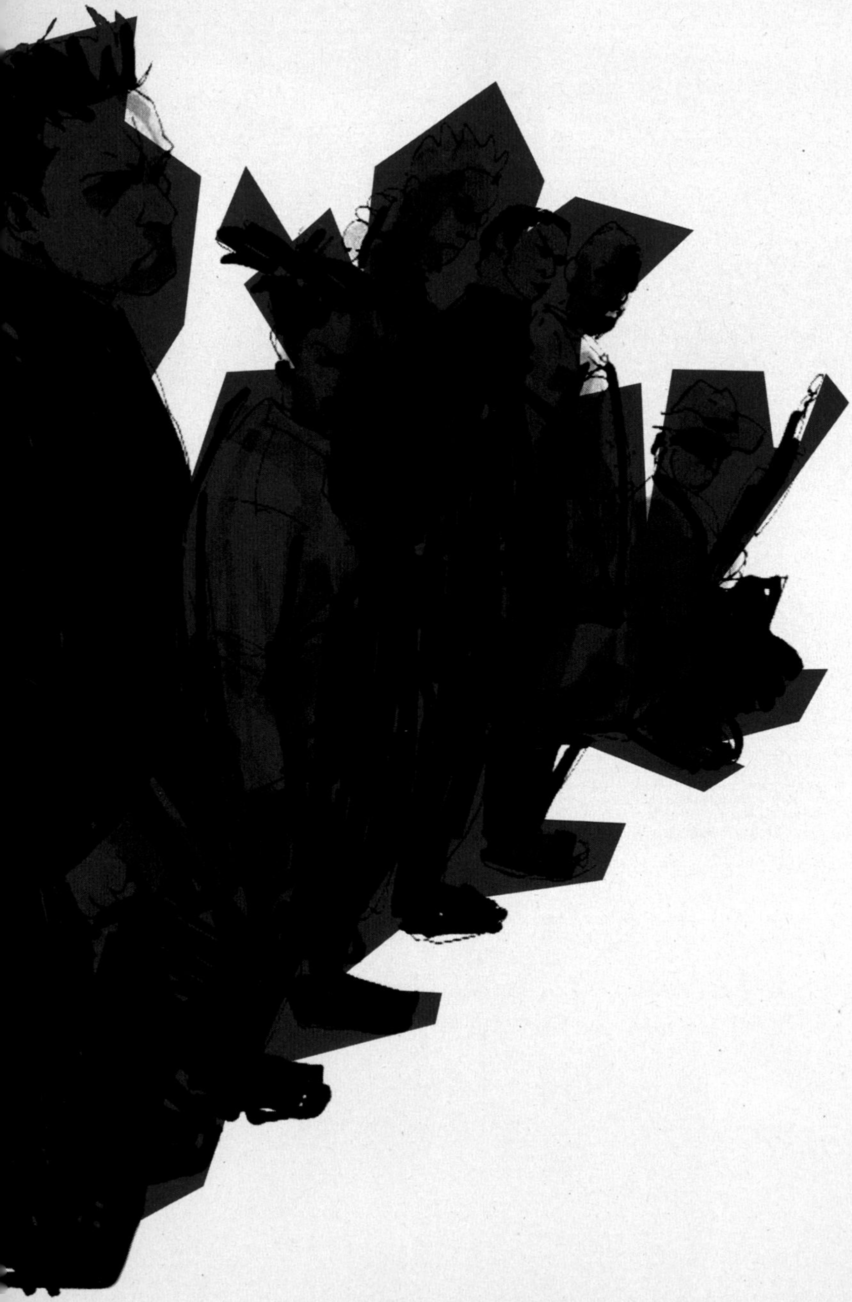

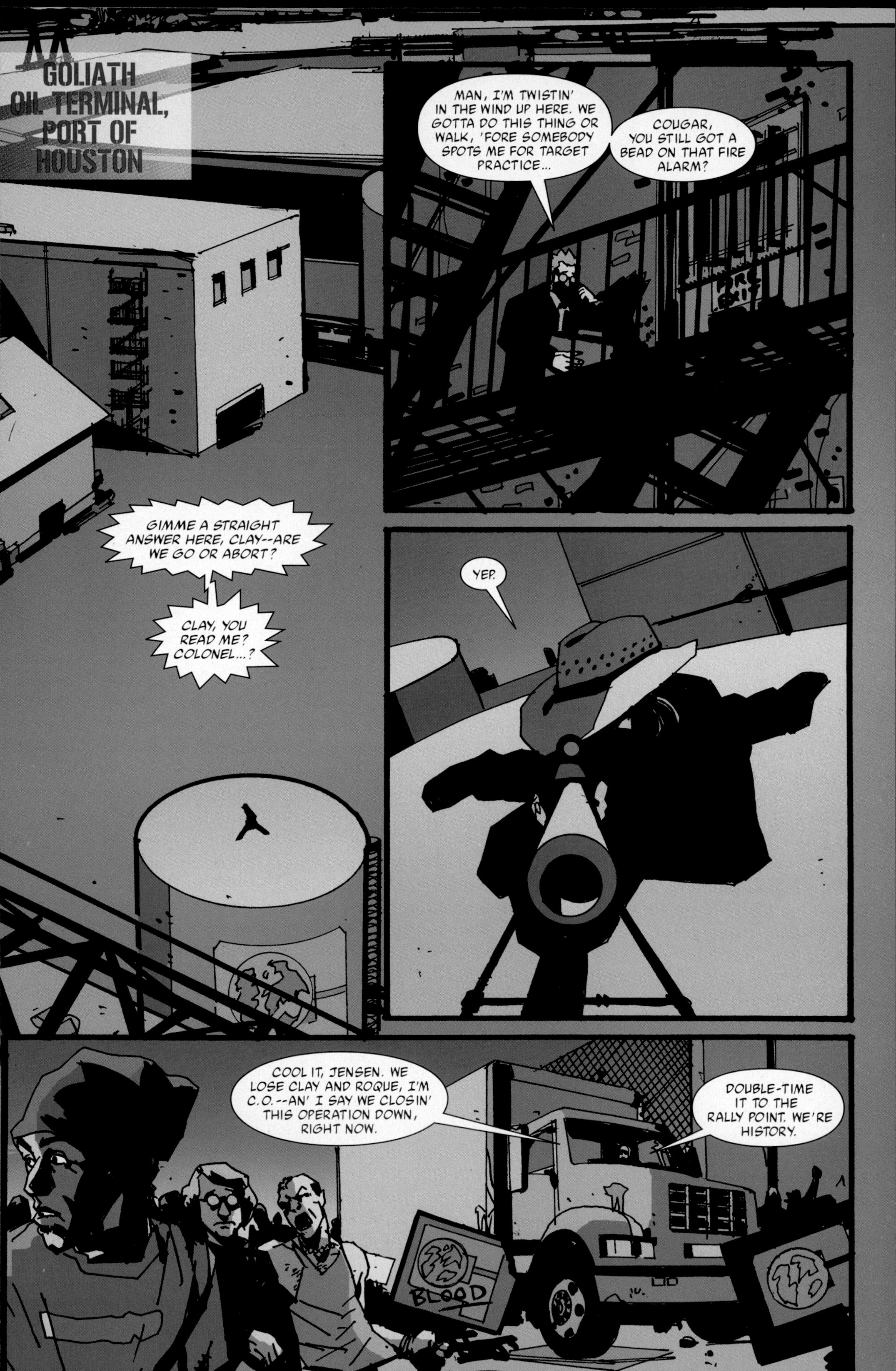
GOLIATH OIL TERMINAL, PORT OF HOUSTON
MAN, I'M TWISTIN' IN THE WIND UP HERE. WE GOTTA DO THIS THING OR WALK, 'FORE SOMEBODY SPOTS ME FOR TARGET PRACTICE...
COUGAR, YOU STILL GOT A BEAD ON THAT FIRE ALARM?
GIMME A STRAIGHT ANSWER HERE, CLAY--ARE WE GO OR ABORT?
CLAY, YOU READ ME? COLONEL...?
YEP.
COOL IT, JENSEN. WE LOSE CLAY AND ROQUE, I'M C.O.--AN' I SAY WE CLOSIN' THIS OPERATION DOWN, RIGHT NOW.
DOUBLE-TIME IT TO THE RALLY POINT. WE'RE HISTORY.
BLOOD

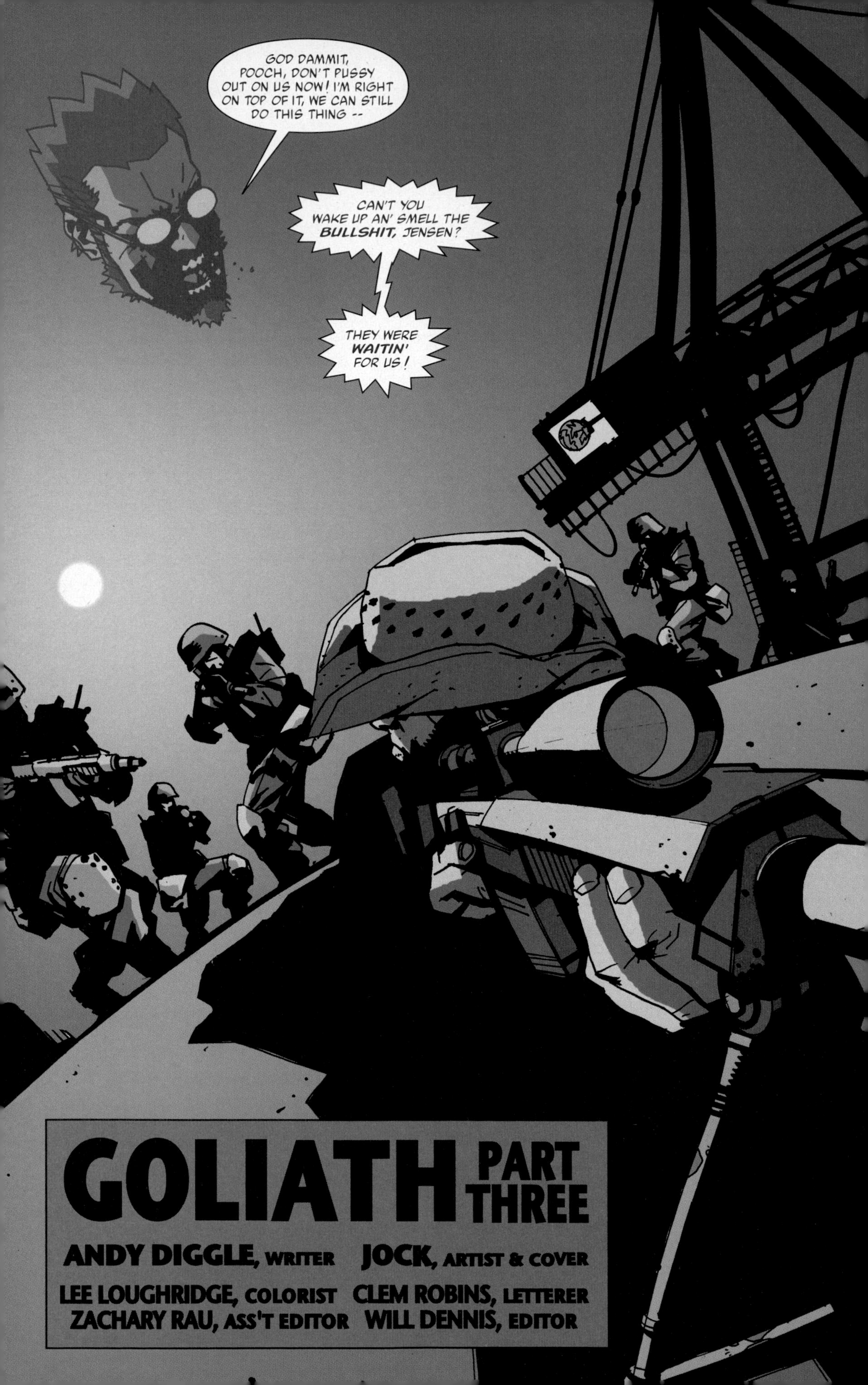
GOD DAMMIT, POOCH, DON'T PUSSY OUT ON US NOW! I'M RIGHT ON TOP OF IT, WE CAN STILL DO THIS THING --
CAN'T YOU WAKE UP AN' SMELL THE BULLSHIT, JENSEN?
THEY WERE WAITIN' FOR US!
GOLIATH PART THREE
ANDY DIGGLE, WRITER JOCK, ARTIST & COVER
LEE LOUGHRIDGE, COLORIST CLEM ROBINS, LETTERER
ZACHARY RAU, ASS'T EDITOR WILL DENNIS, EDITOR

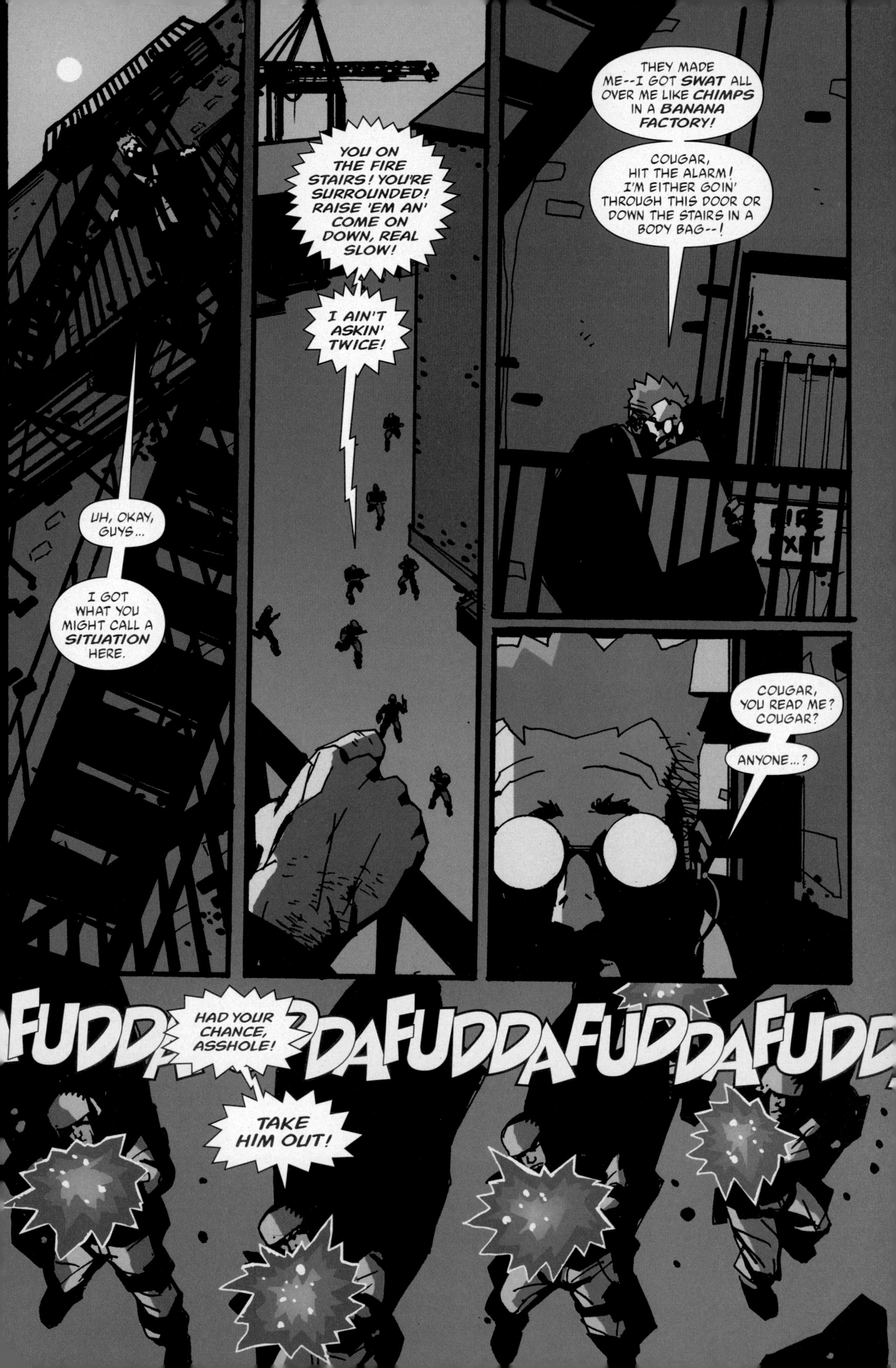
UH, OKAY, GUYS...
I GOT WHAT YOU MIGHT CALL A SITUATION HERE.
YOU ON THE FIRE STAIRS! YOU'RE SURROUNDED! RAISE 'EM AN' COME ON DOWN, REAL SLOW!
I AIN'T ASKIN' TWICE!
THEY MADE ME--I GOT SWAT ALL OVER ME LIKE CHIMPS IN A BANANA FACTORY!
COUGAR, HIT THE ALARM! I'M EITHER GOIN' THROUGH THIS DOOR OR DOWN THE STAIRS IN A BODY BAG--!
FIRE EXIT
COUGAR, YOU READ ME? COUGAR?
ANYONE...?
FUDD
HAD YOUR CHANCE, ASSHOLE!
DAFUDDAFUDDAFUDD
TAKE HIM OUT!

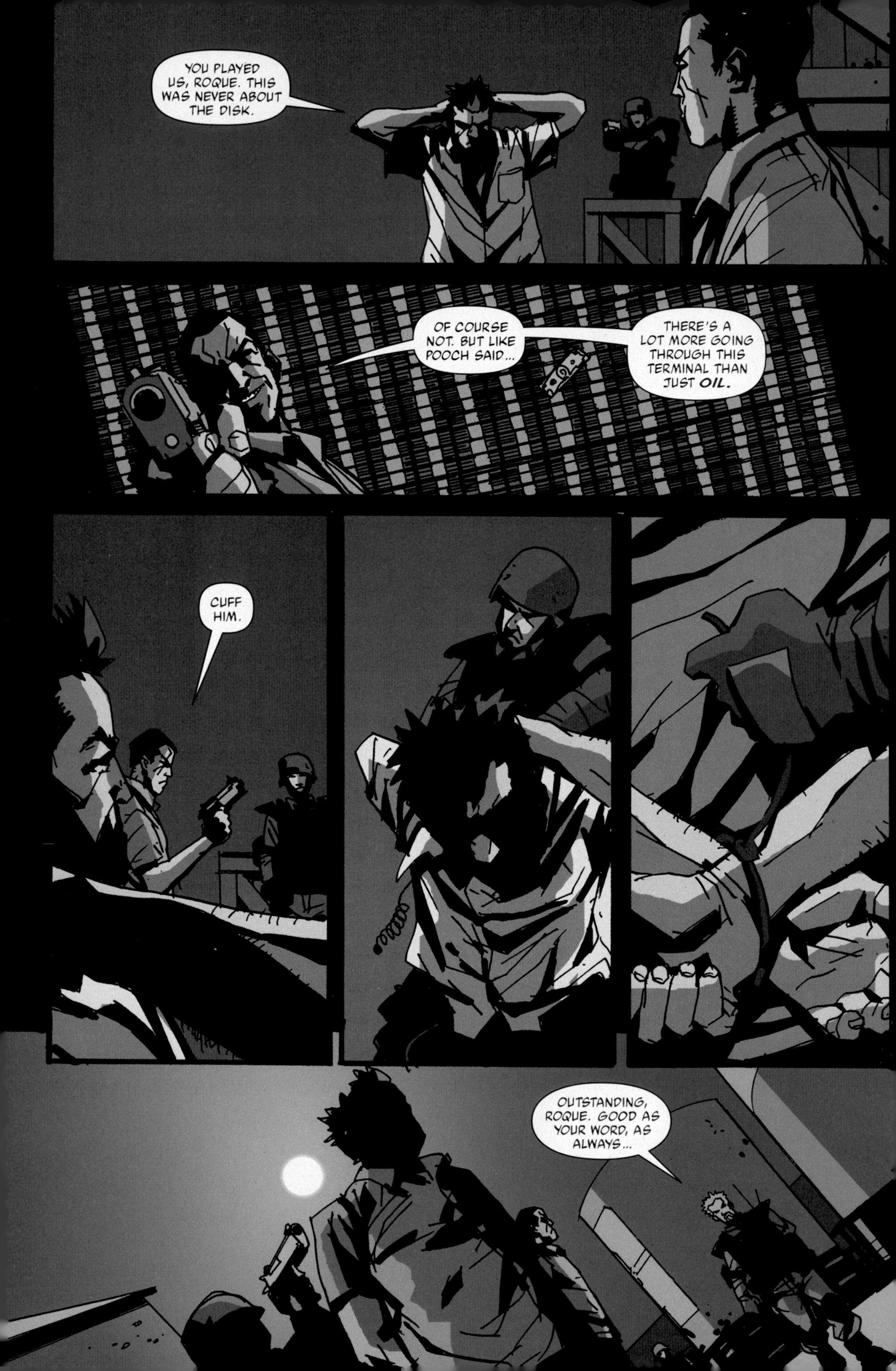
YOU PLAYED US, ROQUE. THIS WAS NEVER ABOUT THE DISK.
OF COURSE NOT. BUT LIKE POOCH SAID...
THERE'S A LOT MORE GOING THROUGH THIS TERMINAL THAN JUST OIL.
CUFF HIM.
OUTSTANDING, ROQUE. GOOD AS YOUR WORD, AS ALWAYS...

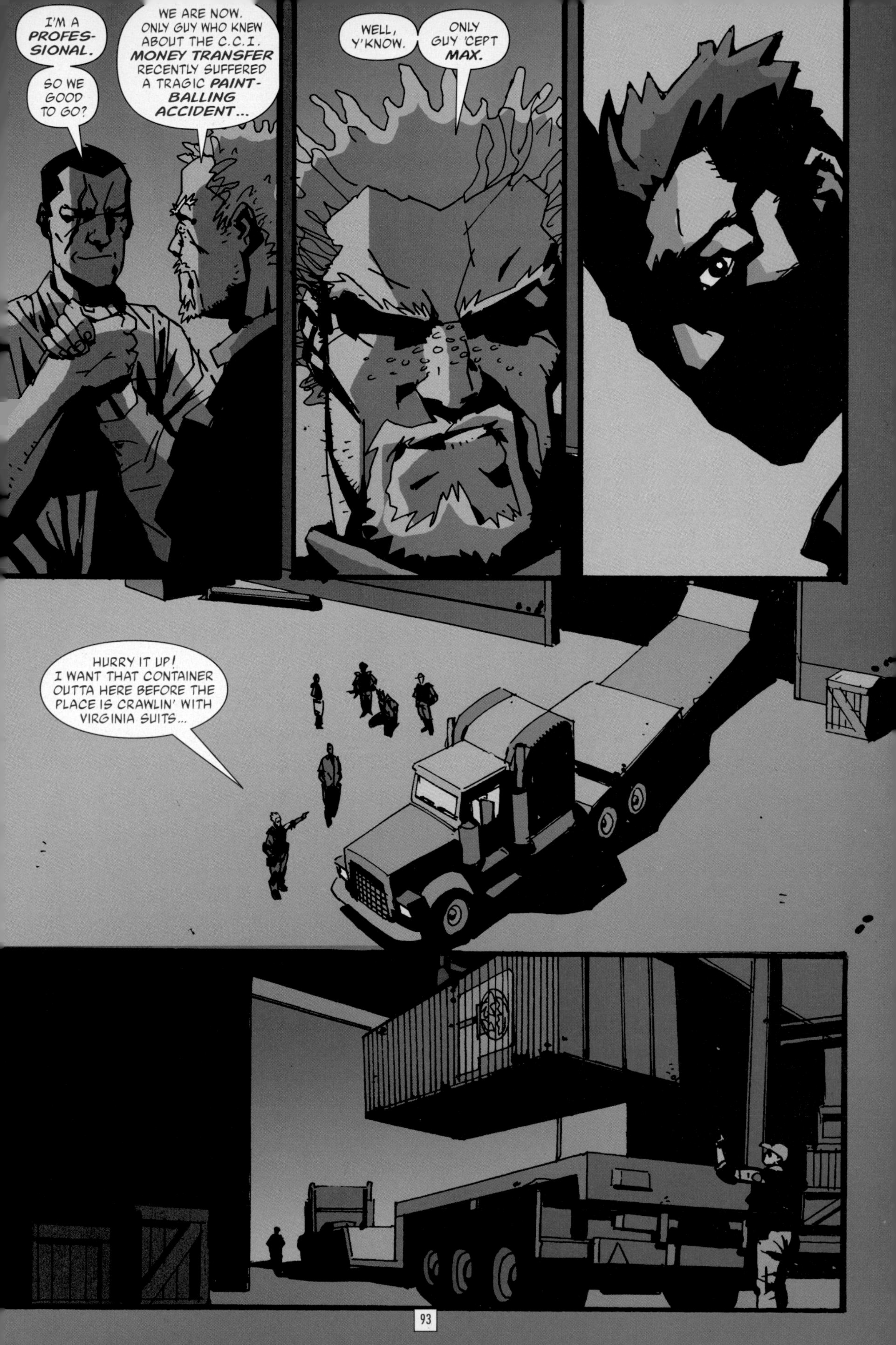
I'M A PROFES-SIONAL.
SO WE GOOD TO GO?
WE ARE NOW. ONLY GUY WHO KNEW ABOUT THE C.C.I. MONEY TRANSFER RECENTLY SUFFERED A TRAGIC PAINT-BALLING ACCIDENT...
WELL, Y'KNOW.
ONLY GUY 'CEPT MAX.
HURRY IT UP! I WANT THAT CONTAINER OUTTA HERE BEFORE THE PLACE IS CRAWLIN' WITH VIRGINIA SUITS...

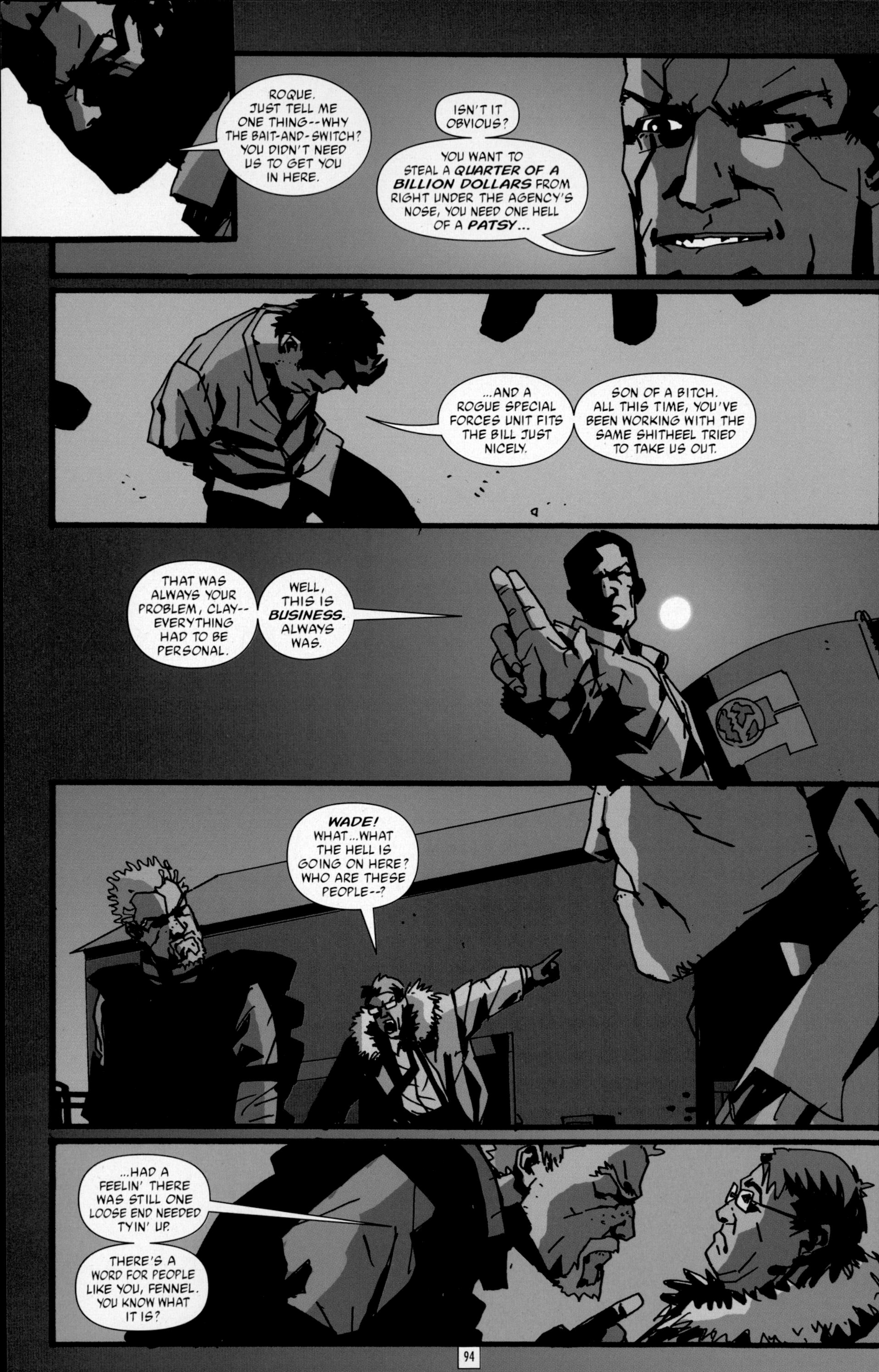
ROQUE. JUST TELL ME ONE THING--WHY THE BAIT-AND-SWITCH? YOU DIDN'T NEED US TO GET YOU IN HERE.
ISN'T IT OBVIOUS?
YOU WANT TO STEAL A QUARTER OF A BILLION DOLLARS FROM RIGHT UNDER THE AGENCY'S NOSE, YOU NEED ONE HELL OF A PATSY...
...AND A ROGUE SPECIAL FORCES UNIT FITS THE BILL JUST NICELY.
SON OF A BITCH. ALL THIS TIME, YOU'VE BEEN WORKING WITH THE SAME SHITHEEL TRIED TO TAKE US OUT.
THAT WAS ALWAYS YOUR PROBLEM, CLAY--EVERYTHING HAD TO BE PERSONAL.
WELL, THIS IS BUSINESS. ALWAYS WAS.
WADE! WHAT...WHAT THE HELL IS GOING ON HERE? WHO ARE THESE PEOPLE--?
...HAD A FEELIN' THERE WAS STILL ONE LOOSE END NEEDED TYIN' UP.
THERE'S A WORD FOR PEOPLE LIKE YOU, FENNEL. YOU KNOW WHAT IT IS?

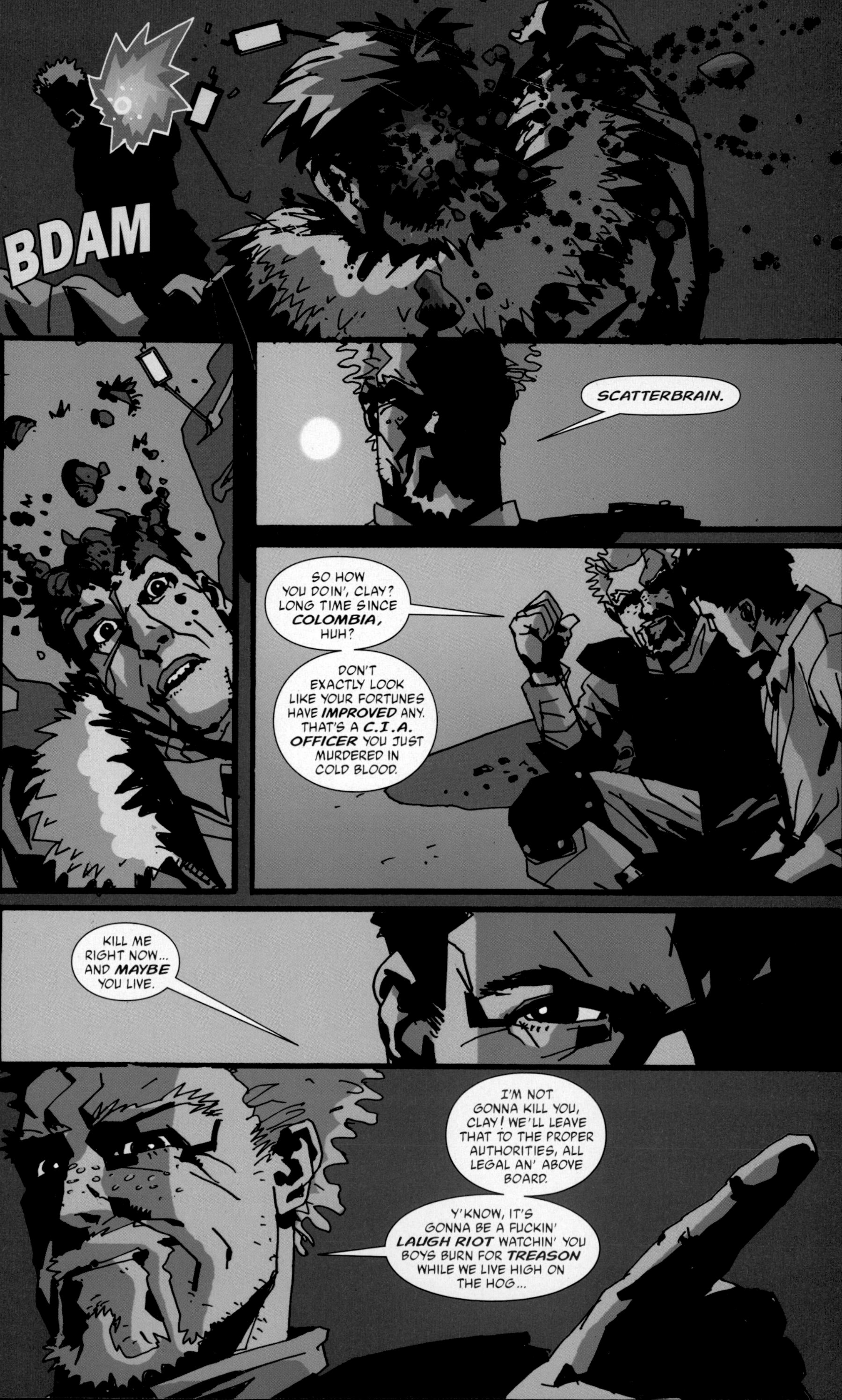
BDAM
SCATTERBRAIN.
SO HOW YOU DOIN', CLAY? LONG TIME SINCE COLOMBIA, HUH?
DON'T EXACTLY LOOK LIKE YOUR FORTUNES HAVE IMPROVED ANY. THAT'S A C.I.A. OFFICER YOU JUST MURDERED IN COLD BLOOD.
KILL ME RIGHT NOW... AND MAYBE YOU LIVE.
I'M NOT GONNA KILL YOU, CLAY! WE'LL LEAVE THAT TO THE PROPER AUTHORITIES, ALL LEGAL AN' ABOVE BOARD.
Y'KNOW, IT'S GONNA BE A FUCKIN' LAUGH RIOT WATCHIN' YOU BOYS BURN FOR TREASON WHILE WE LIVE HIGH ON THE HOG...

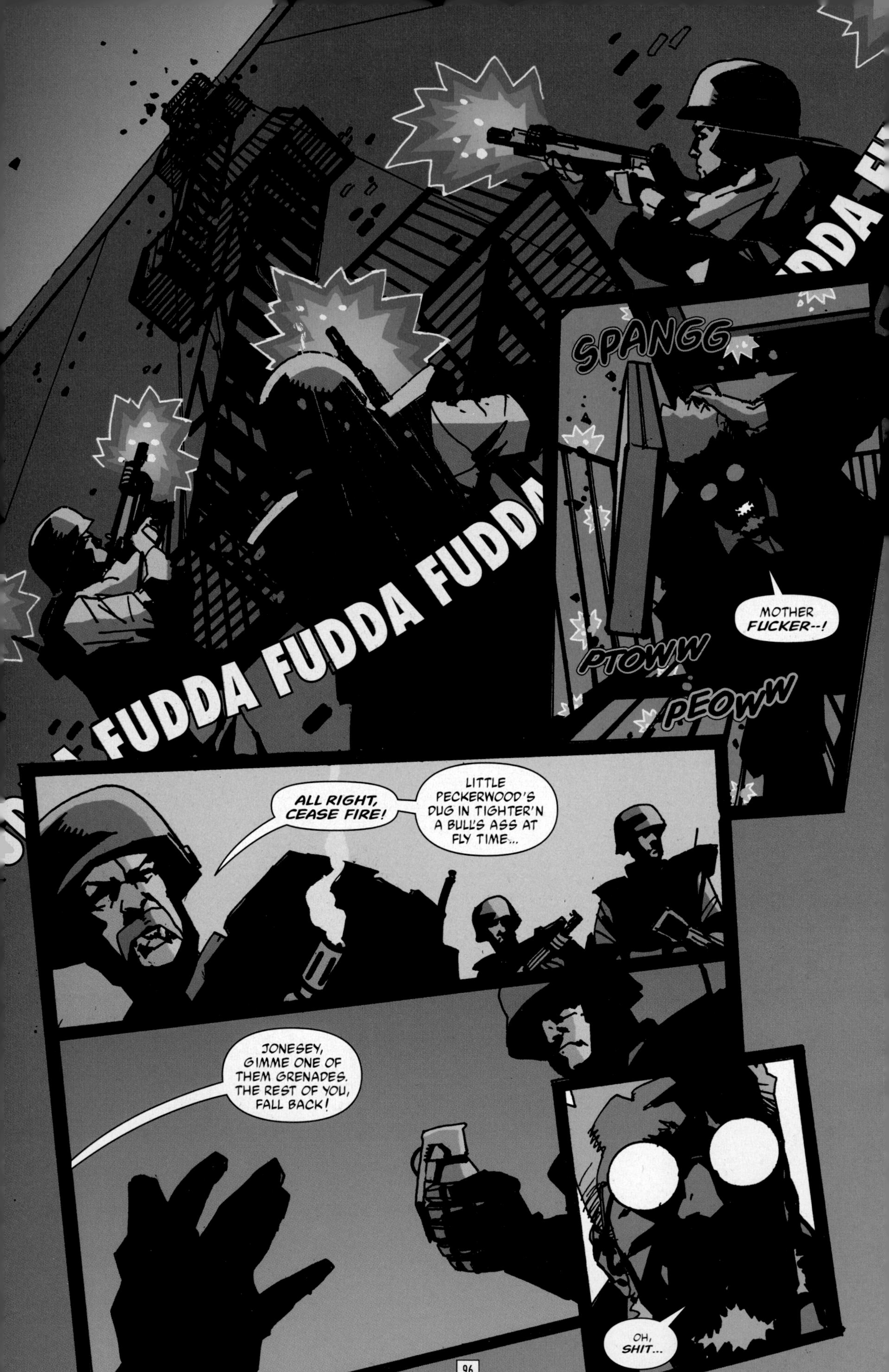
FUDDA FUDDA FUDDA
SPANGG
MOTHER FUCKER--!
PTOWW
PEOWW
ALL RIGHT, CEASE FIRE!
LITTLE PECKERWOOD'S DUG IN TIGHTER'N A BULL'S ASS AT FLY TIME...
JONESEY, GIMME ONE OF THEM GRENADES. THE REST OF YOU, FALL BACK!
OH, SHIT...

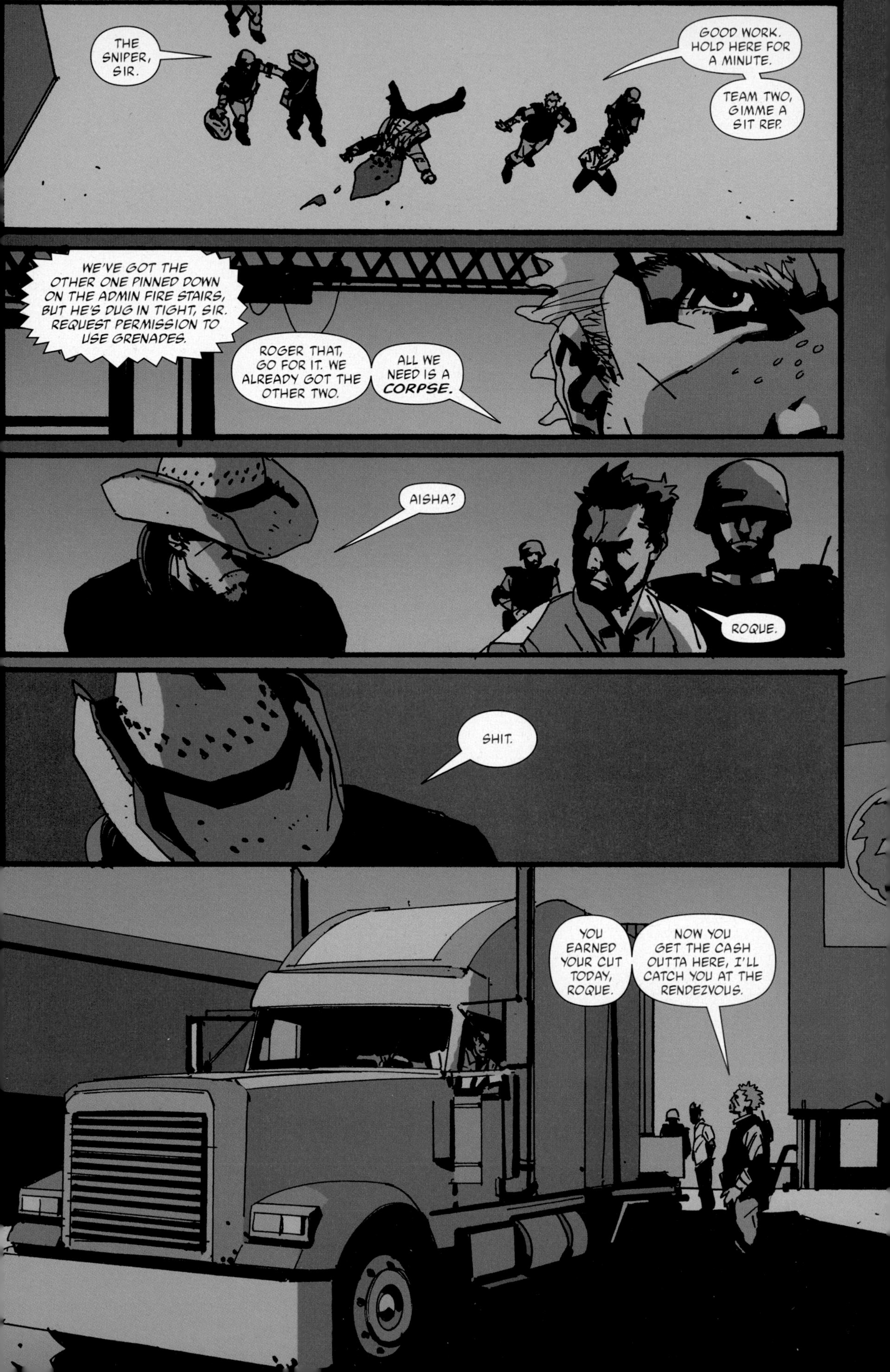
THE SNIPER, SIR.
GOOD WORK. HOLD HERE FOR A MINUTE.
TEAM TWO, GIMME A SIT REP.
WE'VE GOT THE OTHER ONE PINNED DOWN ON THE ADMIN FIRE STAIRS, BUT HE'S DUG IN TIGHT, SIR. REQUEST PERMISSION TO USE GRENADES.
ROGER THAT, GO FOR IT. WE ALREADY GOT THE OTHER TWO.
ALL WE NEED IS A CORPSE.
AISHA?
ROQUE.
SHIT.
YOU EARNED YOUR CUT TODAY, ROQUE.
NOW YOU GET THE CASH OUTTA HERE, I'LL CATCH YOU AT THE RENDEZVOUS.

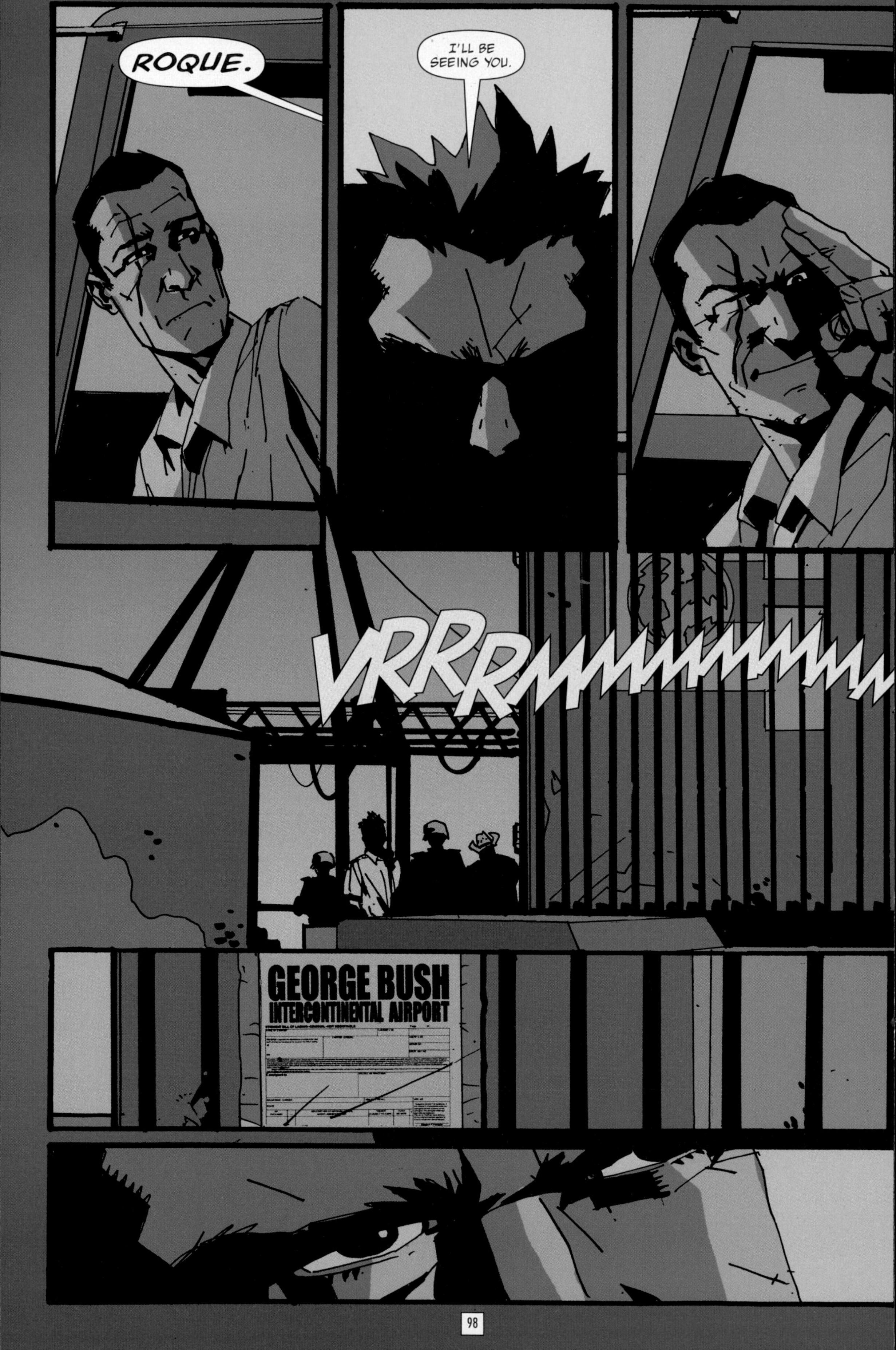
ROQUE.
I'LL BE SEEING YOU.
VRRRMMMMMMMMMM
GEORGE BUSH
INTERCONTINENTAL AIRPORT

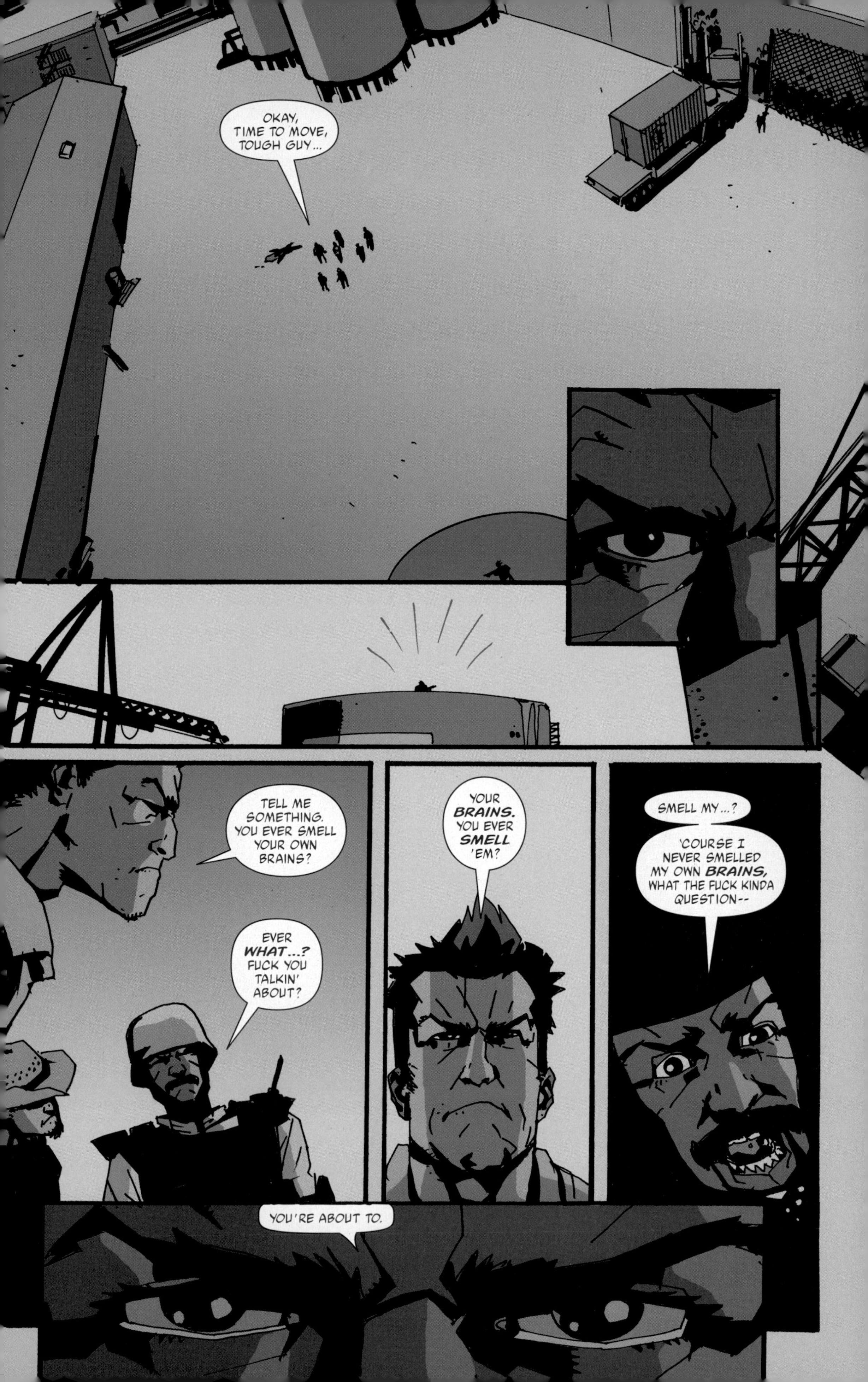
OKAY, TIME TO MOVE, TOUGH GUY...
TELL ME SOMETHING. YOU EVER SMELL YOUR OWN BRAINS?
EVER WHAT...? FUCK YOU TALKIN' ABOUT?
YOUR BRAINS. YOU EVER SMELL 'EM?
SMELL MY...?
'COURSE I NEVER SMELLED MY OWN BRAINS, WHAT THE FUCK KINDA QUESTION--
YOU'RE ABOUT TO.

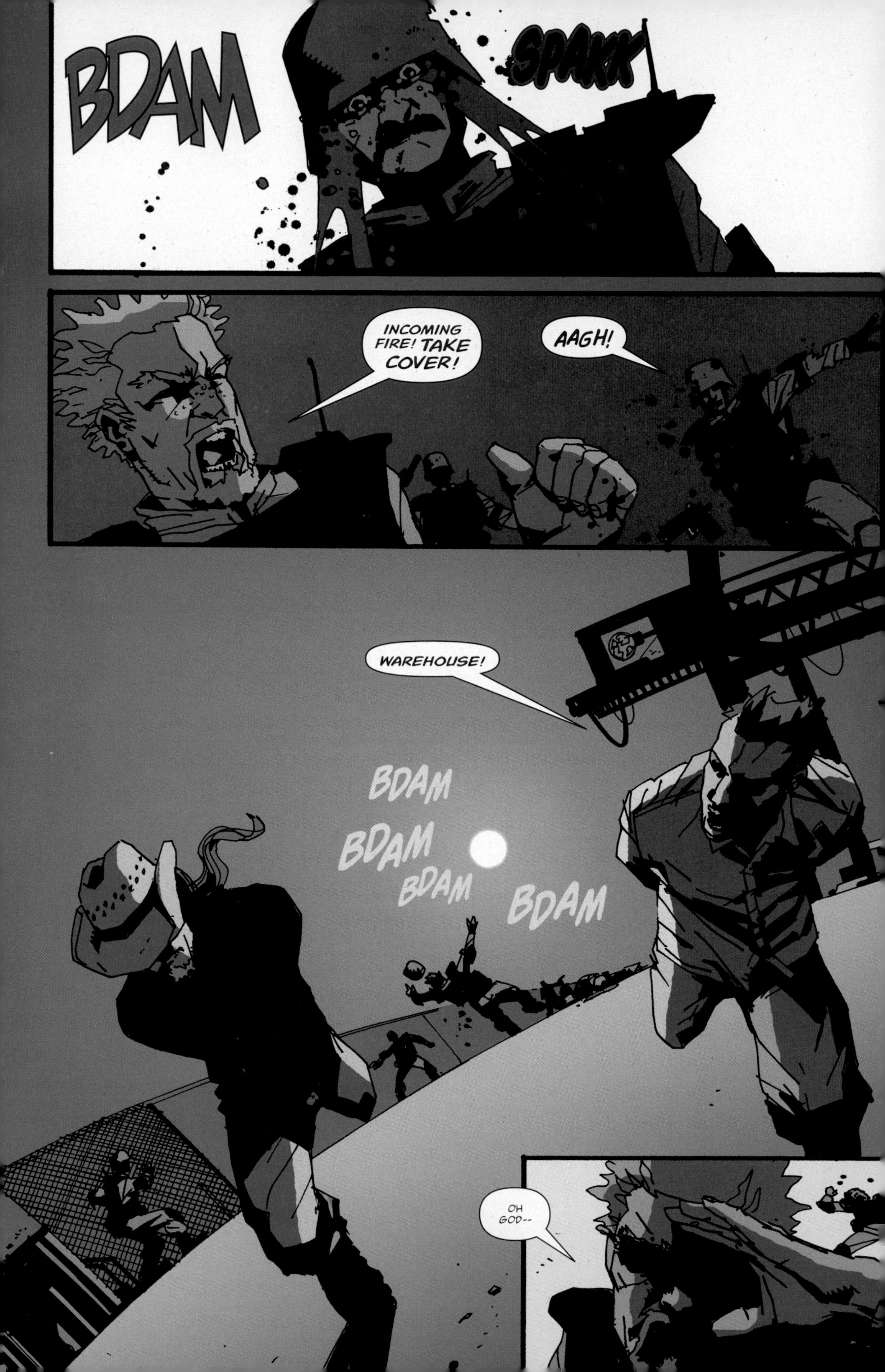
BDAM
SPAKK
INCOMING FIRE! TAKE COVER!
AAGH!
WAREHOUSE!
BDAM
BDAM
BDAM
BDAM
OH GOD--

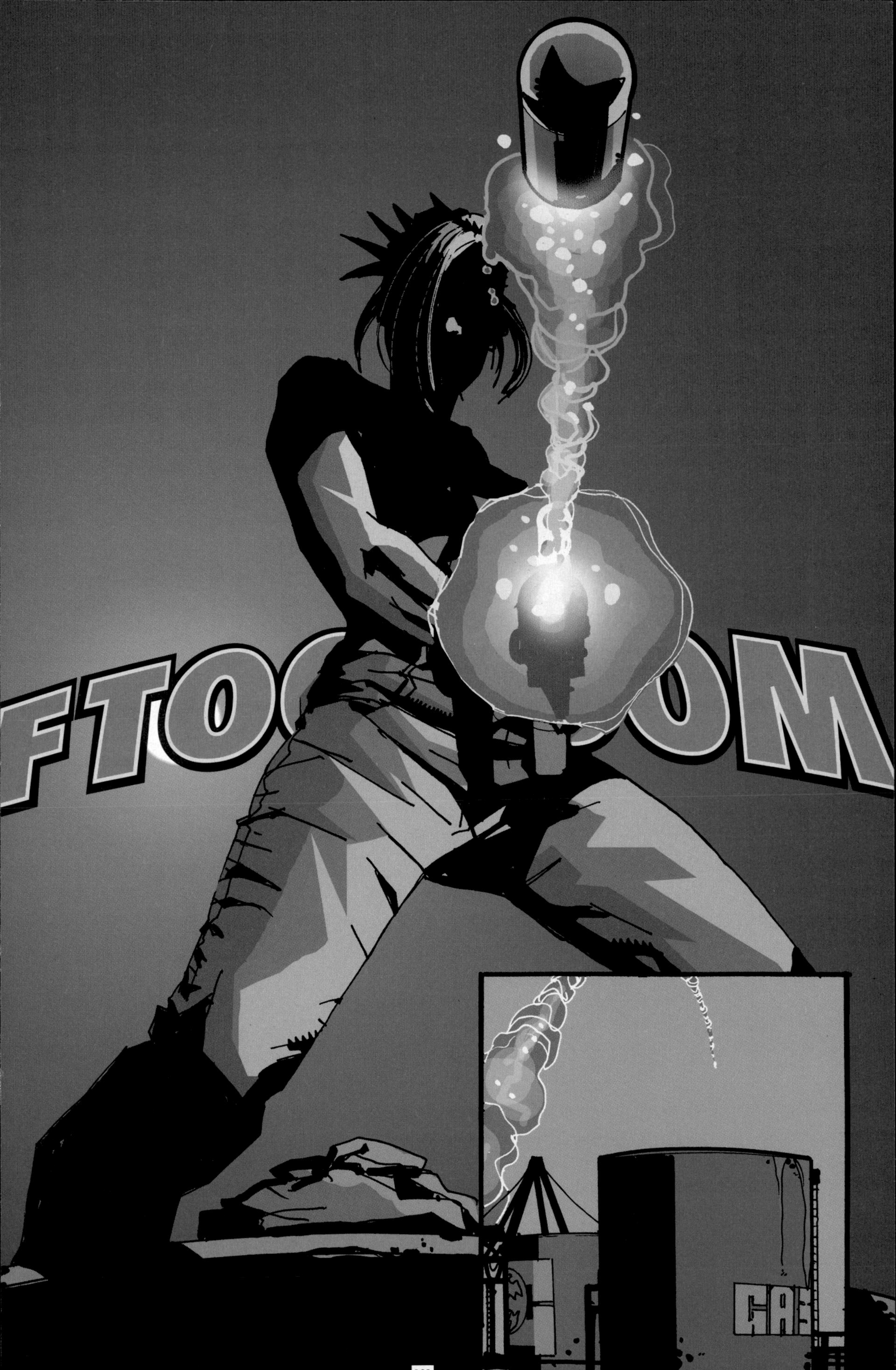

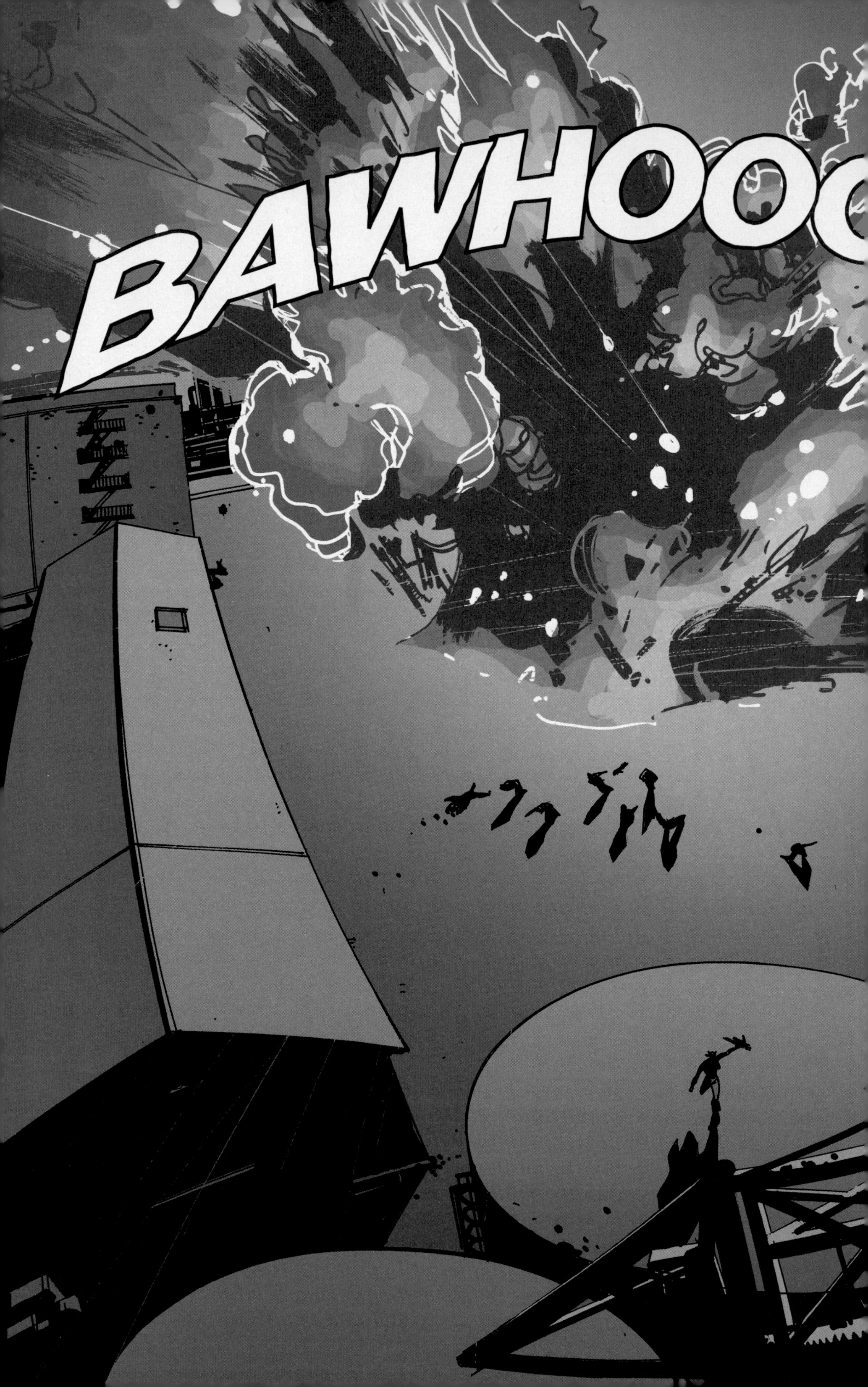
BAWHOOO

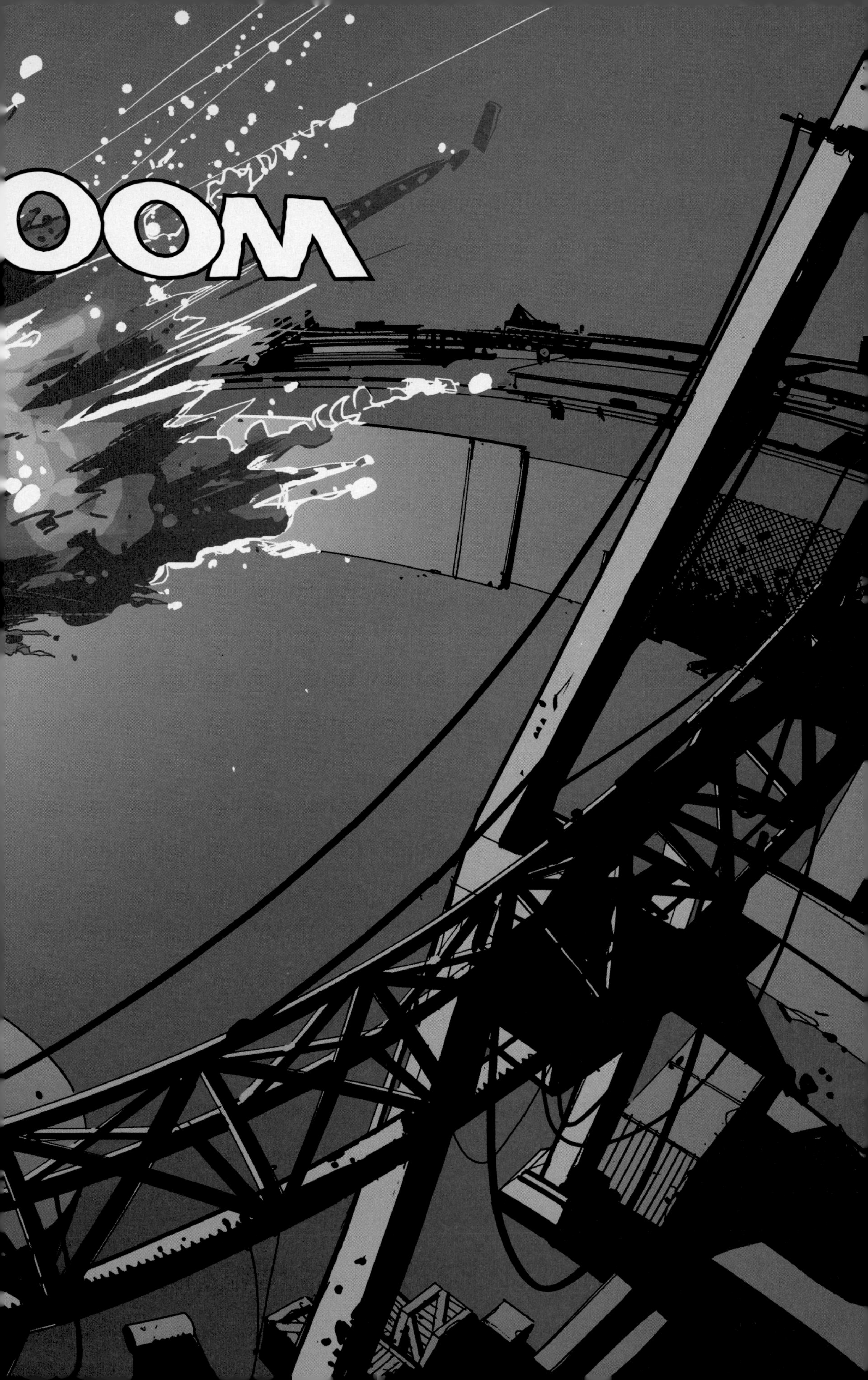
OOM

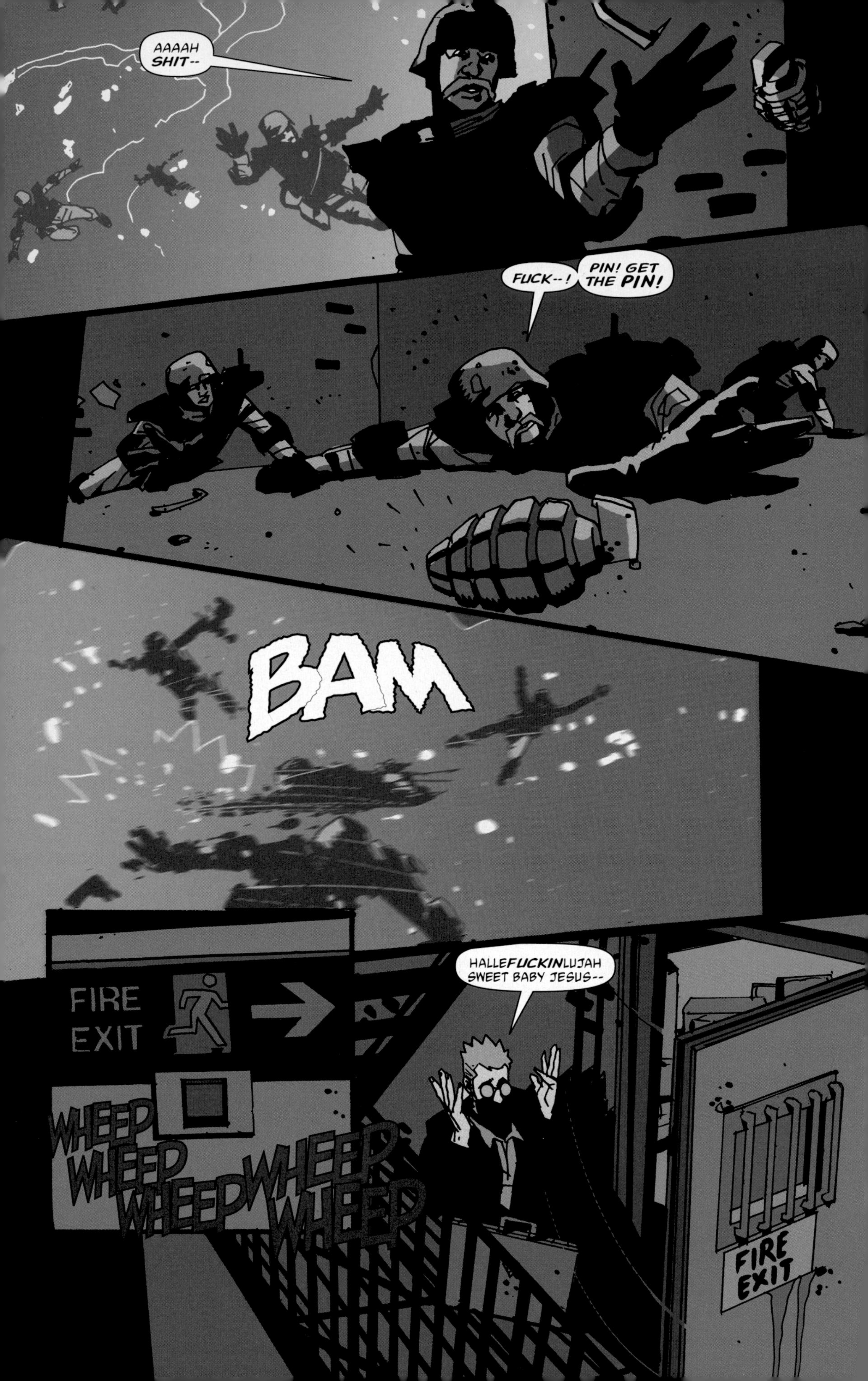
AAAAH SHIT--
FUCK--!
PIN! GET THE PIN!
BAM
HALLEFUCKINLUJAH SWEET BABY JESUS--
FIRE EXIT
WHEEP WHEEP WHEEP WHEEP WHEEP
FIRE EXIT

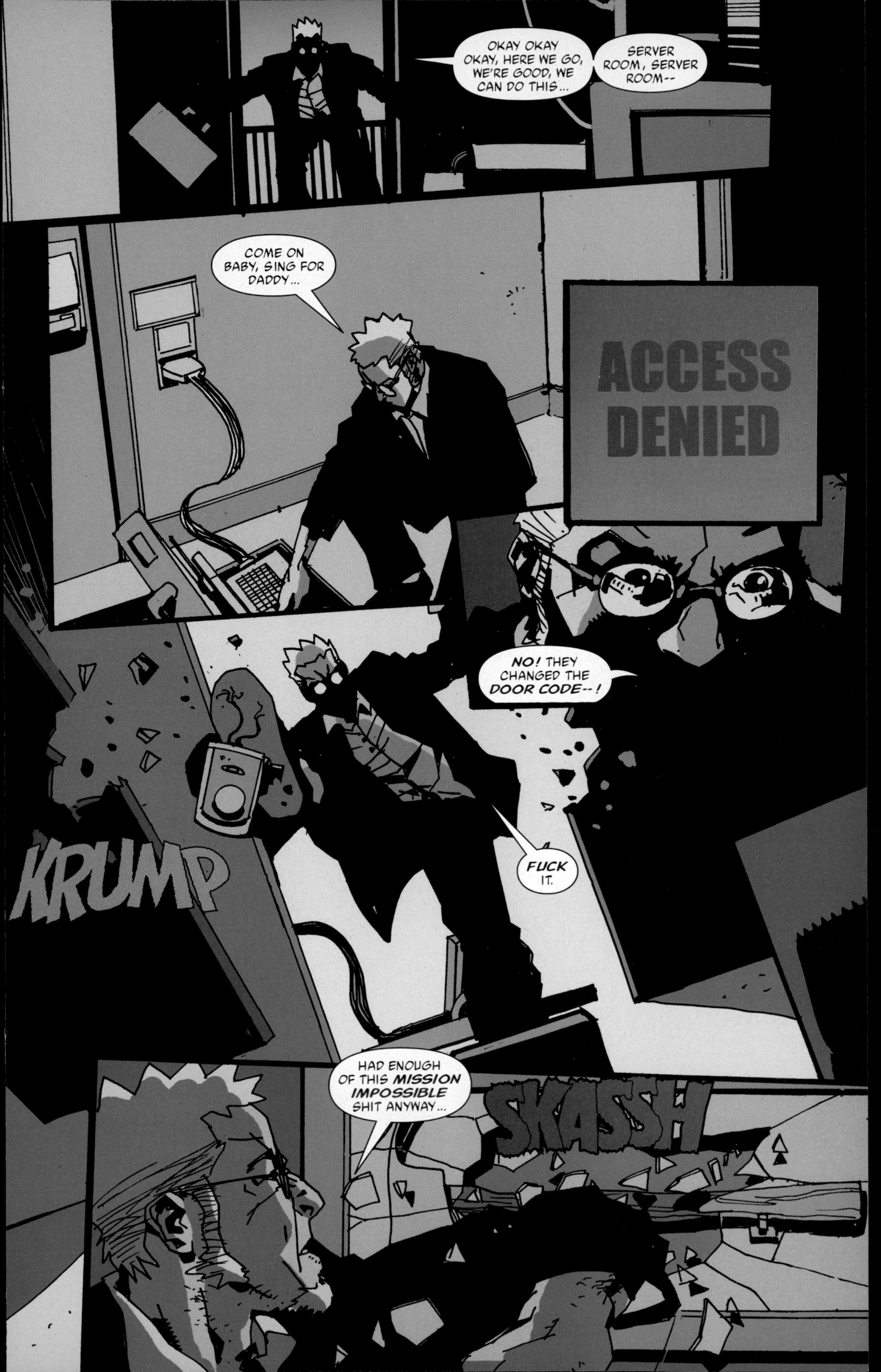
OKAY OKAY OKAY, HERE WE GO, WE'RE GOOD, WE CAN DO THIS...
SERVER ROOM, SERVER ROOM--
COME ON BABY, SING FOR DADDY...
ACCESS DENIED
NO! THEY CHANGED THE DOOR CODE--!
KRUMP
FUCK IT.
HAD ENOUGH OF THIS MISSION IMPOSSIBLE SHIT ANYWAY...
SKASSH

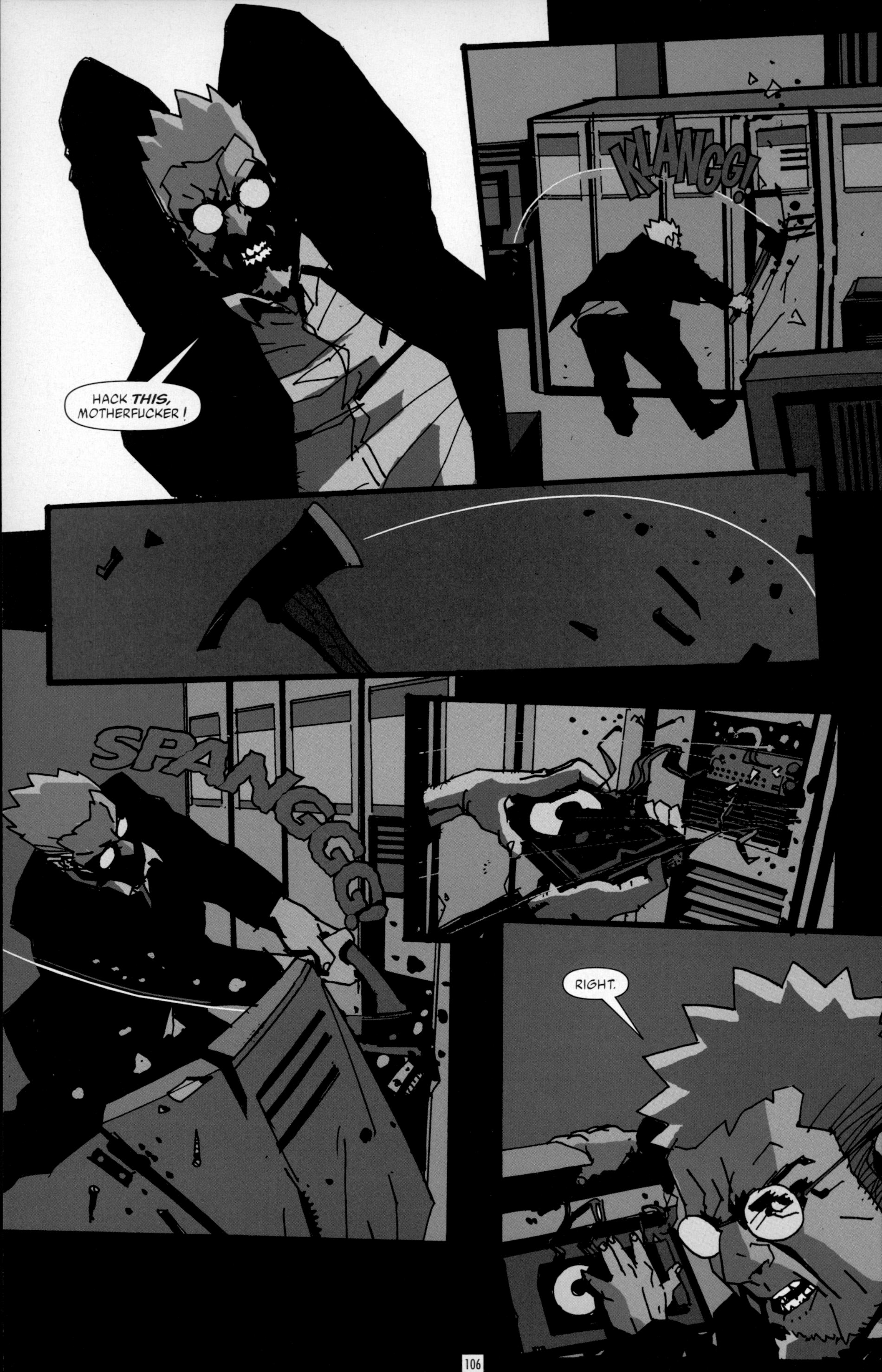
HACK THIS, MOTHERFUCKER!
KLANGG!
SPANGGG
RIGHT.

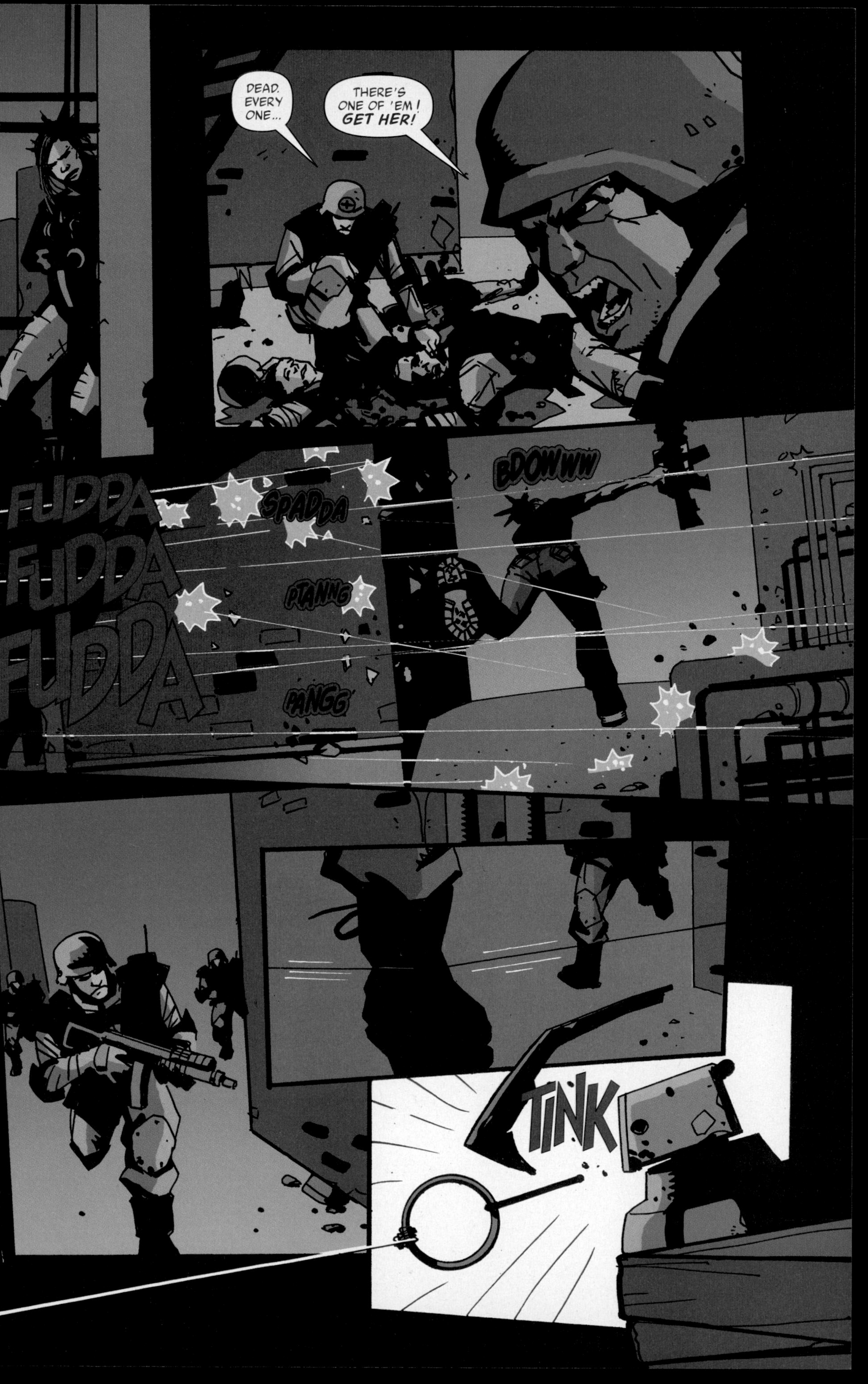
DEAD. EVERY ONE...
THERE'S ONE OF 'EM! GET HER!
FUDDA FUDDA FUDDA
SPADDA
BDOWWW
PTANNG
PANGG
TINK

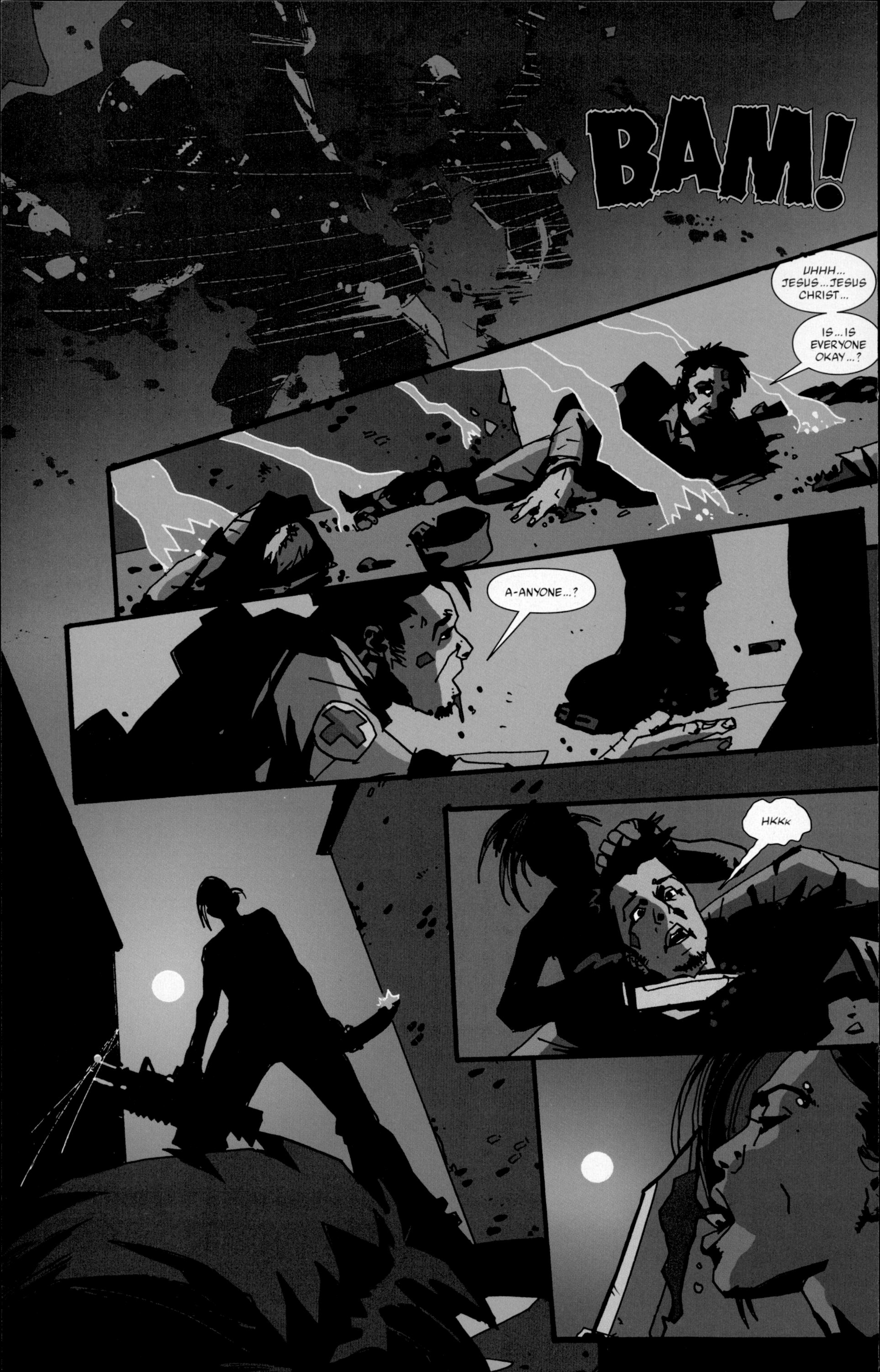
BAM!
UHHH... JESUS...JESUS CHRIST...
IS...IS EVERYONE OKAY...?
A-ANYONE...?
HKKk

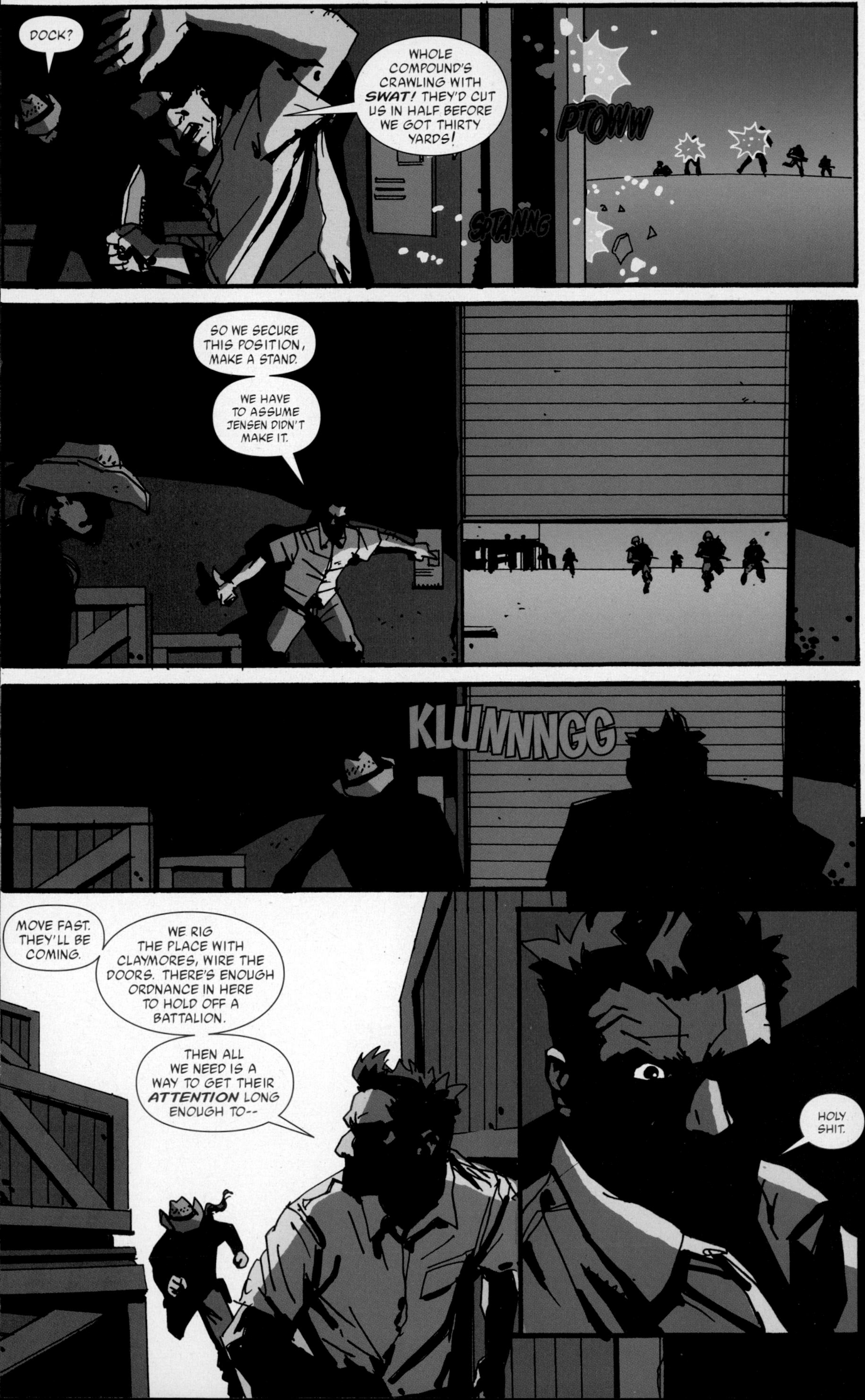
DOCK?
WHOLE COMPOUND'S CRAWLING WITH SWAT! THEY'D CUT US IN HALF BEFORE WE GOT THIRTY YARDS!
PTOWW
SPTANNG
SO WE SECURE THIS POSITION, MAKE A STAND.
WE HAVE TO ASSUME JENSEN DIDN'T MAKE IT.
KLUNNNGG
MOVE FAST. THEY'LL BE COMING.
WE RIG THE PLACE WITH CLAYMORES, WIRE THE DOORS. THERE'S ENOUGH ORDNANCE IN HERE TO HOLD OFF A BATTALION.
THEN ALL WE NEED IS A WAY TO GET THEIR ATTENTION LONG ENOUGH TO--
HOLY SHIT.

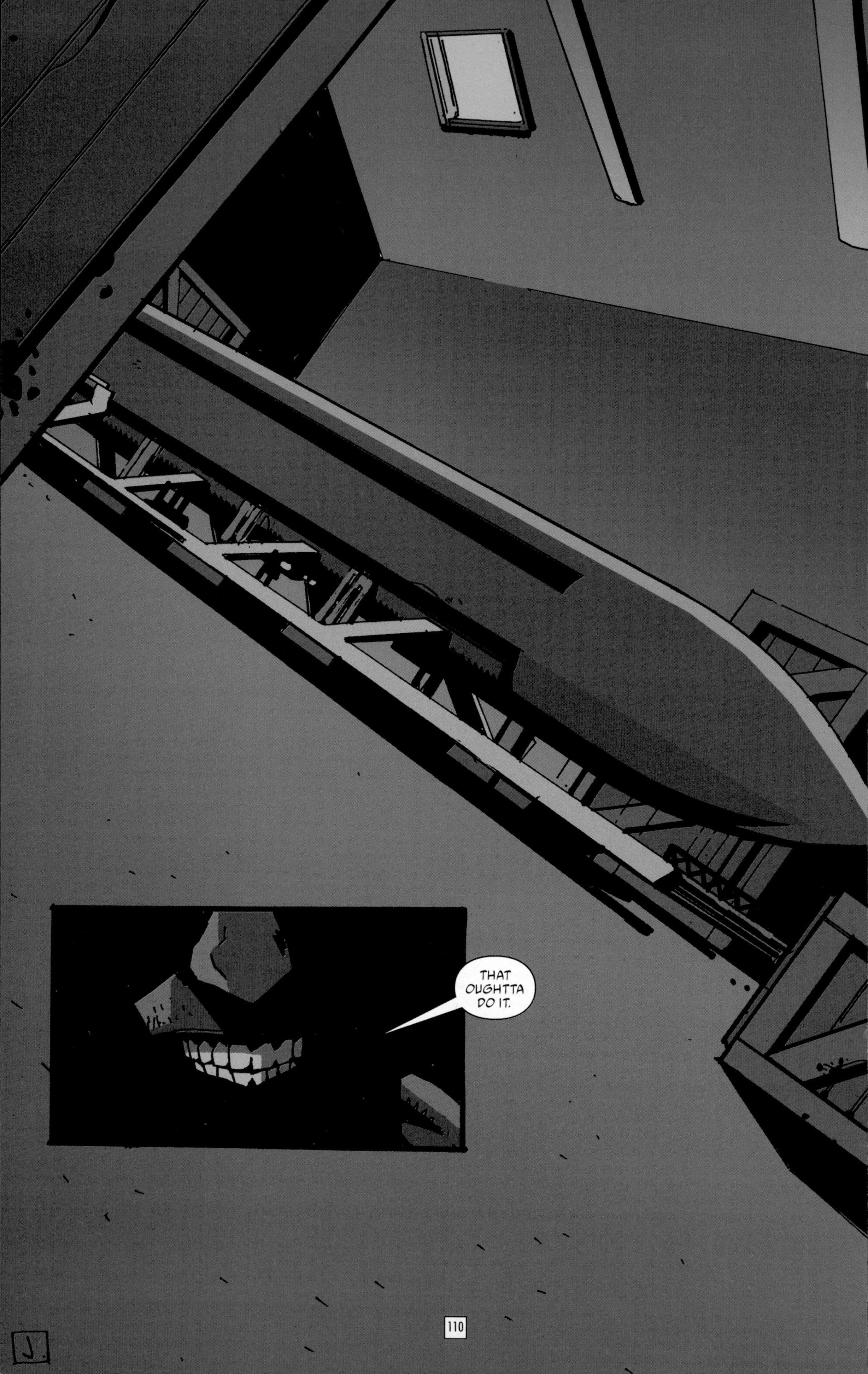
THAT OUGHTTA DO IT.

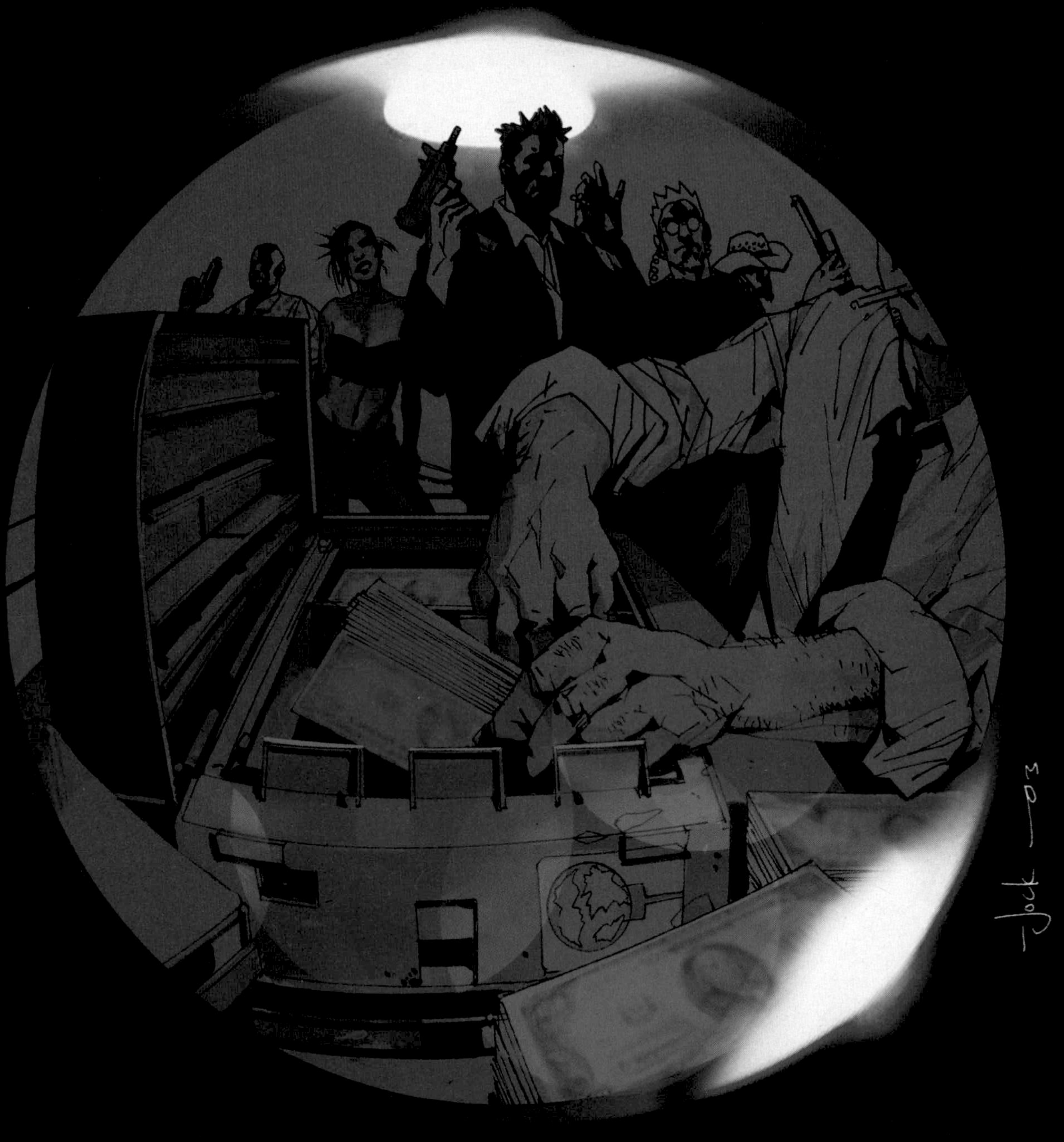

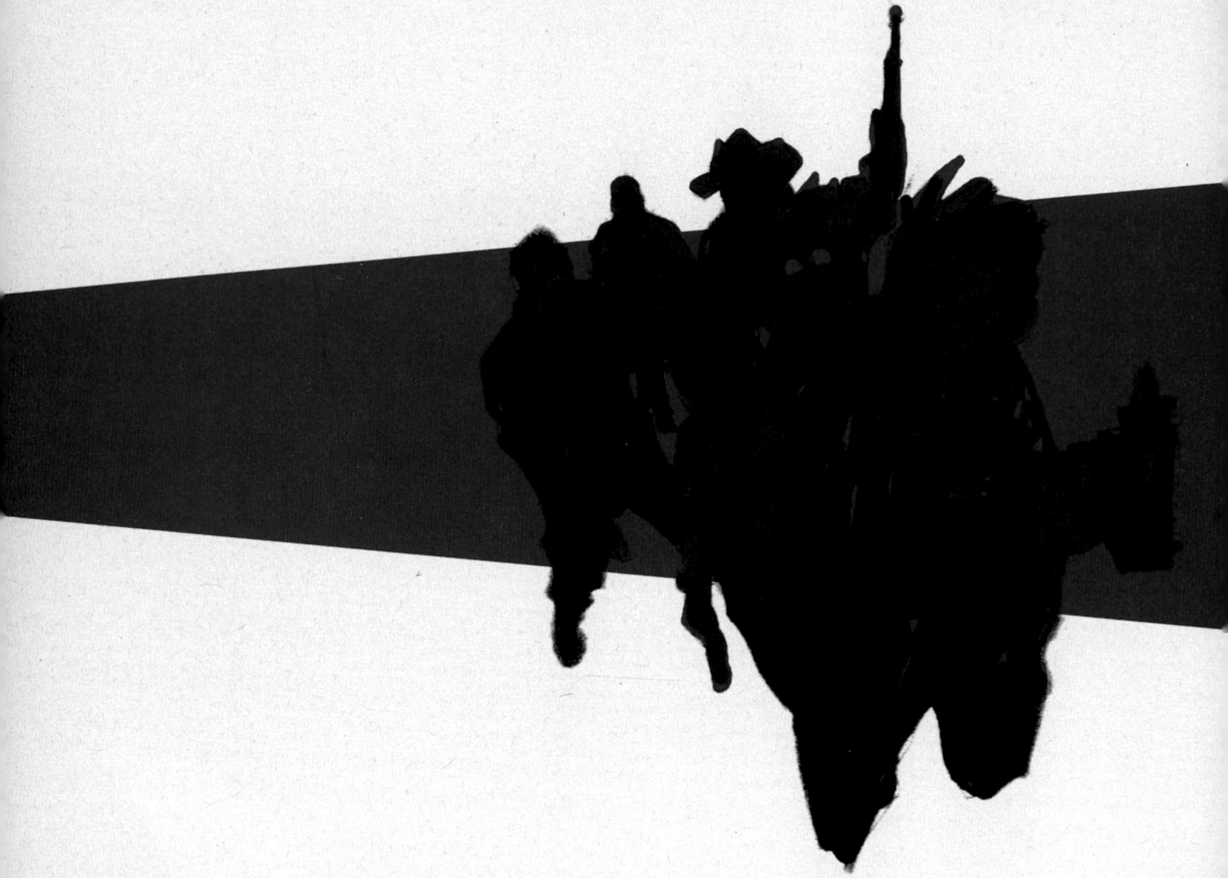

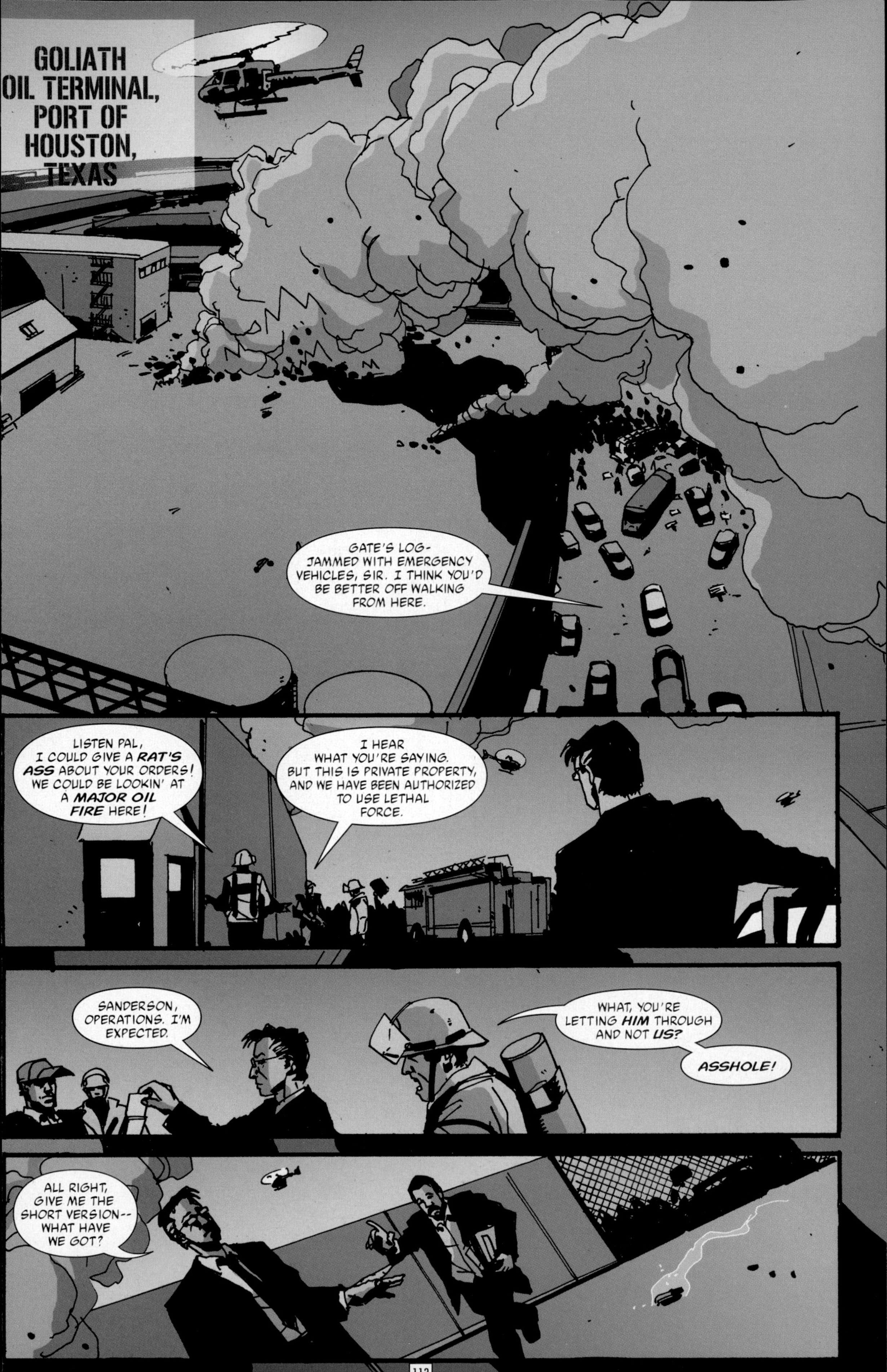
GOLIATH OIL TERMINAL, PORT OF HOUSTON, TEXAS
GATE'S LOG-JAMMED WITH EMERGENCY VEHICLES, SIR. I THINK YOU'D BE BETTER OFF WALKING FROM HERE.
LISTEN PAL, I COULD GIVE A RAT'S ASS ABOUT YOUR ORDERS! WE COULD BE LOOKIN' AT A MAJOR OIL FIRE HERE!
I HEAR WHAT YOU'RE SAYING. BUT THIS IS PRIVATE PROPERTY, AND WE HAVE BEEN AUTHORIZED TO USE LETHAL FORCE.
SANDERSON, OPERATIONS. I'M EXPECTED.
WHAT, YOU'RE LETTING HIM THROUGH AND NOT US?
ASSHOLE!
ALL RIGHT, GIVE ME THE SHORT VERSION-- WHAT HAVE WE GOT?

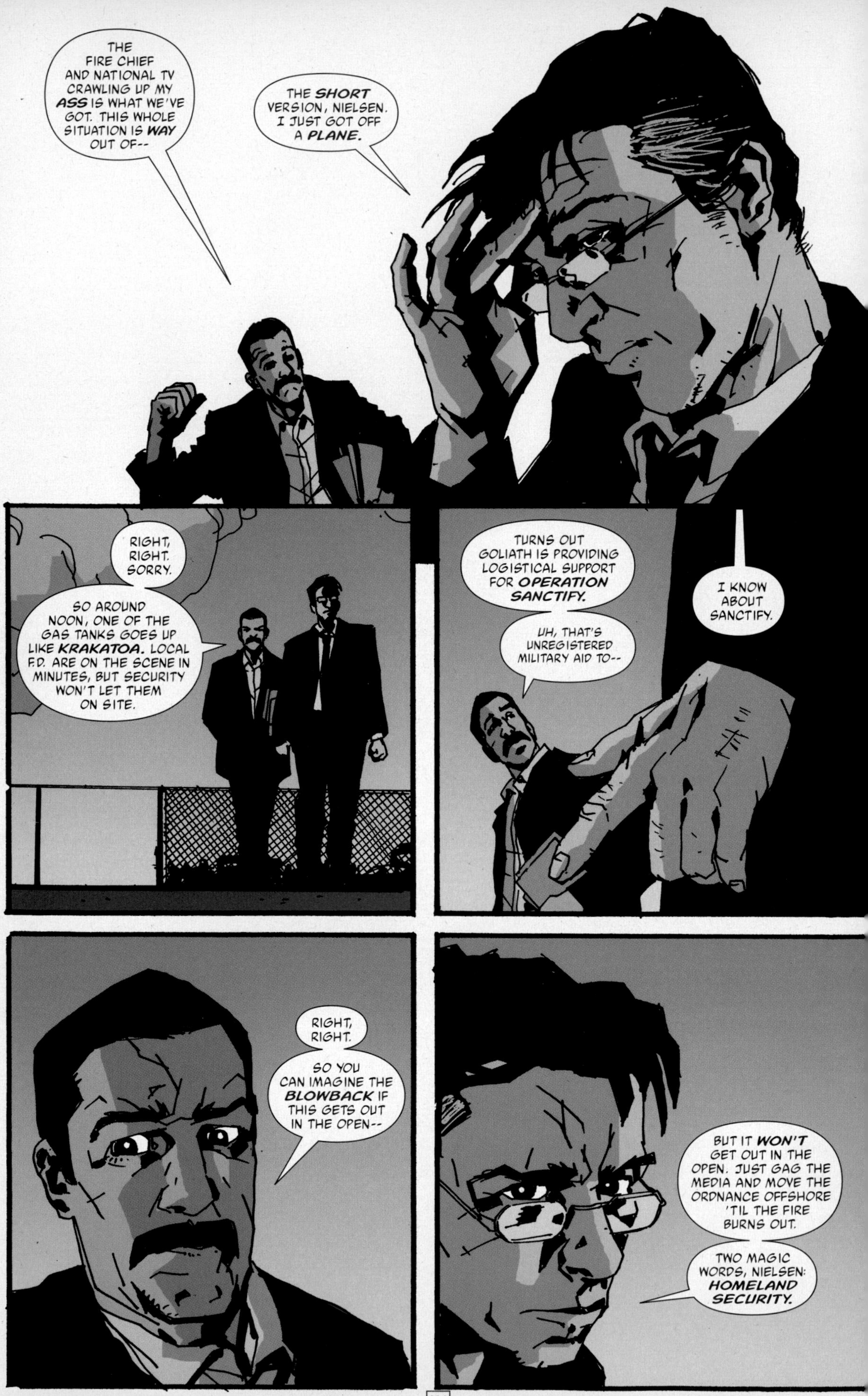
THE FIRE CHIEF AND NATIONAL TV CRAWLING UP MY ASS IS WHAT WE'VE GOT. THIS WHOLE SITUATION IS WAY OUT OF--
THE SHORT VERSION, NIELSEN. I JUST GOT OFF A PLANE.
RIGHT, RIGHT. SORRY.
SO AROUND NOON, ONE OF THE GAS TANKS GOES UP LIKE KRAKATOA. LOCAL F.D. ARE ON THE SCENE IN MINUTES, BUT SECURITY WON'T LET THEM ON SITE.
TURNS OUT GOLIATH IS PROVIDING LOGISTICAL SUPPORT FOR OPERATION SANCTIFY.
UH, THAT'S UNREGISTERED MILITARY AID TO--
I KNOW ABOUT SANCTIFY.
RIGHT, RIGHT.
SO YOU CAN IMAGINE THE BLOWBACK IF THIS GETS OUT IN THE OPEN--
BUT IT WON'T GET OUT IN THE OPEN. JUST GAG THE MEDIA AND MOVE THE ORDNANCE OFFSHORE 'TIL THE FIRE BURNS OUT.
TWO MAGIC WORDS, NIELSEN: HOMELAND SECURITY.

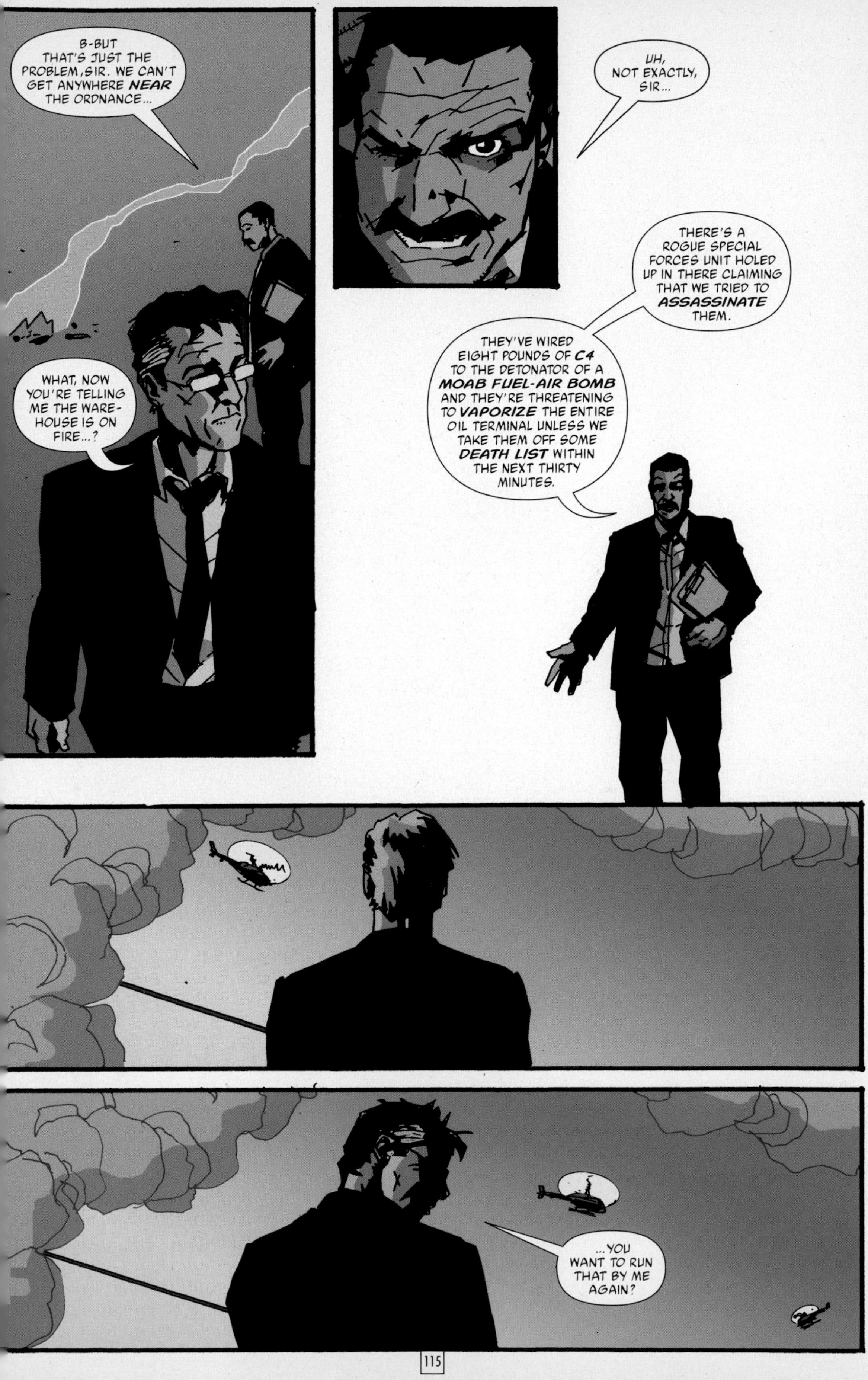
B-BUT THAT'S JUST THE PROBLEM, SIR. WE CAN'T GET ANYWHERE NEAR THE ORDNANCE...
UH, NOT EXACTLY, SIR...
WHAT, NOW YOU'RE TELLING ME THE WARE-HOUSE IS ON FIRE...?
THERE'S A ROGUE SPECIAL FORCES UNIT HOLED UP IN THERE CLAIMING THAT WE TRIED TO ASSASSINATE THEM.
THEY'VE WIRED EIGHT POUNDS OF C4 TO THE DETONATOR OF A MOAB FUEL-AIR BOMB AND THEY'RE THREATENING TO VAPORIZE THE ENTIRE OIL TERMINAL UNLESS WE TAKE THEM OFF SOME DEATH LIST WITHIN THE NEXT THIRTY MINUTES.
...YOU WANT TO RUN THAT BY ME AGAIN?

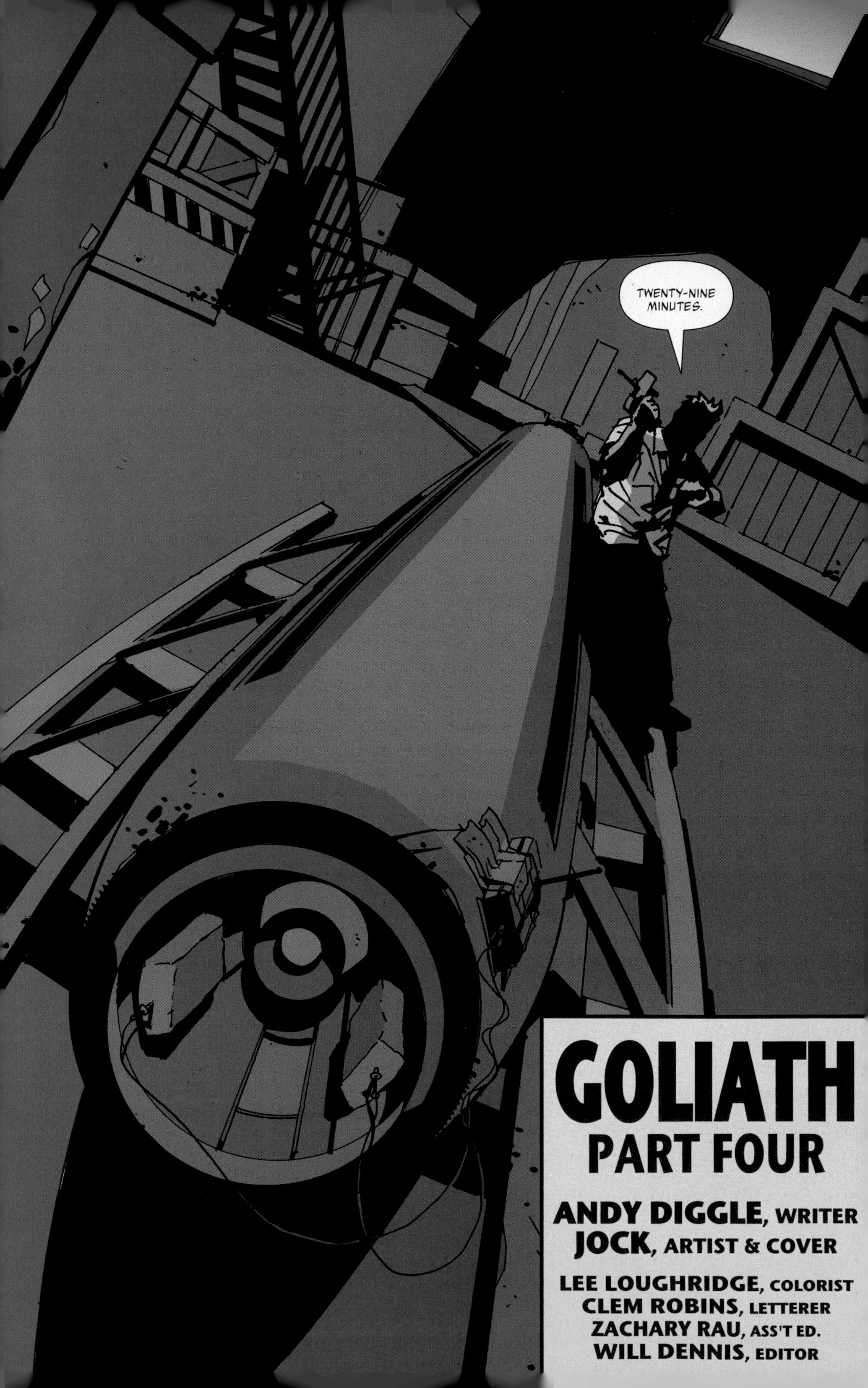
TWENTY-NINE MINUTES.
GOLIATH
PART FOUR
ANDY DIGGLE, WRITER
JOCK, ARTIST & COVER
LEE LOUGHRIDGE, COLORIST
CLEM ROBINS, LETTERER
ZACHARY RAU, ASS'T ED.
WILL DENNIS, EDITOR

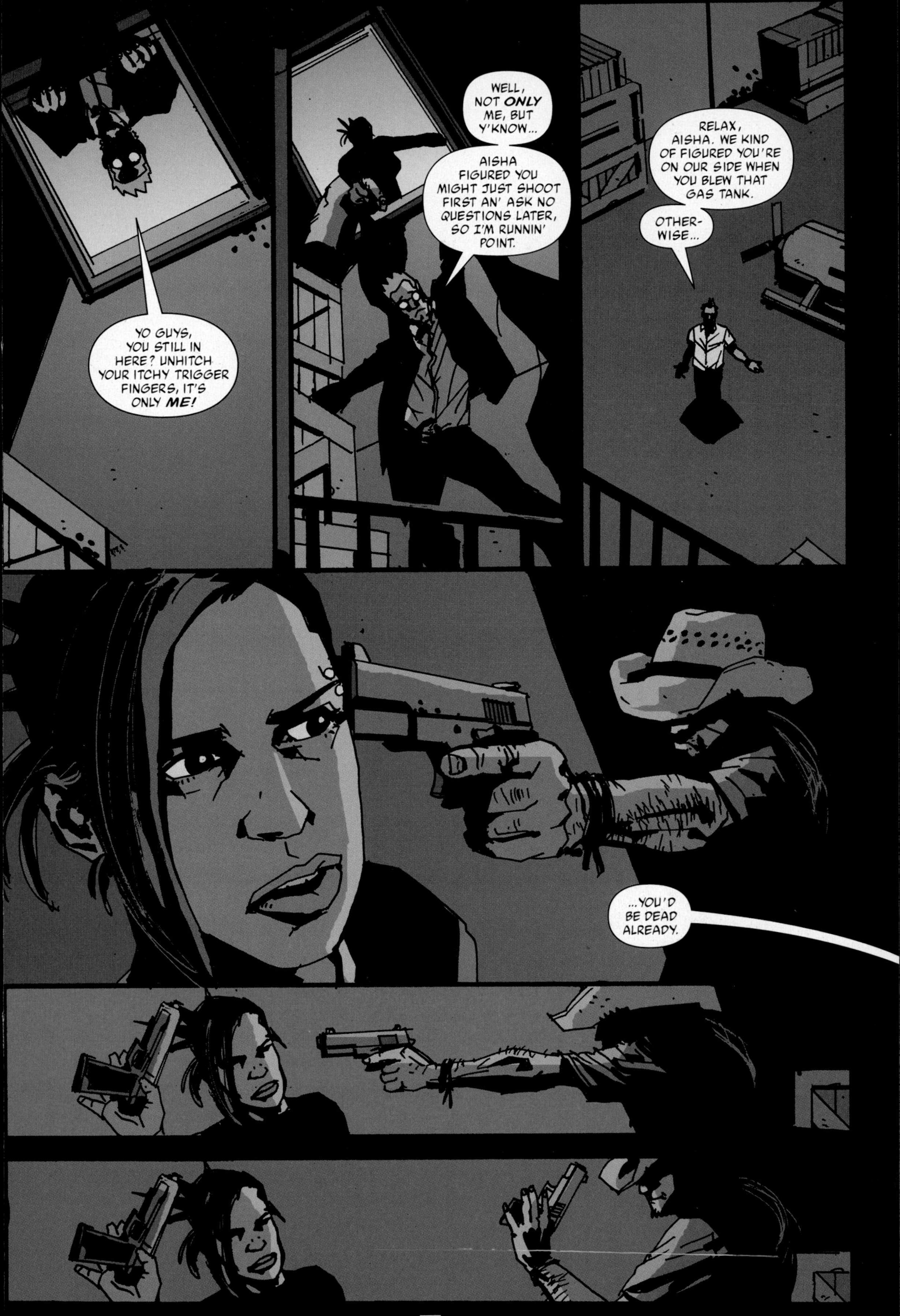
YO GUYS, YOU STILL IN HERE? UNHITCH YOUR ITCHY TRIGGER FINGERS, IT'S ONLY *ME!*
WELL, NOT *ONLY* ME, BUT Y'KNOW...
AISHA FIGURED YOU MIGHT JUST SHOOT FIRST AN' ASK NO QUESTIONS LATER, SO I'M RUNNIN' POINT.
RELAX, AISHA. WE KIND OF FIGURED YOU'RE ON OUR SIDE WHEN YOU BLEW THAT GAS TANK.
OTHER-WISE...
...YOU'D BE DEAD ALREADY.

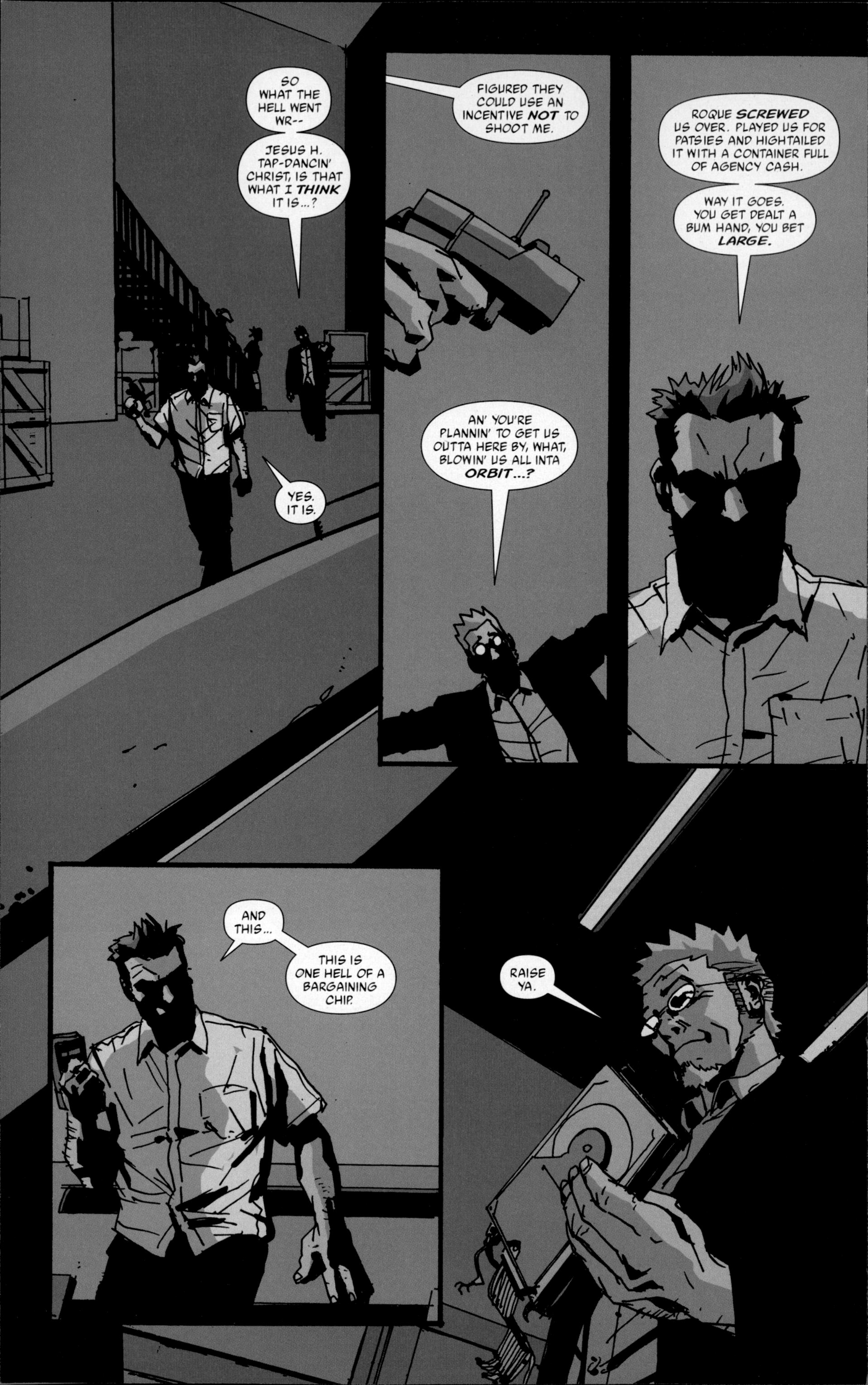
SO WHAT THE HELL WENT WR--
JESUS H. TAP-DANCIN' CHRIST, IS THAT WHAT I THINK IT IS...?
YES. IT IS.
FIGURED THEY COULD USE AN INCENTIVE NOT TO SHOOT ME.
AN' YOU'RE PLANNIN' TO GET US OUTTA HERE BY, WHAT, BLOWIN' US ALL INTA ORBIT...?
ROQUE SCREWED US OVER. PLAYED US FOR PATSIES AND HIGHTAILED IT WITH A CONTAINER FULL OF AGENCY CASH.
WAY IT GOES. YOU GET DEALT A BUM HAND, YOU BET LARGE.
AND THIS...
THIS IS ONE HELL OF A BARGAINING CHIP.
RAISE YA.

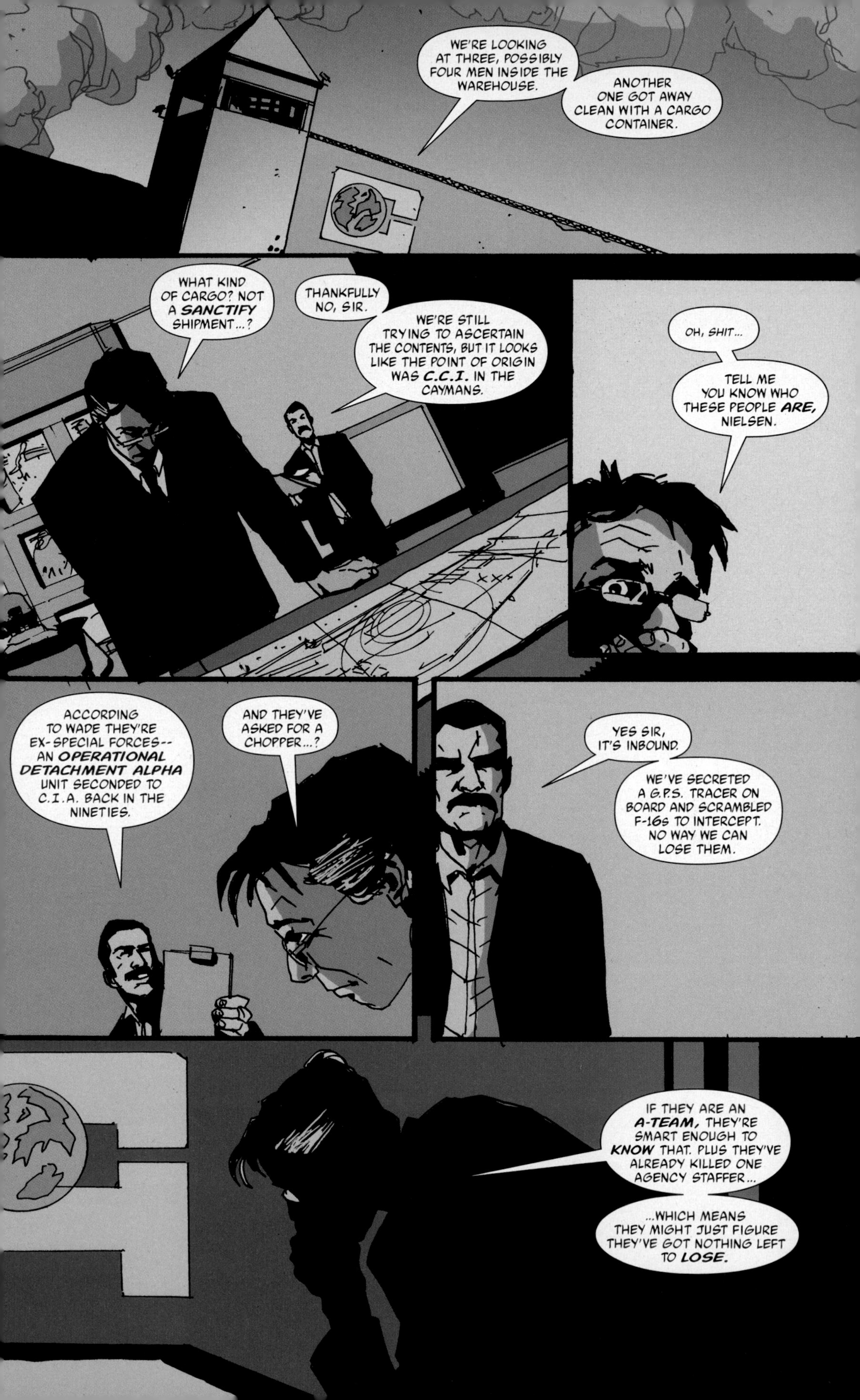
WE'RE LOOKING AT THREE, POSSIBLY FOUR MEN INSIDE THE WAREHOUSE.
ANOTHER ONE GOT AWAY CLEAN WITH A CARGO CONTAINER.
WHAT KIND OF CARGO? NOT A **SANCTIFY** SHIPMENT...?
THANKFULLY NO, SIR.
WE'RE STILL TRYING TO ASCERTAIN THE CONTENTS, BUT IT LOOKS LIKE THE POINT OF ORIGIN WAS **C.C.I.** IN THE CAYMANS.
OH, SHIT...
TELL ME YOU KNOW WHO THESE PEOPLE **ARE,** NIELSEN.
ACCORDING TO WADE THEY'RE EX-SPECIAL FORCES-- AN **OPERATIONAL DETACHMENT ALPHA** UNIT SECONDED TO C.I.A. BACK IN THE NINETIES.
AND THEY'VE ASKED FOR A CHOPPER...?
YES SIR, IT'S INBOUND.
WE'VE SECRETED A G.P.S. TRACER ON BOARD AND SCRAMBLED F-16s TO INTERCEPT. NO WAY WE CAN LOSE THEM.
IF THEY ARE AN **A-TEAM,** THEY'RE SMART ENOUGH TO **KNOW** THAT. PLUS THEY'VE ALREADY KILLED ONE AGENCY STAFFER...
...WHICH MEANS THEY MIGHT JUST FIGURE THEY'VE GOT NOTHING LEFT TO **LOSE.**

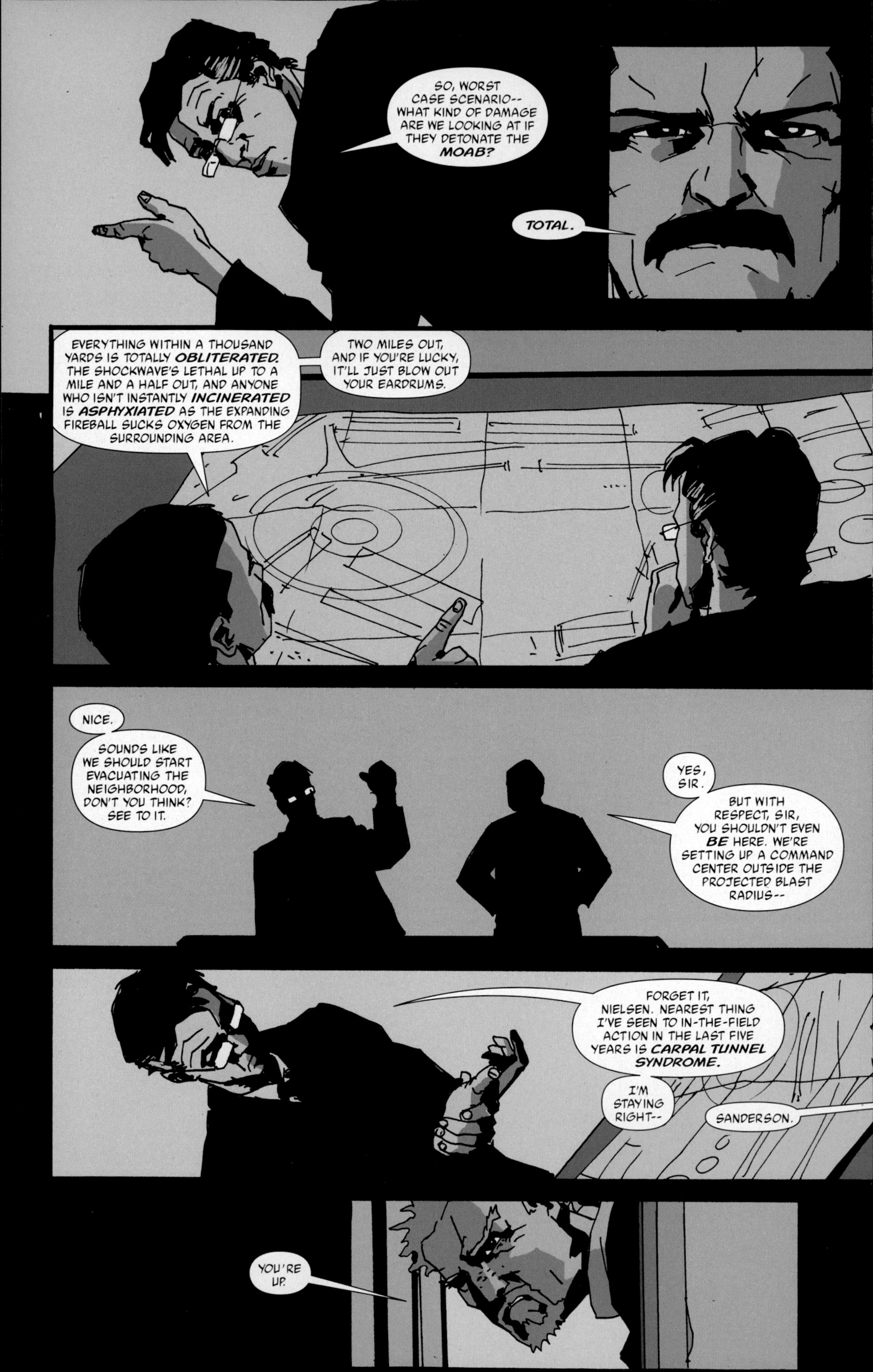
SO, WORST CASE SCENARIO-- WHAT KIND OF DAMAGE ARE WE LOOKING AT IF THEY DETONATE THE **MOAB?**
**TOTAL.**
EVERYTHING WITHIN A THOUSAND YARDS IS TOTALLY **OBLITERATED.** THE SHOCKWAVE'S LETHAL UP TO A MILE AND A HALF OUT, AND ANYONE WHO ISN'T INSTANTLY **INCINERATED** IS **ASPHYXIATED** AS THE EXPANDING FIREBALL SUCKS OXYGEN FROM THE SURROUNDING AREA.
TWO MILES OUT, AND IF YOU'RE LUCKY, IT'LL JUST BLOW OUT YOUR EARDRUMS.
NICE.
SOUNDS LIKE WE SHOULD START EVACUATING THE NEIGHBORHOOD, DON'T YOU THINK? SEE TO IT.
YES, SIR.
BUT WITH RESPECT, SIR, YOU SHOULDN'T EVEN **BE** HERE. WE'RE SETTING UP A COMMAND CENTER OUTSIDE THE PROJECTED BLAST RADIUS--
FORGET IT, NIELSEN. NEAREST THING I'VE SEEN TO IN-THE-FIELD ACTION IN THE LAST FIVE YEARS IS **CARPAL TUNNEL SYNDROME.**
I'M STAYING RIGHT--
SANDERSON.
YOU'RE UP.

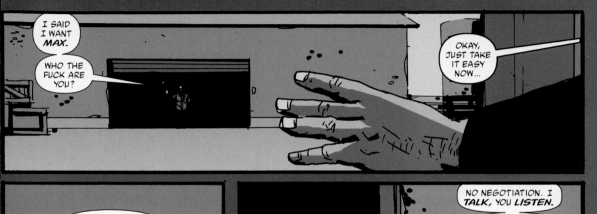

I SAID I WANT **MAX.**

WHO THE FUCK ARE YOU?

OKAY, JUST TAKE IT EASY NOW...

I'M ROBERT SANDERSON, DEPUTY DIRECTOR OF OPERATIONS, CENTRAL INTELLIGENCE AGENCY. I'M HERE TO NEGOTIATE FOR--

NO NEGOTIATION. I **TALK,** YOU **LISTEN.**

ONE: TELL YOUR SNIPERS TO COOL IT. I LET GO THIS TRIGGER-SWITCH, EVERYBODY HERE GETS **FLASH-VAPORIZED.** THINK ABOUT IT.

TWO: **IMMUNITY.**

WE HAVE THE FINANCE RECORDS FOR YOUR LITTLE OPERATION HERE. YOU TRY TO TAKE US OUT AGAIN, GET READY TO BE FAMOUS.

OKAY, NOW YOU'RE GOING TO HAVE TO JUST **BACK UP** A LITTLE HERE...

YOU SEEM TO THINK WE TRIED TO **KILL** YOU? I CAN **ASSURE** YOU THAT'S NOT THE CASE. OUR RECORDS SAY YOUR UNIT DIED IN SOME KIND OF **CHOPPER ACCIDENT...**

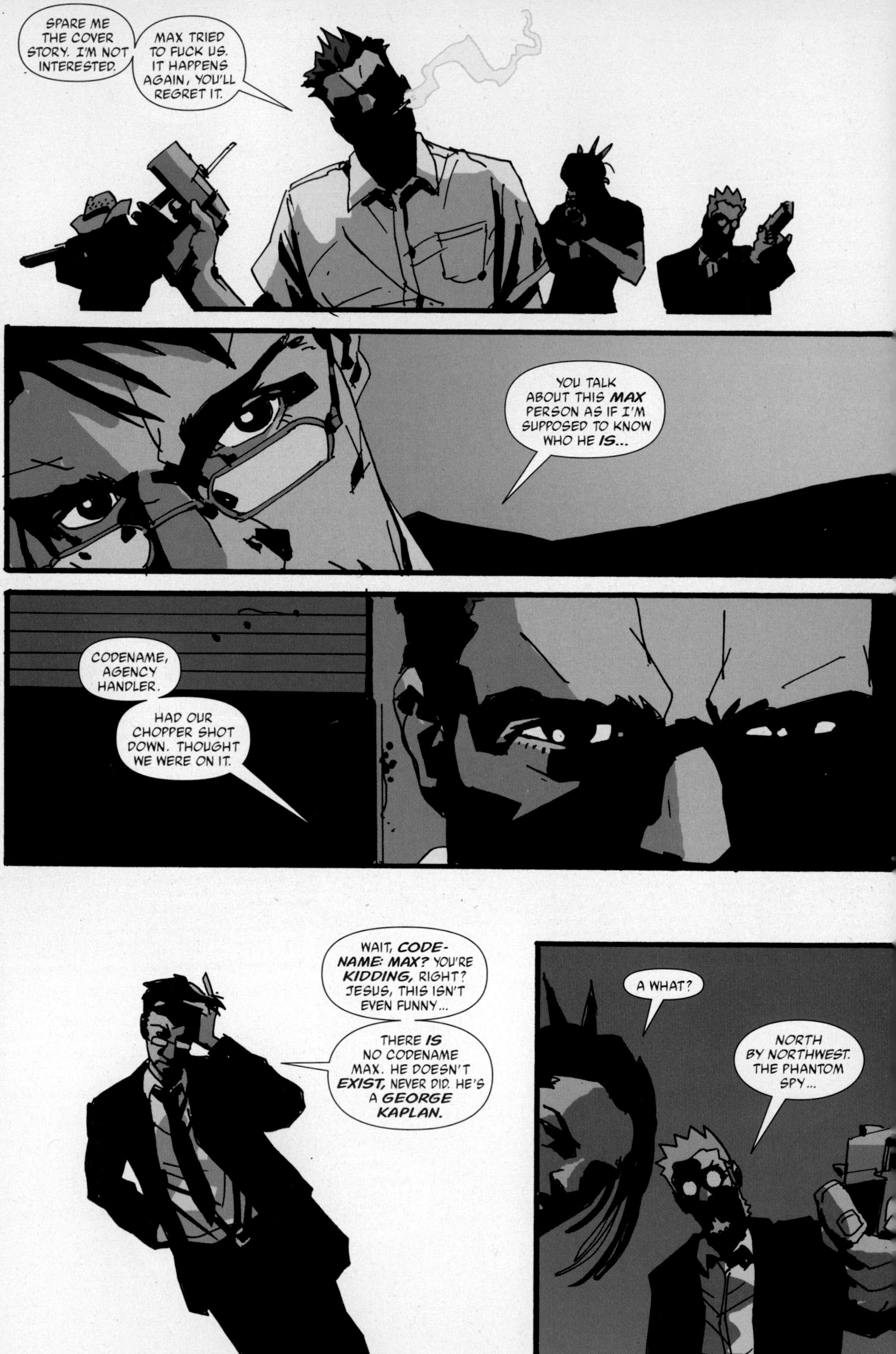
SPARE ME THE COVER STORY. I'M NOT INTERESTED.
MAX TRIED TO FUCK US. IT HAPPENS AGAIN, YOU'LL REGRET IT.
YOU TALK ABOUT THIS MAX PERSON AS IF I'M SUPPOSED TO KNOW WHO HE IS...
CODENAME, AGENCY HANDLER.
HAD OUR CHOPPER SHOT DOWN. THOUGHT WE WERE ON IT.
WAIT, CODE-NAME: MAX? YOU'RE KIDDING, RIGHT? JESUS, THIS ISN'T EVEN FUNNY...
THERE IS NO CODENAME MAX. HE DOESN'T EXIST, NEVER DID. HE'S A GEORGE KAPLAN.
A WHAT?
NORTH BY NORTHWEST. THE PHANTOM SPY...

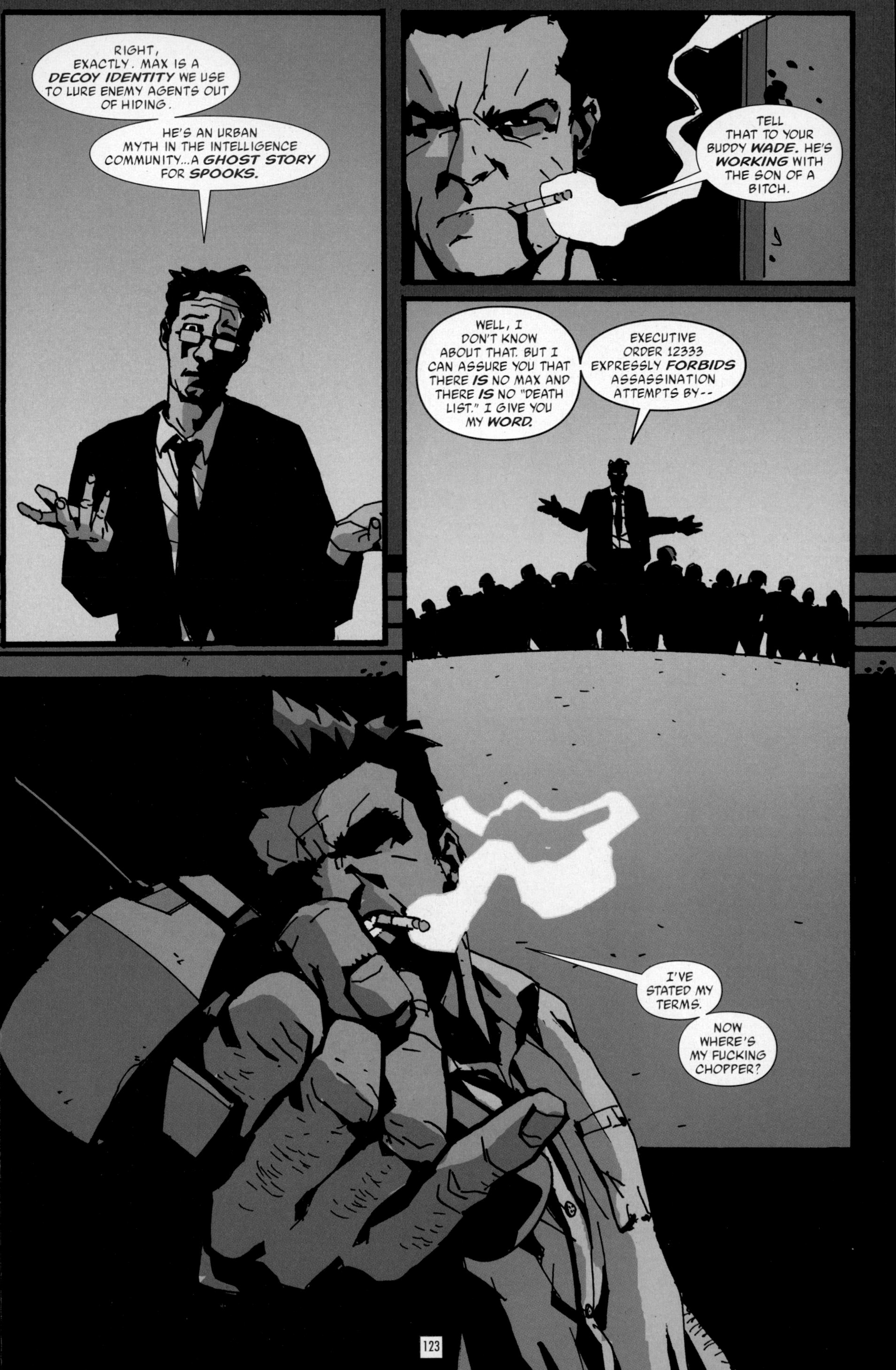
RIGHT, EXACTLY. MAX IS A DECOY IDENTITY WE USE TO LURE ENEMY AGENTS OUT OF HIDING.
HE'S AN URBAN MYTH IN THE INTELLIGENCE COMMUNITY...A GHOST STORY FOR SPOOKS.
TELL THAT TO YOUR BUDDY WADE. HE'S WORKING WITH THE SON OF A BITCH.
WELL, I DON'T KNOW ABOUT THAT. BUT I CAN ASSURE YOU THAT THERE IS NO MAX AND THERE IS NO "DEATH LIST." I GIVE YOU MY WORD.
EXECUTIVE ORDER 12333 EXPRESSLY FORBIDS ASSASSINATION ATTEMPTS BY--
I'VE STATED MY TERMS.
NOW WHERE'S MY FUCKING CHOPPER?

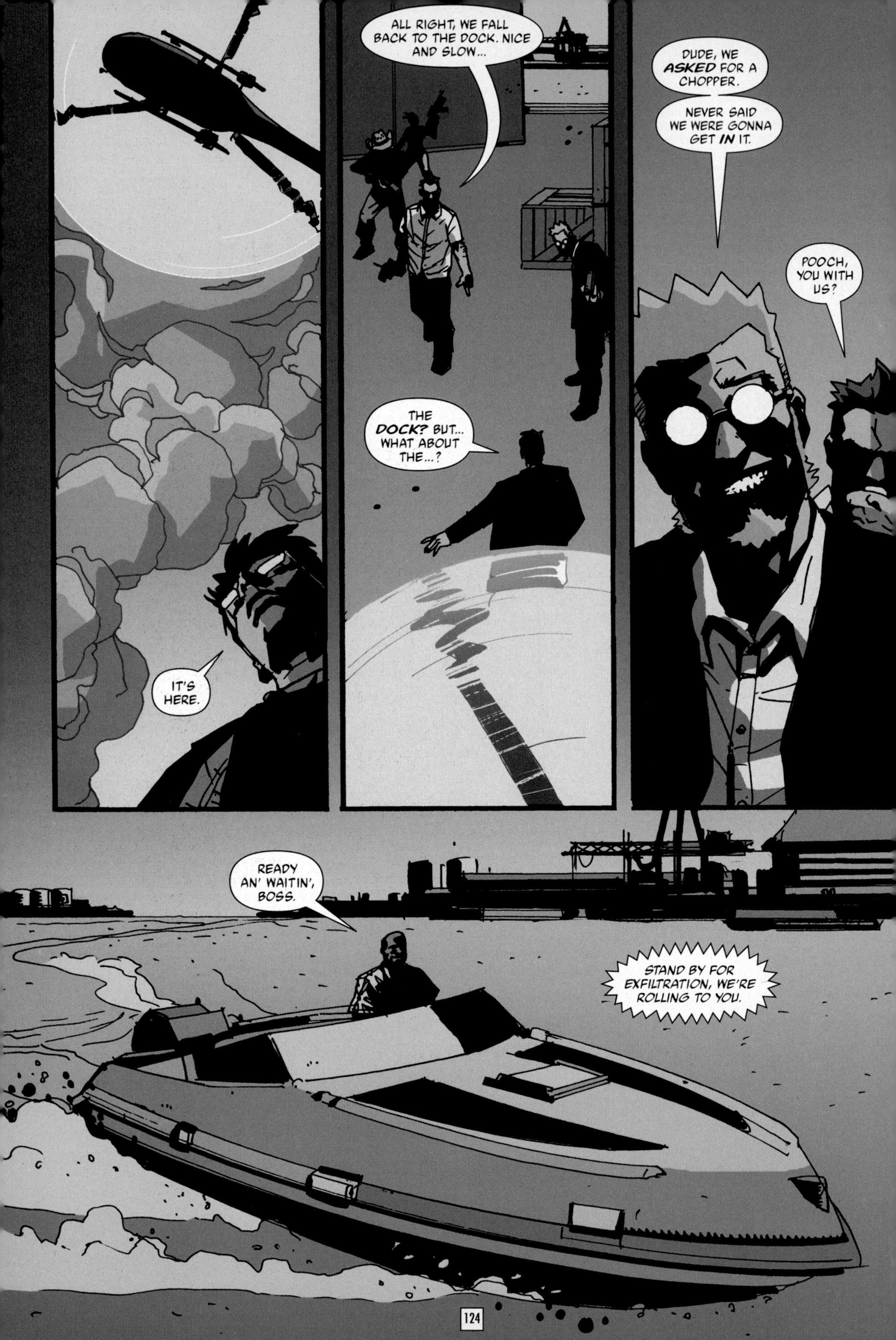

IT'S HERE.
ALL RIGHT, WE FALL BACK TO THE DOCK. NICE AND SLOW...
THE DOCK? BUT... WHAT ABOUT THE...?
DUDE, WE ASKED FOR A CHOPPER.
NEVER SAID WE WERE GONNA GET IN IT.
POOCH, YOU WITH US?
READY AN' WAITIN', BOSS.
STAND BY FOR EXFILTRATION, WE'RE ROLLING TO YOU.

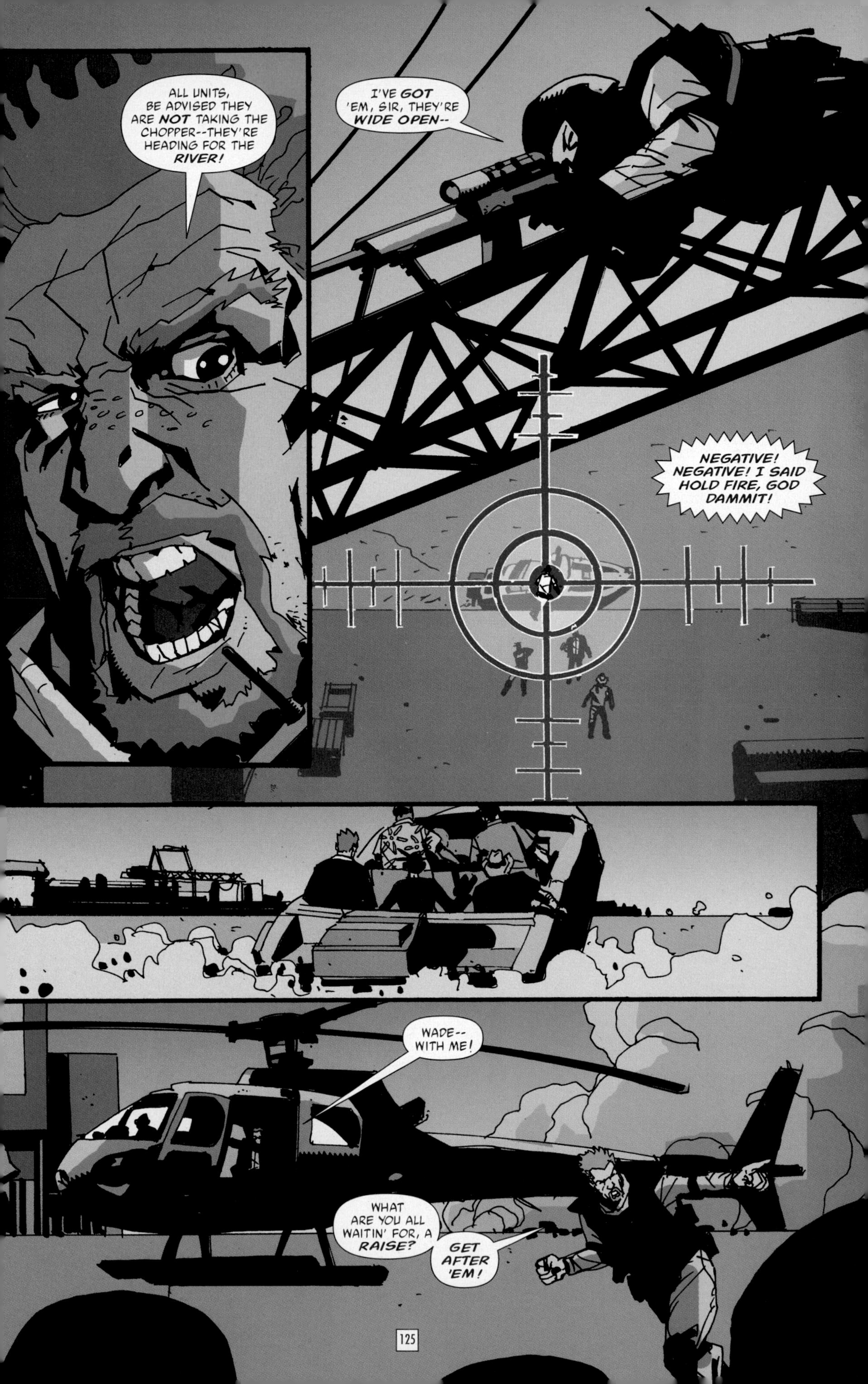
ALL UNITS, BE ADVISED THEY ARE NOT TAKING THE CHOPPER--THEY'RE HEADING FOR THE RIVER!
I'VE GOT 'EM, SIR, THEY'RE WIDE OPEN--
NEGATIVE! NEGATIVE! I SAID HOLD FIRE, GOD DAMMIT!
WADE-- WITH ME!
WHAT ARE YOU ALL WAITIN' FOR, A RAISE?
GET AFTER 'EM!

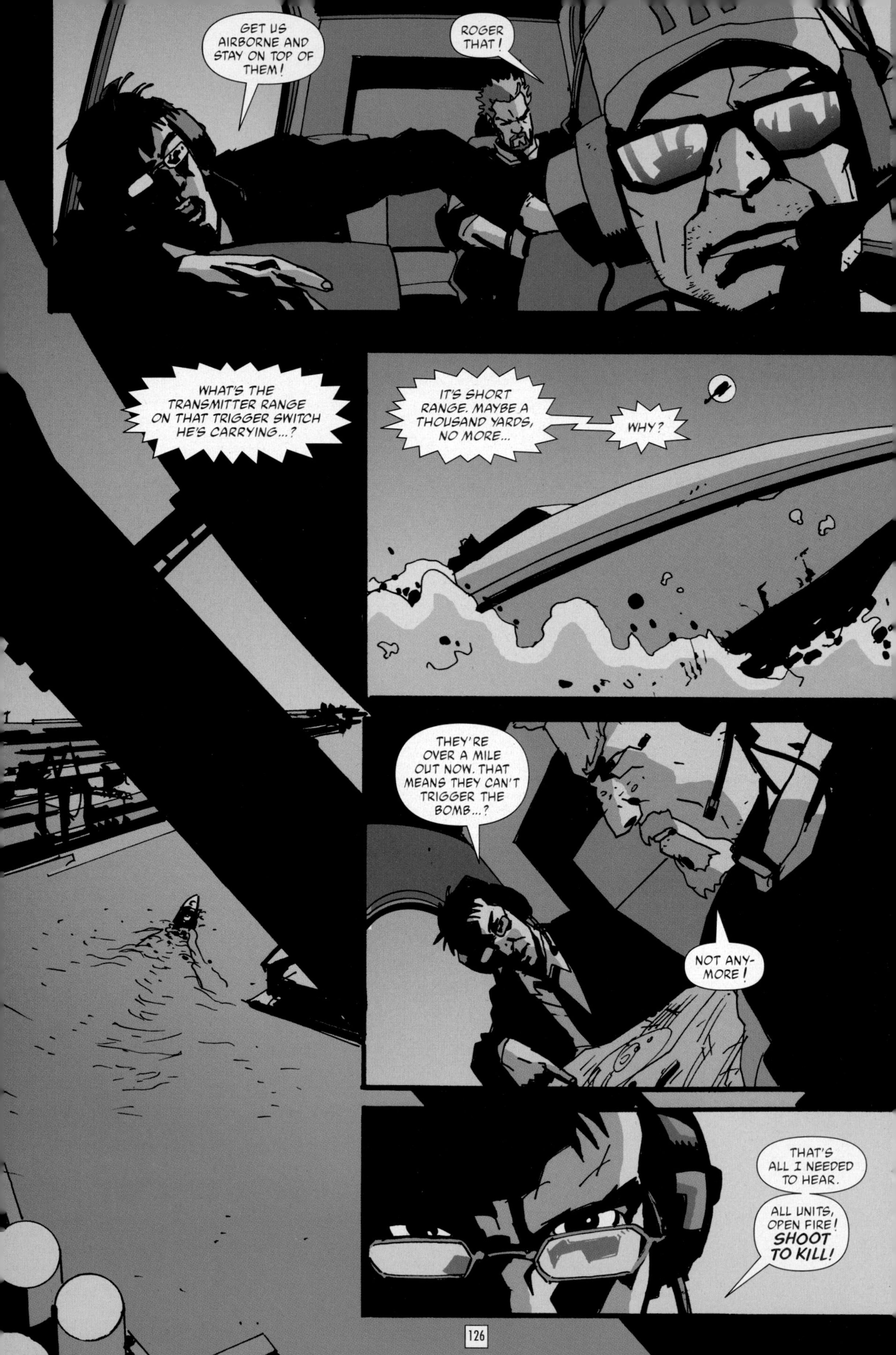
GET US AIRBORNE AND STAY ON TOP OF THEM!
ROGER THAT!
WHAT'S THE TRANSMITTER RANGE ON THAT TRIGGER SWITCH HE'S CARRYING...?
IT'S SHORT RANGE. MAYBE A THOUSAND YARDS, NO MORE...
WHY?
THEY'RE OVER A MILE OUT NOW. THAT MEANS THEY CAN'T TRIGGER THE BOMB...?
NOT ANY-MORE!
THAT'S ALL I NEEDED TO HEAR.
ALL UNITS, OPEN FIRE! **SHOOT TO KILL!**

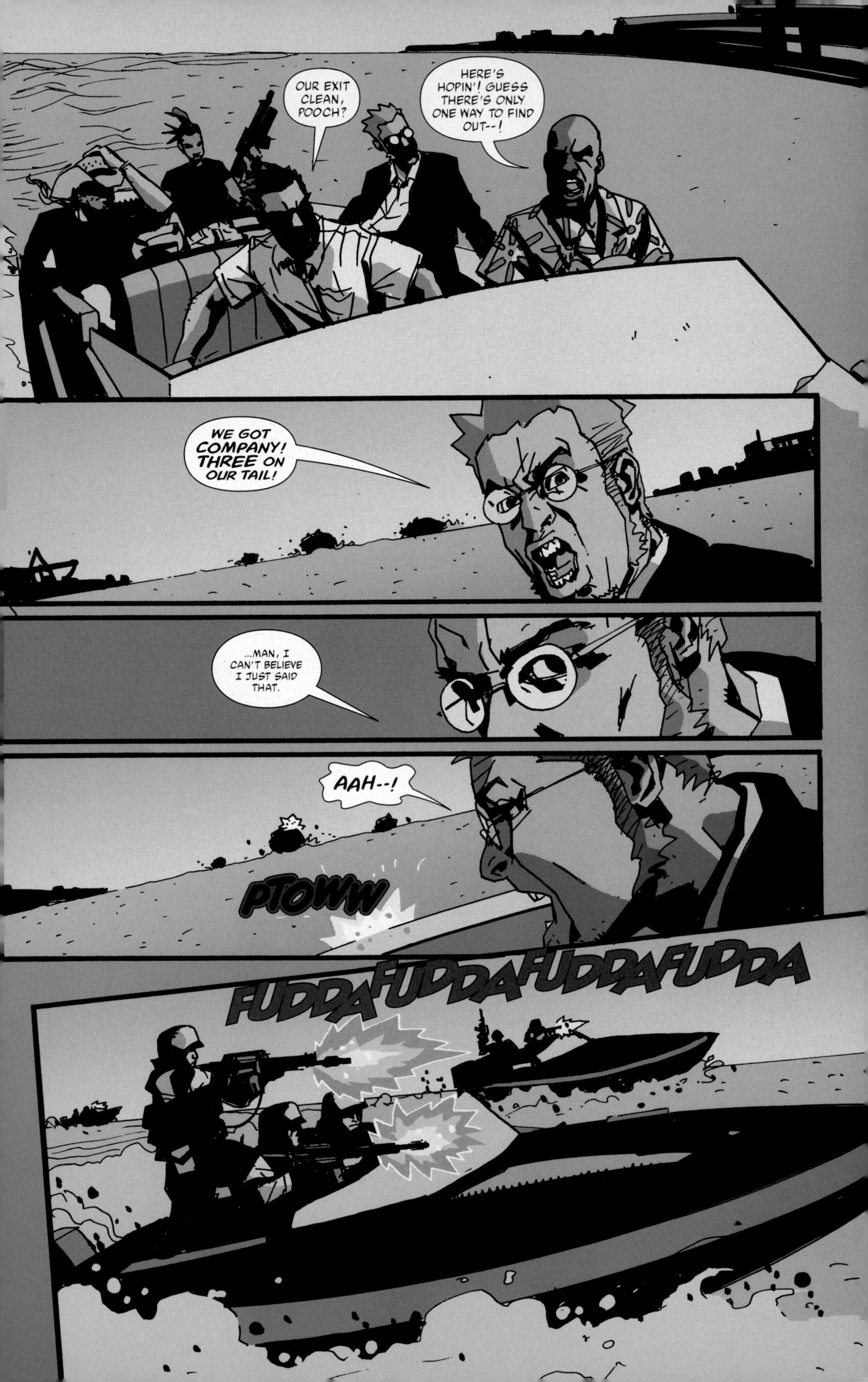
OUR EXIT CLEAN, POOCH?
HERE'S HOPIN'! GUESS THERE'S ONLY ONE WAY TO FIND OUT--!
WE GOT COMPANY! THREE ON OUR TAIL!
...MAN, I CAN'T BELIEVE I JUST SAID THAT.
AAH--!
PTOWW
FUDDAFUDDAFUDDAFUDDA

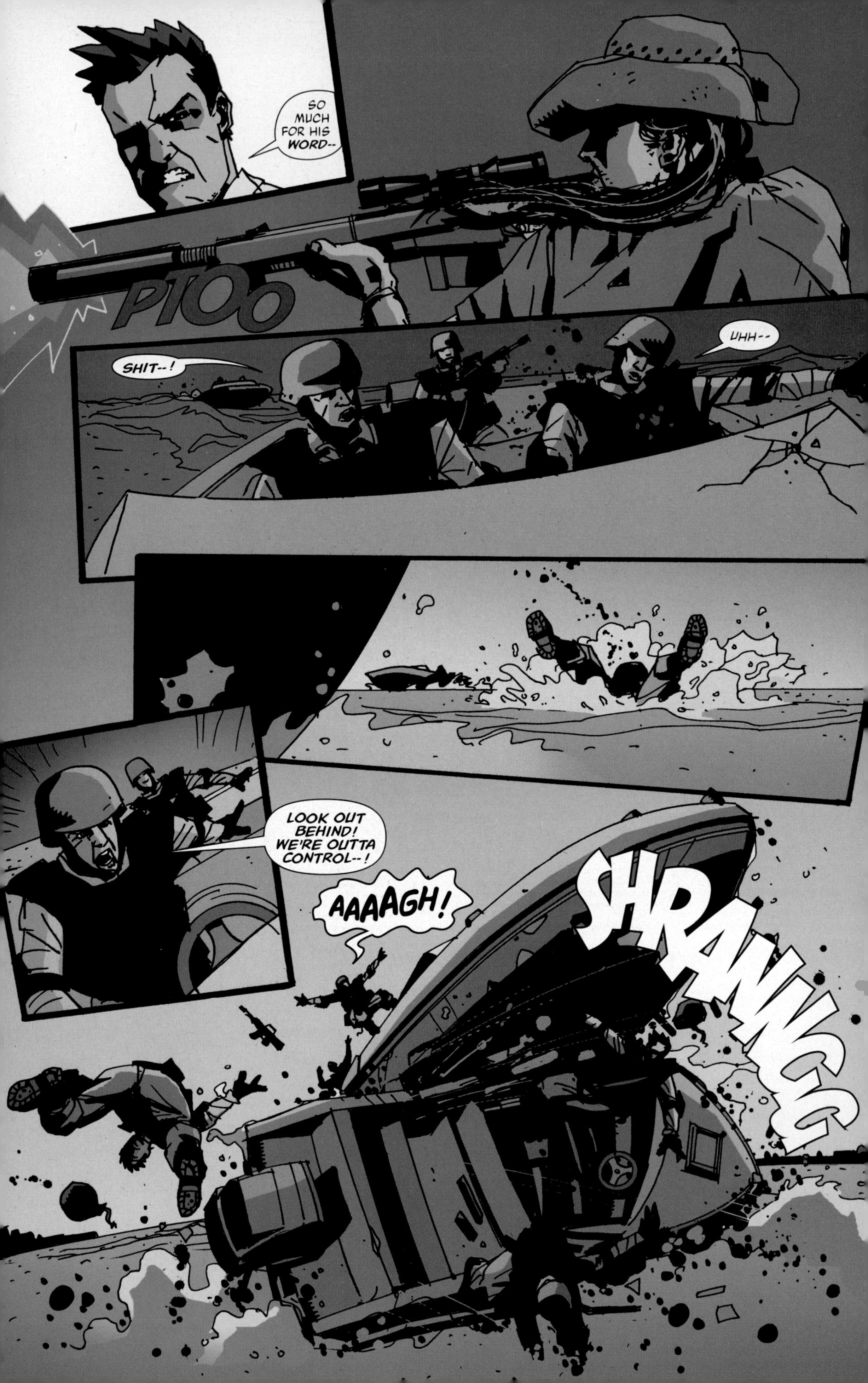
SO MUCH FOR HIS WORD--
PTOO
SHIT--!
UHH--
LOOK OUT BEHIND! WE'RE OUTTA CONTROL--!
AAAAGH!
SHRANNGG

FUDDAFUDDAFUDDAFUDDA
THIS TRIBUTARY'S A DEAD END! WE GOT 'EM BOXED IN!
BDAM BDAM BDAM BDAMBDAM
ONE LEFT! TELL ME YOU HAVE A PLAN TO GET US OUT OF HERE!
COMIN' RIGHT UP, LADY!
HANG ONTO SOMETHIN'--!
SPANNG!
BDANGG!
PTOWW!
YEEEEE-HAAAA!

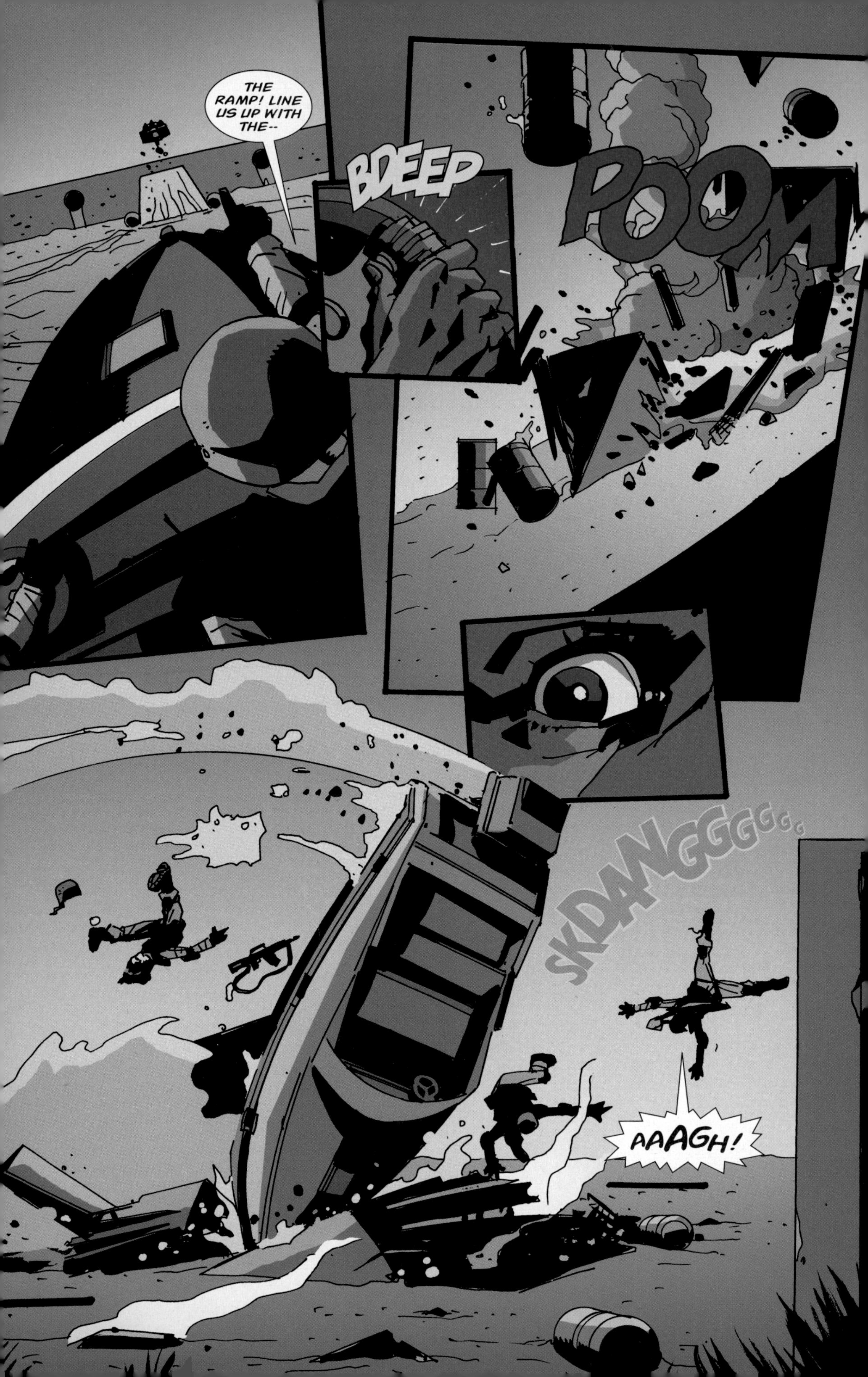
THE RAMP! LINE US UP WITH THE--
BDEEP
POOM
SKDANGGGGG
AAAGH!

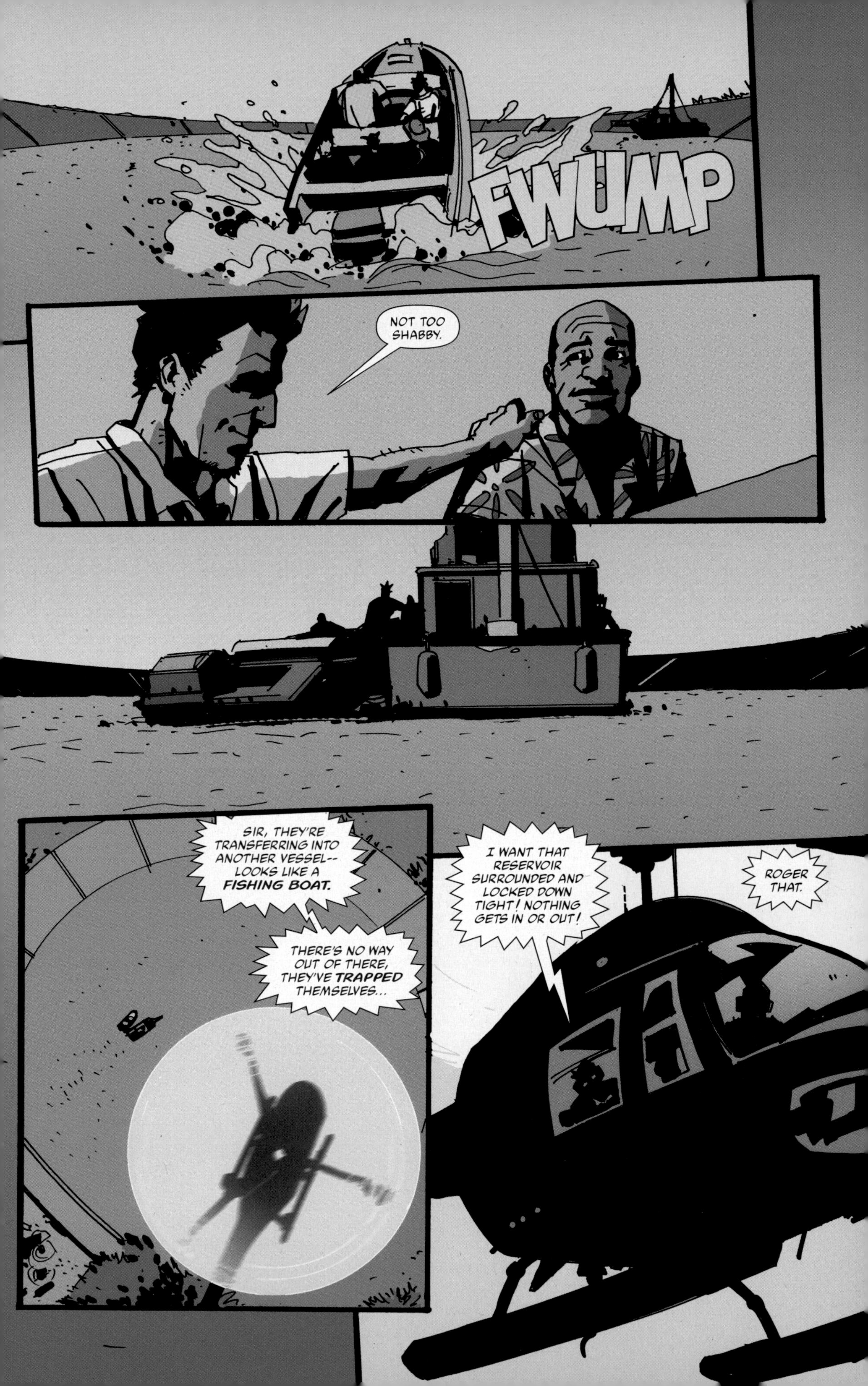
FWUMP
NOT TOO SHABBY.
SIR, THEY'RE TRANSFERRING INTO ANOTHER VESSEL-- LOOKS LIKE A FISHING BOAT.
THERE'S NO WAY OUT OF THERE, THEY'VE TRAPPED THEMSELVES...
I WANT THAT RESERVOIR SURROUNDED AND LOCKED DOWN TIGHT! NOTHING GETS IN OR OUT!
ROGER THAT.

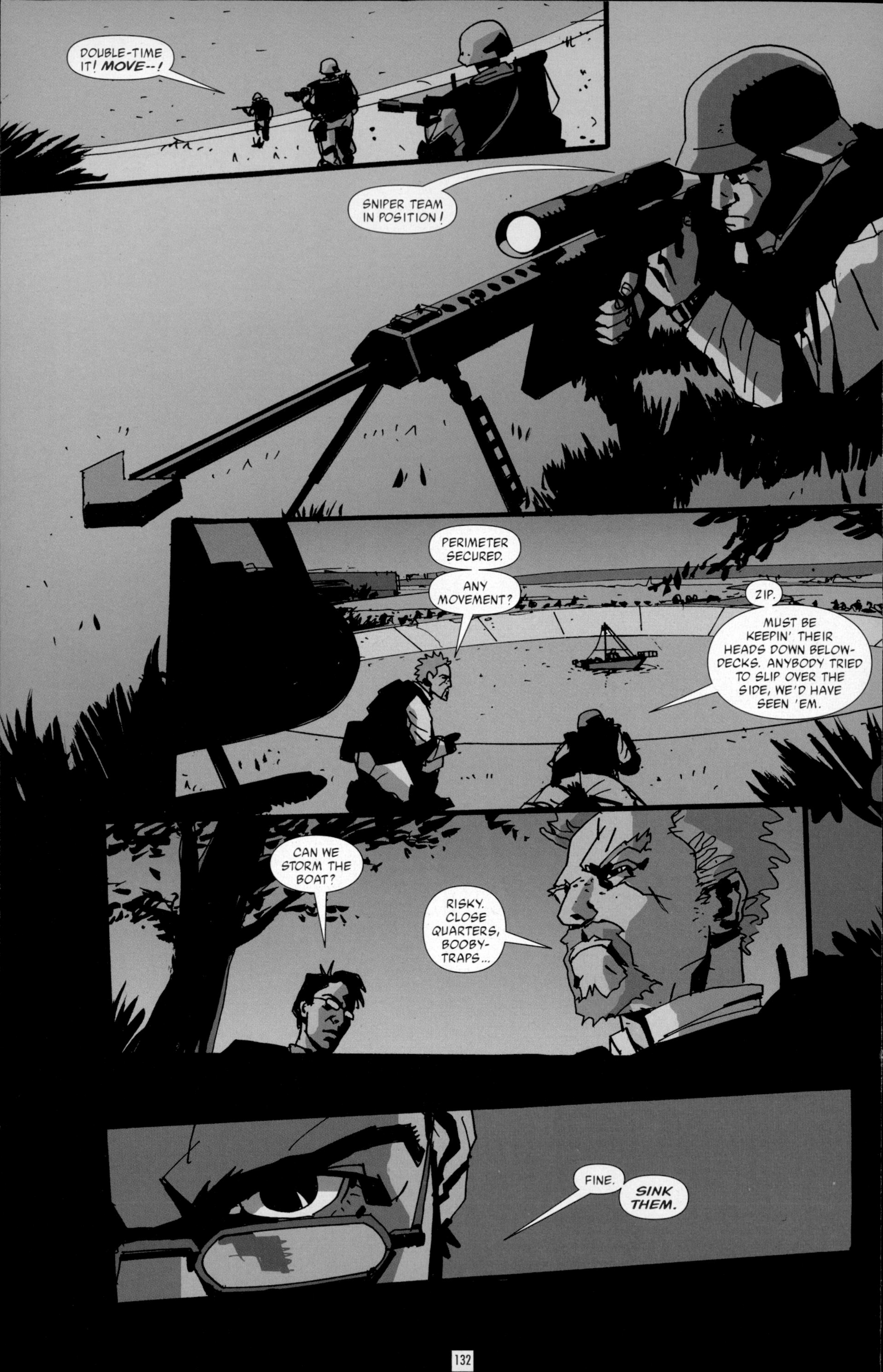
DOUBLE-TIME IT! MOVE--!
SNIPER TEAM IN POSITION!
PERIMETER SECURED.
ANY MOVEMENT?
ZIP.
MUST BE KEEPIN' THEIR HEADS DOWN BELOW-DECKS. ANYBODY TRIED TO SLIP OVER THE SIDE, WE'D HAVE SEEN 'EM.
CAN WE STORM THE BOAT?
RISKY. CLOSE QUARTERS, BOOBY-TRAPS...
FINE. SINK THEM.

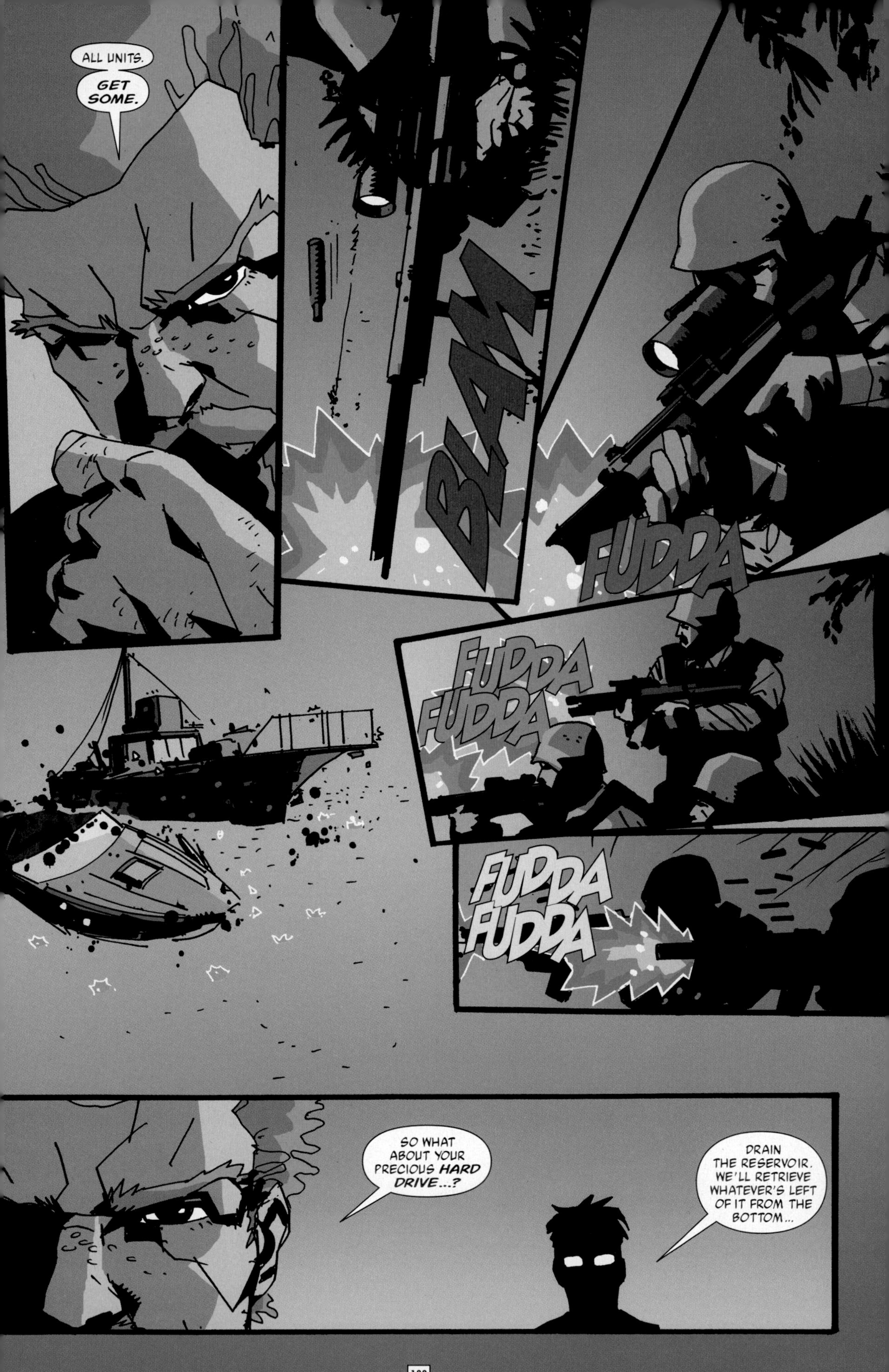
ALL UNITS.
GET SOME.
BLAM
FUDDA
FUDDA FUDDA
FUDDA FUDDA
SO WHAT ABOUT YOUR PRECIOUS HARD DRIVE...?
DRAIN THE RESERVOIR. WE'LL RETRIEVE WHATEVER'S LEFT OF IT FROM THE BOTTOM...

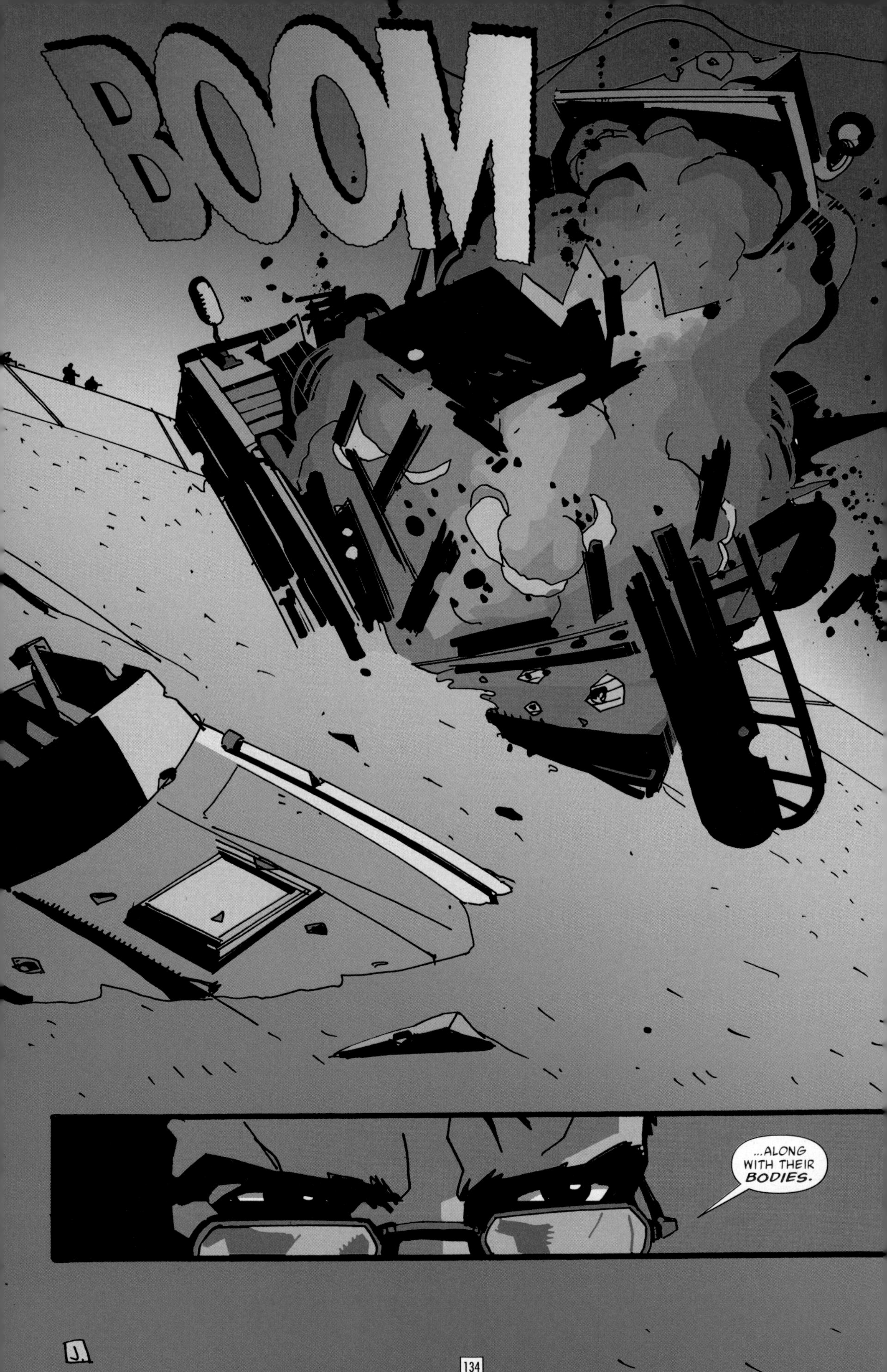
BOOM
...ALONG WITH THEIR BODIES.
J.

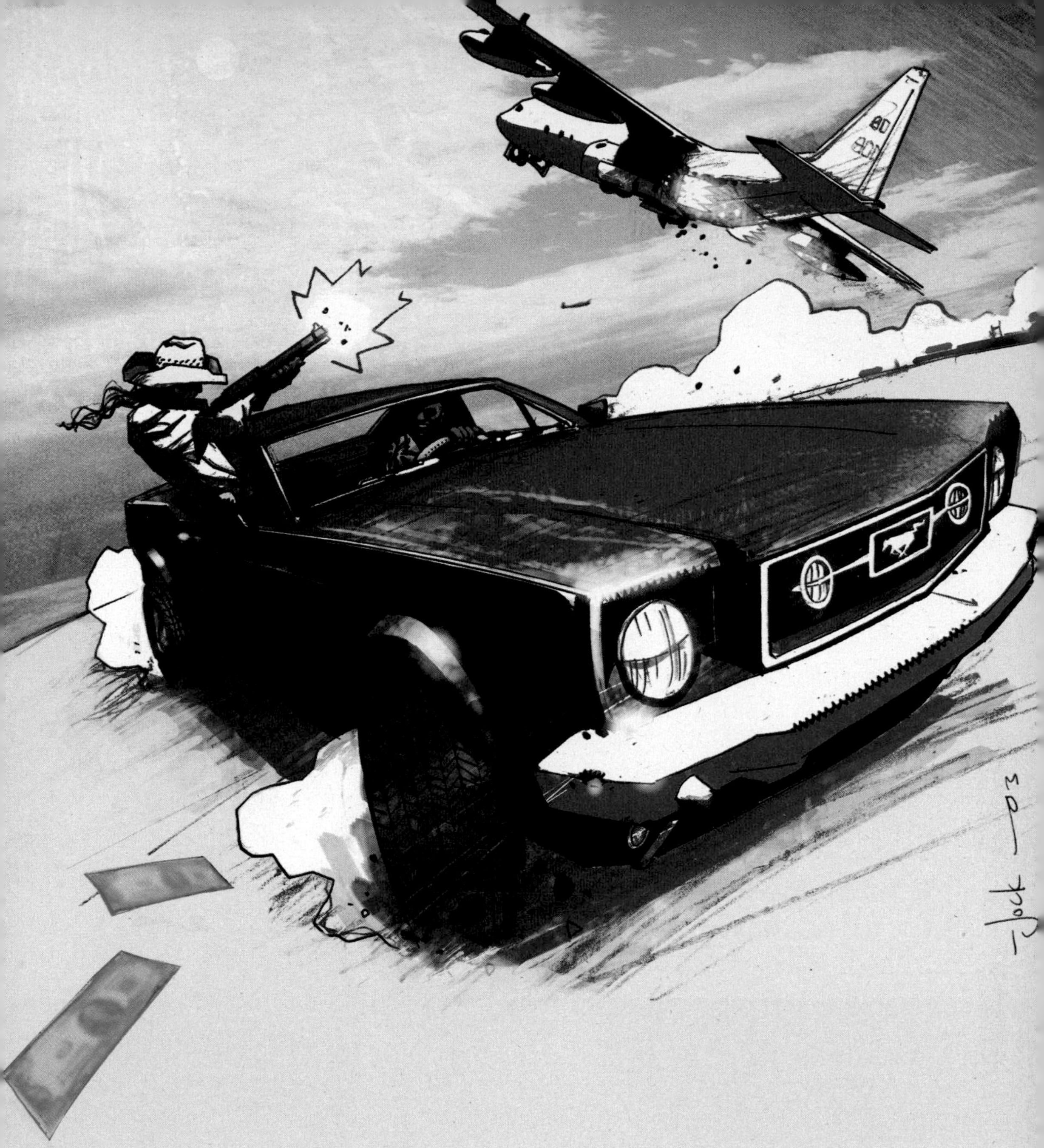
Jock — 03

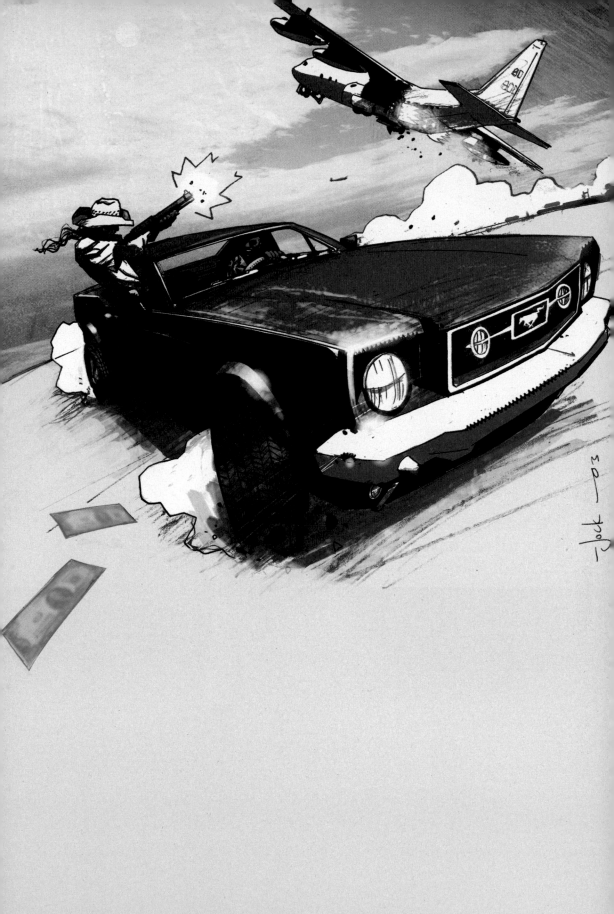

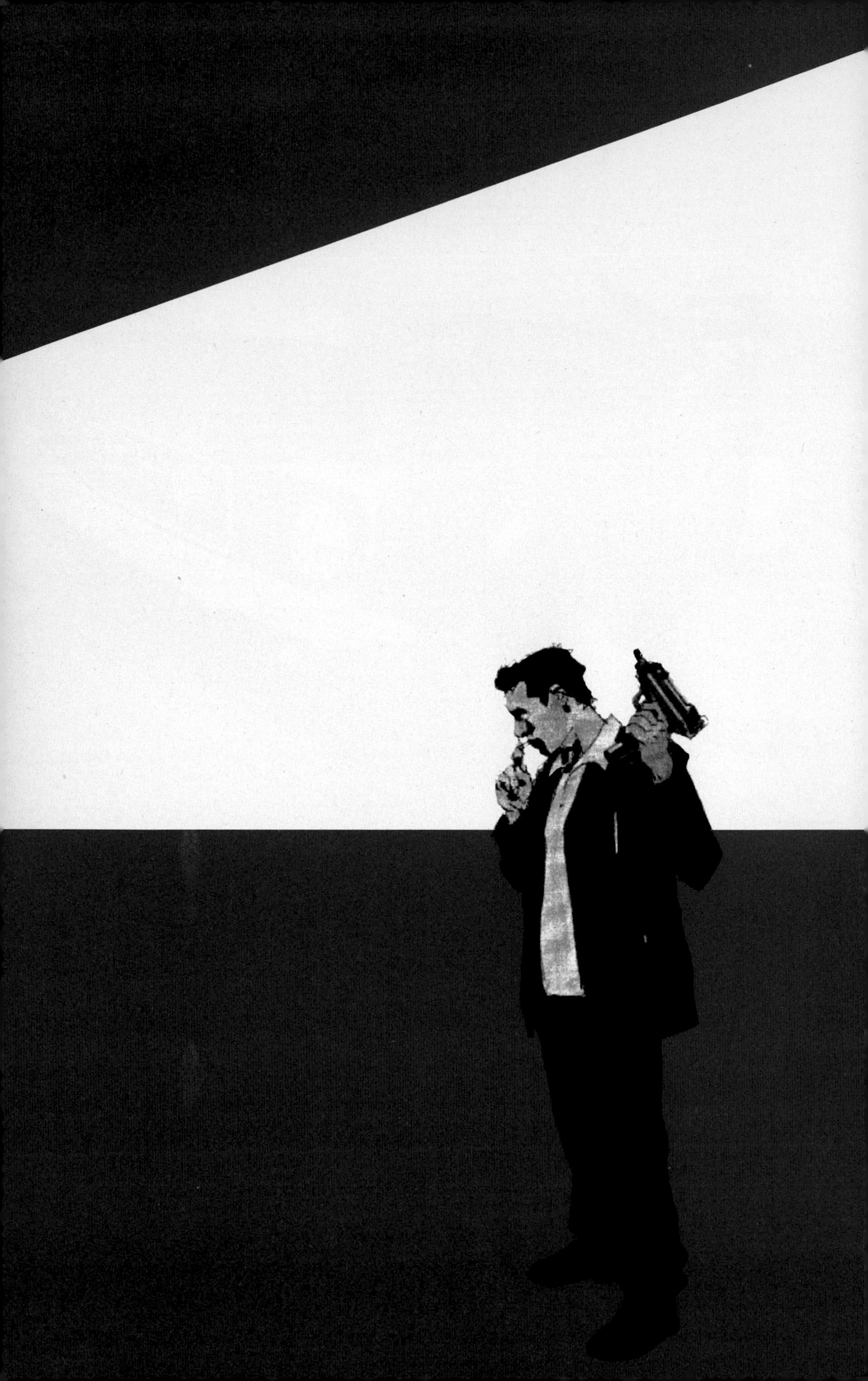

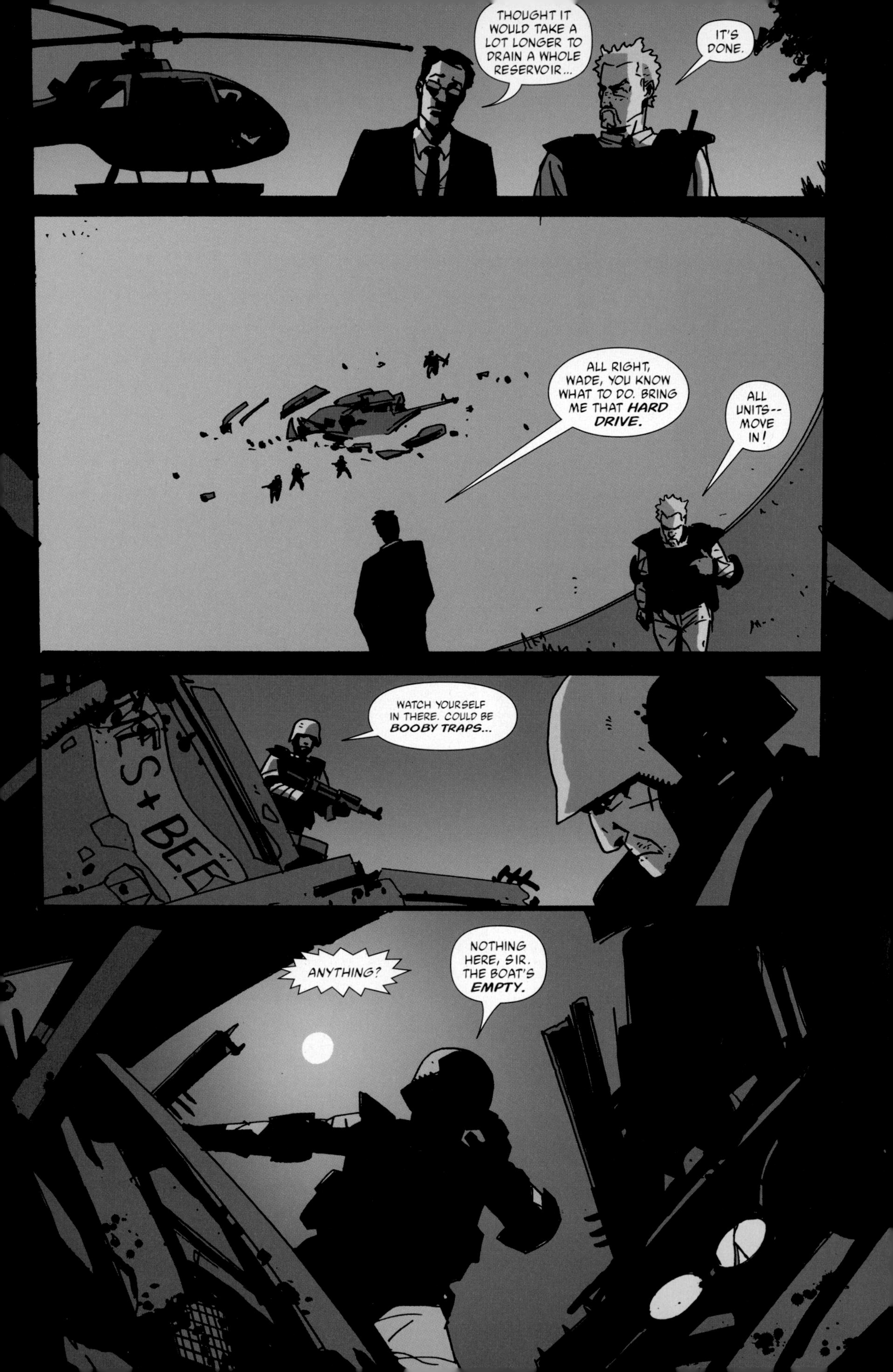
THOUGHT IT WOULD TAKE A LOT LONGER TO DRAIN A WHOLE RESERVOIR...
IT'S DONE.
ALL RIGHT, WADE, YOU KNOW WHAT TO DO. BRING ME THAT **HARD DRIVE.**
ALL UNITS--MOVE IN!
WATCH YOURSELF IN THERE. COULD BE **BOOBY TRAPS...**
ANYTHING?
NOTHING HERE, SIR. THE BOAT'S **EMPTY.**

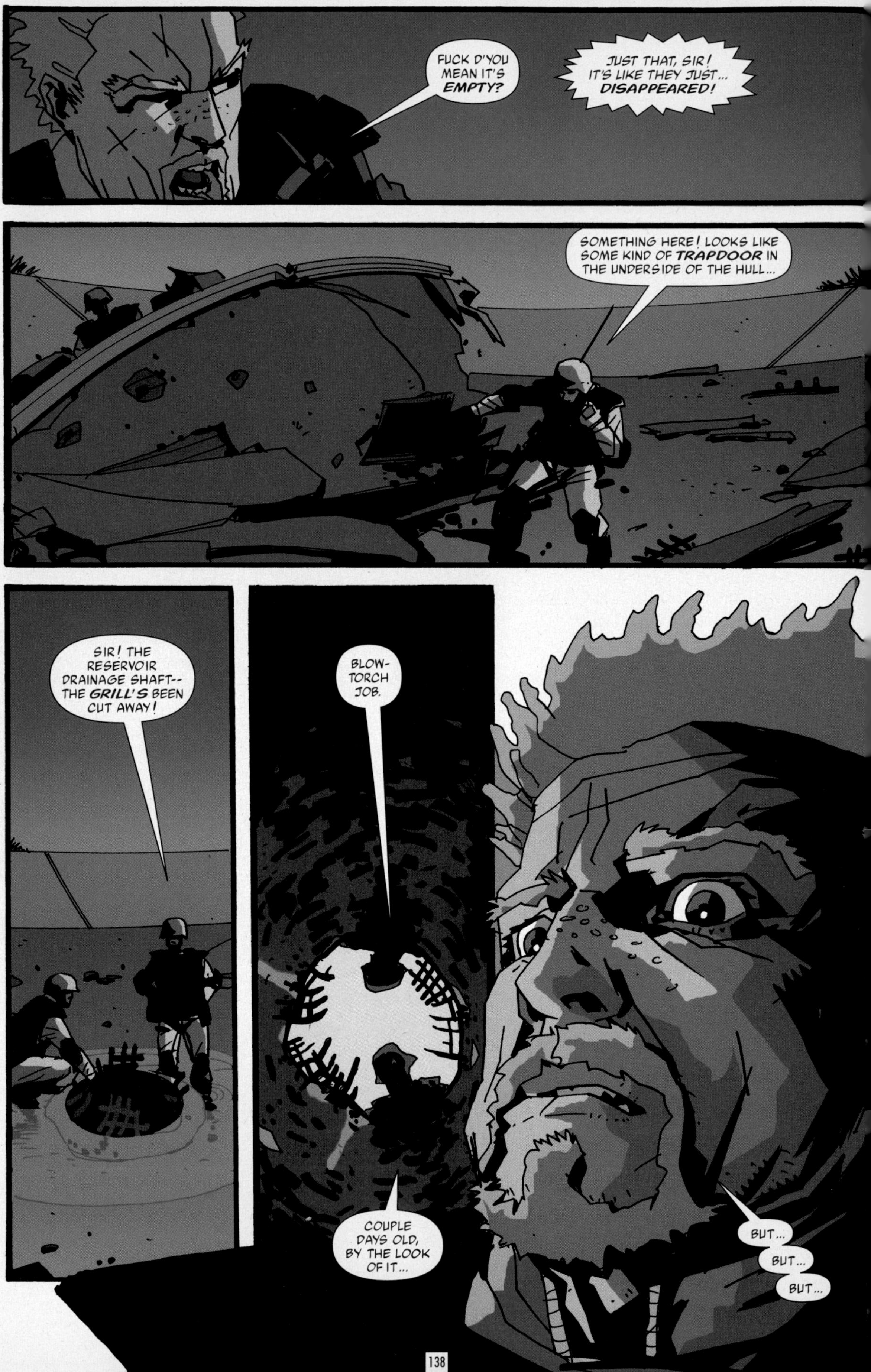
FUCK D'YOU MEAN IT'S EMPTY?
JUST THAT, SIR! IT'S LIKE THEY JUST... DISAPPEARED!
SOMETHING HERE! LOOKS LIKE SOME KIND OF TRAPDOOR IN THE UNDERSIDE OF THE HULL...
SIR! THE RESERVOIR DRAINAGE SHAFT-- THE GRILL'S BEEN CUT AWAY!
BLOW-TORCH JOB.
COUPLE DAYS OLD, BY THE LOOK OF IT...
BUT...
BUT...
BUT...

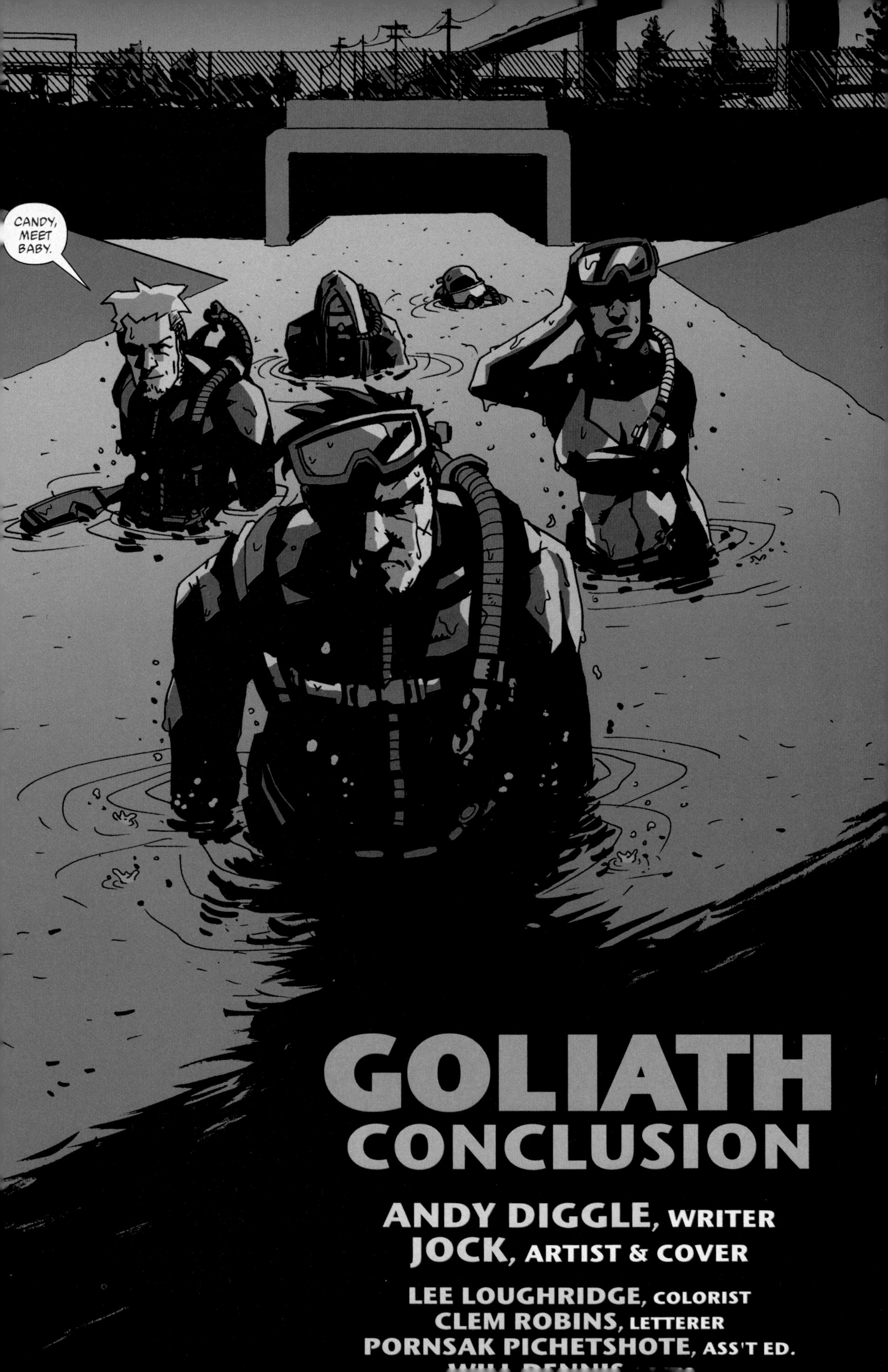
CANDY, MEET BABY.
GOLIATH
CONCLUSION
ANDY DIGGLE, WRITER
JOCK, ARTIST & COVER
LEE LOUGHRIDGE, COLORIST
CLEM ROBINS, LETTERER
PORNSAK PICHETSHOTE, ASS'T ED.

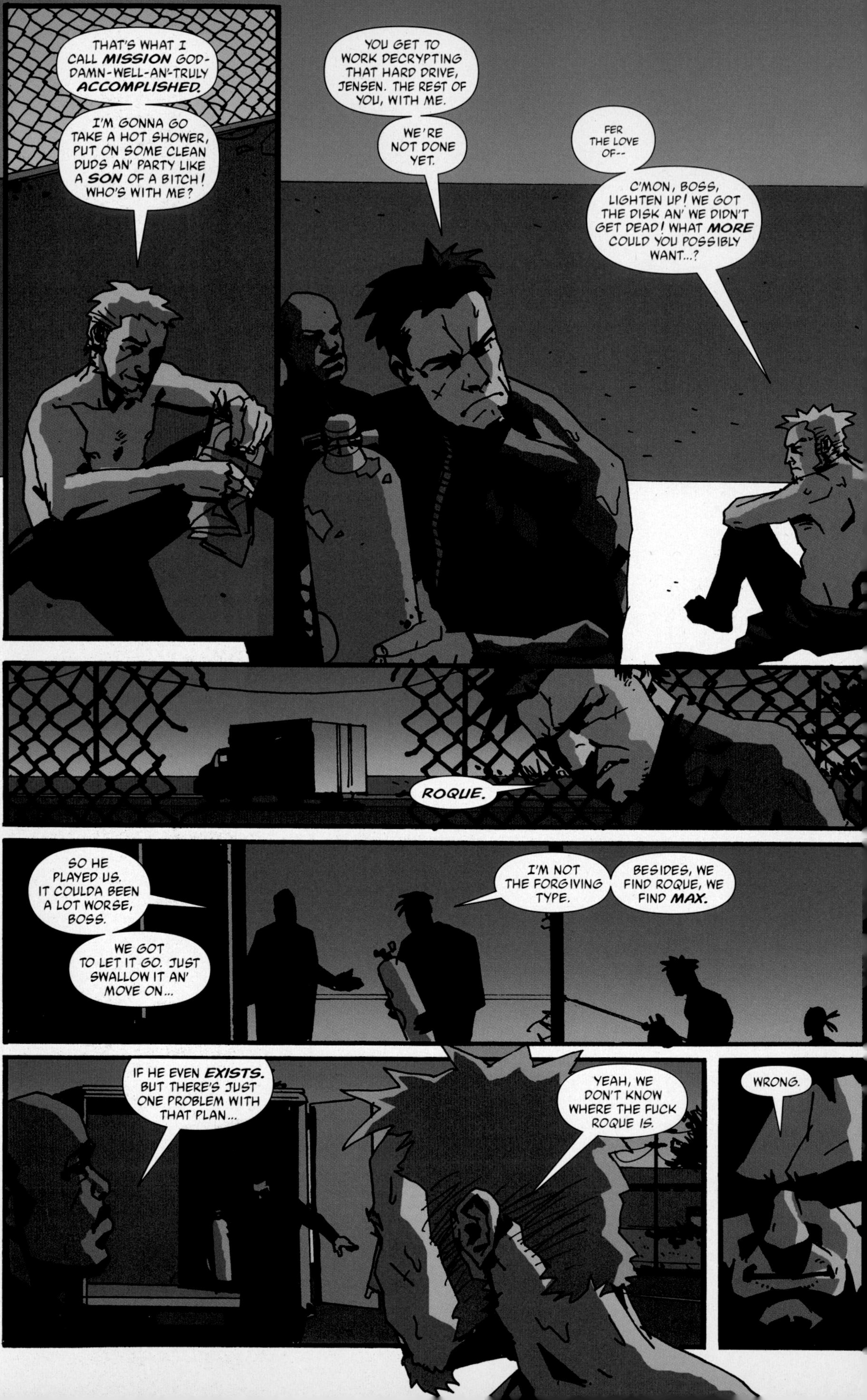

THAT'S WHAT I CALL **MISSION** GOD-DAMN-WELL-AN'-TRULY **ACCOMPLISHED.**
I'M GONNA GO TAKE A HOT SHOWER, PUT ON SOME CLEAN DUDS AN' PARTY LIKE A **SON** OF A BITCH! WHO'S WITH ME?
YOU GET TO WORK DECRYPTING THAT HARD DRIVE, JENSEN. THE REST OF YOU, WITH ME.
WE'RE NOT DONE YET.
FER THE LOVE OF--
C'MON, BOSS, LIGHTEN UP! WE GOT THE DISK AN' WE DIDN'T GET DEAD! WHAT **MORE** COULD YOU POSSIBLY WANT...?
**ROQUE.**
SO HE PLAYED US. IT COULDA BEEN A LOT WORSE, BOSS.
WE GOT TO LET IT GO. JUST SWALLOW IT AN' MOVE ON...
I'M NOT THE FORGIVING TYPE.
BESIDES, WE FIND ROQUE, WE FIND **MAX.**
IF HE EVEN **EXISTS.** BUT THERE'S JUST ONE PROBLEM WITH THAT PLAN...
YEAH, WE DON'T KNOW WHERE THE FUCK ROQUE IS.
WRONG.

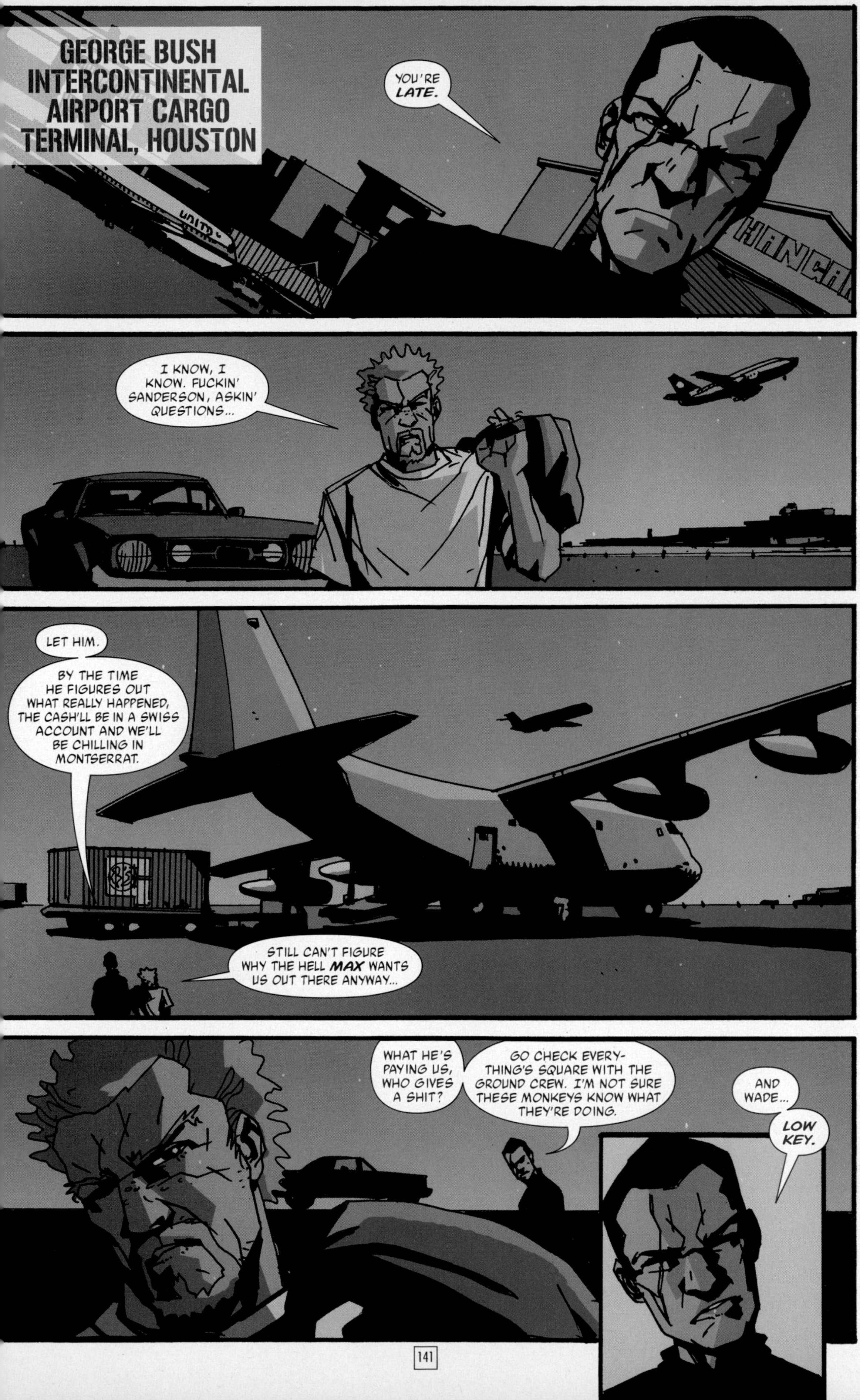
GEORGE BUSH INTERCONTINENTAL AIRPORT CARGO TERMINAL, HOUSTON
YOU'RE LATE.
HANGAR
I KNOW, I KNOW. FUCKIN' SANDERSON, ASKIN' QUESTIONS...
LET HIM.
BY THE TIME HE FIGURES OUT WHAT REALLY HAPPENED, THE CASH'LL BE IN A SWISS ACCOUNT AND WE'LL BE CHILLING IN MONTSERRAT.
STILL CAN'T FIGURE WHY THE HELL MAX WANTS US OUT THERE ANYWAY...
WHAT HE'S PAYING US, WHO GIVES A SHIT?
GO CHECK EVERYTHING'S SQUARE WITH THE GROUND CREW. I'M NOT SURE THESE MONKEYS KNOW WHAT THEY'RE DOING.
AND WADE...
LOW KEY.

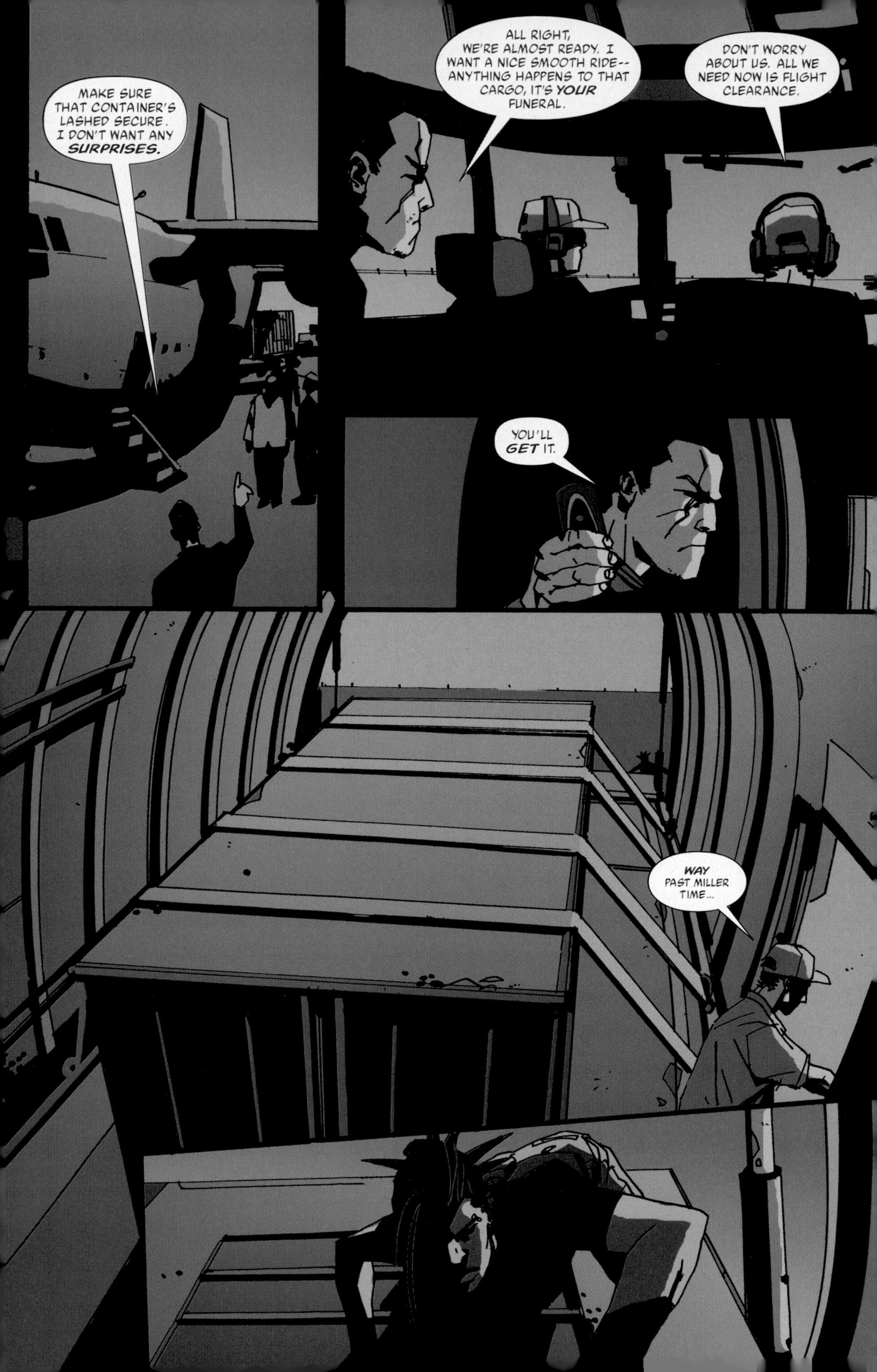
MAKE SURE THAT CONTAINER'S LASHED SECURE. I DON'T WANT ANY SURPRISES.
ALL RIGHT, WE'RE ALMOST READY. I WANT A NICE SMOOTH RIDE-- ANYTHING HAPPENS TO THAT CARGO, IT'S YOUR FUNERAL.
DON'T WORRY ABOUT US. ALL WE NEED NOW IS FLIGHT CLEARANCE.
YOU'LL GET IT.
WAY PAST MILLER TIME...

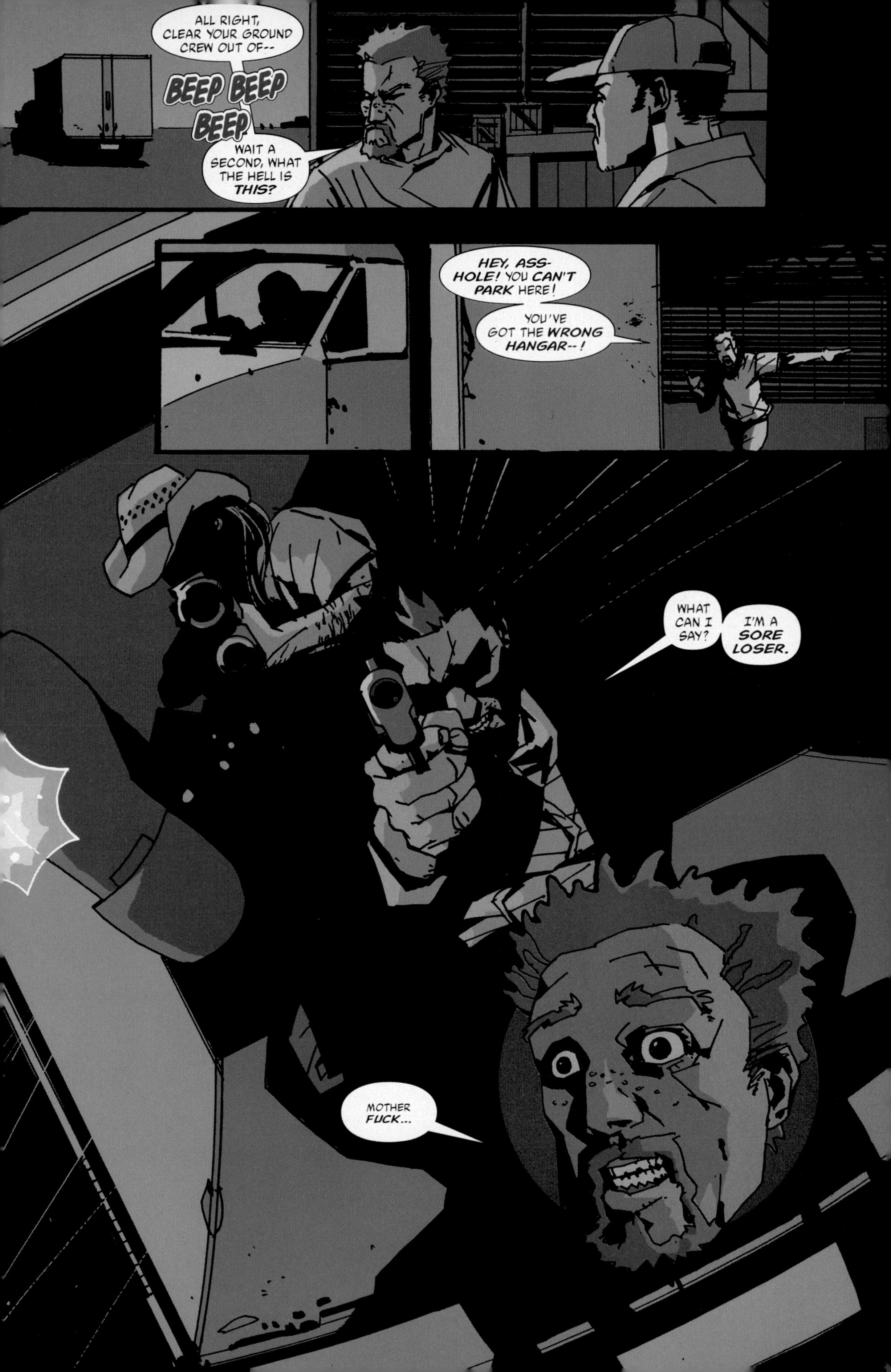
ALL RIGHT, CLEAR YOUR GROUND CREW OUT OF--
BEEP BEEP BEEP
WAIT A SECOND, WHAT THE HELL IS THIS?
HEY, ASS-HOLE! YOU CAN'T PARK HERE!
YOU'VE GOT THE WRONG HANGAR--!
WHAT CAN I SAY?
I'M A SORE LOSER.
MOTHER FUCK...

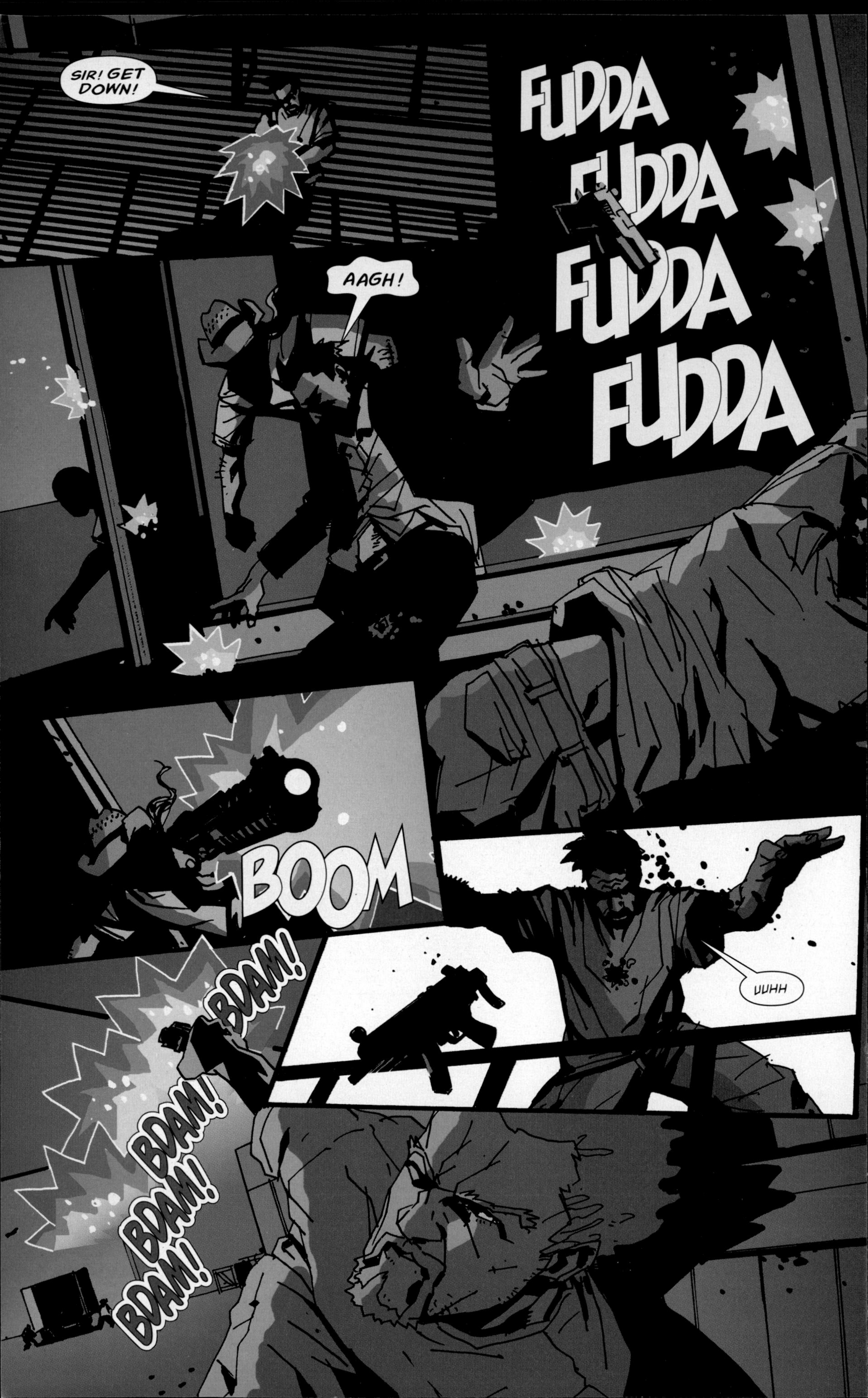

SIR! GET DOWN!
FUDDA FUDDA FUDDA FUDDA
AAGH!
BOOM
UUHH
BDAM! BDAM! BDAM! BDAM!

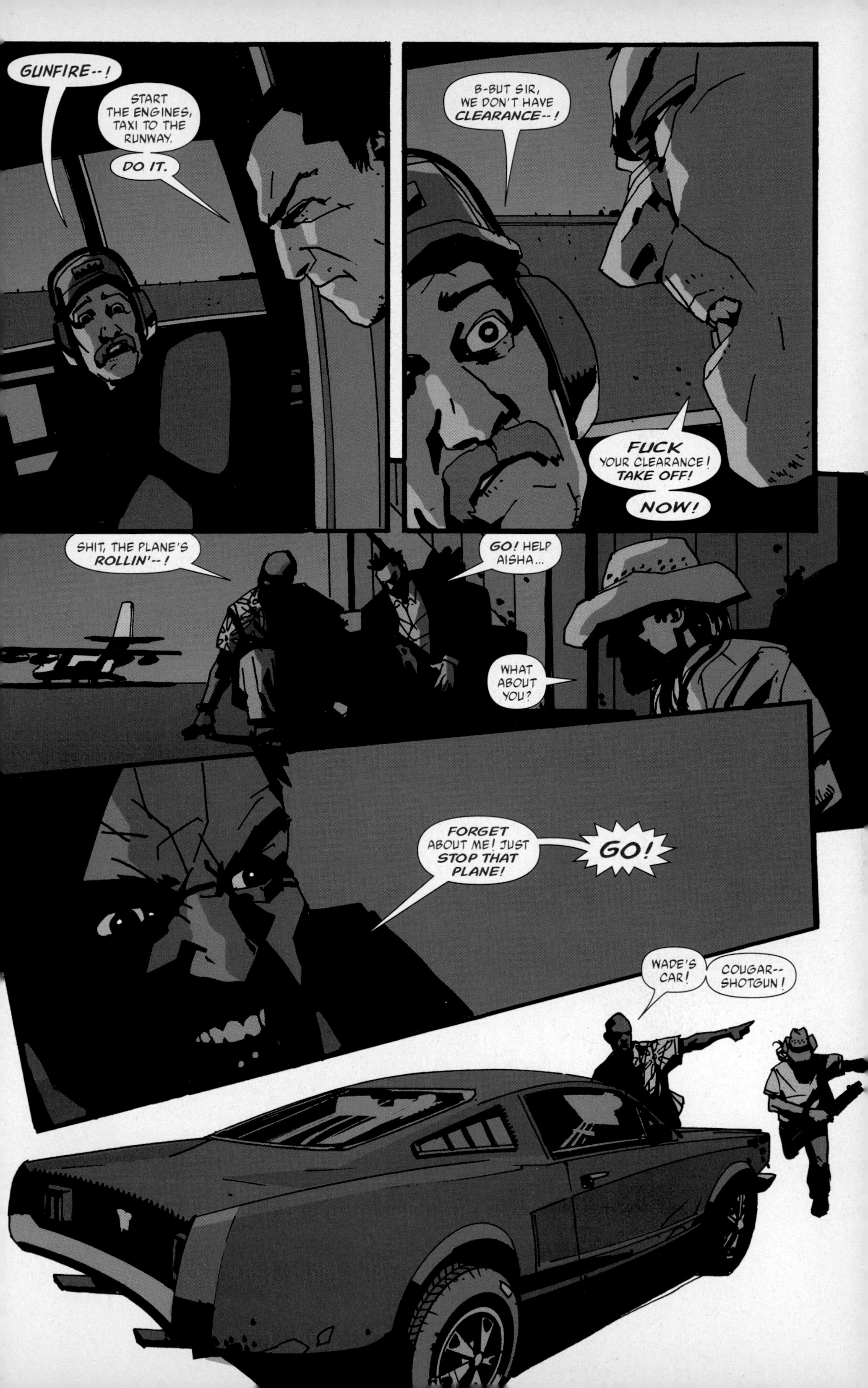
GUNFIRE--!
START THE ENGINES, TAXI TO THE RUNWAY.
DO IT.
B-BUT SIR, WE DON'T HAVE CLEARANCE--!
FUCK YOUR CLEARANCE! TAKE OFF!
NOW!
SHIT, THE PLANE'S ROLLIN'--!
GO! HELP AISHA...
WHAT ABOUT YOU?
FORGET ABOUT ME! JUST STOP THAT PLANE!
GO!
WADE'S CAR!
COUGAR-- SHOTGUN!

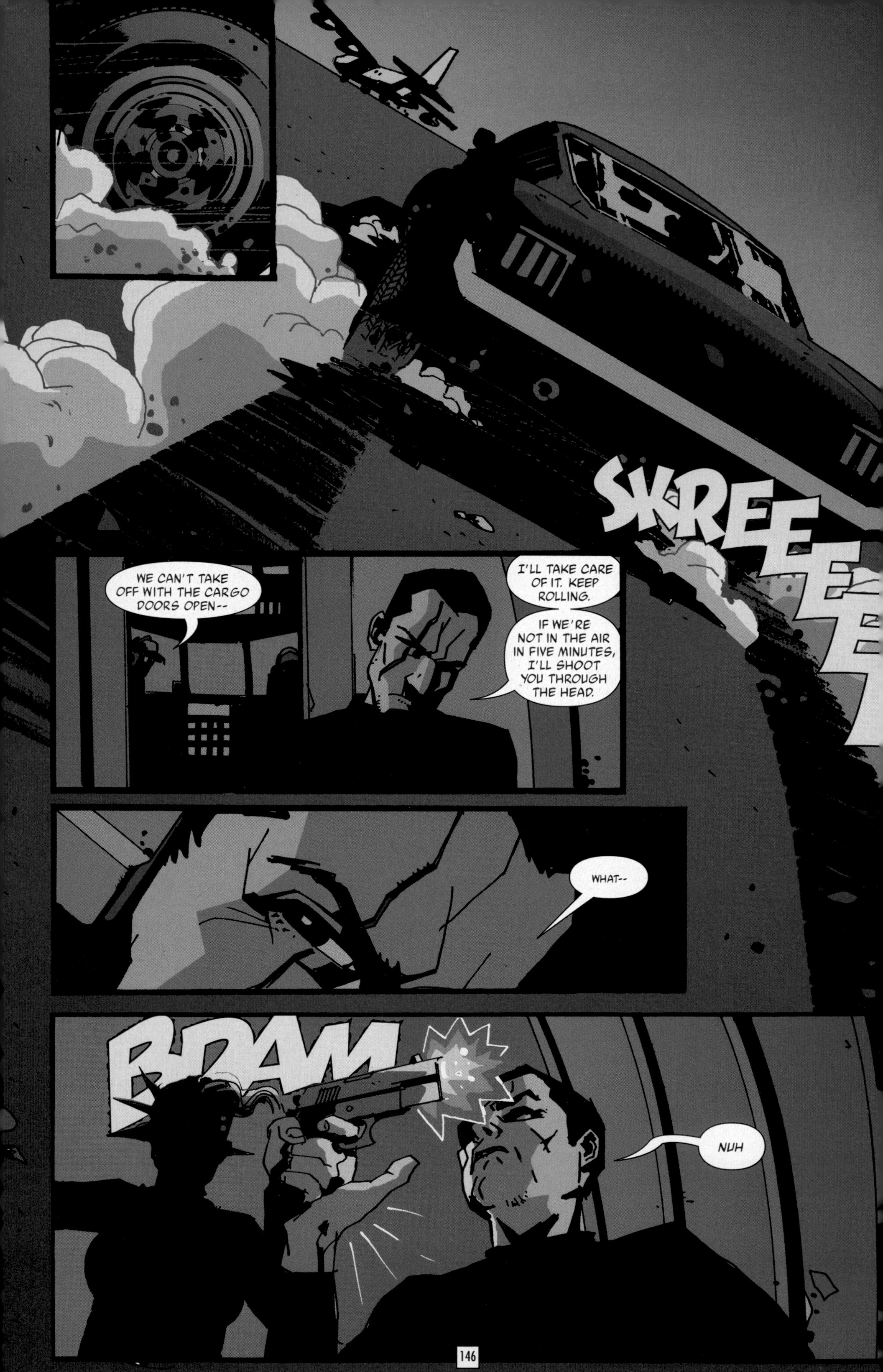
SKREEEEE
WE CAN'T TAKE OFF WITH THE CARGO DOORS OPEN--
I'LL TAKE CARE OF IT. KEEP ROLLING.
IF WE'RE NOT IN THE AIR IN FIVE MINUTES, I'LL SHOOT YOU THROUGH THE HEAD.
WHAT--
BRAM
NUH

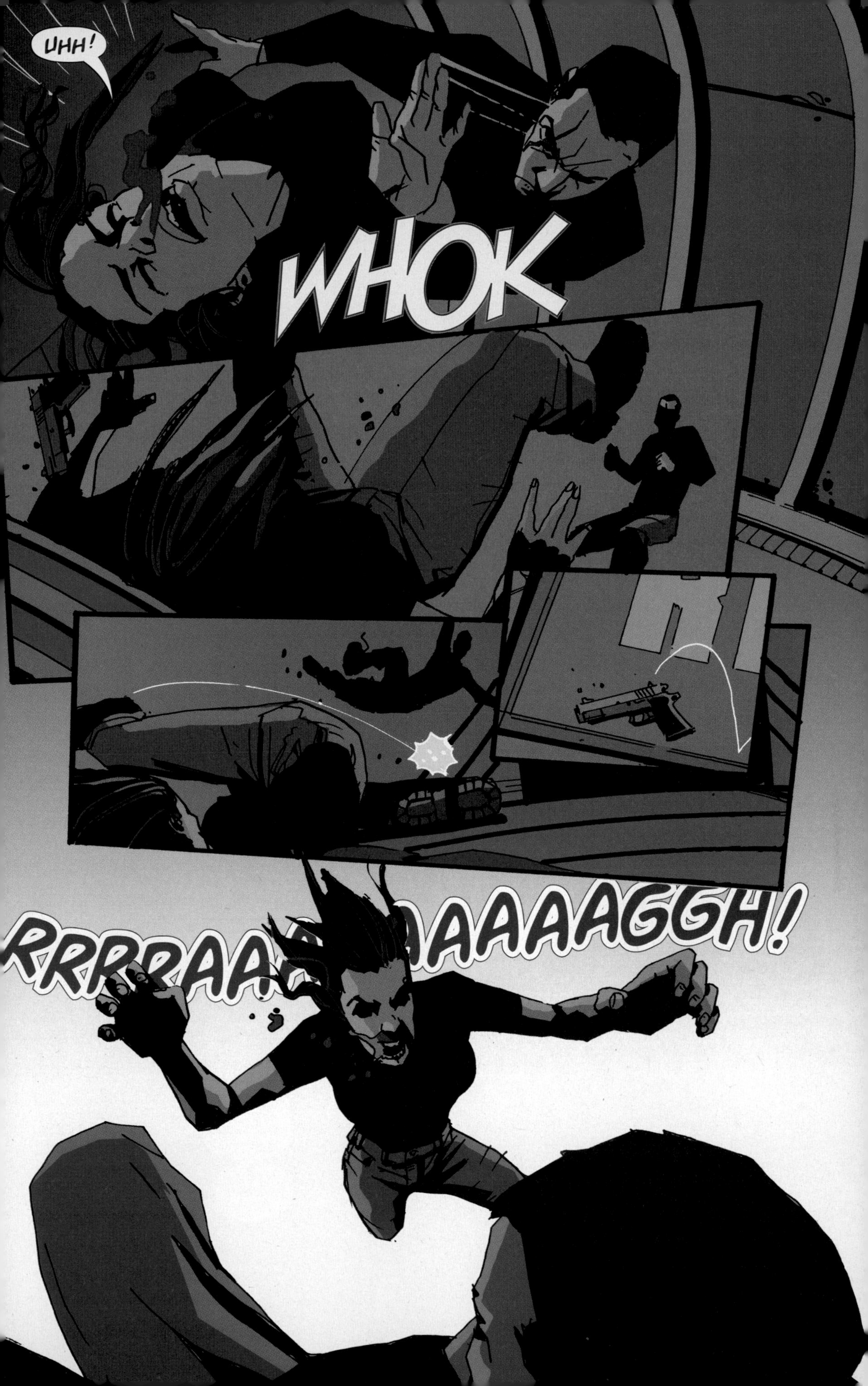
UHH!
WHOK
RRRRAA AAAAAAGGH!

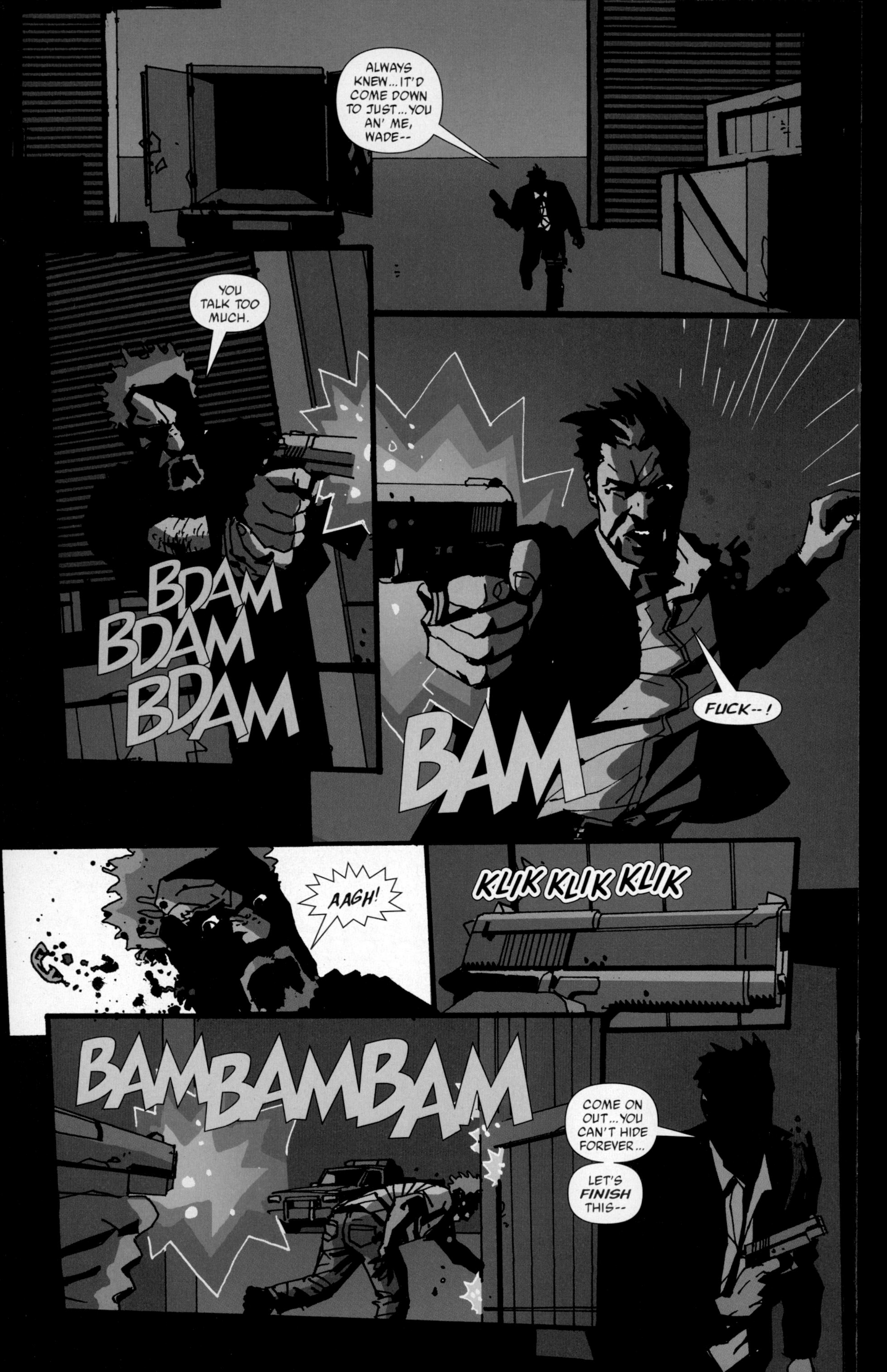
ALWAYS KNEW... IT'D COME DOWN TO JUST... YOU AN' ME, WADE--
YOU TALK TOO MUCH.
BDAM BDAM BDAM
BAM
FUCK--!
AAGH!
KLIK KLIK KLIK
BAMBAMBAM
COME ON OUT... YOU CAN'T HIDE FOREVER...
LET'S FINISH THIS--

KDUNG
FUCKIN' BOY SCOUT BULLSHIT.
I SHOULDA KILLED YOU BACK IN COLOMBIA.
KRUNCH
NO, YOU DON'T GET AWAY--

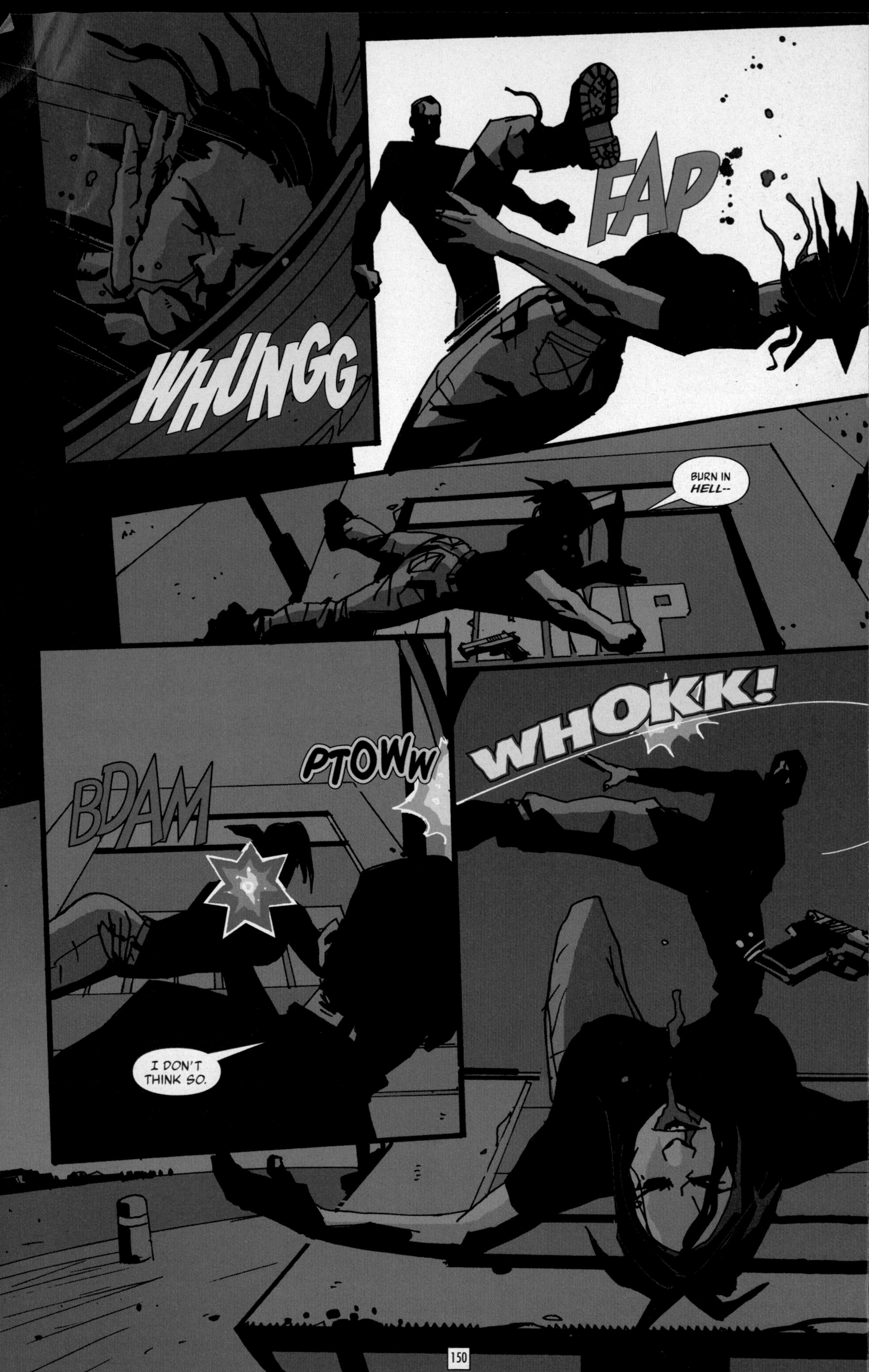
WHUNGG
FAP
BURN IN HELL--
PTOWW
WHOKK!
BDAM
I DON'T THINK SO.

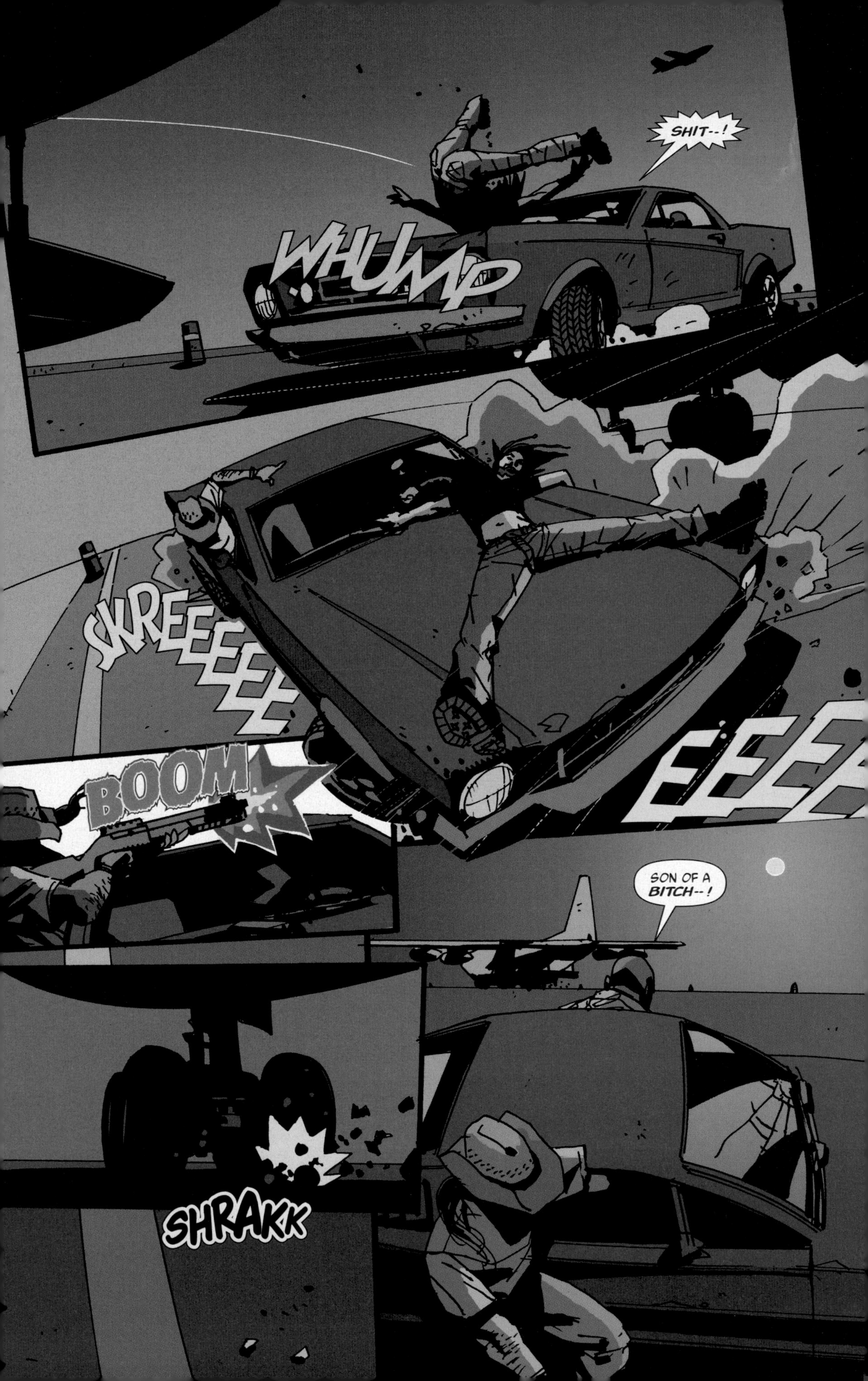
SHIT--!
WHUMP
SKREEEEEEEEEE
BOOM
SON OF A BITCH--!
SHRAKK

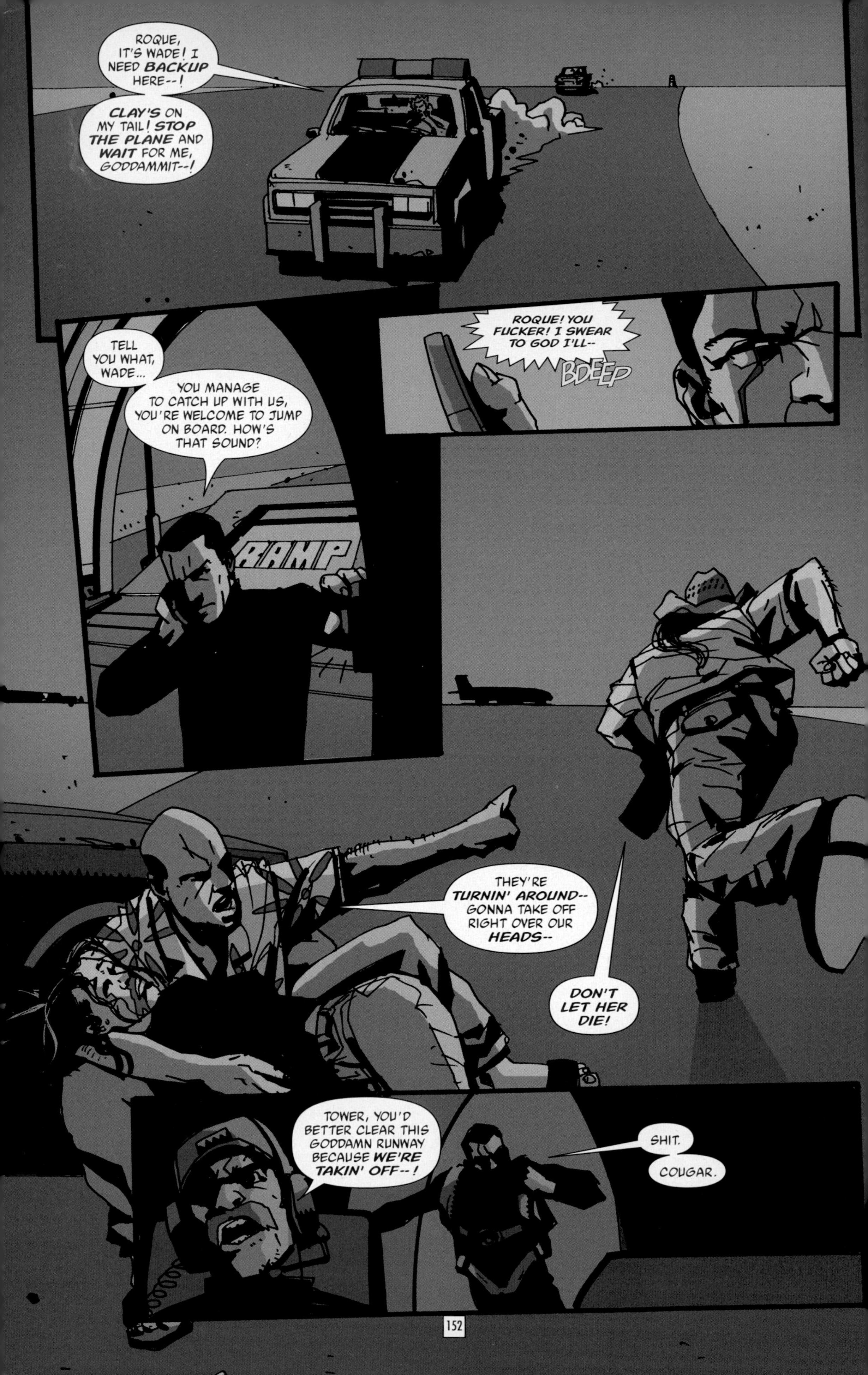
ROQUE, IT'S WADE! I NEED BACKUP HERE--!
CLAY'S ON MY TAIL! STOP THE PLANE AND WAIT FOR ME, GODDAMMIT--!
TELL YOU WHAT, WADE...
YOU MANAGE TO CATCH UP WITH US, YOU'RE WELCOME TO JUMP ON BOARD. HOW'S THAT SOUND?
RAMP
ROQUE! YOU FUCKER! I SWEAR TO GOD I'LL--
BDEEP
THEY'RE TURNIN' AROUND-- GONNA TAKE OFF RIGHT OVER OUR HEADS--
DON'T LET HER DIE!
TOWER, YOU'D BETTER CLEAR THIS GODDAMN RUNWAY BECAUSE WE'RE TAKIN' OFF--!
SHIT.
COUGAR.

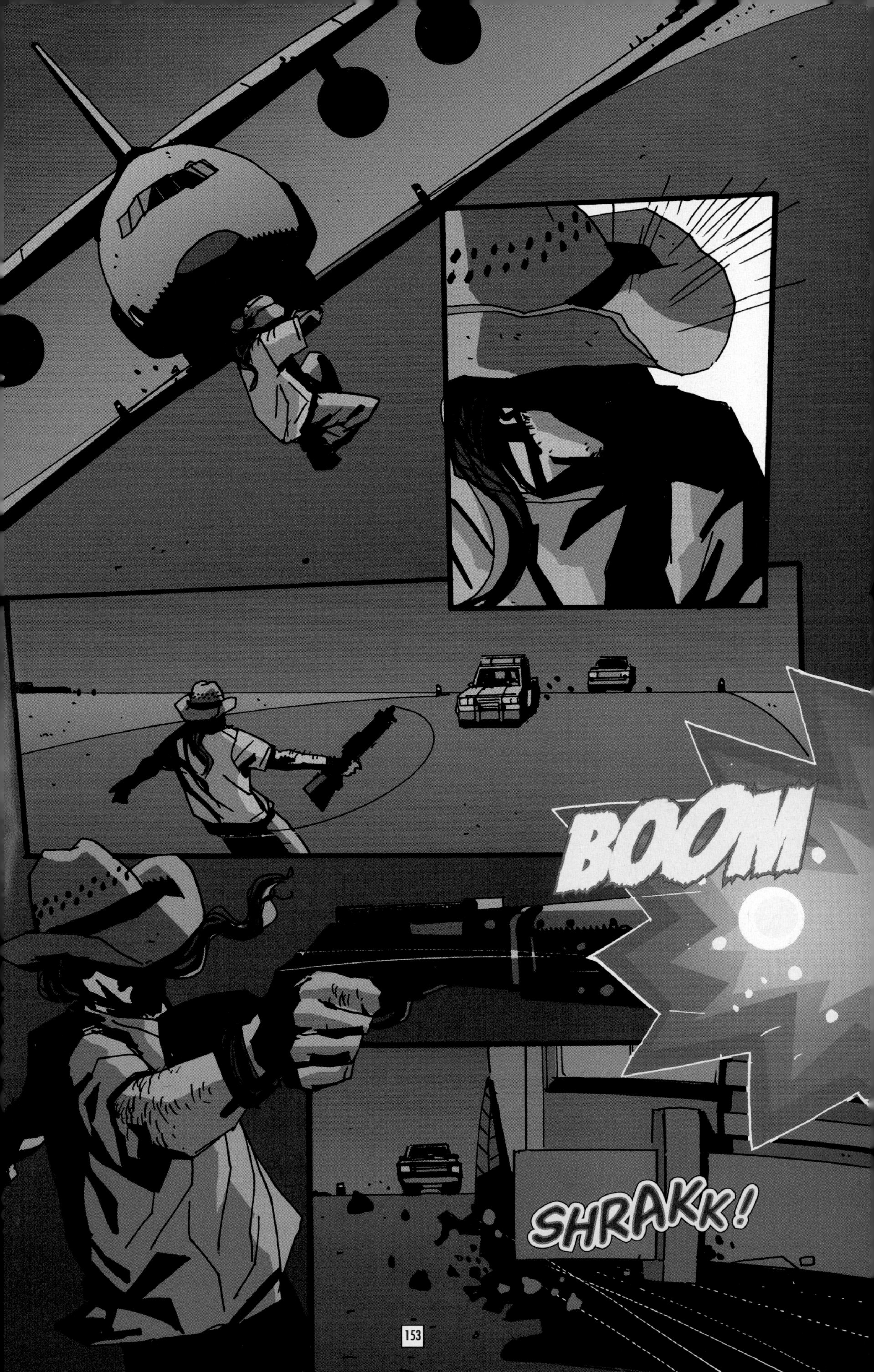
BOOM
SHRAKK!

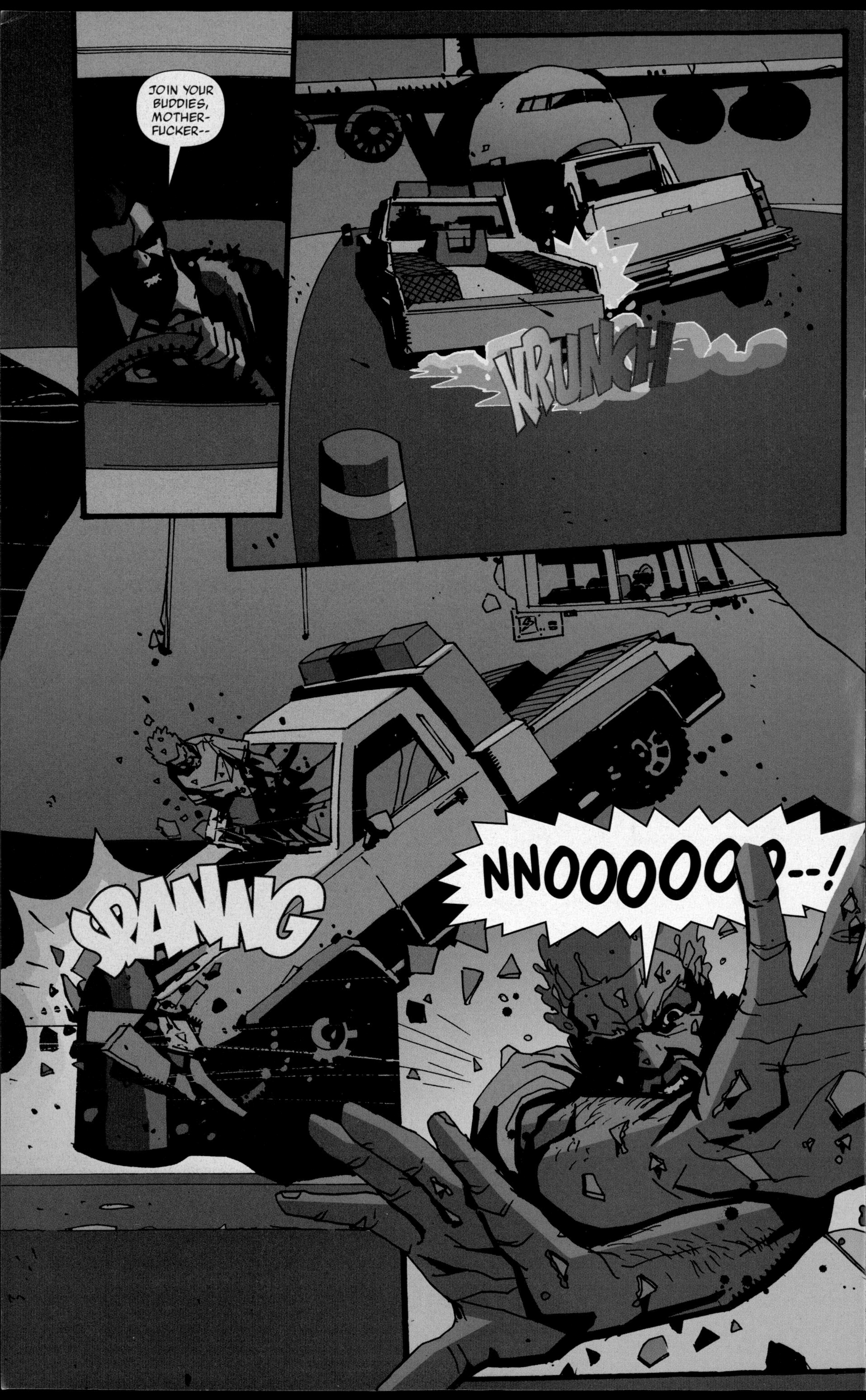
JOIN YOUR BUDDIES, MOTHER-FUCKER--
KRUNCH
SPANNG

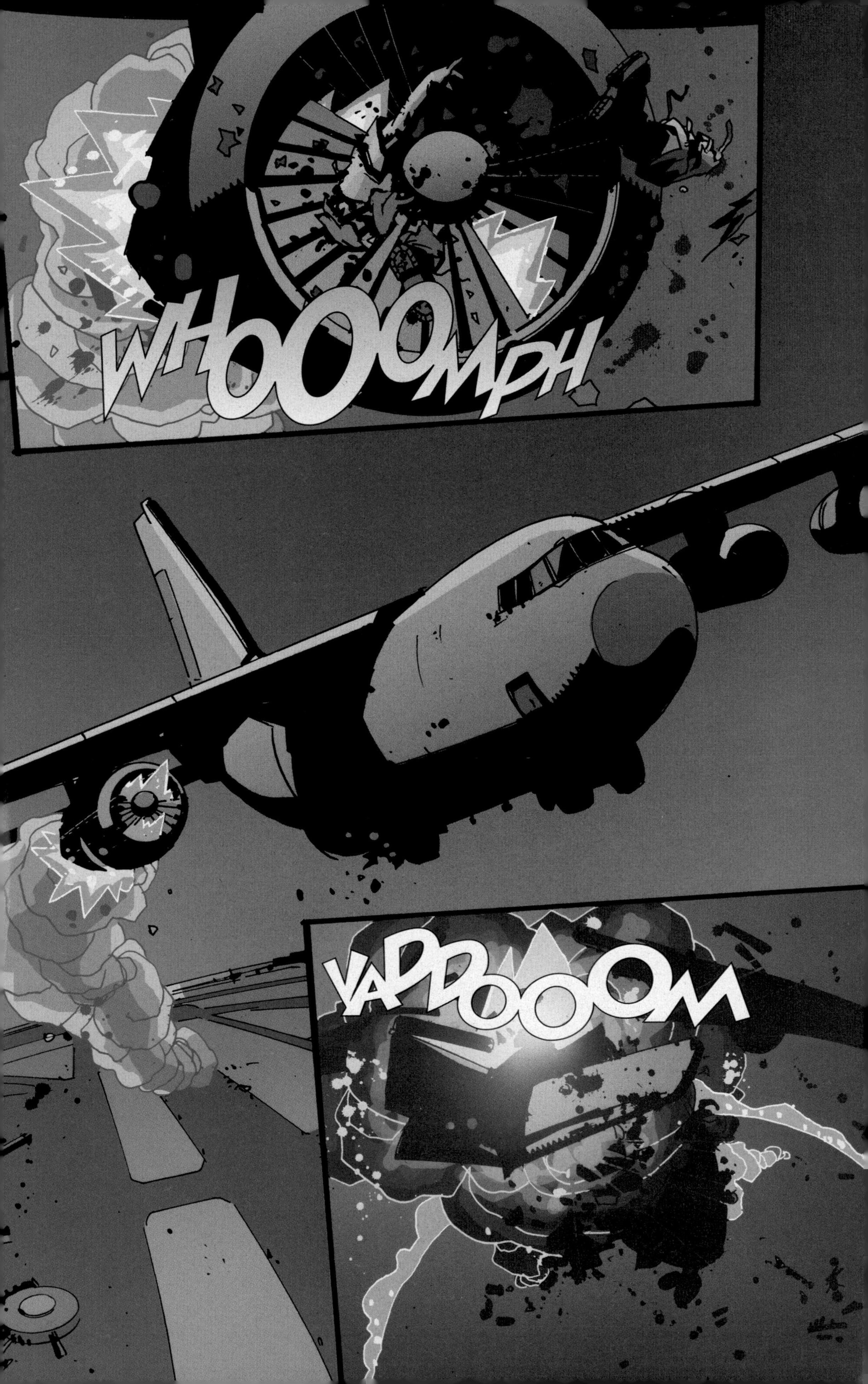
WHOOOMPH
VADDOOOM

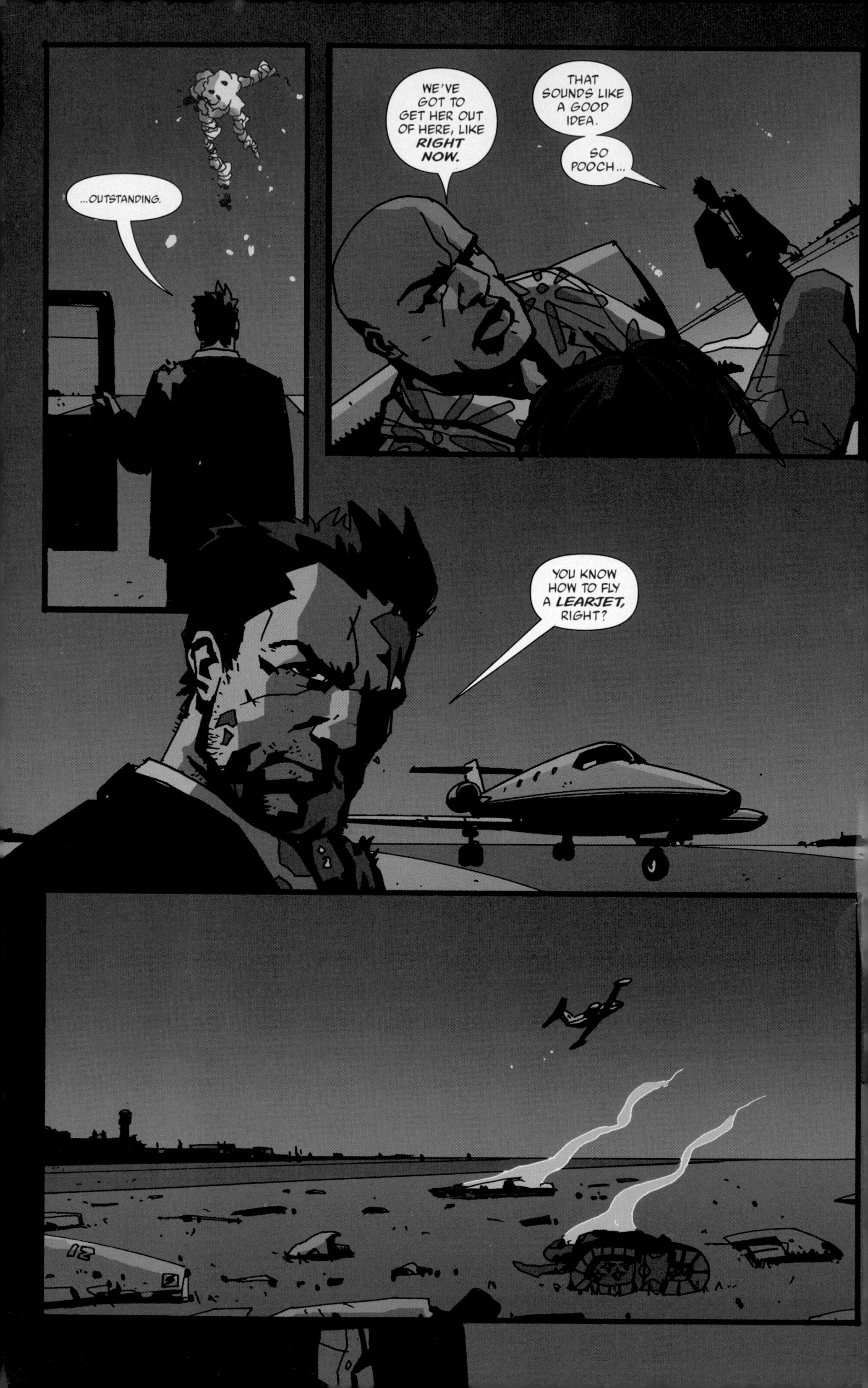
...OUTSTANDING.
WE'VE GOT TO GET HER OUT OF HERE, LIKE **RIGHT NOW.**
THAT SOUNDS LIKE A GOOD IDEA.
SO POOCH...
YOU KNOW HOW TO FLY A **LEARJET,** RIGHT?

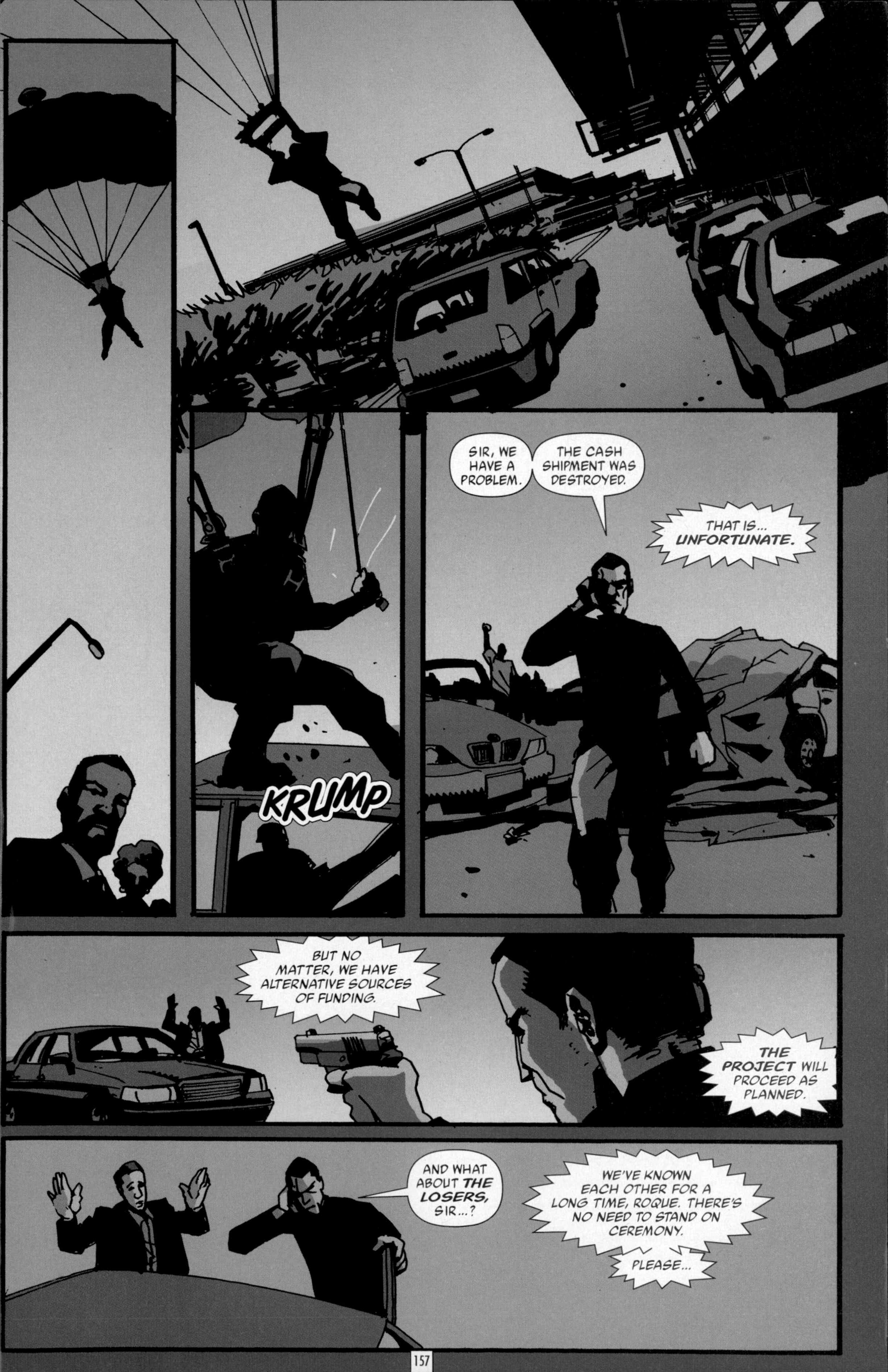
KRUMP
SIR, WE HAVE A PROBLEM.
THE CASH SHIPMENT WAS DESTROYED.
THAT IS... UNFORTUNATE.
BUT NO MATTER, WE HAVE ALTERNATIVE SOURCES OF FUNDING.
THE PROJECT WILL PROCEED AS PLANNED.
AND WHAT ABOUT THE LOSERS, SIR...?
WE'VE KNOWN EACH OTHER FOR A LONG TIME, ROQUE. THERE'S NO NEED TO STAND ON CEREMONY.
PLEASE...

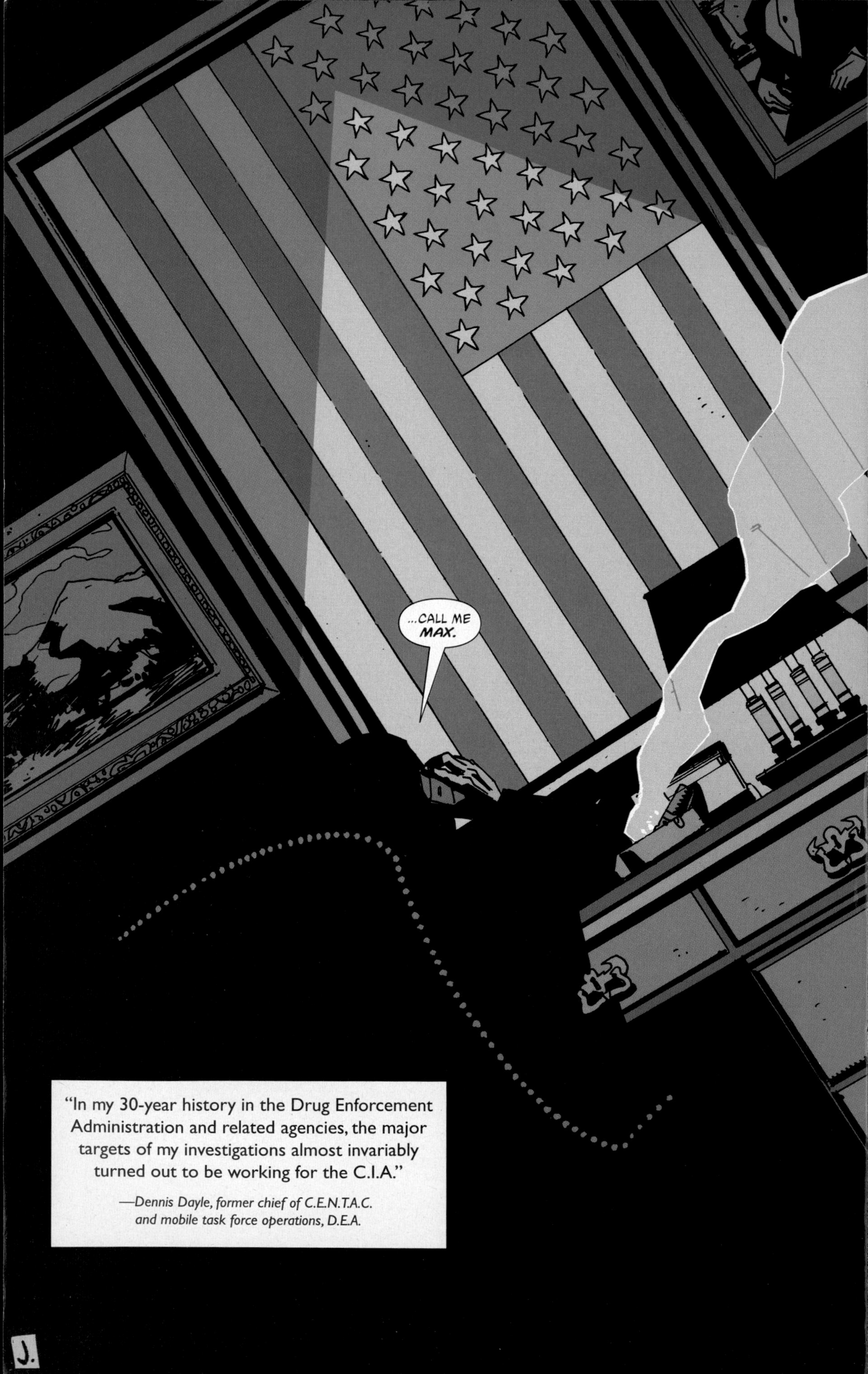
...CALL ME MAX.

"In my 30-year history in the Drug Enforcement Administration and related agencies, the major targets of my investigations almost invariably turned out to be working for the C.I.A."

*—Dennis Dayle, former chief of C.E.N.T.A.C. and mobile task force operations, D.E.A.*